STATUTE, FORM AND PROBLEM SUPPLEMENT

CASES AND MATERIALS ON LAND TRANSFER, DEVELOPMENT AND FINANCE

REAL ESTATE TRANSACTIONS

FIFTH EDITION

by

GERALD KORNGOLD
Professor of Law
New York Law School
and Visiting Fellow
Lincoln Institute of Land Policy

PAUL GOLDSTEIN
Lillick Professor of Law
Stanford University

FOUNDATION PRESS
2009

THOMSON REUTERS

© 1985, 1988, 1993, 1997, 2002 FOUNDATION PRESS

© 2009 By THOMSON REUTERS/FOUNDATION PRESS

    195 Broadway, 9th Floor
    New York, NY 10007
    Phone Toll Free 1–877–888–1330
    Fax (212) 367–6799
    Foundation–press.com
Printed in the United States of America

ISBN 978–1–59941–354–9

[No claim of copyright is made for official U.S. government statutes, rules or regulations.]

 TEXT IS PRINTED ON 10% POST CONSUMER RECYCLED PAPER

TABLE OF CONTENTS

*

STATUTE, FORM AND PROBLEM SUPPLEMENT

REAL ESTATE TRANSACTIONS

*

A. STATUTES

1. REAL ESTATE AGENCY DISCLOSURE STATUTE

———

NEW YORK REAL PROPERTY LAW

§ 443. **Disclosure regarding real estate agency relationship; form**

1. Definitions. As used in this section, the following terms shall have the following meanings:

a. "Agent" means a person who is licensed as a real estate broker or real estate sales associate under section four hundred forty-a of this article and is acting in a fiduciary capacity.

b. "Buyer" means a transferee in a residential real property transaction and includes a person who executes an offer to purchase residential real property from a seller through an agent, or who has engaged the services of an agent with the object of entering into a residential real property transaction as a transferee.

c. "Buyer's agent" means an agent who contracts to locate residential real property for a buyer or who finds a buyer for a property and presents an offer to purchase to the seller or seller's agent and negotiates on behalf of the buyer.

d. "Listing agent" means a person who has entered into a listing agreement to act as an agent of the seller or landlord for compensation.

e. "Listing agreement" means a contract between an owner or owners of residential real property and an agent, by which the agent has been authorized to sell or lease the residential real property or to find or obtain a buyer or lessee therefor.

f. "Residential real property" means real property improved by a one-to-four family dwelling used or occupied, or intended to be used or occupied, wholly or partly, as the home or residence of one or more persons, but shall not refer to (i) unimproved real property upon which such dwellings are to be constructed or (ii) condominium or cooperative apartments in a building containing more than four units.

g. "Seller" means the transferor in a residential real property transaction, and includes an owner who lists residential real property for sale with an agent, whether or not a transfer results, or who receives an offer to purchase residential real property.

h. "Seller's agent" means a listing agent who acts alone, or an agent who acts in cooperation with a listing agent, acts as a seller's subagent or acts as a broker's agent to find or obtain a buyer for residential real property.

i. "Dual agent" means an agent who is acting as a buyer's agent and a seller's agent or a tenant's agent and a landlord's agent in the same transaction.

j. "Designated sales agent" means a licensed real estate salesman or associate broker, working under the supervision of a real estate broker, who has been assigned to represent a client when a different client is also represented by such real estate broker in the same transaction.

1

k. "Broker's agent" means an agent that cooperates or is engaged by a listing agent, buyer's agent or tenant's agent (but does not work for the same firm as the listing agent, buyer's agent or tenant's agent) to assist the listing agent, buyer's agent or tenant's agent in locating a property to sell, buy or lease respectively, for the listing agent's seller or landlord, the buyer agent's buyer or the tenant's agent tenant. The broker's agent does not have a direct relationship with the seller, buyer, landlord or tenant and the seller, buyer, landlord or tenant can not provide instructions or direction directly to the broker's agent. Therefore, the seller, buyer, landlord or tenant do not have vicarious liability for the acts of the broker's agent. The listing agent, buyer's agent or tenant's agent do provide direction and instruction to the broker's agent and therefore the listing agent, buyer's agent or tenant's agent will have liability for the broker's agent.

l. "Tenant" means a lessee in a residential real property transaction and includes a person who executes an offer to lease residential real property from a landlord through an agent, or who has engaged the services of an agent with the object of entering into a residential real property transaction as a lessee.

m. "Landlord" means the lessor in a residential real property transaction, and includes an owner who lists residential real property for lease with an agent, whether or not a lease results, or who receives an offer to lease residential real property.

n. "Tenant's agent" means an agent who contracts to locate residential real property for a tenant or who finds a tenant for a property and presents an offer to lease to the landlord or landlord's agent and negotiates on behalf of the tenant.

o. "Landlord's agent" means a listing agent who acts alone, or an agent who acts in cooperation with a listing agent, acts as a landlord's subagent or acts as a broker's agent to find or obtain a tenant for residential real property.

2. This section shall apply only to transactions involving residential real property.

3. a. A listing agent shall provide the disclosure form set forth in subdivision four of this section to a seller or landlord prior to entering into a listing agreement with the seller or landlord and shall obtain a signed acknowledgment from the seller or landlord, except as provided in paragraph e of this subdivision.

b. A seller's agent or landlord's agent shall provide the disclosure form set forth in subdivision four of this section to a buyer, buyer's agent, tenant or tenant's agent at the time of the first substantive contact with the buyer or tenant and shall obtain a signed acknowledgement from the buyer or tenant, except as provided in paragraph e of this subdivision.

c. A buyer's agent or tenant's agent shall provide the disclosure form to the buyer or tenant prior to entering into an agreement to act as the buyer's agent or tenant's agent and shall obtain a signed acknowledgment from the buyer or tenant, except as provided in paragraph e of this subdivision. A buyer's agent or tenant's agent shall provide the form to the seller, seller's agent, landlord or landlord's agent at the time of the first substantive contact with the seller or landlord and shall obtain a signed acknowledgment from the seller, landlord or the listing agent, except as provided in paragraph e of this subdivision.

d. The agent shall provide to the buyer, seller, tenant or landlord a copy of the signed acknowledgment and shall maintain a copy of the signed acknowledgment for not less than three years.

e.   If the seller, buyer, landlord or tenant refuses to sign an acknowledgment of receipt pursuant to this subdivision, the agent shall set forth under oath or affirmation a written declaration of the facts of the refusal and shall maintain a copy of the declaration for not less than three years.

4.   a. For buyer-seller transactions, the following shall be the disclosure form:

NEW YORK STATE DISCLOSURE FORM
FOR
BUYER AND SELLER
THIS IS NOT A CONTRACT

New York state law requires real estate licensees who are acting as agents of buyers or sellers of property to advise the potential buyers or sellers with whom they work of the nature of their agency relationship and the rights and obligations it creates. This disclosure will help you to make informed choices about your relationship with the real estate broker and its sales associates.

Throughout the transaction you may receive more than one disclosure form. The law requires each agent assisting in the transaction to present you with this disclosure form. A real estate agent is a person qualified to advise about real estate.

If you need legal, tax or other advice, consult with a professional in that field.

DISCLOSURE REGARDING REAL ESTATE AGENCY RELATIONSHIPS
SELLER'S AGENT

A seller's agent is an agent who is engaged by a seller to represent the seller's interests. The seller's agent does this by securing a buyer for the seller's home at a price and on terms acceptable to the seller. A seller's agent has, without limitation, the following fiduciary duties to the seller: reasonable care, undivided loyalty, confidentiality, full disclosure, obedience and duty to account. A seller's agent does not represent the interests of the buyer. The obligations of a seller's agent are also subject to any specific provisions set forth in an agreement between the agent and the seller. In dealings with the buyer, a seller's agent should (a) exercise reasonable skill and care in performance of the agent's duties; (b) deal honestly, fairly and in good faith; and (c) disclose all facts known to the agent materially affecting the value or desirability of property, except as otherwise provided by law.

BUYER'S AGENT

A buyer's agent is an agent who is engaged by a buyer to represent the buyer's interests. The buyer's agent does this by negotiating the purchase of a home at a price and on terms acceptable to the buyer. A buyer's agent has, without limitation, the following fiduciary duties to the buyer: reasonable care, undivided loyalty, confidentiality, full disclosure, obedience and duty to account. A buyer's agent does not represent the interests of the seller. The obligations of a buyer's agent are also subject to any specific provisions set forth in an agreement between the agent and the buyer. In dealings with the seller, a buyer's agent should (a) exercise reasonable skill and care in performance of the agent's duties; (b) deal honestly, fairly and in good faith; and (c) disclose all facts known to the agent materially affecting the buyer's ability and/or willingness to perform a contract to acquire seller's property that are not inconsistent with the agent's fiduciary duties to the buyer.

BROKER'S AGENTS

A broker's agent is an agent that cooperates or is engaged by a listing agent or a buyer's agent (but does not work for the same firm as the listing agent or buyer's agent) to assist the listing agent or buyer's agent in locating a property to sell or buy, respectively, for the listing agent's seller or the buyer agent's buyer. The broker's agent does not have a direct relationship with the buyer or seller and the buyer or seller can not provide instructions or direction directly to the broker's agent. The buyer and the seller therefore do not have vicarious liability for the acts of the broker's agent. The listing agent or buyer's agent do provide direction and instruction to the broker's agent and therefore the listing agent or buyer's agent will have liability for the acts of the broker's agent.

DUAL AGENT

A real estate broker may represent both the buyer and the seller if both the buyer and seller give their informed consent in writing. In such a dual agency situation, the agent will not be able to provide the full range of fiduciary duties to the buyer and seller. The obligations of an agent are also subject to any specific provisions set forth in an agreement between the agent, and the buyer and seller. An agent acting as a dual agent must explain carefully to both the buyer and seller that the agent is acting for the other party as well. The agent should also explain the possible effects of dual representation, including that by consenting to the dual agency relationship the buyer and seller are giving up their right to undivided loyalty. A buyer or seller should carefully consider the possible consequences of a dual agency relationship before agreeing to such representation.

DUAL AGENT
WITH
DESIGNATED SALES AGENTS

If the buyer and the seller provide their informed consent in writing, the principals and the real estate broker who represents both parties as a dual agent may designate a sales agent to represent the buyer and another sales agent to represent the seller to negotiate the purchase and sale of real estate. A sales agent works under the supervision of the real estate broker. With the informed consent of the buyer and the seller in writing, the designated sales agent for the buyer will function as the buyer's agent representing the interests of and advocating on behalf of the buyer and the designated sales agent for the seller will function as the seller's agent representing the interests of and advocating on behalf of the seller in the negotiations between the buyer and seller. A designated sales agent cannot provide the full range of fiduciary duties to the buyer or seller. The designated sales agent must explain that like the dual agent under whose supervision they function, they cannot provide undivided loyalty. A buyer or seller should carefully consider the possible consequences of a dual agency relationship with designated sales agents before agreeing to such representation.

This form was provided to me by .... (print name of licensee) of .... (print name of company, firm or brokerage), a licensed real estate broker acting in the interest of the:

4

( )   Seller as a (check relationship below)   ( )   Buyer as a (check relationship below)

    ( )   Seller's agent   ( )   Buyer's agent

    ( )   Broker's agent   ( )   Broker's agent

          ( ) Dual agent

          ( ) Dual agent with designated sales agents

If dual agent with designated sales agents is checked:

.... is appointed to represent the buyer; and

.... is appointed to represent the seller in this transaction.

(I)(We) acknowledge receipt of a copy of this disclosure form:

Signature of [ ] Buyer(s) and/or [ ] Seller(s):

_____   _____

_____   _____

Date: _____   Date: _____

b.   For landlord-tenant transactions, the following shall be the disclosure form:

NEW YORK STATE DISCLOSURE FORM
FOR
LANDLORD AND TENANT

THIS IS NOT A CONTRACT

New York state law requires real estate licensees who are acting as agents of landlords and tenants of real property to advise the potential landlords and tenants with whom they work of the nature of their agency relationship and the rights and obligations it creates. This disclosure will help you to make informed choices about your relationship with the real estate broker and its sales associates.

Throughout the transaction you may receive more than one disclosure form. The law requires each agent assisting in the transaction to present you with this disclosure form. A real estate agent is a person qualified to advise about real estate. If you need legal, tax or other advice, consult with a professional in that field.

DISCLOSURE REGARDING REAL ESTATE AGENCY RELATIONSHIPS

LANDLORD'S AGENT

A landlord's agent is an agent who is engaged by a landlord to represent the landlord's interest. The landlord's agent does this by securing a tenant for the landlord's apartment or house at a rent and on terms acceptable to the landlord. A landlord's agent has, without limitation, the following fiduciary duties to the landlord: reasonable care, undivided loyalty, confidentiality, full disclosure, obedience and duty to account. A landlord's agent does not represent the interests of the tenant. The obligations of a landlord's agent are also subject to any specific provisions set forth in an agreement between the agent and the landlord. In

5

dealings with the tenant, a landlord's agent should (a) exercise reasonable skill and care in performance of the agent's duties; (b) deal honestly, fairly and in good faith; and (c) disclose all facts known to the agent materially affecting the value or desirability of property, except as otherwise provided by law.

TENANT'S AGENT

A tenant's agent is an agent who is engaged by a tenant to represent the tenant's interest. The tenant's agent does this by negotiating the rental or lease of an apartment or house at a rent and on terms acceptable to the tenant. A tenant's agent has, without limitation, the following fiduciary duties to the tenant: reasonable care, undivided loyalty, confidentiality, full disclosure, obedience and duty to account. A tenant's agent does not represent the interest of the landlord. The obligations of a tenant's agent are also subject to any specific provisions set forth in an agreement between the agent and the tenant. In dealings with the landlord, a tenant's agent should (a) exercise reasonable skill and care in performance of the agent's duties; (b) deal honestly, fairly and in good faith; and (c) disclose all facts known to the tenant's ability and/or willingness to perform a contract to rent or lease landlord's property that are not inconsistent with the agent's fiduciary duties to the buyer.

BROKER'S AGENTS

A broker's agent is an agent that cooperates or is engaged by a listing agent or a tenant's agent (but does not work for the same firm as the listing agent or tenant's agent) to assist the listing agent or tenant's agent in locating a property to rent or lease for the listing agent's landlord or the tenant agent's tenant. The broker's agent does not have a direct relationship with the tenant or landlord and the tenant or landlord can not provide instructions or direction directly to the broker's agent. The tenant and the landlord therefore do not have vicarious liability for the acts of the broker's agent. The listing agent or tenant's agent do provide direction and instruction to the broker's agent and therefore the listing agent or tenant's agent will have liability for the acts of the broker's agent.

DUAL AGENT

A real estate broker may represent both the tenant and the landlord if both the tenant and landlord give their informed consent in writing. In such a dual agency situation, the agent will not be able to provide the full range of fiduciary duties to the landlord and the tenant. The obligations of an agent are also subject to any specific provisions set forth in an agreement between the agent, and the tenant and landlord. An agent acting as a dual agent must explain carefully to both the landlord and tenant that the agent is acting for the other party as well. The agent should also explain the possible effects of dual representation, including that by consenting to the dual agency relationship the landlord and tenant are giving up their right to undivided loyalty. A landlord and tenant should carefully consider the possible consequences of a dual agency relationship before agreeing to such representation.

DUAL AGENT
WITH
DESIGNATED SALES AGENTS

If the tenant and the landlord provide their informed consent in writing, the principals and the real estate broker who represents both parties as a dual agent may designate a sales agent to represent the tenant and another sales agent to represent the landlord. A sales agent works under the supervision of the real estate broker. With the informed consent in writing of the tenant and the landlord, the designated sales agent for the tenant will function as the tenant's agent representing the interests of and advocating on behalf of the tenant and the designated sales agent for the landlord will function as the landlord's agent representing the interests of and advocating on behalf of the landlord in the negotiations between the tenant and the landlord. A designated sales agent cannot provide the full range of fiduciary duties to the landlord or tenant. The designated sales agent must explain that like the dual agent under whose supervision they function, they cannot provide undivided loyalty. A landlord or tenant should carefully consider the possible consequences of a dual agency relationship with designated sales agents before agreeing to such representation.

This form was provided to me by

(print name of licensee) of .... (print name of company, firm or brokerage), a licensed real estate broker acting in the interest of the:

( ) Landlord as a (check relationship be-   ( ) Tenant as a (check relationship below)   low)

    ( ) Landlord's agent   ( ) Tenant's agent

    ( ) Broker's agent   ( ) Broker's agent

        ( ) Dual agent

        ( ) Dual agent with designated sales agents

If dual agent with designated sales agents is checked:

.... is appointed to represent the tenant; and

.... is appointed to represent the landlord in this transaction.

(I)(We) .... acknowledge receipt of a copy of this disclosure form:

Signature of [] Landlord(s) and/or [] Tenant(s):

_____   _____

_____   _____

Date: _____   Date: _____

5. This section shall not apply to a real estate licensee who works with a buyer, seller, tenant or landlord in accordance with terms agreed to by the licensee and buyer, seller, tenant or landlord and in a capacity other than as an agent, as such term is defined in paragraph a of subdivision one of this section.

6. Nothing in this section shall be construed to limit or alter the application of the common law of agency with respect to residential real estate transactions.

2. UNIFORM VENDOR AND PURCHASER RISK ACT

CALIFORNIA CIVIL CODE

§ 1662. Uniform Vendor and Purchaser Risk Act

Any contract hereafter made in this State for the purchase and sale of real property shall be interpreted as including an agreement that the parties shall have the following rights and duties, unless the contract expressly provides otherwise:

(a) If, when neither the legal title nor the possession of the subject matter of the contract has been transferred, all or a material part thereof is destroyed without fault of the purchaser or is taken by eminent domain, the vendor cannot enforce the contract, and the purchaser is entitled to recover any portion of the price that he has paid;

(b) If, when either the legal title or the possession of the subject matter of the contract has been transferred, all or any part thereof is destroyed without fault of the vendor or is taken by eminent domain, the purchaser is not thereby relieved from a duty to pay the price, nor is he entitled to recover any portion thereof that he has paid.

This section shall be so interpreted and construed as to effectuate its general purpose to make uniform the law of those states which enact it.

This section may be cited as the Uniform Vendor and Purchaser Risk Act.

765 ILLINOIS ANNOTATED STATUTES

§ 65/1. Risk of Loss

Any contract hereafter made for the purchase and sale of real property in this State shall be interpreted as including an agreement that the parties shall have the following rights and duties, unless the contract expressly provides otherwise:

(a) If, when neither the legal title nor the possession of the subject matter of the contract has been transferred, all or a material part thereof is destroyed without fault of the purchaser or is taken by eminent domain, the vendor cannot enforce the contract, and the purchaser is entitled to recover any portion of the price that he has paid;

(b) If, when either the legal title or the possession of the subject matter of the contract has been transferred, all or any part thereof is destroyed without fault of the vendor or is taken by eminent domain, the purchaser is not thereby relieved from a duty to pay the price, nor is he entitled to recover any portion thereof that he has paid; provided, however, if the purchase and sale of real property is to be consummated by means of an escrow, title shall not be considered to have been transferred for purposes of this act, despite the delivery and recordation of a deed to such real property, unless the conditions of the escrow relating to the passing of the full legal and equitable title shall have been fulfilled.

§ 65/2. Uniformity of Interpretation

This act shall be so interpreted and construed as to effectuate its general purpose to make uniform the law of those states which enact it.

§ 65/3. Short Title

This act may be cited as the Uniform Vendor and Purchaser Risk Act.

NEW YORK GENERAL OBLIGATIONS LAW

§ 5–1311. Uniform Vendor and Purchaser Risk Act

1. Any contract for the purchase and sale or exchange of realty shall be interpreted, unless the contract expressly provides otherwise, as including an agreement that the parties shall have the following rights and duties:

a. When neither the legal title nor the possession of the subject matter of the contract has been transferred to the purchaser: (1) if all or a material part thereof is destroyed without fault of the purchaser or is taken by eminent domain, the vendor cannot enforce the contract, and the purchaser is entitled to recover any portion of the price that he has paid; but nothing herein contained shall be deemed to deprive the vendor of any right to recover damages against the purchaser for any breach of contract by the purchaser prior to the destruction or taking; (2) if an immaterial part thereof is destroyed without fault of the purchaser or is taken by eminent domain, neither the vendor nor the purchaser is thereby deprived of the right to enforce the contract; but there shall be, to the extent of the destruction or taking, an abatement of the purchase price.

b. When either the legal title or the possession of the subject matter of the contract has been transferred to the purchaser, if all or any part thereof is destroyed without fault of the vendor or is taken by eminent domain, the purchaser is not thereby relieved from a duty to pay the price, nor is he thereby entitled to recover any portion thereof that he has paid; but nothing herein contained shall be deemed to deprive the purchaser of any right to recover damages against the vendor for any breach of contract by the vendor prior to the destruction or taking.

2. This section shall be so interpreted and construed as to effectuate its general purpose to make uniform the law of those states which enact it.

3. This section may be cited as the uniform vendor and purchaser risk act.

3. DEEDS AND DEED COVENANTS

OHIO REVISED CODE

§ 5302.01 Statutory forms; alteration

The forms set forth in sections 5302.05, 5302.07, 5302.09, 5302.11, 5302.12, 5302.14, 5302.17, and 5302.22 of the Revised Code may be used and shall be sufficient for their respective purposes. They shall be known as "Statutory Forms" and may be referred to as such. They may be altered as circumstances require, and the authorization of such forms shall not prevent the use of other forms. Wherever the phrases defined in sections 5302.06, 5302.08, 5302.10, and 5302.13 of the Revised Code are to be incorporated in instruments by reference, the method of incorporation as indicated in the statutory forms shall be sufficient, but shall not preclude other methods.

§ 5302.03 Grant defined

In a conveyance of real estate or any interest therein, the word "grant" is a sufficient word of conveyance without the use of more words. No covenant shall be implied from the use of the word "grant."

§ 5302.05 Deed in fee simple, general warranty deed

A deed in substance following the form set forth in this section, when duly executed in accordance with Chapter 5301. of the Revised Code, has the force and effect of a deed in fee simple to the grantee, the grantee's heirs, assigns, and successors, to the grantee's and the grantee's heirs', assigns', and successors' own use, with covenants on the part of the grantor with the grantee, the grantee's heirs, assigns, and successors, that, at the time of the delivery of that deed the grantor was lawfully seized in fee simple of the granted premises, that the granted premises were free from all encumbrances, that the grantor had good right to sell and convey the same to the grantee and the grantee's heirs, assigns, and successors, and that the grantor does warrant and will defend the same to the grantee and the grantee's heirs, assigns, and successors, forever, against the lawful claims and demands of all persons.

"GENERAL WARRANTY DEED

_____ (marital status), of _____ County, _____ for valuable consideration paid, grant(s), with general warranty covenants, to _____, whose tax-mailing address is _____, the following real property:

(description of land or interest therein and encumbrances, reservations, and exceptions, if any)

Prior Instrument Reference: Volume ___, Page ___

_____, wife (husband) of the grantor, releases all rights of dower therein.

Executed this _____ day of _____.

_____

(Signature of Grantor)

(Execution in accordance with Chapter 5301. of the Revised Code)"

§ 5302.06   General warranty covenants

In a conveyance of real estate, or any interest therein, the words "general warranty covenants" have the full force, meaning, and effect of the following words: "The grantor covenants with the grantee, his heirs, assigns, and successors, that he is lawfully seized in fee simple of the granted premises; that they are free from all encumbrances; that he has good right to sell and convey the same, and that he does warrant and will defend the same to the grantee and his heirs, assigns, and successors, forever, against the lawful claims and demands of all persons."

§ 5302.07   Limited warranty deed

A deed in substance following the form set forth in this section, when duly executed in accordance with Chapter 5301. of the Revised Code, has the force and effect of a deed in fee simple to the grantee, the grantee's heirs, assigns, and successors, to the grantee's and the grantee's heirs', assigns', and successors' own use, with covenants on the part of the grantor with the grantee, the grantee's heirs, assigns, and successors, that, at the time of the delivery of that deed the premises were free from all encumbrances made by the grantor, and that the grantor does warrant and will defend the same to the grantee and the grantee's heirs, assigns, and successors, forever, against the lawful claims and demands of all persons claiming by, through, or under the grantor, but against none other.

"LIMITED WARRANTY DEED

_____ (marital status), of _____ County, _____ for valuable consideration paid, grant(s), with limited warranty covenants, to _____, whose tax-mailing address is _____, the following real property:

(description of land or interest therein and encumbrances, reservations, and exceptions, if any)

Prior Instrument Reference: Volume ___, Page ___

_____, wife (husband) of said grantor, releases to said grantee all rights of dower therein.

Executed this _____ day of _____.

_____

(Signature of Grantor)

(Execution in accordance with Chapter 5301. of the Revised Code)"

§ 5302.08   Limited warranty covenants defined

In a conveyance of real estate, or any interest therein, the words "limited warranty covenants" have the full force, meaning, and effect of the following words: "The grantor covenants with the grantee, his heirs, assigns, and successors, that the granted premises are free from all encumbrances made by the grantor, and that he does warrant and will defend the same to the grantee and his heirs, assigns, and successors, forever, against the lawful claims and demands of all persons claiming by, through, or under the grantor, but against none other."

11

§ 5302.11   Quit-claim deed

A deed in substance following the form set forth in this section, when duly executed in accordance with Chapter 5301. of the Revised Code, has the force and effect of a deed in fee simple to the grantee, the grantee's heirs, assigns, and successors, and to the grantee's and the grantee's heirs', assigns', and successors' own use, but without covenants of any kind on the part of the grantor.

"QUIT–CLAIM DEED

_____ (marital status), of _____ County, _____ for valuable consideration paid, grant(s) to _____, whose tax-mailing address is _____, the following real property:

(description of land or interest therein and encumbrances, reservations, and exceptions, if any)

Prior Instrument Reference: Volume ___, Page ___

_____, wife (husband) of the grantor, releases all rights of dower therein.

Executed this _____ day of _____.

_____

(Signature of Grantor)

(Execution in accordance with Chapter 5301. of the Revised Code)"

4. DISCLOSURES ON SALE OF REALTY STATUTE

CALIFORNIA CIVIL CODE

§ 1102. Application of Article

(a) Except as provided in Section 1102.2, this article applies to any transfer by sale, exchange, installment land sale contract, as defined in Section 2985, lease with an option to purchase, any other option to purchase, or ground lease coupled with improvements, of real property, or residential stock cooperative, improved with or consisting of not less than one nor more than four dwelling units.

(b) This article shall be applicable to the resale on or after January 1, 2000, of a manufactured home, as defined in Section 18007 of the Health and Safety Code, or a mobile home, as defined in Section 18008 of the Health and Safety Code.

(c) Any waiver of the requirements of this article is void as against public policy.

§ 1102.3 Delivery of Required Written Statement From Transferor to Prospective Transferee; . . . Disclosures Delivered After Offer to Purchase; Time to Terminate

The transferor of any real property subject to this article shall deliver to the prospective transferee the written statement required by this article, as follows:

(a) In the case of a sale, as soon as practicable before transfer of title.

(b) In the case of transfer by a real property sales contract, as defined in Section 2985, or by a lease together with an option to purchase, or a ground lease coupled with improvements, as soon as practicable before execution of the contract. For the purpose of this subdivision, "execution" means the making or acceptance of an offer.

. . .

If any disclosure, or any material amendment of any disclosure, required to be made by this article, is delivered after the execution of an offer to purchase, the transferee shall have three days after delivery in person or five days after delivery by deposit in the mail, to terminate his or her offer by delivery of a written notice of termination to the transferor or the transferor's agent.

§ 1102.6 Disclosure Form

The disclosures required by this article pertaining to the property proposed to be transferred are set forth in, and shall be made on a copy of, the following disclosure form:

REAL ESTATE TRANSFER DISCLOSURE STATEMENT

THIS DISCLOSURE STATEMENT CONCERNS THE REAL PROPERTY SITUATED IN THE CITY OF _____, COUNTY OF _____, STATE OF CALIFORNIA, DESCRIBED AS _____. THIS STATEMENT IS A DISCLOSURE OF THE CONDITION OF THE ABOVE DESCRIBED PROPERTY IN COMPLIANCE WITH SECTION 1102 OF THE CIVIL CODE AS _____, 19__. IT IS NOT A WARRANTY OF ANY KIND BY THE

SELLER(S) OR ANY AGENT(S) REPRESENTING ANY PRINCIPAL(S) IN THIS TRANS-
ACTION, AND IS NOT A SUBSTITUTE FOR ANY INSPECTIONS OR WARRANTIES
THE PRINCIPAL(S) MAY WISH TO OBTAIN.

I
COORDINATION WITH OTHER DISCLOSURE FORMS

This Real Estate Transfer Disclosure Statement is made pursuant to Section 1102 of the
Civil Code. Other statutes require disclosures, depending upon the details of the particular
real estate transaction (for example: special study zone and purchase-money liens on
residential property).

Substituted Disclosures: The following disclosures and other disclosures required by law,
including the Natural Hazard Disclosure Report/Statement that may include airport annoy-
ances, earthquake, fire, flood, or special assessment information, have or will be made in
connection with this real estate transfer, and are intended to satisfy the disclosure obligations on this form, where the subject matter is the same:

[ ] Inspection reports completed pursuant to the contract of sale or receipt for deposit.

[ ] Additional inspection reports or disclosures: _____

_____

_____

_____

II
SELLER'S INFORMATION

The Seller discloses the following information with the knowledge that even though this
is not a warranty, prospective Buyers may rely on this information in deciding whether and
on what terms to purchase the subject property. Seller hereby authorizes any agent(s)
representing any principal(s) in this transaction to provide a copy of this statement to any
person or entity in connection with any actual or anticipated sale of the property.

THE FOLLOWING ARE REPRESENTATIONS MADE BY THE SELLER(S) AND ARE
NOT THE REPRESENTATIONS OF THE AGENT(S), IF ANY. THIS INFORMATION IS
A DISCLOSURE AND IS NOT INTENDED TO BE PART OF ANY CONTRACT BE-
TWEEN THE BUYER AND SELLER.

Seller ___ is ___ is not occupying the property.

A. The subject property has the items checked below (read across):

___ Range	___ Oven	___ Microwave
___ Dishwasher	___ Trash Compactor	___ Garbage Disposal
___ Washer/Dryer Hook-ups		___ Rain Gutters
___ Burglar Alarms	___ Smoke Detector(s)	___ Fire Alarm
___ TV Antenna	___ Satellite Dish	___ Intercom
___ Central Heating	___ Central Air Cndtng.	___ Evaporator Cooler(s)
___ Wall/Window Air Cndtng.	___ Sprinklers	___ Public Sewer System
___ Septic Tank	___ Sump Pump	___ Water Softener
___ Patio/Decking	___ Built-in Barbecue	___ Gazebo
___ Sauna		

___ Hot Tub ___Locking Safety Cover*
___ Security Gate(s)

Garage: ___Attached
Pool/Spa Heater: ___Gas
Water Heater: ___Gas

Water Supply: ___City
Gas Supply: ___Utility
___ Window Screens

___ Pool ___Child Resistant Barrier*
___ Automatic Garage Door Opener(s)*
___ Not Attached
___ Solar
___ Water Heater Anchored, Braced, or Strapped*

___ Well
___ Bottled
___ Window Security Bars
___ Quick Release Mechanism on Bedroom Windows*

___ Spa ___Locking Safety Cover*
___ Number Remote Controls
___ Carport
___ Electric
___ Private Utility or Other_____

Exhaust Fan(s) in _____ 220 Volt Wiring in ____ Fireplace(s) in _____
Gas   Starter _____   Roof(s):   Type: _____   Age: _____   (approx.)
Other: _____

Are there, to the best of your (Seller's) knowledge, any of the above that are not in operating condition? ___Yes ___No. If yes, then describe.

(Attach additional sheets if necessary): _____

_____
_____
_____

B. Are you (Seller) aware of any significant defects/malfunctions in any of the following? ___Yes ___No. If yes, check appropriate space(s) below.

___Interior Walls ___Ceilings ___Floors ___Exterior Walls ___Insulation ___Roof(s) ___Windows ___Doors ___Foundation ___Slab(s) ___Driveways ___Sidewalks ___Walls/Fences ___Electrical Systems ___Plumbing/Sewers/Septics ___Other

Structural Components (Describe: _____)
If any of the above is checked, explain. (Attach additional sheets if necessary): _____

_____
_____
_____

C. Are you (Seller) aware of any of the following:
   1. Substances, materials, or products which may be an environmental hazard such as, but not limited to, asbestos, formaldehyde, radon gas, lead-based paint, mold, fuel or chemical storage tanks, and contaminated soil or water on the subject property.................___Yes ___No
   2. Features of the property shared in common with adjoining landowners, such as walls, fences, and driveways, whose use or responsibility for maintenance may have an effect on the subject property . . . . .___Yes ___No

* This garage door opener or child resistant pool barrier may not be in compliance with the safety standards relating to automatic reversing devices as set forth in Chapter 12.5 (commencing with Section 19890) of Part 3 of Division 13 of, or with the pool safety standards of Article 2.5 (commencing with Section 115920) of Chapter 5 of Part 10 of Division 104 of, the Health and Safety Code. The water heater may not be anchored, braced, or strapped in accordance with Section 19211 of the Health and Safety Code. Window security bars may not have quick-release mechanisms in compliance with the 1995 edition of the California Building Standards Code.

3. Any encroachments, easements or similar matters that may affect your interest in the subject property.............................___Yes ___No
4. Room additions, structural modifications, or other alterations or repairs made without necessary permits ....___Yes ___No
5. Room additions, structural modifications, or other alterations or repairs not in compliance with building codes ....___Yes ___No
6. Fill (compacted or otherwise) on the property or any portion thereof ....___Yes ___No
7. Any settling from any cause, or slippage, sliding, or other soil problems..___Yes ___No
8. Flooding, drainage or grading problems...........................___Yes ___No
9. Major damage to the property or any of the structures from fire, earthquake, floods, or landslides ....___Yes ___No
10. Any zoning violations, nonconforming uses, violations of "setback" requirements...___Yes ___No
11. Neighborhood noise problems or other nuisances ....___Yes ___No
12. CC & R's or other deed restrictions or obligations..................___Yes ___No
13. Homeowners' Association which has any authority over the subject property ....___Yes ___No
14. Any "common area" (facilities such as pools, tennis courts, walkways, or other areas co-owned in undivided interest with others) ....___Yes ___No
15. Any notices of abatement or citations against the property ....___Yes ___No
16. Any lawsuits by or against the Seller threatening to or affecting this real property, including any lawsuits alleging a defect or deficiency in this real property or "common areas" (facilities such as pools, tennis courts, walkways, or other areas coowned in undivided interest with others).....................................___Yes ___No

If the answer to any of these is yes, explain. (Attach additional sheets if necessary.):

_____
_____
_____

Seller certifies that the information herein is true and correct to the best of the Seller's knowledge as of the date signed by the Seller.

Seller _____   Date _____
Seller _____   Date _____

III*

AGENT'S INSPECTION DISCLOSURE

(To be completed only if the Seller is represented by an agent in this transaction.)

THE UNDERSIGNED, BASED ON THE ABOVE INQUIRY OF THE SELLER(S) AS TO THE CONDITION OF THE PROPERTY AND BASED ON A REASONABLY COMPETENT AND DILIGENT VISUAL INSPECTION OF THE ACCESSIBLE AREAS OF THE PROPERTY IN CONJUNCTION WITH THAT INQUIRY, STATES THE FOLLOWING:

[ ] Agent notes no items for disclosure.

[ ] Agent notes the following items:

_____

_____

_____

_____

_____

Agent (Broker
Representing Seller) _____ By _____ Date _____
                   (Please Print)   (Associate Licensee
                                   or Broker–Signature)

IV

AGENT'S INSPECTION DISCLOSURE

(To be completed only if the agent who has obtained the offer is other than the agent above.)

THE UNDERSIGNED, BASED ON A REASONABLY COMPETENT AND DILIGENT VISUAL INSPECTION OF THE ACCESSIBLE AREAS OF THE PROPERTY, STATES THE FOLLOWING:

[ ] Agent notes no items for disclosure.

[ ] Agent notes the following items:

_____

_____

_____

_____

Agent (Broker
Representing Seller) _____ By _____ Date _____
                   (Please Print)   (Associate Licensee
                                   or Broker–Signature)

V

BUYER(S) AND SELLER(S) MAY WISH TO OBTAIN PROFESSIONAL ADVICE AND/OR INSPECTIONS OF THE PROPERTY AND TO PROVIDE FOR APPROPRIATE PROVISIONS IN A CONTRACT BETWEEN BUYER AND SELLER(S) WITH RESPECT TO ANY ADVICE/INSPECTIONS/DEFECTS.

I/WE ACKNOWLEDGE RECEIPT OF A COPY OF THIS STATEMENT.

Seller _____ Date _____ Buyer _____ Date _____
Seller _____ Date _____ Buyer _____ Date _____

Agent (Broker
Representing Seller) _____ By _____ Date _____
                                 (Associate Licensee
                                   or Broker–Signature

Agent (Broker
obtaining the Offer) _____ By _____ Date _____

(Associate Licensee
or Broker–Signature)

SECTION 1102.3 OF THE CIVIL CODE PROVIDES A BUYER WITH THE RIGHT TO RESCIND A PURCHASE CONTRACT FOR AT LEAST THREE DAYS AFTER THE DELIVERY OF THIS DISCLOSURE IF DELIVERY OCCURS AFTER THE SIGNING OF AN OFFER TO PURCHASE. IF YOU WISH TO RESCIND THE CONTRACT, YOU MUST ACT WITHIN THE PRESCRIBED PERIOD.

A REAL ESTATE BROKER IS QUALIFIED TO ADVISE ON REAL ESTATE. IF YOU DESIRE LEGAL ADVICE, CONSULT YOUR ATTORNEY.

§ 1102.7   Good Faith Required

Each disclosure required by this article and each act which may be performed in making the disclosure, shall be made in good faith. For purposes of this article, "good faith" means honesty in fact in the conduct of the transaction.

§ 1102.8   Specification of Items for Disclosure Not Limitation on Other Disclosure Obligations

The specification of items for disclosure in this article does not limit or abridge any obligation for disclosure created by any other provision of law or which may exist in order to avoid fraud, misrepresentation, or deceit in the transfer transaction.

§ 1102.13   Failure to Comply With Article; Transfer Not Invalidated; Damages

No transfer subject to this article shall be invalidated solely because of the failure of any person to comply with any provision of this article. However, any person who willfully or negligently violates or fails to perform any duty prescribed by any provision of this article shall be liable in the amount of actual damages suffered by a transferee.

5. RECORDING ACTS

a. RACE TYPE

———

GENERAL STATUTES OF NORTH CAROLINA

§ 47–18. Conveyances, Contracts to Convey, Options and Leases of Land

(a) No (i) conveyance of land, or (ii) contract to convey, or (iii) option to convey, or (iv) lease of land for more than three years shall be valid to pass any property interest as against lien creditors or purchasers for a valuable consideration from the donor, bargainor or lessor but from the time of registration thereof in the county where the land lies, or if the land is located in more than one county, then in each county where any portion of the land lies to be effective as to the land in that county. Unless otherwise stated either on the registered instrument or on a separate registered instrument duly executed by the party whose priority interest is adversely affected, (i) instruments registered in the office of the register of deeds shall have priority based on the order of registration as determined by the time of registration, and (ii) if instruments are registered simultaneously, then the instruments shall be presumed to have priority as determined by:

(1) The earliest document number set forth on the registered instrument.

(2) The sequential book and page number set forth on the registered instrument if no document number is set forth on the registered instrument.

The presumption created by this subsection is rebuttable

(b) This section shall not apply to contracts, leases or deeds executed prior to March 1, 1885, until January 1, 1886; and no purchase from any such donor, bargainor or lessor shall avail or pass title as against any unregistered deed executed prior to December 1, 1885, when the person holding or claiming under such unregistered deed shall be in actual possession and enjoyment of such land, either in person or by his tenant, at the time of the execution of such second deed, or when the person claiming under or taking such second deed had at the time of taking or purchasing under such deed actual or constructive notice of such unregistered deed, or the claim of the person holding or claiming thereunder.

b. NOTICE TYPE

ANNOTATED LAWS OF MASSACHUSETTS c. 183

§ 4. Effect of Recordation or Actual Notice of Deeds or Leases, or Assignment of Rents or Profits

A conveyance of an estate in fee simple, fee tail or for life, or a lease for more than seven years from the making thereof, or an assignment of rents or profits from an estate or lease, shall not be valid as against any person, except the grantor or lessor, his heirs and devisees and persons having actual notice of it, unless it, or an office copy as provided in section thirteen of chapter thirty-six, or, with respect to such a lease or an assignment of rents or profits, a notice of lease or a notice of assignment of rents or profits, as hereinafter defined, is recorded in the registry of deeds for the county or district in which the land to which it relates lies. A "notice of lease", as used in this section, shall mean an instrument in writing executed by all persons who are parties to the lease of which notice is given and shall contain the following information with reference to such lease:—the date of execution thereof and a description, in the form contained in such lease, of the premises demised, and the term of such lease, with the date of commencement of such term and all rights of extension or renewal. A "notice of assignment of rents or profits", as used in this section, shall mean an instrument in writing executed by the assignor and containing the following information:—a description of the premises, the rent or profits of which have been assigned, adequate to identify the premises, the name of assignee, and the rents and profits which have been assigned. A provision in a recorded mortgage assigning or conditionally assigning rents or profits or obligating the mortgagor to assign or conditionally assign existing or future rents or profits shall constitute a "notice of assignment of rents or profits".

c. RACE–NOTICE TYPE

CALIFORNIA CIVIL CODE

§ 1214. Prior Recording of Subsequent Conveyances, Mortgages, Judgments

Every conveyance of real property or an estate for years therein, other than a lease for a term not exceeding one year, is void as against any subsequent purchaser or mortgagee of the same property, or any part thereof, in good faith and for a valuable consideration, whose conveyance is first duly recorded, and as against any judgment affecting the title, unless the conveyance shall have been duly recorded prior to the record of notice of action.

NEW YORK REAL PROPERTY LAW

§ 291. Recording of Conveyances

A conveyance of real property, within the state, on being duly acknowledged by the person executing the same, or proved as required by this chapter, and such acknowledgment or proof duly certified when required by this chapter, may be recorded in the office of the clerk of the county where such real property is situated, and such county clerk shall, upon the request of any party, on tender of the lawful fees therefor, record the same in his said office. Every such conveyance not so recorded is void as against any person who subsequently purchases or acquires by exchange or contracts to purchase or acquire by exchange, the same real property or any portion thereof, or acquires by assignment the rent to accrue therefrom as provided in section two hundred ninety-four-a of the real property law, in good faith and for a valuable consideration, from the same vendor or assignor, his distributees or devisees, and whose conveyance, contract or assignment is first duly recorded, and is void as against the lien upon the same real property or any portion thereof arising from payments made upon the execution of or pursuant to the terms of a contract with the same vendor, his distributees or devisees, if such contract is made in good faith and is first duly recorded. Notwithstanding the foregoing, any increase in the principal balance of a mortgage lien by virtue of the addition thereto of unpaid interest in accordance with the terms of the mortgage shall retain the priority of the original mortgage lien as so increased provided that any such mortgage instrument sets forth its terms of repayment.

6. HOLDER IN DUE COURSE PROVISIONS

a. UNIFORM COMMERCIAL CODE, 1990 OFFICIAL TEXT

§ 3–104. Negotiable Instrument

(a) Except as provided in subsections (c) and (d), "negotiable instrument" means an unconditional promise or order to pay a fixed amount of money, with or without interest or other charges described in the promise or order, if it:

(1) is payable to bearer or to order at the time it is issued or first comes into possession of a holder;

(2) is payable on demand or at a definite time; and

(3) does not state any other undertaking or instruction by the person promising or ordering payment to do any act in addition to the payment of money, but the promise or order may contain (i) an undertaking or power to give, maintain, or protect collateral to secure payment, (ii) an authorization or power to the holder to confess judgment or realize on or dispose of collateral, or (iii) a waiver of the benefit of any law intended for the advantage or protection of an obligor.

(b) "Instrument" means a negotiable instrument.

(c) An order that meets all of the requirements of subsection (a), except paragraph (1), and otherwise falls within the definition of "check" in subsection (f) is a negotiable instrument and a check.

(d) A promise or order other than a check is not an instrument if, at the time it is issued or first comes into possession of a holder, it contains a conspicuous statement, however expressed, to the effect that the promise or order is not negotiable or is not an instrument governed by this Article.

(e) An instrument is a "note" if it is a promise and is a "draft" if it is an order. If an instrument falls within the definition of both "note" and "draft," a person entitled to enforce the instrument may treat it as either.

(f) "Check" means (i) a draft, other than a documentary draft, payable on demand and drawn on a bank or (ii) a cashier's check or teller's check. An instrument may be a check even though it is described on its face by another term, such as "money order."

(g) "Cashier's check" means a draft with respect to which the drawer and drawee are the same bank or branches of the same bank.

(h) "Teller's check" means a draft drawn by a bank (i) on another bank, or (ii) payable at or through a bank.

(i) "Traveler's check" means an instrument that (i) is payable on demand, (ii) is drawn on or payable at or through a bank, (iii) is designated by the term "traveler's check" or by a substantially similar term, and (iv) requires, as a condition to payment, a countersignature by a person whose specimen signature appears on the instrument.

(j) "Certificate of deposit" means an instrument containing an acknowledgment by a bank that a sum of money has been received by the bank and a promise by the bank to repay the sum of money. A certificate of deposit is a note of the bank.

§ 3–106. Unconditional Promise or Order

(a) Except as provided in this section, for the purposes of Section 3–104(a), a promise or order is unconditional unless it states (i) an express condition to payment, (ii) that the promise or order is subject to or governed by another writing, or (iii) that rights or obligations with respect to the promise or order are stated in another writing. A reference to another writing does not of itself make the promise or order conditional.

(b) A promise or order is not made conditional (i) by a reference to another writing for a statement of rights with respect to collateral, prepayment, or acceleration, or (ii) because payment is limited to resort to a particular fund or source.

(c) If a promise or order requires, as a condition to payment, a countersignature by a person whose specimen signature appears on the promise or order, the condition does not make the promise or order conditional for the purposes of Section 3–104(a). If the person whose specimen signature appears on an instrument fails to countersign the instrument, the failure to countersign is a defense to the obligation of the issuer, but the failure does not prevent a transferee of the instrument from becoming a holder of the instrument.

(d) If a promise or order at the time it is issued or first comes into possession of a holder contains a statement, required by applicable statutory or administrative law, to the effect that the rights of a holder or transferee are subject to claims or defenses that the issuer could assert against the original payee, the promise or order is not thereby made conditional for the purposes of Section 3–104(a); but if the promise or order is an instrument, there cannot be a holder in due course of the instrument.

§ 3–302. Holder in Due Course

(a) Subject to subsection (c) and Section 3–106(d), "holder in due course" means the holder of an instrument if:

    (1) the instrument when issued or negotiated to the holder does not bear such apparent evidence of forgery or alteration or is not otherwise so irregular or incomplete as to call into question its authenticity; and

    (2) the holder took the instrument (i) for value, (ii) in good faith, (iii) without notice that the instrument is overdue or has been dishonored or that there is an uncured default with respect to payment of another instrument issued as part of the same series, (iv) without notice that the instrument contains an unauthorized signature or has been altered, (v) without notice of any claim to the instrument described in Section 3–306, and (vi) without notice that any party has a defense or claim in recoupment described in Section 3–305(a).

(b) Notice of discharge of a party, other than discharge in an insolvency proceeding, is not notice of a defense under subsection (a), but discharge is effective against a person who became a holder in due course with notice of the discharge. Public filing or recording of a document does not of itself constitute notice of a defense, claim in recoupment, or claim to the instrument.

(c) Except to the extent a transferor or predecessor in interest has rights as a holder in due course, a person does not acquire rights of a holder in due course of an instrument taken (i) by legal process or by purchase in an execution, bankruptcy, or creditor's sale or similar proceeding, (ii) by purchase as part of a bulk transaction not in ordinary course of business of the transferor, or (iii) as the successor in interest to an estate or other organization.

(d) If, under Section 3–303(a)(1), the promise of performance that is the consideration for an instrument has been partially performed, the holder may assert rights as a holder in due course of the instrument only to the fraction of the amount payable under the instrument equal to the value of the partial performance divided by the value of the promised performance.

(e) If (i) the person entitled to enforce an instrument has only a security interest in the instrument and (ii) the person obliged to pay the instrument has a defense, claim in recoupment, or claim to the instrument that may be asserted against the person who granted the security interest, the person entitled to enforce the instrument may assert rights as a holder in due course only to an amount payable under the instrument which, at the time of enforcement of the instrument, does not exceed the amount of the unpaid obligation secured.

(f) To be effective, notice must be received at a time and in a manner that gives a reasonable opportunity to act on it.

(g) This section is subject to any law limiting status as a holder in due course in particular classes of transactions.

§ 3–303. Value and Consideration

(a) An instrument is issued or transferred for value if:

(1) the instrument is issued or transferred for a promise of performance, to the extent the promise has been performed;

(2) the transferee acquires a security interest or other lien in the instrument other than a lien obtained by judicial proceeding;

(3) the instrument is issued or transferred as payment of, or as security for, an antecedent claim against any person, whether or not the claim is due;

(4) the instrument is issued or transferred in exchange for a negotiable instrument; or

(5) the instrument is issued or transferred in exchange for the incurring of an irrevocable obligation to a third party by the person taking the instrument.

(b) "Consideration" means any consideration sufficient to support a simple contract. The drawer or maker of an instrument has a defense if the instrument is issued without consideration. If an instrument is issued for a promise of performance, the issuer has a defense to the extent performance of the promise is due and the promise has not been performed. If an instrument is issued for value as stated in subsection (a), the instrument is also issued for consideration.

§ 3–305. Defenses and Claims in Recoupment; Claims in Consumer Transactions

(a) Except as stated in subsection (b), the right to enforce the obligation of a party to pay an instrument is subject to the following:

(1) a defense of the obligor based on (i) infancy of the obligor to the extent it is a defense to a simple contract, (ii) duress, lack of legal capacity, or illegality of the transaction which, under other law, nullifies the obligation of the obligor, (iii) fraud that induced the obligor to sign the instrument with neither knowledge nor reasonable opportunity to learn of its character or its essential terms, or (iv) discharge of the obligor in insolvency proceedings;

(2) a defense of the obligor stated in another section of this Article or a defense of the obligor that would be available if the person entitled to enforce the instrument were enforcing a right to payment under a simple contract; and

(3) a claim in recoupment of the obligor against the original payee of the instrument if the claim arose from the transaction that gave rise to the instrument; but the claim of the obligor may be asserted against a transferee of the instrument only to reduce the amount owing on the instrument at the time the action is brought.

(b) The right of a holder in due course to enforce the obligation of a party to pay the instrument is subject to defenses of the obligor stated in subsection (a)(1), but is not subject to defenses of the obligor stated in subsection (a)(2) or claims in recoupment stated in subsection (a)(3) against a person other than the holder.

(c) Except as stated in subsection (d), in an action to enforce the obligation of a party to pay the instrument, the obligor may not assert against the person entitled to enforce the instrument a defense, claim in recoupment, or claim to the instrument (Section 3–306) of another person, but the other person's claim to the instrument may be asserted by the obligor if the other person is joined in the action and personally asserts the claim against the person entitled to enforce the instrument. An obligor is not obliged to pay the instrument if the person seeking enforcement of the instrument does not have rights of a holder in due course and the obligor proves that the instrument is a lost or stolen instrument.

(d) In an action to enforce the obligation of an accommodation party to pay an instrument, the accommodation party may assert against the person entitled to enforce the instrument any defense or claim in recoupment under subsection (a) that the accommodated party could assert against the person entitled to enforce the instrument, except the defenses of discharge in insolvency proceedings, infancy, and lack of legal capacity.

b.   UNIFORM COMMERCIAL CODE, 2001 OFFICIAL TEXT

§ 1–201.   General Definitions.

(a) Unless the context otherwise requires, words or phrases defined in this section, or in the additional definitions contained in other articles of [the Uniform Commercial Code] that apply to particular articles or parts thereof, have the meanings stated.

(b) Subject to definitions contained in other articles of [the Uniform Commercial Code] that apply to particular articles or parts thereof:

(20) "Good faith," except as otherwise provided in Article 5, means honesty in fact and the observance of reasonable commercial standards of fair dealing.

Comment 20. "Good faith." Former Section 1–201(19) defined "good faith" simply as honesty in fact; the definition contained no element of commercial reasonableness. Initially, that definition applied throughout the Code with only one exception. Former Section 2–

103(1)(b) provided that *"in this Article* ... good faith in the case of a merchant means honesty in fact and the observance of reasonable commercial standards of fair dealing in the trade." This alternative definition was limited in applicability in three ways. First, it applied only to transactions within the scope of Article 2. Second, it applied only to merchants. Third, strictly construed it applied only to uses of the phrase "good faith" *in Article 2;* thus, so construed it would not define "good faith" for its most important use-the obligation of good faith imposed by former Section 1–203.

Over time, however, amendments to the Uniform Commercial Code brought the Article 2 merchant concept of good faith (subjective honesty and objective commercial reasonableness) into other Articles. First, Article 2A explicitly incorporated the Article 2 standard. See Section 2A–103(7). Then, other Articles broadened the applicability of that standard by adopting it for all parties rather than just for merchants. *See, e.g.,* Sections 3–103(a)(4), 4A–105(a)(6), 8–102(a)(10), and 9–102(a)(43). All of these definitions are comprised of two elements-honesty in fact *and* the observance of reasonable commercial standards of fair dealing. Only revised Article 5 defines "good faith" solely in terms of subjective honesty, and only Article 6 and Article 7 are without definitions of good faith. (It should be noted that, while revised Article 6 did not define good faith, Comment 2 to revised Section 6–102 states that "this Article adopts the definition of 'good faith' in Article 1 in all cases, even when the buyer is a merchant.") Given these developments, it is appropriate to move the broader definition of "good faith" to Article 1. Of course, this definition is subject to the applicability of the narrower definition in revised Article 5.

c. 16 CODE OF FEDERAL REGULATIONS

§ 433.1 Definitions

(a) Person. An individual, corporation, or any other business organization.

(b) Consumer. A natural person who seeks or acquires goods or services for personal, family, or household use.

(c) Creditor. A person who, in the ordinary course of business, lends purchase money or finances the sale of goods or services to consumers on a deferred payment basis; Provided, such person is not acting, for the purposes of a particular transaction, in the capacity of a credit card issuer.

(d) Purchase money loan. A cash advance which is received by a consumer in return for a "Finance Charge" within the meaning of the Truth in Lending Act and Regulation Z, which is applied, in whole or substantial part, to a purchase of goods or services from a seller who (1) refers consumers to the creditor or (2) is affiliated with the creditor by common control, contract, or business arrangement.

(e) Financing a sale. Extending credit to a consumer in connection with a "Credit Sale" within the meaning of the Truth in Lending Act and Regulation Z.

(f) Contract. Any oral or written agreement, formal or informal, between a creditor and a seller, which contemplates or provides for cooperative or concerted activity in connection with the sale of goods or services to consumers or the financing thereof.

(g) Business arrangement. Any understanding, procedure, course of dealing, or arrangement, formal or informal, between a creditor and a seller, in connection with the sale of goods or services to consumers or the financing thereof.

(h) Credit card issuer. A person who extends to cardholders the right to use a credit card in connection with purchases of goods or services.

(i) Consumer credit contract. Any instrument which evidences or embodies a debt arising from a "Purchase Money Loan" transaction or a "financed sale" as defined in paragraphs (d) and (e) of this section.

(j) Seller. A person who, in the ordinary course of business, sells or leases goods or services to consumers.

§ 433.2 Preservation of consumers' claims and defenses, unfair or deceptive acts or practices

In connection with any sale or lease of goods or services to consumers, in or affecting commerce as "commerce" is defined in the Federal Trade Commission Act, it is an unfair or deceptive act or practice within the meaning of Section 5 of that Act for a seller, directly or indirectly, to:

(a) Take or receive a consumer credit contract which fails to contain the following provision in at least ten point, bold face, type:

NOTICE

ANY HOLDER OF THIS CONSUMER CREDIT CONTRACT IS SUBJECT TO ALL CLAIMS AND DEFENSES WHICH THE DEBTOR COULD ASSERT AGAINST THE SELLER OF GOODS OR SERVICES OBTAINED PURSUANT HERETO OR WITH THE PROCEEDS HEREOF. RECOVERY HEREUNDER BY THE DEBTOR SHALL NOT EXCEED AMOUNTS PAID BY THE DEBTOR HEREUNDER.

or,

(b) Accept, as full or partial payment for such sale or lease, the proceeds of any purchase money loan (as purchase money loan is defined herein), unless any consumer credit contract made in connection with such purchase money loan contains the following provision in at least ten point, bold face, type:

NOTICE

ANY HOLDER OF THIS CONSUMER CREDIT CONTRACT IS SUBJECT TO ALL CLAIMS AND DEFENSES WHICH THE DEBTOR COULD ASSERT AGAINST THE SELLER OF GOODS OR SERVICES OBTAINED WITH THE PROCEEDS HEREOF. RECOVERY HEREUNDER BY THE DEBTOR SHALL NOT EXCEED AMOUNTS PAID BY THE DEBTOR HEREUNDER.

§ 433.3 Exemption of sellers taking or receiving open end consumer credit contracts before November 1, 1977 from requirements of § 433.2(a)

(a) Any seller who has taken or received an open end consumer credit contract before November 1, 1977, shall be exempt from the requirements of 16 CFR part 433 with respect to such contract provided the contract does not cut off consumers' claims and defenses.

(b) Definitions. The following definitions apply to this exemption:

(1) All pertinent definitions contained in 16 CFR 433.1.

(2) Open end consumer credit contract: a consumer credit contract pursuant to which "open end credit" is extended.

(3) "Open end credit": consumer credit extended on an account pursuant to a plan under which a creditor may permit an applicant to make purchases or make loans, from time to time, directly from the creditor or indirectly by use of a credit card, check, or other device, as the plan may provide. The term does not include negotiated advances under an open-end real estate mortgage or a letter of credit.

(4) Contract which does not cut off consumers' claims and defenses: A consumer credit contract which does not constitute or contain a negotiable instrument, or contain any waiver, limitation, term, or condition which has the effect of limiting a consumer's right to assert against any holder of the contract all legally sufficient claims and defenses which the consumer could assert against the seller of goods or services purchased pursuant to the contract.

---

§ 9–313. Priority of Security Interests in Fixtures

(1) In this section and in the provisions of Part 4 of this Article referring to fixture filing, unless the context otherwise requires

(a) goods are "fixtures" when they become so related to particular real estate that an interest in them arises under real estate law

(b) a "fixture filing" is the filing in the office where a mortgage on the real estate would be filed or recorded of a financing statement covering goods which are or are to become fixtures and conforming to the requirements of subsection (5) of Section 9–402

(c) a mortgage is a "construction mortgage" to the extend that it secures an obligation incurred for the construction of an improvement on land including the acquisition cost of the land, if the recorded writing so indicates.

(2) A security interest under this Article may be created in goods which are fixtures or may continue in goods which become fixtures, but no security interest exists under this Article in ordinary building materials incorporated into an improvement on land.

(3) This Article does not prevent creation of an encumbrance upon fixtures pursuant to real estate law.

(4) A perfected security interest in fixtures has priority over the conflicting interest of an encumbrancer or owner of the real estate where

(a) the security interest is a purchase money security interest, the interest of the encumbrancer or owner arises before the goods become fixtures, the security interest is perfected by a fixture filing before the goods become fixtures or within ten days thereafter, and the debtor has an interest of record in the real estate or is in possession of the real estate; or

(b) the security interest is perfected by a fixture filing before the interest of the encumbrancer or owner is of record, the security interest has priority over any conflicting interest of a predecessor in title of the encumbrancer or owner, and the debtor has an interest of record in the real estate or is in possession of the real estate; or

(c) the fixtures are readily removable factory or office machines or readily removable replacements of domestic appliances which are consumer goods, and before the goods become fixtures the security interest is perfected by any method permitted by this Article; or

(d) the conflicting interest is a lien on the real estate obtained by legal or equitable proceedings after the security interest was perfected by any method permitted by this Article.

(5) A security interest in fixtures, whether or not perfected, has priority over the conflicting interest of an encumbrancer or owner of the real estate where

(a) the encumbrancer or owner has consented in writing to the security interest or has disclaimed an interest in the goods as fixtures; or

(b) the debtor has a right to remove the goods as against the encumbrancer or owner. If the debtor's right terminates, the priority of the security interest continues for a reasonable time.

(6) Notwithstanding paragraph (a) of subsection (4) but otherwise subject to subsections (4) and (5), a security interest in fixtures is subordinate to a construction mortgage recorded before the goods becomes fixtures if the goods become fixtures before the completion of the construction. To the extent that it is given to refinance a construction mortgage, a mortgage has this priority to the same extent as the construction mortgage.

(7) In cases not within the preceding subsections, a security interest in fixtures is subordinate to the conflicting interest of an encumbrancer or owner of the related real estate who is not the debtor.

(8) When the secured party has priority over all owners and encumbrancers of the real estate, he may, on default, subject to the provisions of Part 5, remove his collateral from the real estate but he must reimburse any encumbrancer or owner of the real estate who is not the debtor and who has not otherwise agreed for the cost of repair of any physical injury, but not for any diminution in value of the real estate caused by the absence of the goods removed or by any necessity of replacing them. A person entitled to reimbursement may refuse permission to remove until the secured party gives adequate security for the performance of this obligation.

b. 2000 OFFICIAL TEXT

§ 9–334. Priority of Security Interests in Fixtures and Crops

(a) **[Security interest in fixtures under this Article.]** A security interest under this article may be created in goods that are fixtures or may continue in goods that become fixtures. A security interest does not exist under this article in ordinary building materials incorporated into an improvement on land.

(b) **[Security interest in fixtures under real-property law.]** This article does not prevent creation of an encumbrance upon fixtures under real property law.

(c) **[General rule: subordination of security interest in fixtures.]** In cases not governed by subsections (d) through (h), a security interest in fixtures is subordinate to a conflicting interest of an encumbrancer or owner of the related real property other than the debtor.

(d) **[Fixtures purchase-money priority.]** Except as otherwise provided in subsection (h), a perfected security interest in fixtures has priority over a conflicting interest of an encumbrancer or owner of the real property if the debtor has an interest of record in or is in possession of the real property and:

(1) the security interest is a purchase-money security interest;

(2) the interest of the encumbrancer or owner arises before the goods become fixtures; and

(3) the security interest is perfected by a fixture filing before the goods become fixtures or within 20 days thereafter.

29

(e) **[Priority of security interest in fixtures over interests in real property.]** A perfected security interest in fixtures has priority over a conflicting interest of an encumbrancer or owner of the real property if:

(1) the debtor has an interest of record in the real property or is in possession of the real property and the security interest:

(A) is perfected by a fixture filing before the interest of the encumbrancer or owner is of record; and

(B) has priority over any conflicting interest of a predecessor in title of the encumbrancer or owner;

(2) before the goods become fixtures, the security interest is perfected by any method permitted by this article and the fixtures are readily removable:

(A) factory or office machines;

(B) equipment that is not primarily used or leased for use in the operation of the real property; or

(C) replacements of domestic appliances that are consumer goods;

(3) the conflicting interest is a lien on the real property obtained by legal or equitable proceedings after the security interest was perfected by any method permitted by this article; or

(4) the security interest is:

(A) created in a manufactured home in a manufactured-home transaction; and

(B) perfected pursuant to a statute described in Section 9–311(a)(2).

(f) **[Priority based on consent, disclaimer, or right to remove.]** A security interest in fixtures, whether or not perfected, has priority over a conflicting interest of an encumbrancer or owner of the real property if:

(1) the encumbrancer or owner has, in an authenticated record, consented to the security interest or disclaimed an interest in the goods as fixtures; or

(2) the debtor has a right to remove the goods as against the encumbrancer or owner.

(g) **[Continuation of paragraph (f)(2) priority.]** The priority of the security interest under paragraph (f)(2) continues for a reasonable time if the doctor's right to remove the goods as against the encumbrancer or owner terminates.

(h) **[Priority of construction mortgage.]** A mortgage is a construction mortgage to the extent that it secures an obligation incurred for the construction of an improvement on land, including the acquisition cost of the land, if a recorded record of the mortgage so indicates. Except as otherwise provided in subsections (e) and (f), a security interest in fixtures is subordinate to a construction mortgage if a record of the mortgage is recorded before the goods become fixtures and the goods become fixtures before the completion of the construction. A mortgage has this priority to the same extent as a construction mortgage to the extent that it is given to refinance a construction mortgage.

(i) **[Priority of security interest in crops.]** A perfected security interest in crops growing on real property has priority over a conflicting interest of an encumbrancer or owner of the real property if the debtor has an interest of record in or is in possession of the real property.

30

(j) **[Subsection (i) prevails.]** Subsection (i) prevails over any inconsistent provisions of the following statutes:

[List here any statutes containing provisions inconsistent with subsection (i).]

§ 9–604. Procedure if Security Agreement Covers Real Property or Fixtures

(a) **[Enforcement: personal and real property.]** If a security agreement covers both personal and real property, a secured party may proceed:

(1) under this part as to the personal property without prejudicing any rights with respect to the real property; or

(2) as to both the personal property and the real property in accordance with the rights with respect to the real property, in which case the other provisions of this part do not apply.

(b) **[Enforcement: fixtures.]** Subject to subsection (c), if a security agreement covers goods that are or become fixtures, a secured party may proceed:

(1) under this part; or

(2) in accordance with the rights with respect to real property, in which case the other provisions of this part do not apply.

(c) **[Removal of fixtures.]** Subject to the other provisions of this part, if a secured party holding a security interest in fixtures has priority over all owners and encumbrancers of the real property, the secured party, after default, may remove the collateral from the real property.

(d) **[Injury caused by removal.]** A secured party that removes collateral shall promptly reimburse any encumbrancer or owner of the real property, other than the debtor, for the cost of repair of any physical injury caused by the removal. The secured party need not reimburse the encumbrancer or owner for any diminution in value of the real property caused by the absence of the goods removed or by any necessity of replacing them. A person entitled to reimbursement may refuse permission to remove until the secured party gives adequate assurance for the performance of the obligation to reimburse.

§ 9–605. Unknown Debtor or Secondary Obligor

A secured party does not owe a duty based on its status as secured party:

(1) to a person that is a debtor or obligor, unless the secured party knows:

(A) that the person is a debtor or obligor;

(B) the identity of the person; and

(C) how to communicate with the person; or

(2) to a secured party or lienholder that has filed a financing statement against a person, unless the secured party knows:

(A) that the person is a debtor; and

(B) the identity of the person.

8. PRIORITY OF MORTGAGE LIENS AND ADVANCES STATUTE

42 PENNSYLVANIA CONSOLIDATED STATUTES ANNOTATED

§ 8143. Open–End Mortgages

(a) General rule.—Whether or not it secures any other debt or obligation, an open-end mortgage, other than a purchase money mortgage as defined in section 8141 (relating to time from which liens have priority), may secure unpaid balances of advances made after such open-end mortgage is left for record. The validity and enforceability of the lien of an open-end mortgage shall not be affected by the fact that the first advance is made after the date of recording of the mortgage or that there may be no outstanding indebtedness for a period of time after an advance or advances may have been made and repaid.

(b) Unobligated advance after notice.—An open-end mortgage securing unpaid balances of advances referred to in subsection (a) is a lien on the premises described therein from the time the mortgage is left for record for the full amount of the total unpaid indebtedness, including the unpaid balances of the advances that are made under the mortgage plus interest thereon, regardless of the time when the advances are made. However, if an advance is made after the holder of the mortgage receives written notice which complies with subsection (d) of a lien or encumbrance on the mortgaged premises which is subordinate to the lien of the mortgage and if the holder is not obligated to make the advance at the time the notice is received, then the lien of the mortgage for the unpaid balance of the advance so made is subordinate to the lien or encumbrance unless the advance so made is in order to pay toward, or to provide funds to the mortgagor to pay toward, all or part of the cost of completing any erection, construction, alteration or repair of any part of the mortgaged premises, the financing of which, in whole or in part, the mortgage was given to secure. If an advance is made after the holder of an open-end mortgage receives written notice of labor performed or to be performed or materials furnished or to be furnished for the erection, construction, alteration or repair of any part of the mortgaged premises and if the holder is not obligated to make the advance at the time the notice is received, then the lien of the mortgage for the unpaid balance of the advance so made is subordinate to a valid mechanic's lien for the labor actually performed or materials actually furnished as specified in the notice unless the advance so made is in order to pay toward, or to provide funds to the mortgagor to pay toward, all or part of the cost of completing any erection, construction, alteration or repair of any part of the mortgaged premises, the financing of which, in whole or in part, the mortgage was given to secure.

(c) Mortgagor may limit indebtedness.—The mortgagor may limit the indebtedness secured by an open-end mortgage, and release the obligation of the mortgagee to make any further payments, to that in existence at the time of the delivery of a written notice to that effect to the recorder for record, if the notice is executed by the mortgagor, is acknowledged according to law and states the volume and initial page of the record or the recorder's file number of the mortgage, and a copy thereof is served upon the holder of the mortgage more than three days prior to the delivery of the notice to the recorder for record. The notice shall be recorded and indexed by the recorder as an amendment of the mortgage and shall be noted on the margin of the record of the mortgage, giving the book and page number where

32

the notice is recorded. The right of the mortgagor to limit indebtedness secured by the mortgage is not applicable to interest subsequently accruing on indebtedness or advances made after the delivery of the notice to the recorder for record in order to pay for all or part of the cost of completing any erection, construction, alteration or repair of any part of the mortgaged premises, the financing of which, in whole or in part, the mortgage was given to secure.

(d) Notice.—The written notices provided for in subsection (b) shall be signed by the holder of the lien or encumbrance or the person who has performed or intends to perform the labor or who has furnished or intends to furnish materials, or by his agent or attorney, and shall set forth a description of the real property to which the notice relates, the date, the parties to, the volume and initial page of the record or the recorder's file number of the mortgage over which priority is claimed for the lien or encumbrance and the amount and nature of the claim to which the lien or encumbrance relates or the nature of the labor performed or to be performed or materials furnished or to be furnished and the amount claimed or to be claimed therefor. The written notices provided for in subsections (b) and (c) shall be deemed to have been received by or served upon the holder of the mortgage when delivered to the holder personally or by registered or certified mail at the address of the holder appearing in the mortgage or an assignment thereof or, if no address is so given, at the principal place of business or residence of the holder or the agent of the holder within this Commonwealth or, if the holder has no principal place of business or residence or agent within this Commonwealth, when posted in some conspicuous place on the mortgaged premises.

(e) Section not exclusive.—This section is not exclusive and shall not be construed to change existing law with respect to the priority of the lien of advances made pursuant to a mortgage except to the extent that it gives priority to the lien for advances under an open-end mortgage complying with the requirements of this section which would not have such priority in the absence of this section.

(f) Definitions.—As used in this section, the following words and phrases shall have the meanings given to them in this subsection:

"Holder of the mortgage." The holder of the mortgage as disclosed by the records of the recorder or recorders of the county or counties in which the mortgaged premises are situated.

"Indebtedness." The unpaid principal balance of advances exclusive of interest and unpaid balances of advances and other extensions of credit secured by the mortgage made for the payment of taxes, assessments, maintenance charges, insurance premiums and costs incurred for the protection of the mortgaged premises.

"Mortgage." Includes a mortgage, deed of trust or other instrument in the nature of a mortgage.

"Mortgagor." Includes the mortgagor's successors in interest as disclosed by the records of the recorder or recorders of the county or counties in which the mortgaged premises are situated.

"Open-end mortgage." A mortgage which secures advances, up to a maximum amount of indebtedness outstanding at any time stated in the mortgage, plus accrued and unpaid interest. Such a mortgage shall be identified at the beginning thereof as an "open-end mortgage" and shall clearly state that it secures future advances, which in the

33

case of a home equity plan, the lender has a contractual obligation to make on the terms and conditions set forth in the mortgage and open-end loan agreement with the borrower. Such open-end mortgage shall be deemed to secure obligatory future advances even though the mortgage or loan agreement contains some or all of the limitations and conditions on the obligation to make advances which are permitted for home equity plans under the Home Equity Loan Consumer Protection Act of 1988 (Public Law 100–709, 102 Stat. 4725), as implemented by Regulation Z issued thereunder in 12 CFR 226.5(b) (relating to general disclosure requirements).

"Recorder." The recorder of deeds or other official in charge of recording mortgages in each county in which the mortgaged premises are located.

§ 8144. Mortgages to Secure Certain Advances

In addition to any other indebtedness, a mortgage may secure unpaid balances of advances made, with respect to the mortgaged premises, for the payment of taxes, assessments, maintenance charges, insurance premiums or costs incurred for the protection of the mortgaged premises or the lien of the mortgage, expenses incurred by the mortgagee by reason of default by the mortgagor under the mortgage or advances made under a construction loan to enable completion of the improvements for which the construction loan was originally made, if such mortgage states that it shall secure such unpaid balances. A mortgage complying with this section is a lien on the premises described therein from the time the mortgage is left for record or the time of delivery to the mortgagee of a purchase money mortgage which is recorded within ten days after its date for the full amount of the unpaid balances of such advances that are made under the mortgage, plus interest thereon, regardless of the time when the advances are made.

9. INTERNAL REVENUE CODE

26 U.S.C.A.

§ 109. Improvements by Lessee on Lessor's Property

Gross income does not include income (other than rent) derived by a lessor of real property on the termination of a lease, representing the value of such property attributable to buildings erected or other improvements made by the lessee.

§ 121. Exclusion of gain from sale of principal residence

(a) Exclusion.—Gross income shall not include gain from the sale or exchange of property if, during the 5–year period ending on the date of the sale or exchange, such property has been owned and used by the taxpayer as the taxpayer's principal residence for periods aggregating 2 years or more.

(b) Limitations.—

(1) In general.—The amount of gain excluded from gross income under subsection (a) with respect to any sale or exchange shall not exceed $250,000.

(2) Special rules for joint returns.—In the case of a husband and wife who make a joint return for the taxable year of the sale or exchange of the property—

(A) $500,000 limitation for certain joint returns.—Paragraph (1) shall be applied by substituting "$500,000" for "$250,000" if.—

(i) either spouse meets the ownership requirements of subsection (a) with respect to such property;

(ii) both spouses meet the use requirements of subsection (a) with respect to such property; and

(iii) neither spouse is ineligible for the benefits of subsection (a) with respect to such property by reason of paragraph (3).

(B) Other joint returns.—If such spouses do not meet the requirements of subparagraph (A), the limitation under paragraph (1) shall be the sum of the limitations under paragraph (1) to which each spouse would be entitled if such spouses had not been married. For purposes of the preceding sentence, each spouse shall be treated as owning the property during the period that either spouse owned the property.

(3) Application to only 1 sale or exchange every 2 years.—

(A) In general.—Subsection (a) shall not apply to any sale or exchange by the taxpayer if, during the 2–year period ending on the date of such sale or exchange, there was any other sale or exchange by the taxpayer to which subsection (a) applied.

(B) Pre–May 7, 1997, sales not taken into account.—Subparagraph (A) shall be applied without regard to any sale or exchange before May 7, 1997.

(4)[1] **Special rule for certain sales by surviving spouses.**—In the case of a sale or exchange of property by an unmarried individual whose spouse is deceased on the date of such sale, paragraph (1) shall be applied by substituting "$500,000" for "$250,000" if such

---

1. So in original. Two pars. (4) enacted.

sale occurs not later than 2 years after the date of death of such spouse and the requirements of paragraph (2)(A) were met immediately before such date of death.

(4)[1] Exclusion of gain allocated to nonqualified use.—

(A) In general.—Subsection (a) shall not apply to so much of the gain from the sale or exchange of property as is allocated to periods of nonqualified use.

(B) Gain allocated to periods of nonqualified use.—For purposes of subparagraph (A), gain shall be allocated to periods of nonqualified use based on the ratio which—

(i) the aggregate periods of nonqualified use during the period such property was owned by the taxpayer, bears to

(ii) the period such property was owned by the taxpayer.

(C) Period of nonqualified use.—For purposes of this paragraph—

(i) In general.—The term "period of nonqualified use" means any period (other than the portion of any period preceding January 1, 2009) during which the property is not used as the principal residence of the taxpayer or the taxpayer's spouse or former spouse.

(ii) Exceptions.—The term "period of nonqualified use" does not include—

(I) any portion of the 5–year period described in subsection (a) which is after the last date that such property is used as the principal residence of the taxpayer or the taxpayer's spouse,

(II) any period (not to exceed an aggregate period of 10 years) during which the taxpayer or the taxpayer's spouse is serving on qualified official extended duty (as defined in subsection (d)(9)(C)) described in clause (i), (ii), or (iii) of subsection (d)(9)(A), and

(III) any other period of temporary absence (not to exceed an aggregate period of 2 years) due to change of employment, health conditions, or such other unforeseen circumstances as may be specified by the Secretary.

(D) Coordination with recognition of gain attributable to depreciation.—For purposes of this paragraph—

(i) subparagraph (A) shall be applied after the application of subsection (d)(6), and

(ii) subparagraph (B) shall be applied without regard to any gain to which subsection (d)(6) applies.

(c) Exclusion for taxpayers failing to meet certain requirements.—

(1) In general.—In the case of a sale or exchange to which this subsection applies, the ownership and use requirements of subsection (a), and subsection (b)(3), shall not apply; but the dollar limitation under paragraph (1) or (2) of subsection (b), whichever is applicable, shall be equal to—

(A) the amount which bears the same ratio to such limitation (determined without regard to this paragraph) as

(B)(i) the shorter of—

---

1. So in original. Two pars. (4) enacted.

(I) the aggregate periods, during the 5–year period ending on the date of such sale or exchange, such property has been owned and used by the taxpayer as the taxpayer's principal residence; or

(II) the period after the date of the most recent prior sale or exchange by the taxpayer to which subsection (a) applied and before the date of such sale or exchange, bears to

(ii) 2 years.

(2) Sales and exchanges to which subsection applies.—This subsection shall apply to any sale or exchange if—

(A) subsection (a) would not (but for this subsection) apply to such sale or exchange by reason of—

(i) a failure to meet the ownership and use requirements of subsection (a), or

(ii) subsection (b)(3), and

(B) such sale or exchange is by reason of a change in place of employment, health, or, to the extent provided in regulations, unforeseen circumstances.

(d) Special rules.—

(1) Joint returns.—If a husband and wife make a joint return for the taxable year of the sale or exchange of the property, subsections (a) and (c) shall apply if either spouse meets the ownership and use requirements of subsection (a) with respect to such property.

(2) Property of deceased spouse.—For purposes of this section, in the case of an unmarried individual whose spouse is deceased on the date of the sale or exchange of property, the period such unmarried individual owned and used such property shall include the period such deceased spouse owned and used such property before death.

(3) Property owned by spouse or former spouse.—For purposes of this section—

(A) Property transferred to individual from spouse or former spouse.—In the case of an individual holding property transferred to such individual in a transaction described in section 1041(a), the period such individual owns such property shall include the period the transferor owned the property.

(B) Property used by former spouse pursuant to divorce decree, etc.—Solely for purposes of this section, an individual shall be treated as using property as such individual's principal residence during any period of ownership while such individual's spouse or former spouse is granted use of the property under a divorce or separation instrument (as defined in section 71(b)(2)).

(4) Tenant-stockholder in cooperative housing corporation.—For purposes of this section, if the taxpayer holds stock as a tenant-stockholder (as defined in section 216) in a cooperative housing corporation (as defined in such section), then—

(A) the holding requirements of subsection (a) shall be applied to the holding of such stock, and

(B) the use requirements of subsection (a) shall be applied to the house or apartment which the taxpayer was entitled to occupy as such stockholder.

(5) Involuntary conversions.—

(A) In general.—For purposes of this section, the destruction, theft, seizure, requisition, or condemnation of property shall be treated as the sale of such property.

(B) Application of section 1033.—In applying section 1033 (relating to involuntary conversions), the amount realized from the sale or exchange of property shall be treated as being the amount determined without regard to this section, reduced by the amount of gain not included in gross income pursuant to this section.

(C) Property acquired after involuntary conversion.—If the basis of the property sold or exchanged is determined (in whole or in part) under section 1033(b) (relating to basis of property acquired through involuntary conversion), then the holding and use by the taxpayer of the converted property shall be treated as holding and use by the taxpayer of the property sold or exchanged.

(6) Recognition of gain attributable to depreciation.—Subsection (a) shall not apply to so much of the gain from the sale of any property as does not exceed the portion of the depreciation adjustments (as defined in section 1250(b)(3)) attributable to periods after May 6, 1997, in respect of such property.

(7) Determination of use during periods of out-of-residence care.—In the case of a taxpayer who—

(A) becomes physically or mentally incapable of selfcare, and

(B) owns property and uses such property as the taxpayer's principal residence during the 5–year period described in subsection (a) for periods aggregating at least 1 year,

then the taxpayer shall be treated as using such property as the taxpayer's principal residence during any time during such 5–year period in which the taxpayer owns the property and resides in any facility (including a nursing home) licensed by a State or political subdivision to care for an individual in the taxpayer's condition.

(8) Sales of remainder interests.—For purposes of this section—

(A) In general.—At the election of the taxpayer, this section shall not fail to apply to the sale or exchange of an interest in a principal residence by reason of such interest being a remainder interest in such residence, but this section shall not apply to any other interest in such residence which is sold or exchanged separately.

(B) Exception for sales to related parties.—Subparagraph (A) shall not apply to any sale to, or exchange with, any person who bears a relationship to the taxpayer which is described in section 267(b) or 707(b).

(9) Uniformed services, foreign service, and intelligence community.—

(A) In general.—At the election of an individual with respect to a property, the running of the 5–year period described in subsections (a) and (c)(1)(B) and paragraph (7) of this subsection with respect to such property shall be suspended during any period that such individual or such individual's spouse is serving on qualified official extended duty—

(i) as a member of the uniformed services,

(ii) as a member of the Foreign Service of the United States, or

(iii) as an employee of the intelligence community.

(B) Maximum period of suspension.—The 5–year period described in subsection (a) shall not be extended more than 10 years by reason of subparagraph (A).

(C) Qualified official extended duty.—For purposes of this paragraph—

(i) In general.—The term "qualified official extended duty" means any extended duty while serving at a duty station which is at least 50 miles from such property or while residing under Government orders in Government quarters.

(ii) Uniformed services.—The term "uniformed services" has the meaning given such term by section 101(a)(5) of title 10, United States Code, as in effect on the date of the enactment of this paragraph.

(iii) Foreign service of the United States.—The term "member of the Foreign Service of the United States" has the meaning given the term "member of the Service" by paragraph (1), (2), (3), (4), or (5) of section 103 of the Foreign Service Act of 1980, as in effect on the date of the enactment of this paragraph.

(iv) Employee of intelligence community.—The term "employee of the intelligence community" means an employee (as defined by section 2105 of title 5, United States Code) of—

(I) the Office of the Director of National Intelligence,

(II) the Central Intelligence Agency,

(III) the National Security Agency,

(IV) the Defense Intelligence Agency,

(V) the National Geospatial–Intelligence Agency,

(VI) the National Reconnaissance Office,

(VII) any other office within the Department of Defense for the collection of specialized national intelligence through reconnaissance programs,

(VIII) any of the intelligence elements of the Army, the Navy, the Air Force, the Marine Corps, the Federal Bureau of Investigation, the Department of Treasury, the Department of Energy, and the Coast Guard,

(IX) the Bureau of Intelligence and Research of the Department of State, or

(X) any of the elements of the Department of Homeland Security concerned with the analyses of foreign intelligence information.

(v) Extended duty.—The term "extended duty" means any period of active duty pursuant to a call or order to such duty for a period in excess of 90 days or for an indefinite period.

[**(vi) Repealed.** Pub.L. 110–245, Title I, § 113(b), June 17, 2008, 122 Stat. 1635]

(D) Special rules relating to election.—

(i) Election limited to 1 property at a time.—An election under subparagraph (A) with respect to any property may not be made if such an election is in effect with respect to any other property.

(ii) Revocation of election.—An election under subparagraph (A) may be revoked at any time.

[**(E) Repealed.** Pub.L. 110–245, Title I, § 113(a), June 17, 2008, 122 Stat. 1635]

(10) Property acquired in like-kind exchange.—If a taxpayer acquires property in an exchange with respect to which gain is not recognized (in whole or in part) to the taxpayer under subsection (a) or (b) of section 1031, subsection (a) shall not apply to the sale or exchange of such property by such taxpayer (or by any person whose basis in such property is determined, in whole or in part, by reference to the basis in the hands of such taxpayer) during the 5–year period beginning with the date of such acquisition.[1]

(12) Peace Corps.—

(A) In general.—At the election of an individual with respect to a property, the running of the 5–year period described in subsections (a) and (c)(1)(B) and paragraph (7) of this subsection with respect to such property shall be suspended during any period that such individual or such individual's spouse is serving outside the United States—

(i) on qualified official extended duty (as defined in paragraph (9)(C)) as an employee of the Peace Corps, or

(ii) as an enrolled volunteer or volunteer leader under section 5 or 6 (as the case may be) of the Peace Corps Act (22 U.S.C. 2504, 2505).

(B) Applicable rules.—For purposes of subparagraph (A), rules similar to the rules of subparagraphs (B) and (D) shall apply.

(e) Denial of exclusion for expatriates.—This section shall not apply to any sale or exchange by an individual if the treatment provided by section 877(a)(1) applies to such individual.

(f) Election to have section not apply.—This section shall not apply to any sale or exchange with respect to which the taxpayer elects not to have this section apply.

(g) Residences acquired in rollovers under section 1034.—For purposes of this section, in the case of property the acquisition of which by the taxpayer resulted under section 1034 (as in effect on the day before the date of the enactment of this section) in the nonrecognition of any part of the gain realized on the sale or exchange of another residence, in determining the period for which the taxpayer has owned and used such property as the taxpayer's principal residence, there shall be included the aggregate periods for which such other residence (and each prior residence taken into account under section 1223(6) in determining the holding period of such property) had been so owned and used.

§ 163. Interest

(a) General rule.—There shall be allowed as a deduction all interest paid or accrued within the taxable year on indebtedness.

(b) Installment purchases where interest charge is not separately stated.—

(1) General rule.—If personal property or educational services are purchased under a contract—

(A) which provides that payment of part or all of the purchase price is to be made in installments, and

---

1. No par. (11) enacted for effective date.

(B) in which carrying charges are separately stated but the interest charge cannot be ascertained,

then the payments made during the taxable year under the contract shall be treated for purposes of this section as if they included interest equal to 6 percent of the average unpaid balance under the contract during the taxable year. For purposes of the preceding sentence, the average unpaid balance is the sum of the unpaid balance outstanding on the first day of each month beginning during the taxable year, divided by 12. For purposes of this paragraph, the term "educational services" means any service (including lodging) which is purchased from an educational organization described in section 170(b)(1)(A)(ii) and which is provided for a student of such organization.

(2) Limitation.—In the case of any contract to which paragraph (1) applies, the amount treated as interest for any taxable year shall not exceed the aggregate carrying charges which are properly attributable to such taxable year.

(c) Redeemable ground rents.—For purposes of this subtitle, any annual or periodic rental under a redeemable ground rent (excluding amounts in redemption thereof) shall be treated as interest on an indebtedness secured by a mortgage.

(d) Limitation on investment interest.—

(1) In general.—In the case of a taxpayer other than a corporation, the amount allowed as a deduction under this chapter for investment interest for any taxable year shall not exceed the net investment income of the taxpayer for the taxable year.

(2) Carryforward of disallowed interest.—The amount not allowed as a deduction for any taxable year by reason of paragraph (1) shall be treated as investment interest paid or accrued by the taxpayer in the succeeding taxable year.

(3) Investment interest.—For purposes of this subsection—

(A) In general.—The term "investment interest" means any interest allowable as a deduction under this chapter (determined without regard to paragraph (1)) which is paid or accrued on indebtedness properly allocable to property held for investment.

(B) Exceptions.—The term "investment interest" shall not include—

(i) any qualified residence interest (as defined in subsection (h)(3)), or

(ii) any interest which is taken into account under section 469 in computing income or loss from a passive activity of the taxpayer.

(C) Personal property used in short sale.—For purposes of this paragraph, the term "interest" includes any amount allowable as a deduction in connection with personal property used in a short sale.

(4) Net investment income.—For purposes of this subsection—

(A) In general.—The term "net investment income" means the excess of—

(i) investment income, over

(ii) investment expenses.

(B) Investment income.—The term "investment income" means the sum of—

(i) gross income from property held for investment (other than any gain taken into account under clause (ii)(I)),

(ii) the excess (if any) of—

(I) the net gain attributable to the disposition of property held for investment, over

(II) the net capital gain determined by only taking into account gains and losses from dispositions of property held for investment, plus

(iii) so much of the net capital gain referred to in clause (ii)(II) (or, if lesser, the net gain referred to in clause (ii)(I)) as the taxpayer elects to take into account under this clause.

Such term shall include qualified dividend income (as defined in section 1(h)(11)(B)) only to the extent the taxpayer elects to treat such income as investment income for purposes of this subsection.

(C) Investment expenses.—The term "investment expenses" means the deductions allowed under this chapter (other than for interest) which are directly connected with the production of investment income.

(D) Income and expenses from passive activities.—Investment income and investment expenses shall not include any income or expenses taken into account under section 469 in computing income or loss from a passive activity.

(E) Reduction in investment income during phase-in of passive loss rules.— Investment income of the taxpayer for any taxable year shall be reduced by the amount of the passive activity loss to which section 469(a) does not apply for such taxable year by reason of section 469(m). The preceding sentence shall not apply to any portion of such passive activity loss which is attributable to a rental real estate activity with respect to which the taxpayer actively participates (within the meaning of section 469(i)(6)) during such taxable year.

(5) Property held for investment.—For purposes of this subsection—

(A) In general.—The term "property held for investment" shall include—

(i) any property which produces income of a type described in section 469(e)(1), and

(ii) any interest held by a taxpayer in an activity involving the conduct of a trade or business—

(I) which is not a passive activity, and

(II) with respect to which the taxpayer does not materially participate.

(B) Investment expenses.—In the case of property described in subparagraph (A)(i), expenses shall be allocated to such property in the same manner as under section 469.

(C) Terms.—For purposes of this paragraph, the terms "activity", "passive activity", and "materially participate" have the meanings given such terms by section 469.

(6) Phase-in of disallowance.—In the case of any taxable year beginning in calendar years 1987 through 1990—

(A) In general.—The amount of interest paid or accrued during any such taxable year which is disallowed under this subsection shall not exceed the sum of—

(i) the amount which would be disallowed under this subsection if—

(I) paragraph (1) were applied by substituting "the sum of the ceiling amount and the net investment income" for "the net investment income", and

(II) paragraphs (4)(E) and (5)(A)(ii) did not apply, and

(ii) the applicable percentage of the excess of—

(I) the amount which (without regard to this paragraph) is not allowable as a deduction under this subsection for the taxable year, over

(II) the amount described in clause (i).

The preceding sentence shall not apply to any interest treated as paid or accrued during the taxable year under paragraph (2).

(B) Applicable percentage.—For purposes of this paragraph, the applicable percentage shall be determined in accordance with the following table:

In the case of taxable years beginning in:	The applicable percentage is:
1987	35
1988	60
1989	80
1990	90

(C) Ceiling amount.—For purposes of this paragraph, the term "ceiling amount" means—

(i) $10,000 in the case of a taxpayer not described in clause (ii) or (iii),

(ii) $5,000 in the case of a married individual filing a separate return, and

(iii) zero in the case of a trust.

(e) Original issue discount.—

(1) In general.—In the case of any debt instrument issued after July 1, 1982, the portion of the original issue discount with respect to such debt instrument which is allowable as a deduction to the issuer for any taxable year shall be equal to the aggregate daily portions of the original issue discount for days during such taxable year.

(2) Definitions and special rules.—For purposes of this subsection—

(A) Debt instrument.—The term "debt instrument" has the meaning given such term by section 1275(a)(1).

(B) Daily portions.—The daily portion of the original issue discount for any day shall be determined under section 1272(a) (without regard to paragraph (7) thereof and without regard to section 1273(a)(3)).

(C) Short-term obligations.—In the case of an obligor of a short-term obligation (as defined in section 1283(a)(1)(A)) who uses the cash receipts and disbursements method of accounting, the original issue discount (and any other interest payable) on such obligation shall be deductible only when paid.

(3) Special rule for original issue discount on obligation held by related foreign person.—

(A) In general.—If any debt instrument having original issue discount is held by a related foreign person, any portion of such original issue discount shall not be allowable as a deduction to the issuer until paid. The preceding sentence shall not apply to the extent that the original issue discount is effectively connected with the conduct by such foreign related person of a trade or business within the United States unless such original issue discount is exempt from taxation (or is subject to a reduced rate of tax) pursuant to a treaty obligation of the United States.

(B) Special rule for certain foreign entities.—

(i) In general.—In the case of any debt instrument having original issue discount which is held by a related foreign person which is a controlled foreign corporation (as defined in section 957) or a passive foreign investment company (as defined in section 1297), a deduction shall be allowable to the issuer with respect to such original issue discount for any taxable year before the taxable year in which paid only to the extent such original issue discount is includible (determined without regard to properly allocable deductions and qualified deficits under section 952(c)(1)(B)) during such prior taxable year in the gross income of a United States person who owns (within the meaning of section 958(a)) stock in such corporation.

(ii) Secretarial authority.—The Secretary may by regulation exempt transactions from the application of clause (i), including any transaction which is entered into by a payor in the ordinary course of a trade or business in which the payor is predominantly engaged.

(C) Related foreign person.—For purposes of subparagraph (A), the term "related foreign person" means any person—

(i) who is not a United States person, and

(ii) who is related (within the meaning of section 267(b)) to the issuer.

(4) Exceptions.—This subsection shall not apply to any debt instrument described in—

(A) subparagraph (D) of section 1272(a)(2) (relating to obligations issued by natural persons before March 2, 1984), and

(B) subparagraph (E) of section 1272(a)(2) (relating to loans between natural persons).

(5) Special rules for original issue discount on certain high yield obligations.—

(A) In general.—In the case of an applicable high yield discount obligation issued by a corporation—

(i) no deduction shall be allowed under this chapter for the disqualified portion of the original issue discount on such obligation, and

(ii) the remainder of such original issue discount shall not be allowable as a deduction until paid.

For purposes of this paragraph, rules similar to the rules of subsection (i)(3)(B) shall apply in determining the amount of the original issue discount and when the original issue discount is paid.

(B) Disqualified portion treated as stock distribution for purposes of dividend received deduction.—

(i) In general.—Solely for purposes of sections 243, 245, 246, and 246A, the dividend equivalent portion of any amount includible in gross income of a corporation under section 1272(a) in respect of an applicable high yield discount obligation shall be treated as a dividend received by such corporation from the corporation issuing such obligation.

(ii) Dividend equivalent portion.—For purposes of clause (i), the dividend equivalent portion of any amount includible in gross income under section 1272(a) in respect of an applicable high yield discount obligation is the portion of the amount so includible—

(I) which is attributable to the disqualified portion of the original issue discount on such obligation, and

(II) which would have been treated as a dividend if it had been a distribution made by the issuing corporation with respect to stock in such corporation.

(C) Disqualified portion.—

(i) In general.—For purposes of this paragraph, the disqualified portion of the original issue discount on any applicable high yield discount obligation is the lesser of—

(I) the amount of such original issue discount, or

(II) the portion of the total return on such obligation which bears the same ratio to such total return as the disqualified yield on such obligation bears to the yield to maturity on such obligation.

(ii) Definitions.—For purposes of clause (i), the term "disqualified yield" means the excess of the yield to maturity on the obligation over the sum referred to[2] subsection (i)(1)(B) plus 1 percentage point, and the term "total return" is the amount which would have been the original issue discount on the obligation if interest described in the parenthetical in section 1273(a)(2) were included in the stated redemption price at maturity.

(D) Exception for S corporations.—This paragraph shall not apply to any obligation issued by any corporation for any period for which such corporation is an S corporation.

(E) Effect on earnings and profits.—This paragraph shall not apply for purposes of determining earnings and profits; except that, for purposes of determining the dividend equivalent portion of any amount includible in gross income under section 1272(a) in respect of an applicable high yield discount obligation, no reduction shall be made for any amount attributable to the disqualified portion of any original issue discount on such obligation.

(F) Cross reference.—For definition of applicable high yield discount obligation, see subsection (i).

(6) Cross references.—For provision relating to deduction of original issue discount on tax-exempt obligation, see section 1288.

---

2. So in original. Probably should be followed by "in".

For special rules in the case of the borrower under certain loans for personal use, see section 1275(b).

(f) Denial of deduction for interest on certain obligations not in registered form.—

(1) In general.—Nothing in subsection (a) or in any other provision of law shall be construed to provide a deduction for interest on any registration-required obligation unless such obligation is in registered form.

(2) Registration-required obligation.—For purposes of this section—

(A) In general.—The term "registration-required obligation" means any obligation (including any obligation issued by a governmental entity) other than an obligation which—

(i) is issued by a natural person,

(ii) is not of a type offered to the public,

(iii) has a maturity (at issue) of not more than 1 year, or

(iv) is described in subparagraph (B).

(B) Certain obligations not included.—An obligation is described in this subparagraph if—

(i) there are arrangements reasonably designed to ensure that such obligation will be sold (or resold in connection with the original issue) only to a person who is not a United States person, and

(ii) in the case of an obligation not in registered form—

(I) interest on such obligation is payable only outside the United States and its possessions, and

(II) on the face of such obligation there is a statement that any United States person who holds such obligation will be subject to limitations under the United States income tax laws.

(C) Authority to include other obligations.—Clauses (ii) and (iii) of subparagraph (A), and subparagraph (B), shall not apply to any obligation if—

(i) in the case of—

(I) subparagraph (A), such obligation is of a type which the Secretary has determined by regulations to be used frequently in avoiding Federal taxes, or

(II) subparagraph (B), such obligation is of a type specified by the Secretary in regulations, and

(ii) such obligation is issued after the date on which the regulations referred to in clause (i) take effect.

(3) Book entries permitted, etc.—For purposes of this subsection, rules similar to the rules of section 149(a)(3) shall apply.

(g) Reduction of deduction where section 25 credit taken.—The amount of the deduction under this section for interest paid or accrued during any taxable year on indebtedness with respect to which a mortgage credit certificate has been issued under section 25 shall be reduced by the amount of the credit allowable with respect to such interest under section 25 (determined without regard to section 26).

(h) Disallowance of deduction for personal interest.—

(1) In general.—In the case of a taxpayer other than a corporation, no deduction shall be allowed under this chapter for personal interest paid or accrued during the taxable year.

(2) Personal interest.—For purposes of this subsection, the term "personal interest" means any interest allowable as a deduction under this chapter other than—

(A) interest paid or accrued on indebtedness properly allocable to a trade or business (other than the trade or business of performing services as an employee),

(B) any investment interest (within the meaning of subsection (d)),

(C) any interest which is taken into account under section 469 in computing income or loss from a passive activity of the taxpayer,

(D) any qualified residence interest (within the meaning of paragraph (3)),

(E) any interest payable under section 6601 on any unpaid portion of the tax imposed by section 2001 for the period during which an extension of time for payment of such tax is in effect under section 6163, and

(F) any interest allowable as a deduction under section 221 (relating to interest on educational loans).

(3) Qualified residence interest.—For purposes of this subsection—

(A) In general.—The term "qualified residence interest" means any interest which is paid or accrued during the taxable year on—

(i) acquisition indebtedness with respect to any qualified residence of the taxpayer, or

(ii) home equity indebtedness with respect to any qualified residence of the taxpayer.

For purposes of the preceding sentence, the determination of whether any property is a qualified residence of the taxpayer shall be made as of the time the interest is accrued.

(B) Acquisition indebtedness.—

(i) In general.—The term "acquisition indebtedness" means any indebtedness which—

(I) is incurred in acquiring, constructing, or substantially improving any qualified residence of the taxpayer, and

(II) is secured by such residence.

Such term also includes any indebtedness secured by such residence resulting from the refinancing of indebtedness meeting the requirements of the preceding sentence (or this sentence); but only to the extent the amount of the indebtedness resulting from such refinancing does not exceed the amount of the refinanced indebtedness.

(ii) $1,000,000 Limitation.—The aggregate amount treated as acquisition indebtedness for any period shall not exceed $1,000,000 ($500,000 in the case of a married individual filing a separate return).

(C) Home equity indebtedness.—

(i) In general.—The term "home equity indebtedness" means any indebtedness (other than acquisition indebtedness) secured by a qualified residence to the extent the aggregate amount of such indebtedness does not exceed—

(I) the fair market value of such qualified residence, reduced by

(II) the amount of acquisition indebtedness with respect to such residence.

(ii) Limitation.—The aggregate amount treated as home equity indebtedness for any period shall not exceed $100,000 ($50,000 in the case of a separate return by a married individual).

(D) Treatment of indebtedness incurred on or before October 13, 1987.—

(i) In general.—In the case of any pre-October 13, 1987, indebtedness—

(I) such indebtedness shall be treated as acquisition indebtedness, and

(II) the limitation of subparagraph (B)(ii) shall not apply.

(ii) Reduction in $1,000,000 limitation.—The limitation of subparagraph (B)(ii) shall be reduced (but not below zero) by the aggregate amount of outstanding pre-October 13, 1987, indebtedness.

(iii) Pre–October 13, 1987, indebtedness.—The term "pre-October 13, 1987, indebtedness" means—

(I) any indebtedness which was incurred on or before October 13, 1987, and which was secured by a qualified residence on October 13, 1987, and at all times thereafter before the interest is paid or accrued, or

(II) any indebtedness which is secured by the qualified residence and was incurred after October 13, 1987, to refinance indebtedness described in subclause (I) (or refinanced indebtedness meeting the requirements of this subclause) to the extent (immediately after the refinancing) the principal amount of the indebtedness resulting from the refinancing does not exceed the principal amount of the refinanced indebtedness (immediately before the refinancing).

(iv) Limitation on period of refinancing.—Subclause (II) of clause (iii) shall not apply to any indebtedness after—

(I) the expiration of the term of the indebtedness described in clause (iii)(I), or

(II) if the principal of the indebtedness described in clause (iii)(I) is not amortized over its term, the expiration of the term of the 1st refinancing of such indebtedness (or if earlier, the date which is 30 years after the date of such 1st refinancing).

(E) Mortgage insurance premiums treated as interest.—

(i) In general.—Premiums paid or accrued for qualified mortgage insurance by a taxpayer during the taxable year in connection with acquisition indebtedness with respect to a qualified residence of the taxpayer shall be treated for purposes of this section as interest which is qualified residence interest.

(ii) Phaseout.—The amount otherwise treated as interest under clause (i) shall be reduced (but not below zero) by 10 percent of such amount for each $1,000 ($500 in the case of a married individual filing a separate return) (or fraction thereof) that the taxpayer's adjusted gross income for the taxable year exceeds $100,000 ($50,000 in the case of a married individual filing a separate return).

(iii) Limitation.—Clause (i) shall not apply with respect to any mortgage insurance contracts issued before January 1, 2007.

(iv) Termination.—Clause (i) shall not apply to amounts—

(I) paid or accrued after December 31, 2010, or

(II) properly allocable to any period after such date.

(4) Other definitions and special rules.—For purposes of this subsection—

(A) Qualified residence.—

(i) In general.—The term "qualified residence" means—

(I) the principal residence (within the meaning of section 121) of the taxpayer, and

(II) 1 other residence of the taxpayer which is selected by the taxpayer for purposes of this subsection for the taxable year and which is used by the taxpayer as a residence (within the meaning of section 280A(d)(1)).

(ii) Married individuals filing separate returns.—If a married couple does not file a joint return for the taxable year—

(I) such couple shall be treated as 1 taxpayer for purposes of clause (i), and

(II) each individual shall be entitled to take into account 1 residence unless both individuals consent in writing to 1 individual taking into account the principal residence and 1 other residence.

(iii) Residence not rented.—For purposes of clause (i)(II), notwithstanding section 280A(d)(1), if the taxpayer does not rent a dwelling unit at any time during a taxable year, such unit may be treated as a residence for such taxable year.

(B) Special rule for cooperative housing corporations.—Any indebtedness secured by stock held by the taxpayer as a tenant-stockholder (as defined in section 216) in a cooperative housing corporation (as so defined) shall be treated as secured by the house or apartment which the taxpayer is entitled to occupy as such a tenant-stockholder. If stock described in the preceding sentence may not be used to secure indebtedness, indebtedness shall be treated as so secured if the taxpayer establishes to the satisfaction of the Secretary that such indebtedness was incurred to acquire such stock.

(C) Unenforceable security interests.—Indebtedness shall not fail to be treated as secured by any property solely because, under any applicable State or local homestead or other debtor protection law in effect on August 16, 1986, the security interest is ineffective or the enforceability of the security interest is restricted.

(D) Special rules for estates and trusts.—For purposes of determining whether any interest paid or accrued by an estate or trust is qualified residence interest, any residence held by such estate or trust shall be treated as a qualified residence of such estate or trust if such estate or trust establishes that such residence is a qualified residence of a beneficiary who has a present interest in such estate or trust or an interest in the residuary of such estate or trust.

(E) Qualified mortgage insurance.—The term "qualified mortgage insurance" means—

> **(i)** mortgage insurance provided by the Veterans Administration, the Federal Housing Administration, or the Rural Housing Administration, and

> **(ii)** private mortgage insurance (as defined by section 2 of the Homeowners Protection Act of 1998 (12 U.S.C. 4901), as in effect on the date of the enactment of this subparagraph).

(F) Special rules for prepaid qualified mortgage insurance.—Any amount paid by the taxpayer for qualified mortgage insurance that is properly allocable to any mortgage the payment of which extends to periods that are after the close of the taxable year in which such amount is paid shall be chargeable to capital account and shall be treated as paid in such periods to which so allocated. No deduction shall be allowed for the unamortized balance of such account if such mortgage is satisfied before the end of its term. The preceding sentences shall not apply to amounts paid for qualified mortgage insurance provided by the Veterans Administration or the Rural Housing Administration.

(5) Phase-in of limitation.—In the case of any taxable year beginning in calendar years 1987 through 1990, the amount of interest with respect to which a deduction is disallowed under this subsection shall be equal to the applicable percentage (within the meaning of subsection (d)(6)(B)) of the amount which (but for this paragraph) would have been so disallowed.

(i) Applicable high yield discount obligation.—

(1) In general.—For purposes of this section, the term "applicable high yield discount obligation" means any debt instrument if—

> **(A)** the maturity date of such instrument is more than 5 years from the date of issue,

> **(B)** the yield to maturity on such instrument equals or exceeds the sum of—

>> **(i)** the applicable Federal rate in effect under section 1274(d) for the calendar month in which the obligation is issued, plus

>> **(ii)** 5 percentage points, and

> **(C)** such instrument has significant original issue discount.

For purposes of subparagraph (B)(i), the Secretary may by regulation permit a rate to be used with respect to any debt instrument which is higher than the applicable Federal rate if the taxpayer establishes to the satisfaction of the Secretary that such higher rate is based on the same principles as the applicable Federal rate and is appropriate for the term of the instrument.

(2) Significant original issue discount.—For purposes of paragraph (1)(C), a debt instrument shall be treated as having significant original issue discount if—

> **(A)** the aggregate amount which would be includible in gross income with respect to such instrument for periods before the close of any accrual period (as defined in section 1272(a)(5)) ending after the date 5 years after the date of issue, exceeds—

> **(B)** the sum of—

50

(i) the aggregate amount of interest to be paid under the instrument before the close of such accrual period, and

(ii) the product of the issue price of such instrument (as defined in sections 1273(b) and 1274(a)) and its yield to maturity.

(3) Special rules.—For purposes of determining whether a debt instrument is an applicable high yield discount obligation—

(A) any payment under the instrument shall be assumed to be made on the last day permitted under the instrument, and

(B) any payment to be made in the form of another obligation of the issuer (or a related person within the meaning of section 453(f)(1)) shall be assumed to be made when such obligation is required to be paid in cash or in property other than such obligation. Except for purposes of paragraph (1)(B), any reference to an obligation in subparagraph (B) of this paragraph shall be treated as including a reference to stock.

(4) Debt instrument.—For purposes of this subsection, the term "debt instrument" means any instrument which is a debt instrument as defined in section 1275(a).

(5) Regulations.—The Secretary shall prescribe such regulations as may be appropriate to carry out the purposes of this subsection and subsection (e)(5), including—

(A) regulations providing for modifications to the provisions of this subsection and subsection (e)(5) in the case of varying rates of interest, put or call options, indefinite maturities, contingent payments, assumptions of debt instruments, conversion rights, or other circumstances where such modifications are appropriate to carry out the purposes of this subsection and subsection (e)(5), and

(B) regulations to prevent avoidance of the purposes of this subsection and subsection (e)(5) through the use of issuers other than C corporations, agreements to borrow amounts due under the debt instrument, or other arrangements.

(j) Limitation on deduction for interest on certain indebtedness.—

(1) Limitation.—

(A) In general.—If this subsection applies to any corporation for any taxable year, no deduction shall be allowed under this chapter for disqualified interest paid or accrued by such corporation during such taxable year. The amount disallowed under the preceding sentence shall not exceed the corporation's excess interest expense for the taxable year.

(B) Disallowed amount carried to succeeding taxable year.—Any amount disallowed under subparagraph (A) for any taxable year shall be treated as disqualified interest paid or accrued in the succeeding taxable year (and clause (ii) of paragraph (2)(A) shall not apply for purposes of applying this subsection to the amount so treated).

(2) Corporations to which subsection applies.—

(A) In general.—This subsection shall apply to any corporation for any taxable year if—

(i) such corporation has excess interest expense for such taxable year, and

(ii) the ratio of debt to equity of such corporation as of the close of such taxable year (or on any other day during the taxable year as the Secretary may by regulations prescribe) exceeds 1.5 to 1.

(B) Excess interest expense.—

(i) In general.—For purposes of this subsection, the term "excess interest expense" means the excess (if any) of—

(I) the corporation's net interest expense, over

(II) the sum of 50 percent of the adjusted taxable income of the corporation plus any excess limitation carryforward under clause (ii).

(ii) Excess limitation carryforward.—If a corporation has an excess limitation for any taxable year, the amount of such excess limitation shall be an excess limitation carryforward to the 1st succeeding taxable year and to the 2nd and 3rd succeeding taxable years to the extent not previously taken into account under this clause. The amount of such a carryforward taken into account for any such succeeding taxable year shall not exceed the excess interest expense for such succeeding taxable year (determined without regard to the carryforward from the taxable year of such excess limitation).

(iii) Excess limitation.—For purposes of clause (ii), the term "excess limitation" means the excess (if any) of—

(I) 50 percent of the adjusted taxable income of the corporation, over

(II) the corporation's net interest expense.

(C) Ratio of debt to equity.—For purposes of this paragraph, the term "ratio of debt to equity" means the ratio which the total indebtedness of the corporation bears to the sum of its money and all other assets reduced (but not below zero) by such total indebtedness. For purposes of the preceding sentence—

(i) the amount taken into account with respect to any asset shall be the adjusted basis thereof for purposes of determining gain,

(ii) the amount taken into account with respect to any indebtedness with original issue discount shall be its issue price plus the portion of the original issue discount previously accrued as determined under the rules of section 1272 (determined without regard to subsection (a)(7) or (b)(4) thereof), and

(iii) there shall be such other adjustments as the Secretary may by regulations prescribe.

(3) Disqualified interest.—For purposes of this subsection, the term "disqualified interest" means—

(A) any interest paid or accrued by the taxpayer (directly or indirectly) to a related person if no tax is imposed by this subtitle with respect to such interest,

(B) any interest paid or accrued by the taxpayer with respect to any indebtedness to a person who is not a related person if—

(i) there is a disqualified guarantee of such indebtedness, and

(ii) no gross basis tax is imposed by this subtitle with respect to such interest, and

(C) any interest paid or accrued (directly or indirectly) by a taxable REIT subsidiary (as defined in section 856(l)) of a real estate investment trust to such trust.

(4) Related person.—For purposes of this subsection—

(A) In general.—Except as provided in subparagraph (B), the term "related person" means any person who is related (within the meaning of section 267(b) or 707(b)(1)) to the taxpayer.

(B) Special rule for certain partnerships.—

(i) In general.—Any interest paid or accrued to a partnership which (without regard to this subparagraph) is a related person shall not be treated as paid or accrued to a related person if less than 10 percent of the profits and capital interests in such partnership are held by persons with respect to whom no tax is imposed by this subtitle on such interest. The preceding sentence shall not apply to any interest allocable to any partner in such partnership who is a related person to the taxpayer.

(ii) Special rule where treaty reduction.—If any treaty between the United States and any foreign country reduces the rate of tax imposed by this subtitle on a partner's share of any interest paid or accrued to a partnership, such partner's interests in such partnership shall, for purposes of clause (i), be treated as held in part by a tax-exempt person and in part by a taxable person under rules similar to the rules of paragraph (5)(B).

(5) Special rules for determining whether interest is subject to tax.—

(A) Treatment of pass-thru entities.—In the case of any interest paid or accrued to a partnership, the determination of whether any tax is imposed by this subtitle on such interest shall be made at the partner level. Rules similar to the rules of the preceding sentence shall apply in the case of any pass-thru entity other than a partnership and in the case of tiered partnerships and other entities.

(B) Interest treated as tax-exempt to extent of treaty reduction.—If any treaty between the United States and any foreign country reduces the rate of tax imposed by this subtitle on any interest paid or accrued by the taxpayer, such interest shall be treated as interest on which no tax is imposed by this subtitle to the extent of the same proportion of such interest as—

(i) the rate of tax imposed without regard to such treaty, reduced by the rate of tax imposed under the treaty, bears to

(ii) the rate of tax imposed without regard to the treaty.

(6) Other definitions and special rules.—For purposes of this subsection—

(A) Adjusted taxable income.—The term "adjusted taxable income" means the taxable income of the taxpayer—

(i) computed without regard to—

(I) any deduction allowable under this chapter for the net interest expense.

(II) the amount of any net operating loss deduction under section 172,

(III) any deduction allowable under section 199, and

(IV) any deduction allowable for depreciation, amortization, or depletion, and

(ii) computed with such other adjustments as the Secretary may by regulations prescribe.

(B) Net interest expense.—The term "net interest expense" means the excess (if any) of—

(i) the interest paid or accrued by the taxpayer during the taxable year, over

(ii) the amount of interest includible in the gross income of such taxpayer for such taxable year.

The Secretary may by regulations provide for adjustments in determining the amount of net interest expense.

(C) Treatment of affiliated group.—All members of the same affiliated group (within the meaning of section 1504(a)) shall be treated as 1 taxpayer.

(D) Disqualified guarantee.—

(i) In general.—Except as provided in clause (ii), the term "disqualified guarantee" means any guarantee by a related person which is—

(I) an organization exempt from taxation under this subtitle, or

(II) a foreign person.

(ii) Exceptions.—The term "disqualified guarantee" shall not include a guarantee—

(I) in any circumstances identified by the Secretary by regulation, where the interest on the indebtedness would have been subject to a net basis tax if the interest had been paid to the guarantor, or

(II) if the taxpayer owns a controlling interest in the guarantor.

For purposes of subclause (II), except as provided in regulations, the term "a controlling interest" means direct or indirect ownership of at least 80 percent of the total voting power and value of all classes of stock of a corporation, or 80 percent of the profit and capital interests in any other entity. For purposes of the preceding sentence, the rules of paragraphs (1) and (5) of section 267(c) shall apply; except that such rules shall also apply to interest in entities other than corporations.

(iii) Guarantee.—Except as provided in regulations, the term "guarantee" includes any arrangement under which a person (directly or indirectly through an entity or otherwise) assures, on a conditional or unconditional basis, the payment of another person's obligation under any indebtedness.

(E) Gross basis and net basis taxation.—

(i) Gross basis tax.—The term "gross basis tax" means any tax imposed by this subtitle which is determined by reference to the gross amount of any item of income without any reduction for any deduction allowed by this subtitle.

(ii) Net basis tax.—The term "net basis tax" means any tax imposed by this subtitle which is not a gross basis tax.

(7) Coordination with passive loss rules, etc.—This subsection shall be applied before sections 465 and 469.

(8) Treatment of corporate partners.—Except to the extent provided by regulations, in applying this subsection to a corporation which owns (directly or indirectly) an interest in a partnership—

(A) such corporation's distributive share of interest income paid or accrued to such partnership shall be treated as interest income paid or accrued to such corporation,

(B) such corporation's distributive share of interest paid or accrued by such partnership shall be treated as interest paid or accrued by such corporation, and

(C) such corporation's share of the liabilities of such partnership shall be treated as liabilities of such corporation.

(9) Regulations.—The Secretary shall prescribe such regulations as may be appropriate to carry out the purposes of this subsection, including—

(A) such regulations as may be appropriate to prevent the avoidance of the purposes of this subsection,

(B) regulations providing such adjustments in the case of corporations which are members of an affiliated group as may be appropriate to carry out the purposes of this subsection,

(C) regulations for the coordination of this subsection with section 884, and

(D) regulations providing for the reallocation of shares of partnership indebtedness, or distributive shares of the partnership's interest income or interest expense.

(k) Section 6166 interest.—No deduction shall be allowed under this section for any interest payable under section 6601 on any unpaid portion of the tax imposed by section 2001 for the period during which an extension of time for payment of such tax is in effect under section 6166.

(*l*) Disallowance of deduction on certain debt instruments of corporations.—

(1) In general.—No deduction shall be allowed under this chapter for any interest paid or accrued on a disqualified debt instrument.

(2) Disqualified debt instrument.—For purposes of this subsection, the term "disqualified debt instrument" means any indebtedness of a corporation which is payable in equity of the issuer or a related party or equity held by the issuer (or any related party) in any other person.

(3) Special rules for amounts payable in equity.—For purposes of paragraph (2), indebtedness shall be treated as payable in equity of the issuer or any other person only if—

(A) a substantial amount of the principal or interest is required to be paid or converted, or at the option of the issuer or a related party is payable in, or convertible into, such equity,

(B) a substantial amount of the principal or interest is required to be determined, or at the option of the issuer or a related party is determined, by reference to the value of such equity, or

(C) the indebtedness is part of an arrangement which is reasonably expected to result in a transaction described in subparagraph (A) or (B).

For purposes of this paragraph, principal or interest shall be treated as required to be so paid, converted, or determined if it may be required at the option of the holder or a related party and there is a substantial certainty the option will be exercised.

(4) Capitalization allowed with respect to equity of persons other than issuer and related parties.—If the disqualified debt instrument of a corporation is payable in equity held by the issuer (or any related party) in any other person (other than a related party), the basis of such equity shall be increased by the amount not allowed as a deduction by reason of paragraph (1) with respect to the instrument.

(5) Exception for certain instruments issued by dealers in securities.—For purposes of this subsection, the term "disqualified debt instrument" does not include indebtedness issued by a dealer in securities (or a related party) which is payable in, or by reference to, equity (other than equity of the issuer or a related party) held by such dealer in its capacity as a dealer in securities. For purposes of this paragraph, the term "dealer in securities" has the meaning given such term by section 475.

(6) Related party.—For purposes of this subsection, a person is a related party with respect to another person if such person bears a relationship to such other person described in section 267(b) or 707(b).

(7) Regulations.—The Secretary shall prescribe such regulations as may be necessary or appropriate to carry out the purposes of this subsection, including regulations preventing avoidance of this subsection through the use of an issuer other than a corporation.

(m) Interest on unpaid taxes attributable to nondisclosed reportable transactions.—No deduction shall be allowed under this chapter for any interest paid or accrued under section 6601 on any underpayment of tax which is attributable to the portion of any reportable transaction understatement (as defined in section 6662A(b)) with respect to which the requirement of section 6664(d)(2)(A) is not met.

(n) Cross references.—

(1) For disallowance of certain amounts paid in connection with insurance, endowment, or annuity contracts, see section 264.

(2) For disallowance of deduction for interest relating to tax-exempt income, see section 265(a)(2).

(3) For disallowance of deduction for carrying charges chargeable to capital account, see section 266.

(4) For disallowance of interest with respect to transactions between related taxpayers, see section 267.

(5) For treatment of redeemable ground rents and real property held subject to liabilities under redeemable ground rents, see section 1055.

§ 165. Losses

(a) General rule.—There shall be allowed as a deduction any loss sustained during the taxable year and not compensated for by insurance or otherwise.

(b) Amount of deduction.—For purposes of subsection (a), the basis for determining the amount of the deduction for any loss shall be the adjusted basis provided in section 1011 for determining the loss from the sale or other disposition of property.

(c) Limitation on losses of individuals.—In the case of an individual, the deduction under subsection (a) shall be limited to—

(1) losses incurred in a trade or business;

(2) losses incurred in any transaction entered into for profit, though not connected with a trade or business; and

(3) except as provided in subsection (h), losses of property not connected with a trade or business or a transaction entered into for profit, if such losses arise from fire, storm, shipwreck, or other casualty, or from theft.

(d) Wagering losses.—Losses from wagering transactions shall be allowed only to the extent of the gains from such transactions.

(e) Theft losses.—For purposes of subsection (a), any loss arising from theft shall be treated as sustained during the taxable year in which the taxpayer discovers such loss.

(f) Capital losses.—Losses from sales or exchanges of capital assets shall be allowed only to the extent allowed in sections 1211 and 1212.

(g) Worthless securities.—

(1) General rule.—If any security which is a capital asset becomes worthless during the taxable year, the loss resulting therefrom shall, for purposes of this subtitle, be treated as a loss from the sale or exchange, on the last day of the taxable year, of a capital asset.

(2) Security defined.—For purposes of this subsection, the term "security" means—

(A) a share of stock in a corporation;

(B) a right to subscribe for, or to receive, a share of stock in a corporation; or

(C) a bond, debenture, note, or certificate, or other evidence of indebtedness, issued by a corporation or by a government or political subdivision thereof, with interest coupons or in registered form.

(3) Securities in affiliated corporation.—For purposes of paragraph (1), any security in a corporation affiliated with a taxpayer which is a domestic corporation shall not be treated as a capital asset. For purposes of the preceding sentence, a corporation shall be treated as affiliated with the taxpayer only if—

(A) the taxpayer owns directly stock in such corporation meeting the requirements of section 1504(a)(2), and

(B) more than 90 percent of the aggregate of its gross receipts for all taxable years has been from sources other than royalties, rents (except rents derived from rental of properties to employees of the corporation in the ordinary course of its operating business), dividends, interest (except interest received on deferred purchase price of operating assets sold), annuities, and gains from sales or exchanges of stocks and securities.

In computing gross receipts for purposes of the preceding sentence, gross receipts from sales or exchanges of stocks and securities shall be taken into account only to the extent of gains therefrom.

(h) Treatment of casualty gains and losses.—

(1) $100 limitation per casualty.—Any loss of an individual described in subsection (c)(3) shall be allowed only to the extent that the amount of the loss to such individual arising from each casualty, or from each theft, exceeds $500 ($100 for taxable years beginning after December 31, 2009).

(2) Net casualty loss allowed only to the extent it exceeds 10 percent of adjusted gross income.—

(A) In general.—If the personal casualty losses for any taxable year exceed the personal casualty gains for such taxable year, such losses shall be allowed for the taxable year only to the extent of the sum of—

(i) the amount of the personal casualty gains for the taxable year, plus

(ii) so much of such excess as exceeds 10 percent of the adjusted gross income of the individual.

(B) Special rule where personal casualty gains exceed personal casualty losses.—If the personal casualty gains for any taxable year exceed the personal casualty losses for such taxable year—

(i) all such gains shall be treated as gains from sales or exchanges of capital assets, and

(ii) all such losses shall be treated as losses from sales or exchanges of capital assets.

(3) Special rule for losses in federally declared disasters.—

(A) In general.—If an individual has a net disaster loss for any taxable year, the amount determined under paragraph (2)(A)(ii) shall be the sum of—

(i) such net disaster loss, and

(ii) so much of the excess referred to in the matter preceding clause (i) of paragraph (2)(A) (reduced by the amount in clause (i) of this subparagraph) as exceeds 10 percent of the adjusted gross income of the individual.

(B) Net disaster loss.—For purposes of subparagraph (A), the term "net disaster loss" means the excess of—

(i) the personal casualty losses—

(I) attributable to a federally declared disaster occurring before January 1, 2010, and

(II) occurring in a disaster area, over

(ii) personal casualty gains.

(C) Federally declared disaster.—For purposes of this paragraph—

(i) Federally declared disaster.—**The term "federally declared disaster" means any disaster subsequently determined by the President of the United States to warrant assistance by the Federal Government under the Robert T. Stafford Disaster Relief and Emergency Assistance Act.**

(ii) Disaster area.—**The term "disaster area" means the area so determined to warrant such assistance.**

(4) Definitions of personal casualty gain and personal casualty loss.—For purposes of this subsection—

    (A) Personal casualty gain.—The term "personal casualty gain" means the recognized gain from any involuntary conversion of property which is described in subsection (c)(3) arising from fire, storm, shipwreck, or other casualty, or from theft.

    (B) Personal casualty loss.—The term "personal casualty loss" means any loss described in subsection (c)(3). For purposes of paragraphs (2) and (3), the amount of any personal casualty loss shall be determined after the application of paragraph (1).

(5) Special rules.—

    (A) Personal casualty losses allowable in computing adjusted gross income to the extent of personal casualty gains.—In any case to which paragraph (2)(A) applies, the deduction for personal casualty losses for any taxable year shall be treated as a deduction allowable in computing adjusted gross income to the extent such losses do not exceed the personal casualty gains for the taxable year.

    (B) Joint returns.—For purposes of this subsection, a husband and wife making a joint return for the taxable year shall be treated as 1 individual.

    (C) Determination of adjusted gross income in case of estates and trusts.—For purposes of paragraph (2), the adjusted gross income of an estate or trust shall be computed in the same manner as in the case of an individual, except that the deductions for costs paid or incurred in connection with the administration of the estate or trust shall be treated as allowable in arriving at adjusted gross income.

    (D) Coordination with estate tax.—No loss described in subsection (c)(3) shall be allowed if, at the time of filing the return, such loss has been claimed for estate tax purposes in the estate tax return.

    (E) Claim required to be filed in certain cases.—Any loss of an individual described in subsection (c)(3) to the extent covered by insurance shall be taken into account under this section only if the individual files a timely insurance claim with respect to such loss.

(i) Disaster losses.—

(1) Election to take deduction for preceding year.—Notwithstanding the provisions of subsection (a), any loss occurring in a disaster area (as defined by clause (ii) of subsection (h)(3)(C)) and attributable to a federally declared disaster (as defined by clause (i) of such subsection) may, at the election of the taxpayer, be taken into account for the taxable year immediately preceding the taxable year in which the disaster occurred.

(2) Year of loss.—If an election is made under this subsection, the casualty resulting in the loss shall be treated for purposes of this title as having occurred in the taxable year for which the deduction is claimed.

(3) Amount of loss.—The amount of the loss taken into account in the preceding taxable year by reason of paragraph (1) shall not exceed the uncompensated amount determined on the basis of the facts existing at the date the taxpayer claims the loss.

(4) Use of disaster loan appraisals to establish amount of loss.—Nothing in this title shall be construed to prohibit the Secretary from prescribing regulations or other guidance under which an appraisal for the purpose of obtaining a loan of Federal funds or a loan guarantee from the Federal Government as a result of a federally declared disaster (as defined by subsection (h)(3)(C)(i))[3] may be used to establish the amount of any loss described in paragraph (1) or (2).

(j) Denial of deduction for losses on certain obligations not in registered form.—

(1) In general.—Nothing in subsection (a) or in any other provision of law shall be construed to provide a deduction for any loss sustained on any registration-required obligation unless such obligation is in registered form (or the issuance of such obligation was subject to tax under section 4701).

(2) Definitions.—For purposes of this subsection—

(A) Registration-required obligation.—The term "registration-required obligation" has the meaning given to such term by section 163(f)(2) except that clause (iv) of subparagraph (A), and subparagraph (B), of such section shall not apply.

(B) Registered form.—The term "registered form" has the same meaning as when used in section 163(f).

(3) Exceptions.—The Secretary may, by regulations, provide that this subsection and section 1287 shall not apply with respect to obligations held by any person if—

(A) such person holds such obligations in connection with a trade or business outside the United States,

(B) such person holds such obligations as a broker dealer (registered under Federal or State law) for sale to customers in the ordinary course of his trade or business,

(C) such person complies with reporting requirements with respect to ownership, transfers, and payments as the Secretary may require, or

(D) such person promptly surrenders the obligation to the issuer for the issuance of a new obligation in registered form,

but only if such obligations are held under arrangements provided in regulations or otherwise which are designed to assure that such obligations are not delivered to any United States person other than a person described in subparagraph (A), (B), or (C).

(k) Treatment as disaster loss where taxpayer ordered to demolish or relocate residence in disaster area because of disaster.—In the case of a taxpayer whose residence is located in an area which has been determined by the President of the United States to warrant assistance by the Federal Government under the Robert T. Stafford Disaster Relief and Emergency Assistance Act, if—

(1) not later than the 120th day after the date of such determination, the taxpayer is ordered, by the government of the State or any political subdivision thereof in which such residence is located, to demolish or relocate such residence, and

(2) the residence has been rendered unsafe for use as a residence by reason of the disaster,

any loss attributable to such disaster shall be treated as a loss which arises from a casualty and which is described in subsection (i).

---

3.   So in original. A closing parenthesis should probably follow "subsection (h)(3)(C)(i)".

(*l*) Treatment of certain losses in insolvent financial institutions.—

(1) In general.—If—

(A) as of the close of the taxable year, it can reasonably be estimated that there is a loss on a qualified individual's deposit in a qualified financial institution, and

(B) such loss is on account of the bankruptcy or insolvency of such institution,

then the taxpayer may elect to treat the amount so estimated as a loss described in subsection (c)(3) incurred during the taxable year.

(2) Qualified individual defined.—For purposes of this subsection, the term "qualified individual" means any individual, except an individual—

(A) who owns at least 1 percent in value of the outstanding stock of the qualified financial institution,

(B) who is an officer of the qualified financial institution,

(C) who is a sibling (whether by the whole or half blood), spouse, aunt, uncle, nephew, niece, ancestor, or lineal descendant of an individual described in subparagraph (A) or (B), or

(D) who otherwise is a related person (as defined in section 267(b)) with respect to an individual described in subparagraph (A) or (B).

(3) Qualified financial institution.—For purposes of this subsection, the term "qualified financial institution" means—

(A) any bank (as defined in section 581),

(B) any institution described in section 591,

(C) any credit union the deposits or accounts in which are insured under Federal or State law or are protected or guaranteed under State law, or

(D) any similar institution chartered and supervised under Federal or State law.

(4) Deposit.—For purposes of this subsection, the term "deposit" means any deposit, withdrawable account, or withdrawable or repurchasable share.

(5) Election to treat as ordinary loss.—

(A) In general.—In lieu of any election under paragraph (1), the taxpayer may elect to treat the amount referred to in paragraph (1) for the taxable year as an ordinary loss described in subsection (c)(2) incurred during the taxable year.

(B) Limitations.—

(i) Deposit may not be Federally insured.—No election may be made under subparagraph (A) with respect to any loss on a deposit in a qualified financial institution if part or all of such deposit is insured under Federal law.

(ii) Dollar limitation.—With respect to each financial institution, the aggregate amount of losses attributable to deposits in such financial institution to which an election under subparagraph (A) may be made by the taxpayer for any taxable year shall not exceed $20,000 ($10,000 in the case of a separate return by a married individual). The limitation of the preceding sentence shall be reduced by the amount of any insurance proceeds under any State law which can reasonably be expected to be received with respect to losses on deposits in such institution.

(6) Election.—Any election by the taxpayer under this subsection for any taxable year—

(A) shall apply to all losses for such taxable year of the taxpayer on deposits in the institution with respect to which such election was made, and

(B) may be revoked only with the consent of the Secretary.

(7) Coordination with section 166.—Section 166 shall not apply to any loss to which an election under this subsection applies.

(m) Cross references.—

(1) For special rule for banks with respect to worthless securities, see section 582.

(2) For disallowance of deduction for worthlessness of securities to which subsection (g)(2)(C) applies, if issued by a political party or similar organization, see section 271.

(3) For special rule for losses on stock in a small business investment company, see section 1242.

(4) For special rule for losses of a small business investment company, see section 1243.

(5) For special rule for losses on small business stock, see section 1244.

§ 167. Depreciation

(a) General rule.—There shall be allowed as a depreciation deduction a reasonable allowance for the exhaustion, wear and tear (including a reasonable allowance for obsolescence)—

(1) of property used in the trade or business, or

(2) of property held for the production of income.

(b) Cross Reference.—

For determination of depreciation deduction in case of property to which section 168 applies, see section 168.

(c) Basis for depreciation.—

(1) In general.—The basis on which exhaustion, wear and tear, and obsolescence are to be allowed in respect of any property shall be the adjusted basis provided in section 1011, for the purpose of determining the gain on the sale or other disposition of such property.

(2) Special rule for property subject to lease.—If any property is acquired subject to a lease—

(A) no portion of the adjusted basis shall be allocated to the leasehold interest, and

(B) the entire adjusted basis shall be taken into account in determining the depreciation deduction (if any) with respect to the property subject to the lease.

(d) Life tenants and beneficiaries of trusts and estates.—In the case of property held by one person for life with remainder to another person, the deduction shall be computed as if the life tenant were the absolute owner of the property and shall be allowed to the life tenant. In the case of property held in trust, the allowable deduction shall be apportioned between the income beneficiaries and the trustee in accordance with the pertinent provisions of the instrument creating the trust, or, in the absence of such provisions, on the basis of the trust income allocable to each. In the case of an estate, the allowable deduction shall be apportioned between the estate and the heirs, legatees, and devisees on the basis of the income of the estate allocable to each.

(e) Certain term interests not depreciable.—

(1) In general.—No depreciation deduction shall be allowed under this section (and no depreciation or amortization deduction shall be allowed under any other provision of this subtitle) to the taxpayer for any term interest in property for any period during which the remainder interest in such property is held (directly or indirectly) by a related person.

(2) Coordination with other provisions.—

(A) Section 273.—This subsection shall not apply to any term interest to which section 273 applies.

(B) Section 305(e).—This subsection shall not apply to the holder of the dividend rights which were separated from any stripped preferred stock to which section 305(e)(1) applies.

(3) Basis adjustments.—If, but for this subsection, a depreciation or amortization deduction would be allowable to the taxpayer with respect to any term interest in property—

(A) the taxpayer's basis in such property shall be reduced by any depreciation or amortization deductions disallowed under this subsection, and

(B) the basis of the remainder interest in such property shall be increased by the amount of such disallowed deductions (properly adjusted for any depreciation deductions allowable under subsection (d) to the taxpayer).

(4) Special rules.—

(A) Denial of increase in basis of remainderman.—No increase in the basis of the remainder interest shall be made under paragraph (3)(B) for any disallowed deductions attributable to periods during which the term interest was held—

(i) by an organization exempt from tax under this subtitle, or

(ii) by a nonresident alien individual or foreign corporation but only if income from the term interest is not effectively connected with the conduct of a trade or business in the United States.

(B) Coordination with subsection (d).—If, but for this subsection, a depreciation or amortization deduction would be allowable to any person with respect to any term interest in property, the principles of subsection (d) shall apply to such person with respect to such term interest.

(5) Definitions.—For purposes of this subsection—

(A) Term interest in property.—The term "term interest in property" has the meaning given such term by section 1001(e)(2).

(B) Related persons.—The term "related person" means any person bearing a relationship to the taxpayer described in subsection (b) or (e) of section 267.

(6) Regulations.—The Secretary shall prescribe such regulations as may be necessary to carry out the purposes of this subsection, including regulations preventing avoidance of this subsection through cross-ownership arrangements or otherwise.

(f) Treatment of certain property excluded from section 197.—

(1) Computer software.—

(A) In general.—If a depreciation deduction is allowable under subsection (a) with respect to any computer software, such deduction shall be computed by using the straight line method and a useful life of 36 months.

(B) Computer software.—For purposes of this section, the term "computer software" has the meaning given to such term by section 197(e)(3)(B); except that such term shall not include any such software which is an amortizable section 197 intangible.

(C) Tax-exempt use property subject to lease.—In the case of computer software which would be tax-exempt use property as defined in subsection (h) of section 168 if such section applied to computer software, the useful life under subparagraph (A) shall not be less than 125 percent of the lease term (within the meaning of section 168(i)(3)).

(2) Certain interests or rights acquired separately.—If a depreciation deduction is allowable under subsection (a) with respect to any property described in subparagraph (B), (C), or (D) of section 197(e)(4), such deduction shall be computed in accordance with regulations prescribed by the Secretary. If such property would be tax-exempt use property as defined in subsection (h) of section 168 if such section applied to such property, the useful life under such regulations shall not be less than 125 percent of the lease term (within the meaning of section 168(i)(3)).

(3) Mortgage servicing rights.—If a depreciation deduction is allowable under subsection (a) with respect to any right described in section 197(e)(6), such deduction shall be computed by using the straight line method and a useful life of 108 months.

(g) Depreciation under income forecast method.—

(1) In general.—If the depreciation deduction allowable under this section to any taxpayer with respect to any property is determined under the income forecast method or any similar method—

(A) the income from the property to be taken into account in determining the depreciation deduction under such method shall be equal to the amount of income earned in connection with the property before the close of the 10th taxable year following the taxable year in which the property was placed in service,

(B) the adjusted basis of the property shall only include amounts with respect to which the requirements of section 461(h) are satisfied,

(C) the depreciation deduction under such method for the 10th taxable year beginning after the taxable year in which the property was placed in service shall be equal to the adjusted basis of such property as of the beginning of such 10th taxable year, and

(D) such taxpayer shall pay (or be entitled to receive) interest computed under the look-back method of paragraph (2) for any recomputation year.

(2) Look-back method.—The interest computed under the look-back method of this paragraph for any recomputation year shall be determined by—

(A) first determining the depreciation deductions under this section with respect to such property which would have been allowable for prior taxable years if the determination of the amounts so allowable had been made on the basis of the sum of the following (instead of the estimated income from such property)—

(i) the actual income earned in connection with such property for periods before the close of the recomputation year, and

(ii) an estimate of the future income to be earned in connection with such property for periods after the recomputation year and before the close of the 10th taxable year following the taxable year in which the property was placed in service,

(B) second, determining (solely for purposes of computing such interest) the overpayment or underpayment of tax for each such prior taxable year which would result solely from the application of subparagraph (A), and

(C) then using the adjusted overpayment rate (as defined in section 460(b)(7)), compounded daily, on the overpayment or underpayment determined under subparagraph (B).

For purposes of the preceding sentence, any cost incurred after the property is placed in service (which is not treated as a separate property under paragraph (5)) shall be taken into account by discounting (using the Federal mid-term rate determined under section 1274(d) as of the time such cost is incurred) such cost to its value as of the date the property is placed in service. The taxpayer may elect with respect to any property to have the preceding sentence not apply to such property.

(3) Exception from look-back method.—Paragraph (1)(D) shall not apply with respect to any property which had a cost basis of $100,000 or less.

(4) Recomputation year.—For purposes of this subsection, except as provided in regulations, the term "recomputation year" means, with respect to any property, the 3d and the 10th taxable years beginning after the taxable year in which the property was placed in service, unless the actual income earned in connection with the property for the period before the close of such 3d or 10th taxable year is within 10 percent of the income earned in connection with the property for such period which was taken into account under paragraph (1)(A).

(5) Special rules.—

(A) Certain costs treated as separate property.—For purposes of this subsection, the following costs shall be treated as separate properties:

(i) Any costs incurred with respect to any property after the 10th taxable year beginning after the taxable year in which the property was placed in service.

(ii) Any costs incurred after the property is placed in service and before the close of such 10th taxable year if such costs are significant and give rise to a significant increase in the income from the property which was not included in the estimated income from the property.

(B) Syndication income from television series.—In the case of property which is 1 or more episodes in a television series, income from syndicating such series shall not be required to be taken into account under this subsection before the earlier of—

(i) the 4th taxable year beginning after the date the first episode in such series is placed in service, or

(ii) the earliest taxable year in which the taxpayer has an arrangement relating to the future syndication of such series.

(C) Special rules for financial exploitation of characters, etc.—For purposes of this subsection, in the case of television and motion picture films, the income from the property shall include income from the exploitation of characters, designs, scripts, scores, and other incidental income associated with such films, but only to the extent that such income is earned in connection with the ultimate use of such items by, or the ultimate sale of merchandise to, persons who are not related persons (within the meaning of section 267(b)) to the taxpayer.

(D) Collection of interest.—For purposes of subtitle F (other than sections 6654 and 6655), any interest required to be paid by the taxpayer under paragraph (1) for any recomputation year shall be treated as an increase in the tax imposed by this chapter for such year.

(E) Treatment of distribution costs.—For purposes of this subsection, the income with respect to any property shall be the taxpayer's gross income from such property.

(F) Determinations.—For purposes of paragraph (2), determinations of the amount of income earned in connection with any property shall be made in the same manner as for purposes of applying the income forecast method; except that any income from the disposition of such property shall be taken into account.

(G) Treatment of pass-thru entities.—Rules similar to the rules of section 460(b)(4) shall apply for purposes of this subsection.

(6) Limitation on property for which income forecast method may be used.— The depreciation deduction allowable under this section may be determined under the income forecast method or any similar method only with respect to—

  (A) property described in paragraph (3) or (4) of section 168(f),

  (B) copyrights,

  (C) books,

  (D) patents, and

  (E) other property specified in regulations.

Such methods may not be used with respect to any amortizable section 197 intangible (as defined in section 197(c)).

(7) Treatment of participations and residuals.—

  (A) In general.—For purposes of determining the depreciation deduction allowable with respect to a property under this subsection, the taxpayer may include participations and residuals with respect to such property in the adjusted basis of such property for the taxable year in which the property is placed in service, but only to the extent that such participations and residuals relate to income estimated (for purposes of this subsection) to be earned in connection with the property before the close of the 10th taxable year referred to in paragraph (1)(A).

  (B) Participations and residuals.—For purposes of this paragraph, the term "participations and residuals" means, with respect to any property, costs the amount of which by contract varies with the amount of income earned in connection with such property.

(C) Special rules relating to recomputation years.—If the adjusted basis of any property is determined under this paragraph, paragraph (4) shall be applied by substituting "for each taxable year in such period" for "for such period".

(D) Other special rules.—

(i) **Participations and residuals.**—Notwithstanding subparagraph (A), the taxpayer may exclude participations and residuals from the adjusted basis of such property and deduct such participations and residuals in the taxable year that such participations and residuals are paid.

(ii) **Coordination with other rules.**—Deductions computed in accordance with this paragraph shall be allowable notwithstanding paragraph (1)(B), section 263, 263A, 404, 419, or 461(h).

(E) Authority to make adjustments.—The Secretary shall prescribe appropriate adjustments to the basis of property and to the look-back method for the additional amounts allowable as a deduction solely by reason of this paragraph.

(8) Special rules for certain musical works and copyrights.—

(A) In general.—If an election is in effect under this paragraph for any taxable year, then, notwithstanding paragraph (1), any expense which—

(i) is paid or incurred by the taxpayer in creating or acquiring any applicable musical property placed in service during the taxable year, and

(ii) is otherwise properly chargeable to capital account,

shall be amortized ratably over the 5–year period beginning with the month in which the property was placed in service. The preceding sentence shall not apply to any expense which, without regard to this paragraph, would not be allowable as a deduction.

(B) Exclusive method.—Except as provided in this paragraph, no depreciation or amortization deduction shall be allowed with respect to any expense to which subparagraph (A) applies.

(C) Applicable musical property.—For purposes of this paragraph—

(i) **In general.**—The term "applicable musical property" means any musical composition (including any accompanying words), or any copyright with respect to a musical composition, which is property to which this subsection applies without regard to this paragraph.

(ii) **Exceptions.**—Such term shall not include any property—

(I) with respect to which expenses are treated as qualified creative expenses to which section 263A(h) applies,

(II) to which a simplified procedure established under section 263A(i)(2) applies, or

(III) which is an amortizable section 197 intangible (as defined in section 197(c)).

(D) Election.—An election under this paragraph shall be made at such time and in such form as the Secretary may prescribe and shall apply to all applicable musical property placed in service during the taxable year for which the election applies.

(E) Termination.—An election may not be made under this paragraph for any taxable year beginning after December 31, 2010.

(h) Amortization of geological and geophysical expenditures.—

(1) In general.—Any geological and geophysical expenses paid or incurred in connection with the exploration for, or development of, oil or gas within the United States (as defined in section 638) shall be allowed as a deduction ratably over the 24–month period beginning on the date that such expense was paid or incurred.

(2) Half-year convention.—For purposes of paragraph (1), any payment paid or incurred during the taxable year shall be treated as paid or incurred on the mid-point of such taxable year.

(3) Exclusive method.—Except as provided in this subsection, no depreciation or amortization deduction shall be allowed with respect to such payments.

(4) Treatment upon abandonment.—If any property with respect to which geological and geophysical expenses are paid or incurred is retired or abandoned during the 24–month period described in paragraph (1), no deduction shall be allowed on account of such retirement or abandonment and the amortization deduction under this subsection shall continue with respect to such payment.

(5) Special rule for major integrated oil companies.—

(A) In general.—In the case of a major integrated oil company, paragraphs (1) and (4) shall be applied by substituting "7–year" for "24 month".

(B) Major integrated oil company.—For purposes of this paragraph, the term "major integrated oil company" means, with respect to any taxable year, a producer of crude oil—

(i) which has an average daily worldwide production of crude oil of at least 500,000 barrels for the taxable year,

(ii) which had gross receipts in excess of $1,000,000,000 for its last taxable year ending during calendar year 2005, and

(iii) to which subsection (c) of section 613A does not apply by reason of paragraph (4) of section 613A(d), determined—

(I) by substituting "15 percent" for "5 percent" each place it occurs in paragraph (3) of section 613A(d), and

(II) without regard to whether subsection (c) of section 613A does not apply by reason of paragraph (2) of section 613A(d).

For purposes of clauses (i) and (ii), all persons treated as a single employer under subsections (a) and (b) of section 52 shall be treated as 1 person and, in case of a short taxable year, the rule under section 448(c)(3) (B) shall apply.

(i) Cross references.—

(1) For additional rule applicable to depreciation of improvements in the case of mines, oil and gas wells, other natural deposits, and timber, see section 611.

(2) For amortization of goodwill and certain other intangibles, see section 197.

§ 168. Accelerated Cost Recovery System

(a) General rule.—Except as otherwise provided in this section, the depreciation deduction provided by section 167(a) for any tangible property shall be determined by using—

(1) the applicable depreciation method,

(2) the applicable recovery period, and

(3) the applicable convention.

(b) Applicable depreciation method.—For purposes of this section—

(1) In general.—Except as provided in paragraphs (2) and (3), the applicable depreciation method is—

 (A) the 200 percent declining balance method,

 (B) switching to the straight line method for the 1st taxable year for which using the straight line method with respect to the adjusted basis as of the beginning of such year will yield a larger allowance.

(2) 150 percent declining balance method in certain cases.—Paragraph (1) shall be applied by substituting "150 percent" for "200 percent" in the case of—

 (A) any 15–year or 20–year property not referred to in paragraph (3),

 (B) any property used in a farming business (within the meaning of section 263A(e)(4)),

 (C) any property (other than property described in paragraph (3)) which is a qualified smart electric meter or qualified smart electric grid system, or

 (D) any property (other than property described in paragraph (3)) with respect to which the taxpayer elects under paragraph (5) to have the provisions of this paragraph apply.

(3) Property to which straight line method applies.—The applicable depreciation method shall be the straight line method in the case of the following property:

 (A) Nonresidential real property.

 (B) Residential rental property.

 (C) Any railroad grading or tunnel bore.

 (D) Property with respect to which the taxpayer elects under paragraph (5) to have the provisions of this paragraph apply.

 (E) Property described in subsection (e)(3)(D)(ii).

 (F) Water utility property described in subsection (e)(5).

 (G) Qualified leasehold improvement property described in subsection (e)(6).

 (H) Qualified restaurant property described in subsection (e)(7).

 (I) Qualified retail improvement property described in subsection (e)(8).

(4) Salvage value treated as zero.—Salvage value shall be treated as zero.

(5) Election.—An election under paragraph (2)(C) or (3)(D) may be made with respect to 1 or more classes of property for any taxable year and once made with respect to any class shall apply to all property in such class placed in service during such taxable year. Such an election, once made, shall be irrevocable.

(c) Applicable recovery period.—For purposes of this section, the applicable recovery period shall be determined in accordance with the following table:

In the case of:	The applicable recovery period is:
3–year property	3 years
5–year property	5 years
7–year property	7 years
10–year property	10 years
15–year property	15 years
20–year property	20 years
Water utility property	25 years
Residential rental property	27.5 years
Nonresidential real property	39 years
Any railroad grading or tunnel bore	50 years.

(d) Applicable convention.—For purposes of this section—

(1) In general.—Except as otherwise provided in this subsection, the applicable convention is the half-year convention.

(2) Real property.—In the case of—

(A) nonresidential real property,

(B) residential rental property, and

(C) any railroad grading or tunnel bore, the applicable convention is the mid-month convention.

(3) Special rule where substantial property placed in service during last 3 months of taxable year.—

(A) In general.—Except as provided in regulations, if during any taxable year—

(i) the aggregate bases of property to which this section applies placed in service during the last 3 months of the taxable year, exceed

(ii) 40 percent of the aggregate bases of property to which this section applies placed in service during such taxable year,

the applicable convention for all property to which this section applies placed in service during such taxable year shall be the mid-quarter convention.

(B) Certain property not taken into account.—For purposes of subparagraph (A), there shall not be taken into account—

(i) any nonresidential real property residential rental property[1], and railroad grading or tunnel bore, and

(ii) any other property placed in service and disposed of during the same taxable year.

---

1. So in original. Probably should be ''nonresidential real property, residential rental property''.

(4) Definitions.—

   (A) Half-year convention.—The half-year convention is a convention which treats all property placed in service during any taxable year (or disposed of during any taxable year) as placed in service (or disposed of) on the mid-point of such taxable year.

   (B) Mid-month convention.—The mid-month convention is a convention which treats all property placed in service during any month (or disposed of during any month) as placed in service (or disposed of) on the mid-point of such month.

   (C) Mid-quarter convention.—The mid-quarter convention is a convention which treats all property placed in service during any quarter of a taxable year (or disposed of during any quarter of a taxable year) as placed in service (or disposed of) on the mid-point of such quarter.

(e) Classification of property.—For purposes of this section—

(1) In general.—Except as otherwise provided in this subsection, property shall be classified under the following table:

Property shall be treated as:	If such property has a class life (in years) of:
3–year property	4 or less
5–year property	More than 4 but less than 10
7–year property	10 or more but less than 16
10–year property	16 or more but less than 20
15–year property	20 or more but less than 25
20–year property	25 or more.

(2) Residential rental or nonresidential real property.—

   (A) Residential rental property.—

     (i) Residential rental property.—The term "residential rental property" means any building or structure if 80 percent or more of the gross rental income from such building or structure for the taxable year is rental income from dwelling units.

     (ii) Definitions.—For purposes of clause (i)—

       (I) the term "dwelling unit" means a house or apartment used to provide living accommodations in a building or structure, but does not include a unit in a hotel, motel, or other establishment more than one-half of the units in which are used on a transient basis, and

       (II) if any portion of the building or structure is occupied by the taxpayer, the gross rental income from such building or structure shall include the rental value of the portion so occupied.

   (B) Nonresidential real property.—The term "nonresidential real property" means section 1250 property which is not—

     (i) residential rental property, or

     (ii) property with a class life of less than 27.5 years.

(3) Classification of certain property.—

   (A) 3–year property.—The term "3–year property" includes—

(**i**) any race horse—

(**I**) which is placed in service before January 1, 2014, and

(**II**) which is placed in service after December 31, 2013, and which is more than 2 years old at the time such horse is placed in service by such purchaser,

(**ii**) any horse other than a race horse which is more than 12 years old at the time it is placed in service, and

(**iii**) any qualified rent-to-own property.

(**B**) **5–year property.**—The term "5–year property" includes—

(**i**) any automobile or light general purpose truck,

(**ii**) any semi-conductor manufacturing equipment,

(**iii**) any computer-based telephone central office switching equipment,

(**iv**) any qualified technological equipment,

(**v**) any section 1245 property used in connection with research and experimentation,

(**vi**) any property which—

(**I**) is described in subparagraph (A) of section 48(a)(3) (or would be so described if "solar or wind energy" were substituted for "solar energy" in clause (i) thereof and the last sentence of such section did not apply to such subparagraph),

(**II**) is described in paragraph (15) of section 48(*l*) (as in effect on the day before the date of the enactment of the Revenue Reconciliation Act of 1990) and is a qualifying small power production facility within the meaning of section 3(17)(C) of the Federal Power Act (16 U.S.C. 796(17)(C)), as in effect on September 1, 1986, or

(**III**) is described in section 48(*l*)(3)(A)(ix) (as in effect on the day before the date of the enactment of the Revenue Reconciliation Act of 1990), and

(**vii**) any machinery or equipment (other than any grain bin, cotton ginning asset, fence, or other land improvement) which is used in a farming business (as defined in section 263A(e)(4)), the original use of which commences with the taxpayer after December 31, 2008, and which is placed in service before January 1, 2010.

Nothing in any provision of law shall be construed to treat property as not being described in clause (vi)(I) (or the corresponding provisions of prior law) by reason of being public utility property (within the meaning of section 48(a)(3)).

(**C**) **7–year property.**—The term "7–year property" includes—

(**i**) any railroad track, and[2]

(**ii**) any motorsports entertainment complex,

(**iii**) any Alaska natural gas pipeline,

2. So in original. The word "and" probably should not appear.

(iv) any natural gas gathering line the original use of which commences with the taxpayer after April 11, 2005, and

(v) any property which—

(I) does not have a class life, and

(II) is not otherwise classified under paragraph (2) or this paragraph.

(D) 10–year property.—The term "10–year property" includes—

(i) any single purpose agricultural or horticultural structure (within the meaning of subsection (i)(13)),

(ii) any tree or vine bearing fruit or nuts,

(iii) any qualified smart electric meter, and

(iv) any qualified smart electric grid system.

(E) 15–year property.—The term "15–year property" includes—

(i) any municipal wastewater treatment plant,

(ii) any telephone distribution plant and comparable equipment used for 2–way exchange of voice and data communications,

(iii) any section 1250 property which is a retail motor fuels outlet (whether or not food or other convenience items are sold at the outlet),

(iv) any qualified leasehold improvement property placed in service before January 1, 2010,

(v) any qualified restaurant property placed in service before January 1, 2010,

(vi) initial clearing and grading land improvements with respect to gas utility property,

(vii) any section 1245 property (as defined in section 1245(a)(3)) used in the transmission at 69 or more kilovolts of electricity for sale and the original use of which commences with the taxpayer after April 11, 2005,

(viii) any natural gas distribution line the original use of which commences with the taxpayer after April 11, 2005, and which is placed in service before January 1, 2011, and

(ix) any qualified retail improvement property placed in service after December 31, 2008, and before January 1, 2010.

(F) 20–year property.—The term "20–year property" means initial clearing and grading land improvements with respect to any electric utility transmission and distribution plant.

(4) Railroad grading or tunnel bore.—The term "railroad grading or tunnel bore" means all improvements resulting from excavations (including tunneling), construction of embankments, clearings, diversions of roads and streams, sodding of slopes, and from similar work necessary to provide, construct, reconstruct, alter, protect, improve, replace, or restore a roadbed or right-of-way for railroad track.

(5) Water utility property.—The term "water utility property" means property—

(A) which is an integral part of the gathering, treatment, or commercial distribution of water, and which, without regard to this paragraph, would be 20–year property, and

(B) any municipal sewer.

(6) Qualified leasehold improvement property.—The term "qualified leasehold improvement property" has the meaning given such term in section 168(k)(3) except that the following special rules shall apply:

(A) Improvements made by lessor.—In the case of an improvement made by the person who was the lessor of such improvement when such improvement was placed in service, such improvement shall be qualified leasehold improvement property (if at all) only so long as such improvement is held by such person.

(B) Exception for changes in form of business.—Property shall not cease to be qualified leasehold improvement property under subparagraph (A) by reason of—

(i) death,

(ii) a transaction to which section 381(a) applies,

(iii) a mere change in the form of conducting the trade or business so long as the property is retained in such trade or business as qualified leasehold improvement property and the taxpayer retains a substantial interest in such trade or business,

(iv) the acquisition of such property in an exchange described in section 1031, 1033, or 1038 to the extent that the basis of such property includes an amount representing the adjusted basis of other property owned by the taxpayer or a related person, or

(v) the acquisition of such property by the taxpayer in a transaction described in section 332, 351, 361, 721, or 731 (or the acquisition of such property by the taxpayer from the transferee or acquiring corporation in a transaction described in such section), to the extent that the basis of the property in the hands of the taxpayer is determined by reference to its basis in the hands of the transferor or distributor.

(7) Qualified restaurant property.—

(A) In general.—The term "qualified restaurant property" means any section 1250 property which is—

(i) a building, if such building is placed in service after December 31, 2008, and before January 1, 2010, or

(ii) an improvement to a building,

if more than 50 percent of the building's square footage is devoted to preparation of, and seating for on-premises consumption of, prepared meals.

(B) Exclusion from bonus depreciation.—Property described in this paragraph shall not be considered qualified property for purposes of subsection (k).

(8) Qualified retail improvement property.—

(A) In general.—The term "qualified retail improvement property" means any improvement to an interior portion of a building which is nonresidential real property if—

(i) such portion is open to the general public and is used in the retail trade or business of selling tangible personal property to the general public, and

(ii) such improvement is placed in service more than 3 years after the date the building was first placed in service.

(B) Improvements made by owner.—In the case of an improvement made by the owner of such improvement, such improvement shall be qualified retail improvement property (if at all) only so long as such improvement is held by such owner. Rules similar to the rules under paragraph (6)(B) shall apply for purposes of the preceding sentence.

(C) Certain improvements not included.—Such term shall not include any improvement for which the expenditure is attributable to—

(i) the enlargement of the building,

(ii) any elevator or escalator,

(iii) any structural component benefitting a common area, or

(iv) the internal structural framework of the building.

(D) Exclusion from bonus depreciation.—Property described in this paragraph shall not be considered qualified property for purposes of subsection (k).

(E) Termination.—Such term shall not include any improvement placed in service after December 31, 2009.

(f) Property to which section does not apply.—This section shall not apply to—

(1) Certain methods of depreciation.—Any property if—

(A) the taxpayer elects to exclude such property from the application of this section, and

(B) for the 1st taxable year for which a depreciation deduction would be allowable with respect to such property in the hands of the taxpayer, the property is properly depreciated under the unit-of-production method or any method of depreciation not expressed in a term of years (other than the retirement-replacement-betterment method or similar method).

(2) Certain public utility property.—Any public utility property (within the meaning of subsection (i)(10)) if the taxpayer does not use a normalization method of accounting.

(3) Films and video tape.—Any motion picture film or video tape.

(4) Sound recordings.—Any works which result from the fixation of a series of musical, spoken, or other sounds, regardless of the nature of the material (such as discs, tapes, or other phonorecordings) in which such sounds are embodied.

(5) Certain property placed in service in churning transactions.—

(A) In general.—Property—

(i) described in paragraph (4) of section 168(e) (as in effect before the amendments made by the Tax Reform Act of 1986), or

(ii) which would be described in such paragraph if such paragraph were applied by substituting "1987" for "1981" and "1986" for "1980" each place such terms appear.

(B) Subparagraph (A)(ii) not to apply.—Clause (ii) of subparagraph (A) shall not apply to—

(i) any residential rental property or nonresidential real property,

(ii) any property if, for the 1st taxable year in which such property is placed in service—

(I) the amount allowable as a deduction under this section (as in effect before the date of the enactment of this paragraph) with respect to such property is greater than,

(II) the amount allowable as a deduction under this section (as in effect on or after such date and using the half-year convention) for such taxable year, or

(iii) any property to which this section (as amended by the Tax Reform Act of 1986) applied in the hands of the transferor.

(C) Special rule.—In the case of any property to which this section would apply but for this paragraph, the depreciation deduction under section 167 shall be determined under the provisions of this section as in effect before the amendments made by section 201 of the Tax Reform Act of 1986.

(g) Alternative depreciation system for certain property.—

(1) In general.—In the case of—

(A) any tangible property which during the taxable year is used predominantly outside the United States,

(B) any tax-exempt use property,

(C) any tax-exempt bond financed property,

(D) any imported property covered by an Executive order under paragraph (6), and

(E) any property to which an election under paragraph (7) applies,

the depreciation deduction provided by section 167(a) shall be determined under the alternative depreciation system.

(2) Alternative depreciation system.—For purposes of paragraph (1), the alternative depreciation system is depreciation determined by using—

(A) the straight line method (without regard to salvage value),

(B) the applicable convention determined under subsection (d), and

(C) a recovery period determined under the following table:

In the case of:	The recovery period shall be:
(i) Property not described in clause (ii) or (iii)	The class life.
(ii) Personal property with no class life	12 years.
(iii) Nonresidential real and residential rental property	40 years.
(iv) Any railroad grading or tunnel bore or water utility property	50 years.

(3) Special rules for determining class life.—

(A) Tax-exempt use property subject to lease.—In the case of any tax-exempt use property subject to a lease, the recovery period used for purposes of paragraph (2) shall (notwithstanding any other subparagraph of this paragraph) in no event be less than 125 percent of the lease term.

(B) Special rule for certain property assigned to classes.—For purposes of paragraph (2), in the case of property described in any of the following subparagraphs of subsection (e)(3), the class life shall be determined as follows:

If property is described in subparagraph:	The class life is:
(A)(iii)	4
(B)(ii)	5
(B)(iii)	9.5
(B)(vii)	10
(C)(i)[3]	10
(C)(iii)[3]	22
(C)(iv)	14
(D)(i)	15
(D)(ii)	20
(E)(i)	24
(E)(ii)	24
(E)(iii)	20
(E)(vi)	39
(E)(v)	39
(E)(vi)	20
(E)(vii)	30
(E)(viii)	35
(E)(ix)	39
(F)	25

(C) Qualified technological equipment.—In the case of any qualified technological equipment, the recovery period used for purposes of paragraph (2) shall be 5 years.

(D) Automobiles, etc.—In the case of any automobile or light general purpose truck, the recovery period used for purposes of paragraph (2) shall be 5 years.

(E) Certain real property.—In the case of any section 1245 property which is real property with no class life, the recovery period used for purposes of paragraph (2) shall be 40 years.

(4) Exception for certain property used outside United States.—Subparagraph (A) of paragraph (1) shall not apply to—

(A) any aircraft which is registered by the Administrator of the Federal Aviation Agency and which is operated to and from the United States or is operated under contract with the United States;

(B) rolling stock which is used within and without the United States and which is—

---

3. So in original. No table item relating to subparagraph "(C)(ii)" has been enacted.

(**i**) of a rail carrier subject to part A of subtitle IV of title 49, or

(**ii**) of a United States person (other than a corporation described in clause (i)) but only if the rolling stock is not leased to one or more foreign persons for periods aggregating more than 12 months in any 24–month period;

(**C**) any vessel documented under the laws of the United States which is operated in the foreign or domestic commerce of the United States;

(**D**) any motor vehicle of a United States person (as defined in section 7701(a)(30)) which is operated to and from the United States;

(**E**) any container of a United States person which is used in the transportation of property to and from the United States;

(**F**) any property (other than a vessel or an aircraft) of a United States person which is used for the purpose of exploring for, developing, removing, or transporting resources from the outer Continental Shelf (within the meaning of section 2 of the Outer Continental Shelf Lands Act, as amended and supplemented; (43 U.S.C. 1331));

(**G**) any property which is owned by a domestic corporation (other than a corporation which has an election in effect under section 936) or by a United States citizen (other than a citizen entitled to the benefits of section 931 or 933) and which is used predominantly in a possession of the United States by such a corporation or such a citizen, or by a corporation created or organized in, or under the law of, a possession of the United States;

(**H**) any communications satellite (as defined in section 103(3) of the Communications Satellite Act of 1962, 47 U.S.C. 702(3)), or any interest therein, of a United States person;

(**I**) any cable, or any interest therein, of a domestic corporation engaged in furnishing telephone service to which section 168(i)(10)(C) applies (or of a wholly owned domestic subsidiary of such a corporation), if such cable is part of a submarine cable system which constitutes part of a communication link exclusively between the United States and one or more foreign countries;

(**J**) any property (other than a vessel or an aircraft) of a United States person which is used in international or territorial waters within the northern portion of the Western Hemisphere for the purpose of exploring for, developing, removing, or transporting resources from ocean waters or deposits under such waters;

(**K**) any property described in section 48(*l*)(3)(A)(ix) (as in effect on the day before the date of the enactment of the Revenue Reconciliation Act of 1990) which is owned by a United States person and which is used in international or territorial waters to generate energy for use in the United States; and

(**L**) any satellite (not described in subparagraph (H)) or other spacecraft (or any interest therein) held by a United States person if such satellite or other spacecraft was launched from within the United States.

For purposes of subparagraph (J), the term "northern portion of the Western Hemisphere" means the area lying west of the 30th meridian west of Greenwich, east of the international dateline, and north of the Equator, but not including any foreign country which is a country of South America.

(5) Tax-exempt bond financed property.—For purposes of this subsection—

(A) In general.—Except as otherwise provided in this paragraph, the term "tax-exempt bond financed property" means any property to the extent such property is financed (directly or indirectly) by an obligation the interest on which is exempt from tax under section 103(a).

(B) Allocation of bond proceeds.—For purposes of subparagraph (A), the proceeds of any obligation shall be treated as used to finance property acquired in connection with the issuance of such obligation in the order in which such property is placed in service.

(C) Qualified residential rental projects.—The term "tax-exempt bond financed property" shall not include any qualified residential rental project (within the meaning of section 142(a)(7)).

(6) Imported property.—

(A) Countries maintaining trade restrictions or engaging in discriminatory acts.—If the President determines that a foreign country—

(i) maintains nontariff trade restrictions, including variable import fees, which substantially burden United States commerce in a manner inconsistent with provisions of trade agreements, or

(ii) engages in discriminatory or other acts (including tolerance of international cartels) or policies unjustifiably restricting United States commerce,

the President may by Executive order provide for the application of paragraph (1)(D) to any article or class of articles manufactured or produced in such foreign country for such period as may be provided by such Executive order. Any period specified in the preceding sentence shall not apply to any property ordered before (or the construction, reconstruction, or erection of which began before) the date of the Executive order unless the President determines an earlier date to be in the public interest and specifies such date in the Executive order.

(B) Imported property.—For purposes of this subsection, the term "imported property" means any property if—

(i) such property was completed outside the United States, or

(ii) less than 50 percent of the basis of such property is attributable to value added within the United States.

For purposes of this subparagraph, the term "United States" includes the Commonwealth of Puerto Rico and the possessions of the United States.

(7) Election to use alternative depreciation system.—

(A) In general.—If the taxpayer makes an election under this paragraph with respect to any class of property for any taxable year, the alternative depreciation system under this subsection shall apply to all property in such class placed in service during such taxable year. Notwithstanding the preceding sentence, in the case of nonresidential real property or residential rental property, such election may be made separately with respect to each property.

(B) Election irrevocable.—An election under subparagraph (A), once made, shall be irrevocable.

(h) Tax-exempt use property.—

(1) In general.—For purposes of this section—

(A) Property other than nonresidential real property.—Except as otherwise provided in this subsection, the term "tax-exempt use property" means that portion of any tangible property (other than nonresidential real property) leased to a tax-exempt entity.

(B) Nonresidential real property.—

(i) In general.—In the case of nonresidential real property, the term "tax-exempt use property" means that portion of the property leased to a tax-exempt entity in a disqualified lease.

(ii) Disqualified lease.—For purposes of this subparagraph, the term "disqualified lease" means any lease of the property to a tax-exempt entity, but only if—

(I) part or all of the property was financed (directly or indirectly) by an obligation the interest on which is exempt from tax under section 103(a) and such entity (or a related entity) participated in such financing,

(II) under such lease there is a fixed or determinable price purchase or sale option which involves such entity (or a related entity) or there is the equivalent of such an option,

(III) such lease has a lease term in excess of 20 years, or

(IV) such lease occurs after a sale (or other transfer) of the property by, or lease of the property from, such entity (or a related entity) and such property has been used by such entity (or a related entity) before such sale (or other transfer) or lease.

(iii) 35–percent threshold test.—Clause (i) shall apply to any property only if the portion of such property leased to tax-exempt entities in disqualified leases is more than 35 percent of the property.

(iv) Treatment of improvements.—For purposes of this subparagraph, improvements to a property (other than land) shall not be treated as a separate property.

(v) Leasebacks during 1st 3 months of use not taken into account.—Subclause (IV) of clause (ii) shall not apply to any property which is leased within 3 months after the date such property is first used by the tax-exempt entity (or a related entity).

(C) Exception for short-term leases.—

(i) In general.—Property shall not be treated as tax-exempt use property merely by reason of a short-term lease.

(ii) Short-term lease.—For purposes of clause (i), the term "short-term lease" means any lease the term of which is—

(I) less than 3 years, and

(II) less than the greater of 1 year or 30 percent of the property's present class life.

In the case of nonresidential real property and property with no present class life, subclause (II) shall not apply.

(D) Exception where property used in unrelated trade or business.—The term "tax-exempt use property" shall not include any portion of a property if such portion is predominantly used by the tax-exempt entity (directly or through a partnership of which such entity is a partner) in an unrelated trade or business the income of which is subject to tax under section 511. For purposes of subparagraph (B)(iii), any portion of a property so used shall not be treated as leased to a tax-exempt entity in a disqualified lease.

(E) Nonresidential real property defined.—For purposes of this paragraph, the term "nonresidential real property" includes residential rental property.

(2) Tax-exempt entity.—

(A) In general.—For purposes of this subsection, the term "tax-exempt entity" means—

(i) the United States, any State or political subdivision thereof, any possession of the United States, or any agency or instrumentality of any of the foregoing,

(ii) an organization (other than a cooperative described in section 521) which is exempt from tax imposed by this chapter,

(iii) any foreign person or entity, and

(iv) any Indian tribal government described in section 7701(a)(40).

For purposes of applying this subsection, any Indian tribal government referred to in clause (iv) shall be treated in the same manner as a State.

(B) Exception for certain property subject to United States tax and used by foreign person or entity.—Clause (iii) of subparagraph (A) shall not apply with respect to any property if more than 50 percent of the gross income for the taxable year derived by the foreign person or entity from the use of such property is—

(i) subject to tax under this chapter, or

(ii) included under section 951 in the gross income of a United States shareholder for the taxable year with or within which ends the taxable year of the controlled foreign corporation in which such income was derived.

For purposes of the preceding sentence, any exclusion or exemption shall not apply for purposes of determining the amount of the gross income so derived, but shall apply for purposes of determining the portion of such gross income subject to tax under this chapter.

(C) Foreign person or entity.—For purposes of this paragraph, the term "foreign person or entity" means—

(i) any foreign government, any international organization, or any agency or instrumentality of any of the foregoing, and

(ii) any person who is not a United States person.

Such term does not include any foreign partnership or other foreign pass-thru entity.

81

(D) Treatment of certain taxable instrumentalities.—For purposes of this subsection, a corporation shall not be treated as an instrumentality of the United States or of any State or political subdivision thereof if—

(i) all of the activities of such corporation are subject to tax under this chapter, and

(ii) a majority of the board of directors of such corporation is not selected by the United States or any State or political subdivision thereof.

(E) Certain previously tax-exempt organizations.—

(i) In general.—For purposes of this subsection, an organization shall be treated as an organization described in subparagraph (A)(ii) with respect to any property (other than property held by such organization) if such organization was an organization (other than a cooperative described in section 521) exempt from tax imposed by this chapter at any time during the 5–year period ending on the date such property was first used by such organization. The preceding sentence and subparagraph (D)(ii) shall not apply to the Federal Home Loan Mortgage Corporation.

(ii) Election not to have clause (I) apply.—

(I) In general.—In the case of an organization formerly exempt from tax under section 501(a) as an organization described in section 501(c)(12), clause (i) shall not apply to such organization with respect to any property if such organization elects not to be exempt from tax under section 501(a) during the tax-exempt use period with respect to such property.

(II) Tax-exempt use period.—For purposes of subclause (I), the term "tax-exempt use period" means the period beginning with the taxable year in which the property described in subclause (I) is first used by the organization and ending with the close of the 15th taxable year following the last taxable year of the applicable recovery period of such property.

(III) Election.—Any election under subclause (I), once made, shall be irrevocable.

(iii) Treatment of successor organizations.—Any organization which is engaged in activities substantially similar to those engaged in by a predecessor organization shall succeed to the treatment under this subparagraph of such predecessor organization.

(iv) First used.—For purposes of this subparagraph, property shall be treated as first used by the organization—

(I) when the property is first placed in service under a lease to such organization, or

(II) in the case of property leased to (or held by) a partnership (or other pass-thru entity) in which the organization is a member, the later of when such property is first used by such partnership or pass-thru entity or when such organization is first a member of such partnership or pass-thru entity.

(3) Special rules for certain high technology equipment.—

(A) Exemption where lease term is 5 years or less.—For purposes of this section, the term "tax-exempt use property" shall not include any qualified technological equipment if the lease to the tax-exempt entity has a lease term of 5 years or less. Notwithstanding subsection (i)(3)(A)(i), in determining a lease term for purposes of the preceding sentence, there shall not be taken into account any option of the lessee to renew at the fair market value rent determined at the time of renewal; except that the aggregate period not taken into account by reason of this sentence shall not exceed 24 months.

(B) Exception for certain property.—

(i) In general.—For purposes of subparagraph (A), the term "qualified technological equipment" shall not include any property leased to a tax-exempt entity if—

(I) part or all of the property was financed (directly or indirectly) by an obligation the interest on which is exempt from tax under section 103(a),

(II) such lease occurs after a sale (or other transfer) of the property by, or lease of such property from, such entity (or related entity) and such property has been used by such entity (or a related entity) before such sale (or other transfer) or lease, or

(III) such tax-exempt entity is the United States or any agency or instrumentality of the United States.

(ii) Leasebacks during 1st 3 months of use not taken into account.— Subclause (II) of clause (i) shall not apply to any property which is leased within 3 months after the date such property is first used by the tax-exempt entity (or a related entity).

(4) Related entities.—For purposes of this subsection—

(A)(i) Each governmental unit and each agency or instrumentality of a governmental unit is related to each other such unit, agency, or instrumentality which directly or indirectly derives its powers, rights, and duties in whole or in part from the same sovereign authority.

(ii) For purposes of clause (i), the United States, each State, and each possession of the United States shall be treated as a separate sovereign authority.

(B) Any entity not described in subparagraph (A)(i) is related to any other entity if the 2 entities have—

(i) significant common purposes and substantial common membership, or

(ii) directly or indirectly substantial common direction or control.

(C)(i) An entity is related to another entity if either entity owns (directly or through 1 or more entities) a 50 percent or greater interest in the capital or profits of the other entity.

(ii) For purposes of clause (i), entities treated as related under subparagraph (A) or (B) shall be treated as 1 entity.

(D) An entity is related to another entity with respect to a transaction if such transaction is part of an attempt by such entities to avoid the application of this subsection.

(5) Tax-exempt use of property leased to partnerships, etc., determined at partner level.—For purposes of this subsection—

(A) In general.—In the case of any property which is leased to a partnership, the determination of whether any portion of such property is tax-exempt use property shall be made by treating each tax-exempt entity partner's proportionate share (determined under paragraph (6)(C)) of such property as being leased to such partner.

(B) Other pass-thru entities; tiered entities.—Rules similar to the rules of subparagraph (A) shall also apply in the case of any pass-thru entity other than a partnership and in the case of tiered partnerships and other entities.

(C) Presumption with respect to foreign entities.—Unless it is otherwise established to the satisfaction of the Secretary, it shall be presumed that the partners of a foreign partnership (and the beneficiaries of any other foreign pass-thru entity) are persons who are not United States persons.

(6) Treatment of property owned by partnerships, etc.—

(A) In general.—For purposes of this subsection, if—

(i) any property which (but for this subparagraph) is not tax-exempt use property is owned by a partnership which has both a tax-exempt entity and a person who is not a tax-exempt entity as partners, and

(ii) any allocation to the tax-exempt entity of partnership items is not a qualified allocation,

an amount equal to such tax-exempt entity's proportionate share of such property shall (except as provided in paragraph (1)(D)) be treated as tax-exempt use property.

(B) Qualified allocation.—For purposes of subparagraph (A), the term "qualified allocation" means any allocation to a tax-exempt entity which—

(i) is consistent with such entity's being allocated the same distributive share of each item of income, gain, loss, deduction, credit, and basis and such share remains the same during the entire period the entity is a partner in the partnership, and

(ii) has substantial economic effect within the meaning of section 704(b)(2).

For purposes of this subparagraph, items allocated under section 704(c) shall not be taken into account.

(C) Determination of proportionate share.—

(i) In general.—For purposes of subparagraph (A), a tax-exempt entity's proportionate share of any property owned by a partnership shall be determined on the basis of such entity's share of partnership items of income or gain (excluding gain allocated under section 704(c)), whichever results in the largest proportionate share.

(ii) Determination where allocations vary.—For purposes of clause (i), if a tax-exempt entity's share of partnership items of income or gain (excluding gain allocated under section 704(c)) may vary during the period such entity is a partner in the partnership, such share shall be the highest share such entity may receive.

(D) Determination of whether property used in unrelated trade or business.—For purposes of this subsection, in the case of any property which is owned by a partnership which has both a tax-exempt entity and a person who is not a tax-exempt entity as partners, the determination of whether such property is used in an unrelated trade or business of such an entity shall be made without regard to section 514.

(E) Other pass-thru entities; tiered entities.—Rules similar to the rules of subparagraphs (A), (B), (C), and (D) shall also apply in the case of any pass-thru entity other than a partnership and in the case of tiered partnerships and other entities.

(F) Treatment of certain taxable entities.—

(i) In general.—For purposes of this paragraph and paragraph (5), except as otherwise provided in this subparagraph, any tax-exempt controlled entity shall be treated as a tax-exempt entity.

(ii) Election.—If a tax-exempt controlled entity makes an election under this clause—

(I) such entity shall not be treated as a tax-exempt entity for purposes of this paragraph and paragraph (5), and

(II) any gain recognized by a tax-exempt entity on any disposition of an interest in such entity (and any dividend or interest received or accrued by a tax-exempt entity from such tax-exempt controlled entity) shall be treated as unrelated business taxable income for purposes of section 511.

Any such election shall be irrevocable and shall bind all tax-exempt entities holding interests in such tax-exempt controlled entity. For purposes of subclause (II), there shall only be taken into account dividends which are properly allocable to income of the tax-exempt controlled entity which was not subject to tax under this chapter.

(iii) Tax-exempt controlled entity.—

(I) In general.—The term "tax-exempt controlled entity" means any corporation (which is not a tax-exempt entity determined without regard to this subparagraph and paragraph (2)(E)) if 50 percent or more (in value) of the stock in such corporation is held by 1 or more tax-exempt entities (other than a foreign person or entity).

(II) Only 5–percent shareholders taken into account in case of publicly traded stock.—For purposes of subclause (I), in the case of a corporation the stock of which is publicly traded on an established securities market, stock held by a tax-exempt entity shall not be taken into account unless such entity holds at least 5 percent (in value) of the stock in such corporation. For purposes of this subclause, related entities (within the meaning of paragraph (4)) shall be treated as 1 entity.

(III) Section 318 to apply.—For purposes of this clause, a tax-exempt entity shall be treated as holding stock which it holds through application of section 318 (determined without regard to the 50–percent limitation contained in subsection (a)(2)(C) thereof).

(G) Regulations.—For purposes of determining whether there is a qualified allocation under subparagraph (B), the regulations prescribed under paragraph (8) for purposes of this paragraph—

(i) shall set forth the proper treatment for partnership guaranteed payments, and

(ii) may provide for the exclusion or segregation of items.

85

(7) Lease.—For purposes of this subsection, the term "lease" includes any grant of a right to use property.

(8) Regulations.—The Secretary shall prescribe such regulations as may be necessary or appropriate to carry out the purposes of this subsection.

(i) Definitions and special rules.—For purposes of this section—

(1) Class life.—Except as provided in this section, the term "class life" means the class life (if any) which would be applicable with respect to any property as of January 1, 1986, under subsection (m) of section 167 (determined without regard to paragraph (4) and as if the taxpayer had made an election under such subsection). The Secretary, through an office established in the Treasury, shall monitor and analyze actual experience with respect to all depreciable assets. The reference in this paragraph to subsection (m) of section 167 shall be treated as a reference to such subsection as in effect on the day before the date of the enactment of the Revenue Reconciliation Act of 1990.

(2) Qualified technological equipment.—

    (A) In general.—The term "qualified technological equipment" means—

        (i) any computer or peripheral equipment,

        (ii) any high technology telephone station equipment installed on the customer's premises, and

        (iii) any high technology medical equipment.

    (B) Computer or peripheral equipment defined.—For purposes of this paragraph—

        (i) In general.—The term "computer or peripheral equipment" means—

            (I) any computer, and

            (II) any related peripheral equipment.

        (ii) Computer.—The term "computer" means a programmable electronically activated device which—

            (I) is capable of accepting information, applying prescribed processes to the information, and supplying the results of these processes with or without human intervention, and

            (II) consists of a central processing unit containing extensive storage, logic, arithmetic, and control capabilities.

        (iii) Related peripheral equipment.—The term "related peripheral equipment" means any auxiliary machine (whether on-line or off-line) which is designed to be placed under the control of the central processing unit of a computer.

        (iv) Exceptions.—The term "computer or peripheral equipment" shall not include—

            (I) any equipment which is an integral part of other property which is not a computer,

            (II) typewriters, calculators, adding and accounting machines, copiers, duplicating equipment, and similar equipment, and

(III) equipment of a kind used primarily for amusement or entertainment of the user.

(C) High technology medical equipment.—For purposes of this paragraph, the term "high technology medical equipment" means any electronic, electromechanical, or computer-based high technology equipment used in the screening, monitoring, observation, diagnosis, or treatment of patients in a laboratory, medical, or hospital environment.

(3) Lease term.—

(A) In general.—In determining a lease term—

(i) there shall be taken into account options to renew,

(ii) the term of a lease shall include the term of any service contract or similar arrangement (whether or not treated as a lease under section 7701(e))—

(I) which is part of the same transaction (or series of related transactions) which includes the lease, and

(II) which is with respect to the property subject to the lease or substantially similar property, and

(iii) 2 or more successive leases which are part of the same transaction (or a series of related transactions) with respect to the same or substantially similar property shall be treated as 1 lease.

(B) Special rule for fair rental options on nonresidential real property or residential rental property.—For purposes of clause (i) of subparagraph (A), in the case of nonresidential real property or residential rental property, there shall not be taken into account any option to renew at fair market value, determined at the time of renewal.

(4) General asset accounts.—Under regulations, a taxpayer may maintain 1 or more general asset accounts for any property to which this section applies. Except as provided in regulations, all proceeds realized on any disposition of property in a general asset account shall be included in income as ordinary income.

(5) Changes in use.—The Secretary shall, by regulations, provide for the method of determining the deduction allowable under section 167(a) with respect to any tangible property for any taxable year (and the succeeding taxable years) during which such property changes status under this section but continues to be held by the same person.

(6) Treatments of additions or improvements to property.—In the case of any addition to (or improvement of) any property—

(A) any deduction under subsection (a) for such addition or improvement shall be computed in the same manner as the deduction for such property would be computed if such property had been placed in service at the same time as such addition or improvement, and

(B) the applicable recovery period for such addition or improvement shall begin on the later of—

(i) the date on which such addition (or improvement) is placed in service, or

(ii) the date on which the property with respect to which such addition (or improvement) was made is placed in service.

(7) Treatment of certain transferees.—

(A) In general.—In the case of any property transferred in a transaction described in subparagraph (B), the transferee shall be treated as the transferor for purposes of computing the depreciation deduction determined under this section with respect to so much of the basis in the hands of the transferee as does not exceed the adjusted basis in the hands of the transferor. In any case where this section as in effect before the amendments made by section 201 of the Tax Reform Act of 1986 applied to the property in the hands of the transferor, the reference in the preceding sentence to this section shall be treated as a reference to this section as so in effect.

(B) Transactions covered.—The transactions described in this subparagraph are—

(i) any transaction described in section 332, 351, 361, 721, or 731, and

(ii) any transaction between members of the same affiliated group during any taxable year for which a consolidated return is made by such group.

Subparagraph (A) shall not apply in the case of a termination of a partnership under section 708(b)(1)(B).

(C) Property reacquired by the taxpayer.—Under regulations, property which is disposed of and then reacquired by the taxpayer shall be treated for purposes of computing the deduction allowable under subsection (a) as if such property had not been disposed of.

(8) Treatment of leasehold improvements.—

(A) In general.—In the case of any building erected (or improvements made) on leased property, if such building or improvement is property to which this section applies, the depreciation deduction shall be determined under the provisions of this section.

(B) Treatment of lessor improvements which are abandoned at termination of lease.—An improvement—

(i) which is made by the lessor of leased property for the lessee of such property, and

(ii) which is irrevocably disposed of or abandoned by the lessor at the termination of the lease by such lessee,

shall be treated for purposes of determining gain or loss under this title as disposed of by the lessor when so disposed of or abandoned.

(C) Cross reference.—

For treatment of qualified long-term real property constructed or improved in connection with cash or rent reduction from lessor to lessee, see section 110(b).

(9) Normalization rules.—

(A) In general.—In order to use a normalization method of accounting with respect to any public utility property for purposes of subsection (f)(2)—

(i) the taxpayer must, in computing its tax expense for purposes of establishing its cost of service for rate-making purposes and reflecting operating results in its regulated books of account, use a method of depreciation with respect to such property that is the same as, and a depreciation period for such property that is no shorter than, the method and period used to compute its depreciation expense for such purposes; and

(ii) if the amount allowable as a deduction under this section with respect to such property differs from the amount that would be allowable as a deduction under section 167 using the method (including the period, first and last year convention, and salvage value) used to compute regulated tax expense under clause (i), the taxpayer must make adjustments to a reserve to reflect the deferral of taxes resulting from such difference.

(B) Use of inconsistent estimates and projections, etc.—

(i) **In general.**—One way in which the requirements of subparagraph (A) are not met is if the taxpayer, for ratemaking purposes, uses a procedure or adjustment which is inconsistent with the requirements of subparagraph (A).

(ii) **Use of inconsistent estimates and projections.**—The procedures and adjustments which are to be treated as inconsistent for purposes of clause (i) shall include any procedure or adjustment for ratemaking purposes which uses an estimate or projection of the taxpayer's tax expense, depreciation expense, or reserve for deferred taxes under subparagraph (A)(ii) unless such estimate or projection is also used, for ratemaking purposes, with respect to the other 2 such items and with respect to the rate base.

(iii) **Regulatory authority.**—The Secretary may by regulations prescribe procedures and adjustments (in addition to those specified in clause (ii)) which are to be treated as inconsistent for purposes of clause (i).

(C) Public utility property which does not meet normalization rules.—In the case of any public utility property to which this section does not apply by reason of subsection (f)(2), the allowance for depreciation under section 167(a) shall be an amount computed using the method and period referred to in subparagraph (A)(i).

(10) Public utility property.—The term "public utility property" means property used predominantly in the trade or business of the furnishing or sale of—

(A) electrical energy, water, or sewage disposal services,

(B) gas or steam through a local distribution system,

(C) telephone services, or other communication services if furnished or sold by the Communications Satellite Corporation for purposes authorized by the Communications Satellite Act of 1962 (47 U.S.C. 701), or

(D) transportation of gas or steam by pipeline,

if the rates for such furnishing or sale, as the case may be, have been established or approved by a State or political subdivision thereof, by any agency or instrumentality of the United States, or by a public service or public utility commission or other similar body of any State or political subdivision thereof.

(11) Research and experimentation.—The term "research and experimentation" has the same meaning as the term research and experimental has under section 174.

(12) Section 1245 and 1250 property.—The terms "section 1245 property" and "section 1250 property" have the meanings given such terms by sections 1245(a)(3) and 1250(c), respectively.

(13) Single purpose agricultural or horticultural structure.—

(A) In general.—The term "single purpose agricultural or horticultural structure" means—

(i) a single purpose livestock structure, and

(ii) a single purpose horticultural structure.

(B) Definitions.—For purposes of this paragraph—

(i) Single purpose livestock structure.—The term "single purpose livestock structure" means any enclosure or structure specifically designed, constructed, and used—

(I) for housing, raising, and feeding a particular type of livestock and their produce, and

(II) for housing the equipment (including any replacements) necessary for the housing, raising, and feeding referred to in subclause (I).

(ii) Single purpose horticultural structure.—The term "single purpose horticultural structure" means—

(I) a greenhouse specifically designed, constructed, and used for the commercial production of plants, and

(II) a structure specifically designed, constructed, and used for the commercial production of mushrooms.

(iii) Structures which include work space.—An enclosure or structure which provides work space shall be treated as a single purpose agricultural or horticultural structure only if such work space is solely for—

(I) the stocking, caring for, or collecting of livestock or plants (as the case may be) or their produce,

(II) the maintenance of the enclosure or structure, and

(III) the maintenance or replacement of the equipment or stock enclosed or housed therein.

(iv) Livestock.—The term "livestock" includes poultry.

(14) Qualified rent-to-own property.—

(A) In general.—The term "qualified rent-to-own property" means property held by a rent-to-own dealer for purposes of being subject to a rent-to-own contract.

(B) Rent-to-own dealer.—The term "rent-to-own dealer" means a person that, in the ordinary course of business, regularly enters into rent-to-own contracts with customers for the use of consumer property, if a substantial portion of those contracts terminate and the property is returned to such person before the receipt of all payments required to transfer ownership of the property from such person to the customer.

(C) Consumer property.—The term "consumer property" means tangible personal property of a type generally used within the home for personal use.

(D) Rent-to-own contract.—The term "rent-to-own contract" means any lease for the use of consumer property between a rent-to-own dealer and a customer who is an individual which—

(i) is titled "Rent-to-Own Agreement" or "Lease Agreement with Ownership Option," or uses other similar language,

(ii) provides for level (or decreasing where no payment is less than 40 percent of the largest payment), regular periodic payments (for a payment period which is a week or month),

(iii) provides that legal title to such property remains with the rent-to-own dealer until the customer makes all the payments described in clause (ii) or early purchase payments required under the contract to acquire legal title to the item of property,

(iv) provides a beginning date and a maximum period of time for which the contract may be in effect that does not exceed 156 weeks or 36 months from such beginning date (including renewals or options to extend),

(v) provides for payments within the 156–week or 36–month period that, in the aggregate, generally exceed the normal retail price of the consumer property plus interest,

(vi) provides for payments under the contract that, in the aggregate, do not exceed $10,000 per item of consumer property,

(vii) provides that the customer does not have any legal obligation to make all the payments referred to in clause (ii) set forth under the contract, and that at the end of each payment period the customer may either continue to use the consumer property by making the payment for the next payment period or return such property to the rent-to-own dealer in good working order, in which case the customer does not incur any further obligations under the contract and is not entitled to a return of any payments previously made under the contract, and

(viii) provides that the customer has no right to sell, sublease, mortgage, pawn, pledge, encumber, or otherwise dispose of the consumer property until all the payments stated in the contract have been made.

(15) Motorsports entertainment complex.—

(A) In general.—The term "motorsports entertainment complex" means a racing track facility which—

(i) is permanently situated on land, and

(ii) during the 36–month period following the first day of the month in which the asset is placed in service, hosts 1 or more racing events for automobiles (of any type), trucks, or motorcycles which are open to the public for the price of admission.

(B) Ancillary and support facilities.—Such term shall include, if owned by the taxpayer who owns the complex and provided for the benefit of patrons of the complex—

(i) ancillary facilities and land improvements in support of the complex's activities (including parking lots, sidewalks, waterways, bridges, fences, and landscaping),

(ii) support facilities (including food and beverage retailing, souvenir vending, and other nonlodging accommodations), and (**iii**) appurtenances associated with such facilities and related attractions and amusements (including ticket booths, race track surfaces, suites and hospitality facilities, grandstands and viewing structures, props, walls, facilities that support the delivery of entertainment services, other special purpose structures, facades, shop interiors, and buildings).

(**C**) **Exception.**—Such term shall not include any transportation equipment, administrative services assets, warehouses, administrative buildings, hotels, or motels.

(**D**) **Termination.**—Such term shall not include any property placed in service after December 31, 2009.

(**16**) **Alaska natural gas pipeline.**—The term "Alaska natural gas pipeline" means the natural gas pipeline system located in the State of Alaska which—

(**A**) has a capacity of more than 500,000,000,000 Btu of natural gas per day, and

(**B**) is—

(**i**) placed in service after December 31, 2013, or

(**ii**) treated as placed in service on January 1, 2014, if the taxpayer who places such system in service before January 1, 2014, elects such treatment.

Such term includes the pipe, trunk lines, related equipment, and appurtenances used to carry natural gas, but does not include any gas processing plant.

(**17**) **Natural gas gathering line.**—The term "natural gas gathering line" means—

(**A**) the pipe, equipment, and appurtenances determined to be a gathering line by the Federal Energy Regulatory Commission, and

(**B**) the pipe, equipment, and appurtenances used to deliver natural gas from the wellhead or a commonpoint to the point at which such gas first reaches—

(**i**) a gas processing plant,

(**ii**) an interconnection with a transmission pipeline for which a certificate as an interstate transmission pipeline has been issued by the Federal Energy Regulatory Commission,

(**iii**) an interconnection with an intrastate transmission pipeline, or

(**iv**) a direct interconnection with a local distribution company, a gas storage facility, or an industrial consumer.

(**18**) **Qualified smart electric meters.**—

(**A**) **In general.**—The term "qualified smart electric meter" means any smart electric meter which—

(**i**) is placed in service by a taxpayer who is a supplier of electric energy or a provider of electric energy services, and

(**ii**) does not have a class life (determined without regard to subsection (e)) of less than 10 years.

(**B**) **Smart electric meter.**—For purposes of subparagraph (A), the term "smart electric meter" means any time-based meter and related communication equipment which is capable of being used by the taxpayer as part of a system that—

(i) measures and records electricity usage data on a time-differentiated basis in at least 24 separate time segments per day,

(ii) provides for the exchange of information between supplier or provider and the customer's electric meter in support of time-based rates or other forms of demand response,

(iii) provides data to such supplier or provider so that the supplier or provider can provide energy usage information to customers electronically, and

(iv) provides net metering.

(19) Qualified smart electric grid systems.—

(A) In general.—The term "qualified smart electric grid system" means any smart grid property which—

(i) is used as part of a system for electric distribution grid communications, monitoring, and management placed in service by a taxpayer who is a supplier of electric energy or a provider of electric energy services, and

(ii) does not have a class life (determined without regard to subsection (e)) of less than 10 years.

(B) Smart grid property.—For the purposes of subparagraph (A), the term "smart grid property" means electronics and related equipment that is capable of—

(i) sensing, collecting, and monitoring data of or from all portions of a utility's electric distribution grid,

(ii) providing real-time, two-way communications to monitor or manage such grid, and

(iii) providing real time analysis of and event prediction based upon collected data that can be used to improve electric distribution system reliability, quality, and performance.

(j) Property on Indian reservations.—

(1) In general.—For purposes of subsection (a), the applicable recovery period for qualified Indian reservation property shall be determined in accordance with the table contained in paragraph (2) in lieu of the table contained in subsection (c).

(2) Applicable recovery period for Indian reservation property.—For purposes of paragraph (1)—

In the case of:	The applicable recovery period is:
3–year property	2 years
5–year property	3 years
7–year property	4 years
10–year property	6 years
15–year property	9 years
20–year property	12 years
Nonresidential real property	22 years.

93

(3) Deduction allowed in computing minimum tax.—For purposes of determining alternative minimum taxable income under section 55, the deduction under subsection (a) for property to which paragraph (1) applies shall be determined under this section without regard to any adjustment under section 56.

(4) Qualified Indian reservation property defined.—For purposes of this subsection—

(A) In general.—The term "qualified Indian reservation property" means property which is property described in the table in paragraph (2) and which is—

(i) used by the taxpayer predominantly in the active conduct of a trade or business within an Indian reservation,

(ii) not used or located outside the Indian reservation on a regular basis,

(iii) not acquired (directly or indirectly) by the taxpayer from a person who is related to the taxpayer (within the meaning of section 465(b)(3)(C)), and

(iv) not property (or any portion thereof) placed in service for purposes of conducting or housing class I, II, or III gaming (as defined in section 4 of the Indian Regulatory Act (25 U.S.C. 2703)).

(B) Exception for alternative depreciation property.—The term "qualified Indian reservation property" does not include any property to which the alternative depreciation system under subsection (g) applies, determined—

(i) without regard to subsection (g)(7) (relating to election to use alternative depreciation system), and

(ii) after the application of section 280F(b) (relating to listed property with limited business use).

(C) Special rule for reservation infrastructure investment.—

(i) In general.—Subparagraph (A)(ii) shall not apply to qualified infrastructure property located outside of the Indian reservation if the purpose of such property is to connect with qualified infrastructure property located within the Indian reservation.

(ii) Qualified infrastructure property.—For purposes of this subparagraph, the term "qualified infrastructure property" means qualified Indian reservation property (determined without regard to subparagraph (A)(ii)) which—

(I) benefits the tribal infrastructure,

(II) is available to the general public, and

(III) is placed in service in connection with the taxpayer's active conduct of a trade or business within an Indian reservation.

Such term includes, but is not limited to, roads, power lines, water systems, railroad spurs, and communications facilities.

(5) Real estate rentals.—For purposes of this subsection, the rental to others of real property located within an Indian reservation shall be treated as the active conduct of a trade or business within an Indian reservation.

(6) Indian reservation defined.—For purposes of this subsection, the term "Indian reservation" means a reservation, as defined in—

  (A) section 3(d) of the Indian Financing Act of 1974 (25 U.S.C. 1452(d)), or

  (B) section 4(10) of the Indian Child Welfare Act of 1978 (25 U.S.C. 1903(10)).

For purposes of the preceding sentence, such section 3(d) shall be applied by treating the term "former Indian reservations in Oklahoma" as including only lands which are within the jurisdictional area of an Oklahoma Indian tribe (as determined by the Secretary of the Interior) and are recognized by such Secretary as eligible for trust land status under 25 CFR Part 151 (as in effect on the date of the enactment of this sentence).

(7) Coordination with nonrevenue laws.—Any reference in this subsection to a provision not contained in this title shall be treated for purposes of this subsection as a reference to such provision as in effect on the date of the enactment of this paragraph.

(8) Termination.—This subsection shall not apply to property placed in service after December 31, 2009.

(k) Special allowance for certain property acquired after December 31, 2007, and before January 1, 2009.—

(1) Additional allowance.—In the case of any qualified property—

  (A) the depreciation deduction provided by section 167(a) for the taxable year in which such property is placed in service shall include an allowance equal to 50 percent of the adjusted basis of the qualified property, and

  (B) the adjusted basis of the qualified property shall be reduced by the amount of such deduction before computing the amount otherwise allowable as a depreciation deduction under this chapter for such taxable year and any subsequent taxable year.

(2) Qualified property.—For purposes of this subsection—

  (A) In general.—The term "qualified property" means property—

    (i)(I) to which this section applies which has a recovery period of 20 years or less,

    (II) which is computer software (as defined in section 167(f)(1)(B)) for which a deduction is allowable under section 167(a) without regard to this subsection,

    (III) which is water utility property, or

    (IV) which is qualified leasehold improvement property,

    (ii) the original use of which commences with the taxpayer after December 31, 2007,

    (iii) which is—

      (I) acquired by the taxpayer after December 31, 2007, and before January 1, 2009, but only if no written binding contract for the acquisition was in effect before January 1, 2008, or

      (II) acquired by the taxpayer pursuant to a written binding contract which was entered into after December 31, 2007, and before January 1, 2009, and

    (iv) which is placed in service by the taxpayer before January 1, 2009, or, in the case of property described in subparagraph (B) or (C), before January 1, 2010.

(B) Certain property having longer production periods treated as qualified property.—

(i) In general.—The term "qualified property" includes any property if such property—

(I) meets the requirements of clauses (i), (ii), (iii), and (iv) of subparagraph (A),

(II) has a recovery period of at least 10 years or is transportation property,

(III) is subject to section 263A, and

(IV) meets the requirements of clause (iii) of section 263A(f)(1)(B) (determined as if such clauses also apply to property which has a long useful life (within the meaning of section 263A(f))).

(ii) Only pre-January 1, 2009, basis eligible for additional allowance.—In the case of property which is qualified property solely by reason of clause (i), paragraph (1) shall apply only to the extent of the adjusted basis thereof attributable to manufacture, construction, or production before January 1, 2009.

(iii) Transportation property.—For purposes of this subparagraph, the term "transportation property" means tangible personal property used in the trade or business of transporting persons or property.

(iv) Application of subparagraph.—This subparagraph shall not apply to any property which is described in subparagraph (C).

(C) Certain aircraft.—The term "qualified property" includes property—

(i) which meets the requirements of clauses (ii), (iii), and (iv) of subparagraph (A),

(ii) which is an aircraft which is not a transportation property (as defined in subparagraph (B)(iii)) other than for agricultural or firefighting purposes,

(iii) which is purchased and on which such purchaser, at the time of the contract for purchase, has made a nonrefundable deposit of the lesser of—

(I) 10 percent of the cost, or

(II) $100,000, and

(iv) which has—

(I) an estimated production period exceeding 4 months, and

(II) a cost exceeding $200,000.

(D) Exceptions.—

(i) Alternative depreciation property.—The term "qualified property" shall not include any property to which the alternative depreciation system under subsection (g) applies, determined—

(I) without regard to paragraph (7) of subsection (g) (relating to election to have system apply), and

(II) after application of section 280F(b) (relating to listed property with limited business use).

(ii) Qualified New York Liberty Zone leasehold improvement property.— The term "qualified property" shall not include any qualified New York Liberty Zone leasehold improvement property (as defined in section 1400L(c)(2)).

(iii) Election out.— If a taxpayer makes an election under this clause with respect to any class of property for any taxable year, this subsection shall not apply to all property in such class placed in service during such taxable year.

(E) Special rules.—

(i) Self-constructed property.— In the case of a taxpayer manufacturing, constructing, or producing property for the taxpayer's own use, the requirements of clause (iii) of subparagraph (A) shall be treated as met if the taxpayer begins manufacturing, constructing, or producing the property after December 31, 2007, and before January 1, 2009.

(ii) Sale-leasebacks.— For purposes of clause (iii) and subparagraph (A)(ii), if property is—

(I) originally placed in service after December 31, 2007, by a person, and

(II) sold and leased back by such person within 3 months after the date such property was originally placed in service,

such property shall be treated as originally placed in service not earlier than the date on which such property is used under the leaseback referred to in subclause (II).

(iii) Syndication.— For purposes of subparagraph (A)(ii), if—

(I) property is originally placed in service after December 31, 2007, by the lessor of such property,

(II) such property is sold by such lessor or any subsequent purchaser within 3 months after the date such property was originally placed in service (or, in the case of multiple units of property subject to the same lease, within 3 months after the date the final unit is placed in service, so long as the period between the time the first unit is placed in service and the time the last unit is placed in service does not exceed 12 months), and

(III) the user of such property after the last sale during such 3–month period remains the same as when such property was originally placed in service,

such property shall be treated as originally placed in service not earlier than the date of such last sale.

(iv) Limitations related to users and related parties.— The term "qualified property" shall not include any property if—

(I) the user of such property (as of the date on which such property is originally placed in service) or a person which is related (within the meaning of section 267(b) or 707(b)) to such user or to the taxpayer had a written binding contract in effect for the acquisition of such property at any time on or before December 31, 2007, or

97

(II) in the case of property manufactured, constructed, or produced for such user's or person's own use, the manufacture, construction, or production of such property began at any time on or before December 31, 2007.

(F) Coordination with section 280F.—For purposes of section 280F—

(i) Automobiles.—In the case of a passenger automobile (as defined in section 280F(d)(5)) which is qualified property, the Secretary shall increase the limitation under section 280F(a)(1)(A)(i) by $8,000.

(ii) Listed property.—The deduction allowable under paragraph (1) shall be taken into account in computing any recapture amount under section 280F(b)(2).

(G) Deduction allowed in computing minimum tax.—For purposes of determining alternative minimum taxable income under section 55, the deduction under subsection (a) for qualified property shall be determined under this section without regard to any adjustment under section 56.

(3) Qualified leasehold improvement property.—For purposes of this subsection—

(A) In general.—The term "qualified leasehold improvement property" means any improvement to an interior portion of a building which is nonresidential real property if—

(i) such improvement is made under or pursuant to a lease (as defined in subsection (h)(7))—

(I) by the lessee (or any sublessee) of such portion, or

(II) by the lessor of such portion,

(ii) such portion is to be occupied exclusively by the lessee (or any sublessee) of such portion, and

(iii) such improvement is placed in service more than 3 years after the date the building was first placed in service.

(B) Certain improvements not included.—Such term shall not include any improvement for which the expenditure is attributable to—

(i) the enlargement of the building,

(ii) any elevator or escalator,

(iii) any structural component benefiting a common area, and

(iv) the internal structural framework of the building.

(C) Definitions and special rules.—For purposes of this paragraph—

(i) Commitment to lease treated as lease.—A commitment to enter into a lease shall be treated as a lease, and the parties to such commitment shall be treated as lessor and lessee, respectively.

(ii) Related persons.—A lease between related persons shall not be considered a lease. For purposes of the preceding sentence, the term "related persons" means—

(I) members of an affiliated group (as defined in section 1504), and

(II) persons having a relationship described in subsection (b) of section 267; except that, for purposes of this clause, the phrase "80 percent or more" shall be substituted for the phrase "more than 50 percent" each place it appears in such subsection.

(4) Election to accelerate the AMT and research credits in lieu of bonus depreciation.—

(A) In general.—If a corporation elects to have this paragraph apply for the first taxable year of the taxpayer ending after March 31, 2008, in the case of such taxable year and each subsequent taxable year—

(i) paragraph (1) shall not apply to any eligible qualified property placed in service by the taxpayer,

(ii) the applicable depreciation method used under this section with respect to such property shall be the straight line method, and

(iii) each of the limitations described in subparagraph (B) for any such taxable year shall be increased by the bonus depreciation amount which is—

(I) determined for such taxable year under subparagraph (C), and

(II) allocated to such limitation under subparagraph (E).

(B) Limitations to be increased.—The limitations described in this subparagraph are—

(i) the limitation imposed by section 38(c), and

(ii) the limitation imposed by section 53(c).

(C) Bonus depreciation amount.—For purposes of this paragraph—

(i) In general.—The bonus depreciation amount for any taxable year is an amount equal to 20 percent of the excess (if any) of—

(I) the aggregate amount of depreciation which would be allowed under this section for eligible qualified property placed in service by the taxpayer during such taxable year if paragraph (1) applied to all such property, over

(II) the aggregate amount of depreciation which would be allowed under this section for eligible qualified property placed in service by the taxpayer during such taxable year if paragraph (1) did not apply to any such property.

The aggregate amounts determined under subclauses (I) and (II) shall be determined without regard to any election made under subsection (b)(2)(C), (b)(3)(D), or (g)(7) and without regard to subparagraph (A)(ii).

(ii) Maximum amount.—The bonus depreciation amount for any taxable year shall not exceed the maximum increase amount under clause (iii), reduced (but not below zero) by the sum of the bonus depreciation amounts for all preceding taxable years.

(iii) Maximum increase amount.—For purposes of clause (ii), the term "maximum increase amount" means, with respect to any corporation, the lesser of—

(I) $30,000,000, or

(II) 6 percent of the sum of the business credit increase amount, and the AMT credit increase amount, determined with respect to such corporation under subparagraph (E).

(iv) Aggregation rule.—All corporations which are treated as a single employer under section 52(a) shall be treated—

(I) as 1 taxpayer for purposes of this paragraph, and

(II) as having elected the application of this paragraph if any such corporation so elects.

(D) Eligible qualified property.—For purposes of this paragraph, the term "eligible qualified property" means qualified property under paragraph (2), except that in applying paragraph (2) for purposes of this paragraph—

(i) "March 31, 2008" shall be substituted for "December 31, 2007" each place it appears in subparagraph (A) and clauses (i) and (ii) of subparagraph (E) thereof, and

(ii) only adjusted basis attributable to manufacture, construction, or production after March 31, 2008, and before January 1, 2009, shall be taken into account under subparagraph (B)(ii) thereof.

(E) Allocation of bonus depreciation amounts.—

(i) In general.—Subject to clauses (ii) and (iii), the taxpayer shall, at such time and in such manner as the Secretary may prescribe, specify the portion (if any) of the bonus depreciation amount for the taxable year which is to be allocated to each of the limitations described in subparagraph (B) for such taxable year.

(ii) Limitation on allocations.—The portion of the bonus depreciation amount which may be allocated under clause (i) to the limitations described in subparagraph (B) for any taxable year shall not exceed—

(I) in the case of the limitation described in subparagraph (B)(i), the excess of the business credit increase amount over the bonus depreciation amount allocated to such limitation for all preceding taxable years, and

(II) in the case of the limitation described in subparagraph (B)(ii), the excess of the AMT credit increase amount over the bonus depreciation amount allocated to such limitation for all preceding taxable years.

(iii) Business credit increase amount.—For purposes of this paragraph, the term "business credit increase amount" means the amount equal to the portion of the credit allowable under section 38 (determined without regard to subsection (c) thereof) for the first taxable year ending after March 31, 2008, which is allocable to business credit carryforwards to such taxable year which are—

(I) from taxable years beginning before January 1, 2006, and

(II) properly allocable (determined under the rules of section 38(d)) to the research credit determined under section 41(a).

(iv) AMT credit increase amount.—For purposes of this paragraph, the term "AMT credit increase amount" means the amount equal to the portion of the minimum tax credit under section 53(b) for the first taxable year ending after March 31, 2008, determined by taking into account only the adjusted minimum tax for taxable years beginning before January 1, 2006. For purposes of the preceding sentence, credits shall be treated as allowed on a first-in, first-out basis.

(F) Credit refundable.—For purposes of section 6401(b), the aggregate increase in the credits allowable under part IV of subchapter A for any taxable year resulting from the application of this paragraph shall be treated as allowed under subpart C of such part (and not any other subpart).

(G) Other rules.—

(i) **Election.**—Any election under this paragraph (including any allocation under subparagraph (E)) may be revoked only with the consent of the Secretary.

(ii) **Partnerships with electing partners.**—In the case of a corporation making an election under subparagraph (A) and which is a partner in a partnership, for purposes of determining such corporation's distributive share of partnership items under section 702—

(I) paragraph (1) shall not apply to any eligible qualified property, and

(II) the applicable depreciation method used under this section with respect to such property shall be the straight line method.

(iii) **Special rule for passenger aircraft.**—In the case of any passenger aircraft, the written binding contract limitation under paragraph (2)(A)(iii)(I) shall not apply for purposes of subparagraphs (C)(i)(I) and (D).

(*l*) Special allowance for cellulosic biofuel plant property.—

(1) Additional allowance.—In the case of any qualified cellulosic biofuel plant property—

(A) the depreciation deduction provided by section 167(a) for the taxable year in which such property is placed in service shall include an allowance equal to 50 percent of the adjusted basis of such property, and

(B) the adjusted basis of such property shall be reduced by the amount of such deduction before computing the amount otherwise allowable as a depreciation deduction under this chapter for such taxable year and any subsequent taxable year.

(2) Qualified cellulosic biofuel plant property.—The term "qualified cellulosic biofuel plant property" means property of a character subject to the allowance for depreciation—

(A) which is used in the United States solely to produce cellulosic biofuel,

(B) the original use of which commences with the taxpayer after the date of the enactment of this subsection,

(C) which is acquired by the taxpayer by purchase (as defined in section 179(d)) after the date of the enactment of this subsection, but only if no written binding contract for the acquisition was in effect on or before the date of the enactment of this subsection, and

(D) which is placed in service by the taxpayer before January 1, 2013.

(3) Cellulosic biofuel.—The term "cellulosic biofuel" means any liquid fuel which is produced from any lignocellulosic or hemicellulosic matter that is available on a renewable or recurring basis.

(4) Exceptions.—

(A) Bonus depreciation property under subsection (k).—Such term shall not include any property to which section 168(k) applies.

(B) Alternative depreciation property.—Such term shall not include any property described in section 168(k)(2)(D)(i).[3]

(C) Tax-exempt bond-financed property.—Such term shall not include any property any portion of which is financed with the proceeds of any obligation the interest on which is exempt from tax under section 103.

(D) Election out.—If a taxpayer makes an election under this subparagraph with respect to any class of property for any taxable year, this subsection shall not apply to all property in such class placed in service during such taxable year.

(5) Special rules.—For purposes of this subsection, rules similar to the rules of subparagraph (E) of section 168(k)(2)[4] shall apply, except that such subparagraph shall be applied—

(A) by substituting "the date of the enactment of subsection (*l*)" for "December 31, 2007" each place it appears therein,

(B) by substituting "January 1, 2013" for "January 1, 2009" in clause (i) thereof, and

(C) by substituting "qualified cellulosic biofuel plant property" for "qualified property" in clause (iv) thereof.

(6) Allowance against alternative minimum tax.—For purposes of this subsection, rules similar to the rules of section 168(k)(2)(G)[5] shall apply.

(7) Recapture.—For purposes of this subsection, rules similar to the rules under section 179(d)(10) shall apply with respect to any qualified cellulosic biofuel plant property which ceases to be qualified cellulosic biofuel plant property.

(8) Denial of double benefit.—Paragraph (1) shall not apply to any qualified cellulosic biofuel plant property with respect to which an election has been made under section 179C (relating to election to expense certain refineries).

(m) Special allowance for certain reuse and recycling property.—

(1) In general.—In the case of any qualified reuse and recycling property—

(A) the depreciation deduction provided by section 167(a) for the taxable year in which such property is placed in service shall include an allowance equal to 50 percent of the adjusted basis of the qualified reuse and recycling property, and

(B) the adjusted basis of the qualified reuse and recycling property shall be reduced by the amount of such deduction before computing the amount otherwise allowable as a depreciation deduction under this chapter for such taxable year and any subsequent taxable year.

---

3. So in original. Probably should be "subsection (k)(2)(D)(i) of this section".

4. So in original. Probably should be "subsection (k)(2) of this section".

5. So in original. Probably should be "subsection (k)(2)(G) of this section".

(2) Qualified reuse and recycling property.—For purposes of this subsection—

(A) In general.—The term "qualified reuse and recycling property" means any reuse and recycling property—

(i) to which this section applies,

(ii) which has a useful life of at least 5 years,

(iii) the original use of which commences with the taxpayer after August 31, 2008, and

(iv) which is—

(I) acquired by purchase (as defined in section 179(d)(2)) by the taxpayer after August 31, 2008, but only if no written binding contract for the acquisition was in effect before September 1, 2008, or

(II) acquired by the taxpayer pursuant to a written binding contract which was entered into after August 31, 2008.

(B) Exceptions.—

(i) Bonus depreciation property under subsection (k)—The term "qualified reuse and recycling property" shall not include any property to which section 168(k) applies.

(ii) Alternative depreciation property.—The term "qualified reuse and recycling property" shall not include any property to which the alternative depreciation system under subsection (g) applies, determined without regard to paragraph (7) of subsection (g) (relating to election to have system apply).

(iii) Election out.—If a taxpayer makes an election under this clause with respect to any class of property for any taxable year, this subsection shall not apply to all property in such class placed in service during such taxable year.

(C) Special rule for self-constructed property.—In the case of a taxpayer manufacturing, constructing, or producing property for the taxpayer's own use, the requirements of clause (iv) of subparagraph (A) shall be treated as met if the taxpayer begins manufacturing, constructing, or producing the property after August 31, 2008.

(D) Deduction allowed in computing minimum tax.—For purposes of determining alternative minimum taxable income under section 55, the deduction under subsection (a) for qualified reuse and recycling property shall be determined under this section without regard to any adjustment under section 56.

(3) Definitions.—For purposes of this subsection—

(A) Reuse and recycling property.—

(i) In general.—The term "reuse and recycling property" means any machinery and equipment (not including buildings or real estate), along with all appurtenances thereto, including software necessary to operate such equipment, which is used exclusively to collect, distribute, or recycle qualified reuse and recyclable materials.

(ii) Exclusion.—Such term does not include rolling stock or other equipment used to transport reuse and recyclable materials.

(B) Qualified reuse and recyclable materials.—

    (i) In general.—The term "qualified reuse and recyclable materials" means scrap plastic, scrap glass, scrap textiles, scrap rubber, scrap packaging, recovered fiber, scrap ferrous and nonferrous metals, or electronic scrap generated by an individual or business.

    (ii) Electronic scrap.—For purposes of clause (i), the term "electronic scrap" means—

        (I) any cathode ray tube, flat panel screen, or similar video display device with a screen size greater than 4 inches measured diagonally, or

        (II) any central processing unit.

(C) Recycling or recycle.—The term "recycling" or "recycle" means that process (including sorting) by which worn or superfluous materials are manufactured or processed into specification grade commodities that are suitable for use as a replacement or substitute for virgin materials in manufacturing tangible consumer and commercial products, including packaging.

(n) Special allowance for qualified disaster assistance property.—

(1) In general.—In the case of any qualified disaster assistance property—

    (A) the depreciation deduction provided by section 167(a) for the taxable year in which such property is placed in service shall include an allowance equal to 50 percent of the adjusted basis of the qualified disaster assistance property, and

    (B) the adjusted basis of the qualified disaster assistance property shall be reduced by the amount of such deduction before computing the amount otherwise allowable as a depreciation deduction under this chapter for such taxable year and any subsequent taxable year.

(2) Qualified disaster assistance property.—For purposes of this subsection—

    (A) In general.—The term "qualified disaster assistance property" means any property—

        (i)(I) which is described in subsection (k)(2)(A)(i), or

        (II) which is nonresidential real property or residential rental property,

        (ii) substantially all of the use of which is—

        (I) in a disaster area with respect to a federally declared disaster occurring before January 1, 2010, and

        (II) in the active conduct of a trade or business by the taxpayer in such disaster area,

        (iii) which—

        (I) rehabilitates property damaged, or replaces property destroyed or condemned, as a result of such federally declared disaster, except that, for purposes of this clause, property shall be treated as replacing property destroyed or condemned if, as part of an integrated plan, such property replaces property which is included in a continuous area which includes real property destroyed or condemned, and

(II) is similar in nature to, and located in the same county as, the property being rehabilitated or replaced,

(iv) the original use of which in such disaster area commences with an eligible taxpayer on or after the applicable disaster date,

(v) which is acquired by such eligible taxpayer by purchase (as defined in section 179(d)) on or after the applicable disaster date, but only if no written binding contract for the acquisition was in effect before such date, and

(vi) which is placed in service by such eligible taxpayer on or before the date which is the last day of the third calendar year following the applicable disaster date (the fourth calendar year in the case of nonresidential real property and residential rental property).

(B) Exceptions.—

(i) Other bonus depreciation property.—The term "qualified disaster assistance property" shall not include—

(I) any property to which subsection (k) (determined without regard to paragraph (4)), (*l*), or (m) applies,

(II) any property to which section 1400N(d) applies, and

(III) any property described in section 1400N(p)(3).

(ii) Alternative depreciation property.—The term "qualified disaster assistance property" shall not include any property to which the alternative depreciation system under subsection (g) applies, determined without regard to paragraph (7) of subsection (g) (relating to election to have system apply).

(iii) Tax-exempt bond financed property.—Such term shall not include any property any portion of which is financed with the proceeds of any obligation the interest on which is exempt from tax under section 103.

(iv) Qualified revitalization buildings.—Such term shall not include any qualified revitalization building with respect to which the taxpayer has elected the application of paragraph (1) or (2) of section 1400I(a).

(v) Election out.—If a taxpayer makes an election under this clause with respect to any class of property for any taxable year, this subsection shall not apply to all property in such class placed in service during such taxable year.

(C) Special rules.—For purposes of this subsection, rules similar to the rules of subparagraph (E) of subsection (k)(2) shall apply, except that such subparagraph shall be applied—

(i) by substituting "the applicable disaster date" for "December 31, 2007" each place it appears therein,

(ii) without regard to "and before January 1, 2009" in clause (i) thereof, and

(iii) by substituting "qualified disaster assistance property" for "qualified property" in clause (iv) thereof.

(D) Allowance against alternative minimum tax.—For purposes of this subsection, rules similar to the rules of subsection (k)(2)(G) shall apply.

(3) Other definitions.—For purposes of this subsection—

   (A) Applicable disaster date.—The term "applicable disaster date" means, with respect to any federally declared disaster, the date on which such federally declared disaster occurs.

   (B) Federally declared disaster.—The term "federally declared disaster" has the meaning given such term under section 165(h)(3)(C)(i).

   (C) Disaster area.—The term "disaster area" has the meaning given such term under section 165(h)(3)(C)(ii).

   (D) Eligible taxpayer.—The term "eligible taxpayer" means a taxpayer who has suffered an economic loss attributable to a federally declared disaster.

(4) Recapture.—For purposes of this subsection, rules similar to the rules under section 179(d)(10) shall apply with respect to any qualified disaster assistance property which ceases to be qualified disaster assistance property.

§ 178. Amortization of Cost of Acquiring a Lease

(a) General rule.—In determining the amount of the deduction allowable to a lessee for exhaustion, wear and tear, obsolescence, or amortization in respect of any cost of acquiring the lease, the term of the lease shall be treated as including all renewal options (and any other period for which the parties reasonably expect the lease to be renewed) if less than 75 percent of such cost is attributable to the period of the term of the lease remaining on the date of its acquisition.

(b) Certain periods excluded.—For purposes of subsection (a), in determining the period of the term of the lease remaining on the date of acquisition, there shall not be taken into account any period for which the lease may subsequently be renewed, extended, or continued pursuant to an option exercisable by the lessee.

§ 216. Deduction of Taxes, Interest, and Business Depreciation by Cooperative Housing Corporation Tenant–Stockholder

(a) Allowance of deduction.—In the case of a tenant-stockholder (as defined in subsection (b)(2)), there shall be allowed as a deduction amounts (not otherwise deductible) paid or accrued to a cooperative housing corporation within the taxable year, but only to the extent that such amounts represent the tenant-stockholder's proportionate share of—

(1) the real estate taxes allowable as a deduction to the corporation under section 164 which are paid or incurred by the corporation on the houses or apartment building and on the land on which such houses (or building) are situated, or

(2) the interest allowable as a deduction to the corporation under section 163 which is paid or incurred by the corporation on its indebtedness contracted—

   (A) in the acquisition, construction, alteration, rehabilitation, or maintenance of the houses or apartment building, or

   (B) in the acquisition of the land on which the houses (or apartment building) are situated.

106

(b) Definitions.—For purposes of this section—

(1) Cooperative housing corporation.—The term "cooperative housing corporation" means a corporation—

(A) having one and only one class of stock outstanding,

(B) each of the stockholders of which is entitled, solely by reason of his ownership of stock in the corporation, to occupy for dwelling purposes a house, or an apartment in a building, owned or leased by such corporation,

(C) no stockholder of which is entitled (either conditionally or unconditionally) to receive any distribution not out of earnings and profits of the corporation except on a complete or partial liquidation of the corporation, and

(D) meeting 1 or more of the following requirements for the taxable year in which the taxes and interest described in subsection (a) are paid or incurred:

    (i) 80 percent or more of the corporation's gross income for such taxable year is derived from tenant-stockholders.

    (ii) At all times during such taxable year, 80 percent or more of the total square footage of the corporation's property is used or available for use by the tenant-stockholders for residential purposes or purposes ancillary to such residential use.

    (iii) 90 percent or more of the expenditures of the corporation paid or incurred during such taxable year are paid or incurred for the acquisition, construction, management, maintenance, or care of the corporation's property for the benefit of the tenant-stockholders.

(2) Tenant-stockholder.—The term "tenant-stockholder" means a person who is a stockholder in a cooperative housing corporation, and whose stock is fully paid-up in an amount not less than an amount shown to the satisfaction of the Secretary as bearing a reasonable relationship to the portion of the value of the corporation's equity in the houses or apartment building and the land on which situated which is attributable to the house or apartment which such person is entitled to occupy.

(3) Tenant-stockholder's proportionate share.—

(A) In general.—Except as provided in subparagraph (B), the term "tenant-stockholder's proportionate share" means that proportion which the stock of the cooperative housing corporation owned by the tenant-stockholder is of the total outstanding stock of the corporation (including any stock held by the corporation).

(B) Special rule where allocation of taxes or interest reflect cost to corporation of stockholder's unit.—

    (i) In general.—If, for any taxable year—

        (I) each dwelling unit owned or leased by a cooperative housing corporation is separately allocated a share of such corporation's real estate taxes described in subsection (a)(1) or a share of such corporation's interest described in subsection (a)(2), and

        (II) such allocations reasonably reflect the cost to such corporation of such taxes, or of such interest, attributable to the tenant-stockholder's dwelling unit (and such unit's share of the common areas), then the term "tenant-stockholder's proportionate share" means the shares determined in accordance with the allocations described in subclause (II).

(ii) Election by corporation required.—Clause (i) shall apply with respect to any cooperative housing corporation only if such corporation elects its application. Such an election, once made, may be revoked only with the consent of the Secretary.

(4) Stock owned by governmental units.—For purposes of this subsection, in determining whether a corporation is a cooperative housing corporation, stock owned and apartments leased by the United States or any of its possessions, a State or any political subdivision thereof, or any agency or instrumentality of the foregoing empowered to acquire shares in a cooperative housing corporation for the purpose of providing housing facilities, shall not be taken into account.

(5) Prior approval of occupancy.—For purposes of this section, in the following cases there shall not be taken into account the fact that (by agreement with the cooperative housing corporation) the person or his nominee may not occupy the house or apartment without the prior approval of such corporation:

(A) In any case where a person acquires stock of a cooperative housing corporation by operation of law.

(B) In any case where a person other than an individual acquires stock of a cooperative housing corporation.

(C) In any case where the original seller acquires any stock of the cooperative housing corporation from the corporation not later than 1 year after the date on which the apartments or houses (or leaseholds therein) are transferred by the original seller to the corporation.

(6) Original seller defined.—For purposes of paragraph (5), the term "original seller" means the person from whom the corporation has acquired the apartments or houses (or leaseholds therein).

(c) Treatment as property subject to depreciation.—

(1) In general.—So much of the stock of a tenant-stockholder in a cooperative housing corporation as is allocable, under regulations prescribed by the Secretary, to a proprietary lease or right of tenancy in property subject to the allowance for depreciation under section 167(a) shall, to the extent such proprietary lease or right of tenancy is used by such tenant-stockholder in a trade or business or for the production of income, be treated as property subject to the allowance for depreciation under section 167(a). The preceding sentence shall not be construed to limit or deny a deduction for depreciation under section 167(a) by a cooperative housing corporation with respect to property owned by such a corporation and leased to tenant-stockholders.

(2) Deduction limited to adjusted basis in stock.—

(A) In general.—The amount of any deduction for depreciation allowable under section 167(a) to a tenant-stockholder with respect to any stock for any taxable year by reason of paragraph (1) shall not exceed the adjusted basis of such stock as of the close of the taxable year of the tenant-stockholder in which such deduction was incurred.

(B) Carryforward of disallowed amount.—The amount of any deduction which is not allowed by reason of subparagraph (A) shall, subject to the provisions of subparagraph (A), be treated as a deduction allowable under section 167(a) in the succeeding taxable year.

(d) Disallowance of deduction for certain payments to the corporation.—No deduction shall be allowed to a stockholder in a cooperative housing corporation for any amount paid or accrued to such corporation during any taxable year (in excess of the stockholder's proportionate share of the items described in subsections (a)(1) and (a)(2)) to the extent that, under regulations prescribed by the Secretary, such amount is properly allocable to amounts paid or incurred at any time by the corporation which are chargeable to the corporation's capital account. The stockholder's adjusted basis in the stock in the corporation shall be increased by the amount of such disallowance.

(e) Distributions by cooperative housing corporations.—Except as provided in regulations, no gain or loss shall be recognized on the distribution by a cooperative housing corporation of a dwelling unit to a stockholder in such corporation if such distribution is in exchange for the stockholder's stock in such corporation and such dwelling unit is used as his principal residence (within the meaning of section 121).

§ 280A. Disallowance of Certain Expenses in Connection With Business Use of Home, Rental of Vacation Homes, etc.

(a) General rule.—Except as otherwise provided in this section, in the case of a taxpayer who is an individual or an S corporation, no deduction otherwise allowable under this chapter shall be allowed with respect to the use of a dwelling unit which is used by the taxpayer during the taxable year as a residence.

(b) Exception for interest, taxes, casualty losses, etc.—Subsection (a) shall not apply to any deduction allowable to the taxpayer without regard to its connection with his trade or business (or with his income-producing activity).

(c) Exceptions for certain business or rental use; limitation on deductions for such use.—

(1) Certain business use.—Subsection (a) shall not apply to any item to the extent such item is allocable to a portion of the dwelling unit which is exclusively used on a regular basis—

(A) as the principal place of business for any trade or business of the taxpayer,

(B) as a place of business which is used by patients, clients, or customers in meeting or dealing with the taxpayer in the normal course of his trade or business, or

(C) in the case of a separate structure which is not attached to the dwelling unit, in connection with the taxpayer's trade or business.

In the case of an employee, the preceding sentence shall apply only if the exclusive use referred to in the preceding sentence is for the convenience of his employer. For purposes of subparagraph (A), the term "principal place of business" includes a place of business which is used by the taxpayer for the administrative or management activities of any trade or business of the taxpayer if there is no other fixed location of such trade or business where the taxpayer conducts substantial administrative or management activities of such trade or business.

(2) Certain storage use.—Subsection (a) shall not apply to any item to the extent such item is allocable to space within the dwelling unit which is used on a regular basis as a storage unit for the inventory or product samples of the taxpayer held for use in the taxpayer's trade or business of selling products at retail or wholesale, but only if the dwelling unit is the sole fixed location of such trade or business.

(3) Rental use.—Subsection (a) shall not apply to any item which is attributable to the rental of the dwelling unit or portion thereof (determined after the application of subsection (e)).

(4) Use in providing day care services.—

(A) In general.—Subsection (a) shall not apply to any item to the extent that such item is allocable to the use of any portion of the dwelling unit on a regular basis in the taxpayer's trade or business of providing day care for children, for individuals who have attained age 65, or for individuals who are physically or mentally incapable of caring for themselves.

(B) Licensing, etc., requirement.—Subparagraph (A) shall apply to items accruing for a period only if the owner or operator of the trade or business referred to in subparagraph (A)—

(i) has applied for (and such application has not been rejected),

(ii) has been granted (and such granting has not been revoked), or

(iii) is exempt from having, a license, certification, registration, or approval as a day care center or as a family or group day care home under the provisions of any applicable State law. This subparagraph shall apply only to items accruing in periods beginning on or after the first day of the first month which begins more than 90 days after the date of the enactment of the Tax Reduction and Simplification Act of 1977.

(C) Allocation formula.—If a portion of the taxpayer's dwelling unit used for the purposes described in subparagraph (A) is not used exclusively for those purposes, the amount of the expenses attributable to that portion shall not exceed an amount which bears the same ratio to the total amount of the items allocable to such portion as the number of hours the portion is used for such purposes bears to the number of hours the portion is available for use.

(5) Limitation on deductions.—In the case of a use described in paragraph (1), (2), or (4), and in the case of a use described in paragraph (3) where the dwelling unit is used by the taxpayer during the taxable year as a residence, the deductions allowed under this chapter for the taxable year by reason of being attributed to such use shall not exceed the excess of—

(A) the gross income derived from such use for the taxable year, over

(B) the sum of—

(i) the deductions allocable to such use which are allowable under this chapter for the taxable year whether or not such unit (or portion thereof) was so used, and

(ii) the deductions allocable to the trade or business (or rental activity) in which such use occurs (but which are not allocable to such use) for such taxable year.

Any amount not allowable as a deduction under this chapter by reason of the preceding sentence shall be taken into account as a deduction (allocable to such use) under this chapter for the succeeding taxable year. Any amount taken into account for any taxable year under the preceding sentence shall be subject to the limitation of the 1st sentence of this paragraph whether or not the dwelling unit is used as a residence during such taxable year.

(6) Treatment of rental to employer.—Paragraphs (1) and (3) shall not apply to any item which is attributable to the rental of the dwelling unit (or any portion thereof) by the taxpayer to his employer during any period in which the taxpayer uses the dwelling unit (or portion) in performing services as an employee of the employer.

(d) Use as residence.—

(1) In general.—For purposes of this section, a taxpayer uses a dwelling unit during the taxable year as a residence if he uses such unit (or portion thereof) for personal purposes for a number of days which exceeds the greater of—

(A) 14 days, or

(B) 10 percent of the number of days during such year for which such unit is rented at a fair rental.

For purposes of subparagraph (B), a unit shall not be treated as rented at a fair rental for any day for which it is used for personal purposes.

(2) Personal use of unit.—For purposes of this section, the taxpayer shall be deemed to have used a dwelling unit for personal purposes for a day if, for any part of such day, the unit is used—

(A) for personal purposes by the taxpayer or any other person who has an interest in such unit, or by any member of the family (as defined in section 267(c)(4)) of the taxpayer or such other person;

(B) by any individual who uses the unit under an arrangement which enables the taxpayer to use some other dwelling unit (whether or not a rental is charged for the use of such other unit); or

(C) by any individual (other than an employee with respect to whose use section 119 applies), unless for such day the dwelling unit is rented for a rental which, under the facts and circumstances, is fair rental.

The Secretary shall prescribe regulations with respect to the circumstances under which use of the unit for repairs and annual maintenance will not constitute personal use under this paragraph, except that if the taxpayer is engaged in repair and maintenance on a substantially full time basis for any day, such authority shall not allow the Secretary to treat a dwelling unit as being used for personal use by the taxpayer on such day merely because other individuals who are on the premises on such day are not so engaged.

(3) Rental to family member, etc., for use as principal residence.—

(A) In general.—A taxpayer shall not be treated as using a dwelling unit for personal purposes by reason of a rental arrangement for any period if for such period such dwelling unit is rented, at a fair rental, to any person for use as such person's principal residence.

(B) Special rules for rental to person having interest in unit.—

(i) Rental must be pursuant to shared equity financing agreement.—Subparagraph (A) shall apply to a rental to a person who has an interest in the dwelling unit only if such rental is pursuant to a shared equity financing agreement.

111

(ii) **Determination of fair rental.**—In the case of a rental pursuant to a shared equity financing agreement, fair rental shall be determined as of the time the agreement is entered into and by taking into account the occupant's qualified ownership interest.

(C) **Shared equity financing agreement.**—For purposes of this paragraph, the term "shared equity financing agreement" means an agreement under which—

(i) 2 or more persons acquire qualified ownership interests in a dwelling unit, and

(ii) the person (or persons) holding 1 or more of such interests—

(I) is entitled to occupy the dwelling unit for use as a principal residence, and

(II) is required to pay rent to 1 or more other persons holding qualified ownership interests in the dwelling unit.

(D) **Qualified ownership interest.**—For purposes of this paragraph, the term "qualified ownership interest" means an undivided interest for more than 50 years in the entire dwelling unit and appurtenant land being acquired in the transaction to which the shared equity financing agreement relates.

(4) **Rental of principal residence.—**

(A) **In general.**—For purposes of applying subsection (c)(5) to deductions allocable to a qualified rental period, a taxpayer shall not be considered to have used a dwelling unit for personal purposes for any day during the taxable year which occurs before or after a qualified rental period described in subparagraph (B)(i), or before a qualified rental period described in subparagraph (B)(ii), if with respect to such day such unit constitutes the principal residence (within the meaning of section 121) of the taxpayer.

(B) **Qualified rental period.**—For purposes of subparagraph (A), the term "qualified rental period" means a consecutive period of—

(i) 12 or more months which begins or ends in such taxable year, or

(ii) less than 12 months which begins in such taxable year and at the end of which such dwelling unit is sold or exchanged, and for which such unit is rented, or is held for rental, at a fair rental.

(e) **Expenses attributable to rental.—**

(1) **In general.**—In any case where a taxpayer who is an individual or an S corporation uses a dwelling unit for personal purposes on any day during the taxable year (whether or not he is treated under this section as using such unit as a residence), the amount deductible under this chapter with respect to expenses attributable to the rental of the unit (or portion thereof) for the taxable year shall not exceed an amount which bears the same relationship to such expenses as the number of days during each year that the unit (or portion thereof) is rented at a fair rental bears to the total number of days during such year that the unit (or portion thereof) is used.

(2) **Exception for deductions otherwise allowable.**—This subsection shall not apply with respect to deductions which would be allowable under this chapter for the taxable year whether or not such unit (or portion thereof) was rented.

(f) **Definitions and special rules.—**

(1) **Dwelling unit defined.**—For purposes of this section—

(A) In general.—The term "dwelling unit" includes a house, apartment, condominium, mobile home, boat, or similar property, and all structures or other property appurtenant to such dwelling unit.

(B) Exception.—The term "dwelling unit" does not include that portion of a unit which is used exclusively as a hotel, motel, inn, or similar establishment.

(2) Personal use by shareholders of S corporation.—In the case of an S corporation, subparagraphs (A) and (B) of subsection (d)(2) shall be applied by substituting "any shareholder of the S corporation" for "the taxpayer" each place it appears.

(3) Coordination with section 183.—If subsection (a) applies with respect to any dwelling unit (or portion thereof) for the taxable year—

(A) section 183 (relating to activities not engaged in for profit) shall not apply to such unit (or portion thereof) for such year, but

(B) such year shall be taken into account as a taxable year for purposes of applying subsection (d) of section 183 (relating to 5–year presumption).

(4) Coordination with section 162(a)(2).—Nothing in this section shall be construed to disallow any deduction allowable under section 162(a)(2) (or any deduction which meets the tests of section 162(a)(2) but is allowable under another provision of this title) by reason of the taxpayer's being away from home in the pursuit of a trade or business (other than the trade or business of renting dwelling units).

(g) Special rule for certain rental use.—Notwithstanding any other provision of this section or section 183, if a dwelling unit is used during the taxable year by the taxpayer as a residence and such dwelling unit is actually rented for less than 15 days during the taxable year, then—

(1) no deduction otherwise allowable under this chapter because of the rental use of such dwelling unit shall be allowed, and

(2) the income derived from such use for the taxable year shall not be included in the gross income of such taxpayer under section 61.

§ 453. Installment Method

(a) General rule.—Except as otherwise provided in this section, income from an installment sale shall be taken into account for purposes of this title under the installment method.

(b) Installment sale defined.—For purposes of this section—

(1) In general.—The term "installment sale" means a disposition of property where at least 1 payment is to be received after the close of the taxable year in which the disposition occurs.

(2) Exceptions.—The term "installment sale" does not include—

(A) Dealer dispositions.—Any dealer disposition (as defined in subsection (*l*)).

(B) Inventories of personal property.—A disposition of personal property of a kind which is required to be included in the inventory of the taxpayer if on hand at the close of the taxable year.

113

(c) Installment method defined.—For purposes of this section, the term "installment method" means a method under which the income recognized for any taxable year from a disposition is that proportion of the payments received in that year which the gross profit (realized or to be realized when payment is completed) bears to the total contract price.

(d) Election out.—

(1) In general.—Subsection (a) shall not apply to any disposition if the taxpayer elects to have subsection (a) not apply to such disposition.

(2) Time and manner for making election.—Except as otherwise provided by regulations, an election under paragraph (1) with respect to a disposition may be made only on or before the due date prescribed by law (including extensions) for filing the taxpayer's return of the tax imposed by this chapter for the taxable year in which the disposition occurs. Such an election shall be made in the manner prescribed by regulations.

(3) Election revocable only with consent.—An election under paragraph (1) with respect to any disposition may be revoked only with the consent of the Secretary.

(e) Second dispositions by related persons.—

(1) In general.—If—

(A) any person disposes of property to a related person (hereinafter in this subsection referred to as the "first disposition"), and

(B) before the person making the first disposition receives all payments with respect to such disposition, the related person disposes of the property (hereinafter in this subsection referred to as the "second disposition"), then, for purposes of this section, the amount realized with respect to such second disposition shall be treated as received at the time of the second disposition by the person making the first disposition.

(2) 2–year cutoff for property other than marketable securities.—

(A) In general.—Except in the case of marketable securities, paragraph (1) shall apply only if the date of the second disposition is not more than 2 years after the date of the first disposition.

(B) Substantial diminishing of risk of ownership.—The running of the 2–year period set forth in subparagraph (A) shall be suspended with respect to any property for any period during which the related person's risk of loss with respect to the property is substantially diminished by—

(i) the holding of a put with respect to such property (or similar property),

(ii) the holding by another person of a right to acquire the property, or

(iii) a short sale or any other transaction.

(3) Limitation on amount treated as received.—The amount treated for any taxable year as received by the person making the first disposition by reason of paragraph (1) shall not exceed the excess of—

(A) the lesser of—

(i) the total amount realized with respect to any second disposition of the property occurring before the close of the taxable year, or

(ii) the total contract price for the first disposition, over

114

(B) the sum of—

(i) the aggregate amount of payments received with respect to the first disposition before the close of such year, plus

(ii) the aggregate amount treated as received with respect to the first disposition for prior taxable years by reason of this subsection.

(4) Fair market value where disposition is not sale or exchange.—For purposes of this subsection, if the second disposition is not a sale or exchange, an amount equal to the fair market value of the property disposed of shall be substituted for the amount realized.

(5) Later payments treated as receipt of tax paid amounts.—If paragraph (1) applies for any taxable year, payments received in subsequent taxable years by the person making the first disposition shall not be treated as the receipt of payments with respect to the first disposition to the extent that the aggregate of such payments does not exceed the amount treated as received by reason of paragraph (1).

(6) Exception for certain dispositions.—For purposes of this subsection—

(A) Reacquisitions of stock by issuing corporation not treated as first dispositions.—Any sale or exchange of stock to the issuing corporation shall not be treated as a first disposition.

(B) Involuntary conversions not treated as second dispositions.—A compulsory or involuntary conversion (within the meaning of section 1033) and any transfer thereafter shall not be treated as a second disposition if the first disposition occurred before the threat or imminence of the conversion.

(C) Dispositions after death.—Any transfer after the earlier of—

(i) the death of the person making the first disposition, or

(ii) the death of the person acquiring the property in the first disposition, and any transfer thereafter shall not be treated as a second disposition.

(7) Exception where tax avoidance not a principal purpose.—This subsection shall not apply to a second disposition (and any transfer thereafter) if it is established to the satisfaction of the Secretary that neither the first disposition nor the second disposition had as one of its principal purposes the avoidance of Federal income tax.

(8) Extension of statute of limitations.—The period for assessing a deficiency with respect to a first disposition (to the extent such deficiency is attributable to the application of this subsection) shall not expire before the day which is 2 years after the date on which the person making the first disposition furnishes (in such manner as the Secretary may by regulations prescribe) a notice that there was a second disposition of the property to which this subsection may have applied. Such deficiency may be assessed notwithstanding the provisions of any law or rule of law which would otherwise prevent such assessment.

(f) Definitions and special rules.—For purposes of this section—

(1) Related person.—Except for purposes of subsections (g) and (h), the term "related person" means—

(A) a person whose stock would be attributed under section 318(a) (other than paragraph (4) thereof) to the person first disposing of the property, or

(B) a person who bears a relationship described in section 267(b) to the person first disposing of the property.

(2) Marketable securities.—The term "marketable securities" means any security for which, as of the date of the disposition, there was a market on an established securities market or otherwise.

(3) Payment.—Except as provided in paragraph (4), the term "payment" does not include the receipt of evidences of indebtedness of the person acquiring the property (whether or not payment of such indebtedness is guaranteed by another person).

(4) Purchaser evidences of indebtedness payable on demand or readily tradable.—Receipt of a bond or other evidence of indebtedness which—

(A) is payable on demand, or

(B) is issued by a corporation or a government or political subdivision thereof and is readily tradable, shall be treated as receipt of payment.

(5) Readily tradable defined.—For purposes of paragraph (4), the term "readily tradable" means a bond or other evidence of indebtedness which is issued—

(A) with interest coupons attached or in registered form (other than one in registered form which the taxpayer establishes will not be readily tradable in an established securities market), or

(B) in any other form designed to render such bond or other evidence of indebtedness readily tradable in an established securities market.

(6) Like-kind exchanges.—In the case of any exchange described in section 1031(b)—

(A) the total contract price shall be reduced to take into account the amount of any property permitted to be received in such exchange without recognition of gain,

(B) the gross profit from such exchange shall be reduced to take into account any amount not recognized by reason of section 1031(b), and

(C) the term "payment", when used in any provision of this section other than subsection (b)(1), shall not include any property permitted to be received in such exchange without recognition of gain.

Similar rules shall apply in the case of an exchange which is described in section 356(a) and is not treated as a dividend.

(7) Depreciable property.—The term "depreciable property" means property of a character which (in the hands of the transferee) is subject to the allowance for depreciation provided in section 167.

(8) Payments to be received defined.—The term "payment to be received" includes—

(A) the aggregate amount of all payments which are not contingent as to amount, and

(B) the fair market value of any payments which are contingent as to amount.

(g) Sale of depreciable property to controlled entity.—

(1) In general.—In the case of an installment sale of depreciable property between related persons (within the meaning of section 1239(b))—

(A) subsection (a) shall not apply, and

(B) for purposes of this title—

(i) except as provided in clause (ii), all payments to be received shall be treated as received in the year of the disposition, and

(ii) in the case of any payments which are contingent as to amount but with respect to which the fair market value may not be reasonably ascertained, the basis shall be recovered ratably, and

(C) the purchaser may not increase the basis of any property acquired in such sale by any amount before the time such amount is includible in the gross income of the seller.

(2) Exception where tax avoidance not a principal purpose.—Paragraph (1) shall not apply if it is established to the satisfaction of the Secretary that the disposition did not have as one of its principal purposes the avoidance of Federal income tax.

(3) Related persons.—For purposes of this subsection, the term "related persons" has the meaning given to such term by section 1239(b), except that such term shall include 2 or more partnerships having a relationship to each other described in section 707(b)(1)(B).

(h) Use of installment method by shareholders in certain liquidations.—

(1) Receipt of obligations not treated as receipt of payment.—

(A) In general.—If, in a liquidation to which section 331 applies, the shareholder receives (in exchange for the shareholder's stock) an installment obligation acquired in respect of a sale or exchange by the corporation during the 12–month period beginning on the date a plan of complete liquidation is adopted and the liquidation is completed during such 12–month period, then, for purposes of this section, the receipt of payments under such obligation (but not the receipt of such obligation) by the shareholder shall be treated as the receipt of payment for the stock.

(B) Obligations attributable to sale of inventory must result from bulk sale.—Subparagraph (A) shall not apply to an installment obligation acquired in respect of a sale or exchange of—

(i) stock in trade of the corporation,

(ii) other property of a kind which would properly be included in the inventory of the corporation if on hand at the close of the taxable year, and

(iii) property held by the corporation primarily for sale to customers in the ordinary course of its trade or business, unless such sale or exchange is to 1 person in 1 transaction and involves substantially all of such property attributable to a trade or business of the corporation.

(C) Special rule where obligor and shareholder are related persons.—If the obligor of any installment obligation and the shareholder are married to each other or are related persons (within the meaning of section 1239(b)), to the extent such installment obligation is attributable to the disposition by the corporation of depreciable property—

(i) subparagraph (A) shall not apply to such obligation, and

(ii) for purposes of this title, all payments to be received by the shareholder shall be deemed received in the year the shareholder receives the obligation.

(D) Coordination with subsection (e)(1)(A).—For purposes of subsection (e)(1)(A), disposition of property by the corporation shall be treated also as disposition of such property by the shareholder.

(E) Sales by liquidating subsidiaries.—For purposes of subparagraph (A), in the case of a controlling corporate shareholder (within the meaning of section 368(c)(1)) of a selling corporation, an obligation acquired in respect of a sale or exchange by the selling corporation shall be treated as so acquired by such controlling corporate shareholder. The preceding sentence shall be applied successively to each controlling corporate shareholder above such controlling corporate shareholder.

(2) Distributions received in more than 1 taxable year of shareholder.—If—

(A) paragraph (1) applies with respect to any installment obligation received by a shareholder from a corporation, and

(B) by reason of the liquidation such shareholder receives property in more than 1 taxable year.

then, on completion of the liquidation, basis previously allocated to property so received shall be reallocated for all such taxable years so that the shareholder's basis in the stock of the corporation is properly allocated among all property received by such shareholder in such liquidation.

(i) Recognition of recapture income in year of disposition.—

(1) In general.—In the case of any installment sale of property to which subsection (a) applies—

(A) notwithstanding subsection (a), any recapture income shall be recognized in the year of the disposition, and

(B) any gain in excess of the recapture income shall be taken into account under the installment method.

(2) Recapture income.—For purposes of paragraph (1), the term "recapture income" means, with respect to any installment sale, the aggregate amount which would be treated as ordinary income under section 1245 or 1250 (or so much of section 751 as relates to section 1245 or 1250) for the taxable year of the disposition if all payments to be received were received in the taxable year of disposition.

(j) Regulations—

(1) In general.—The Secretary shall prescribe such regulations as may be necessary or appropriate to carry out the provisions of this section.

(2) Selling price not readily ascertainable.—The regulations prescribed under paragraph (1) shall include regulations providing for ratable basis recovery in transactions where the gross profit or the total contract price (or both) cannot be readily ascertained.

(k) Current inclusion in case of revolving credit plans, etc.—In the case of—

(1) any disposition of personal property under a revolving credit plan, or

(2) any installment obligation arising out of a sale of—

(A) stock or securities which are traded on an established securities market, or

(B) to the extent provided in regulations, property (other than stock or securities) of a kind regularly traded on an established market, subsection (a) shall not apply, and, for purposes of this title, all payments to be received shall be treated as received in the year of disposition. The Secretary may provide for the application of this subsection in whole or in part for transactions in which the rules of this subsection otherwise would be avoided through the use of related parties, pass-thru entities, or intermediaries.

(*l*) Dealer dispositions.—For purposes of subsection (b)(2)(A)—

(1) In general.—The term "dealer disposition" means any of the following dispositions:

(A) Personal property.—Any disposition of personal property by a person who regularly sells or otherwise disposes of personal property on the installment plan.

(B) Real property.—Any disposition of real property which is held by the taxpayer for sale to customers in the ordinary course of the taxpayer's trade or business.

(2) Exceptions.—The term "dealer disposition" does not include—

(A) Farm property.—The disposition on the installment plan of any property used or produced in the trade or business of farming (within the meaning of section 2032A(e)(4) or (5)).

(B) Timeshares and residential lots.—

(i) In general.—Any dispositions described in clause (ii) on the installment plan if the taxpayer elects to have paragraph (3) apply to any installment obligations which arise from such dispositions. An election under this paragraph shall not apply with respect to an installment obligation which is guaranteed by any person other than an individual.

(ii) Dispositions to which subparagraph applies.—A disposition is described in this clause if it is a disposition in the ordinary course of the taxpayer's trade or business to an individual of—

(I) a timeshare right to use or a timeshare ownership interest in residential real property for not more than 6 weeks per year, or a right to use specified campgrounds for recreational purposes, or

(II) any residential lot, but only if the taxpayer (or any related person) is not to make any improvements with respect to such lot.

For purposes of subclause (I), a timeshare right to use (or timeshare ownership interest in) property held by the spouse, children, grandchildren, or parents of an individual shall be treated as held by such individual.

(C) Carrying charges or interest.—Any carrying charges or interest with respect to a disposition described in subparagraph (A) or (B) which are added on the books of account of the seller to the established cash selling price of the property shall be included in the total contract price of the property and, if such charges or interest are not so included, any payments received shall be treated as applying first against such carrying charges or interest.

(3) Payment of interest on timeshares and residential lots.—

(A) In general.—In the case of any installment obligation to which paragraph (2)(B) applies, the tax imposed by this chapter for any taxable year for which payment is received on such obligation shall be increased by the amount of interest determined in the manner provided under subparagraph (B).

(B) Computation of interest.—

(i) In general.—The amount of interest referred to in subparagraph (A) for any taxable year shall be determined—

(I) on the amount of the tax for such taxable year which is attributable to the payments received during such taxable year on installment obligations to which this subsection applies

(II) for the period beginning on the date of sale, and ending on the date such payment is received, and

(III) by using the applicable Federal rate under section 1274 (without regard to subsection (d)(2) thereof) in effect at the time of the sale compounded semiannually.

(ii) Interest not taken into account.—For purposes of clause (i), the portion of any tax attributable to the receipt of any payment shall be determined without regard to any interest imposed under subparagraph (A).

(iii) Taxable year of sale.—No interest shall be determined for any payment received in the taxable year of the disposition from which the installment obligation arises.

(C) Treatment as interest.—Any amount payable under this paragraph shall be taken into account in computing the amount of any deduction allowable to the taxpayer for interest paid or accrued during such taxable year.

§ 453A. Special Rules for Nondealers

(a) General rule.—In the case of an installment obligation to which this section applies—

(1) interest shall be paid on the deferred tax liability with respect to such obligation in the manner provided under subsection (c), and

(2) the pledging rules under subsection (d) shall apply.

(b) Installment obligations to which section applies.—

(1) In general.—This section shall apply to any obligation which arises from the disposition of any property under the installment method, but only if the sales price of such property exceeds $150,000.

(2) Special rule for interest payments.—For purposes of subsection (a)(1), this section shall apply to an obligation described in paragraph (1) arising during a taxable year only if—

(A) such obligation is outstanding as of the close of such taxable year, and

(B) the face amount of all such obligations held by the taxpayer which arose during, and are outstanding as of the close of, such taxable year exceeds $5,000,000.

Except as provided in regulations, all persons treated as a single employer under subsection (a) or (b) of section 52 shall be treated as one person for purposes of this paragraph and subsection (c)(4).

(3) Exception for personal use and farm property.—An installment obligation shall not be treated as described in paragraph (1) if it arises from the disposition—

(A) by an individual of personal use property (within the meaning of section 1275(b)(3)), or

(B) of any property used or produced in the trade or business of farming (within the meaning of section 2032A(e)(4) or (5)).

(4) Special rule for timeshares and residential lots.—An installment obligation shall not be treated as described in paragraph (1) if it arises from a disposition described in section 453(1)(2)(B), but the provisions of section 453(1)(3) (relating to interest payments on timeshares and residential lots) shall apply to such obligation.

(5) Sales price.—For purposes of paragraph (1), all sales or exchanges which are part of the same transaction (or a series of related transactions) shall be treated as 1 sale or exchange.

(c) Interest on deferred tax liability.—

(1) In general.—If an obligation to which this section applies is outstanding as of the close of any taxable year, the tax imposed by this chapter for such taxable year shall be increased by the amount of interest determined in the manner provided under paragraph (2).

(2) Computation of interest.—For purposes of paragraph (1), the interest for any taxable year shall be an amount equal to the product of—

(A) the applicable percentage of the deferred tax liability with respect to such obligation, multiplied by

(B) the underpayment rate in effect under section 6621(a)(2) for the month with or within which the taxable year ends.

(3) Deferred tax liability.—For purposes of this section, the term "deferred tax liability" means, with respect to any taxable year, the product of—

(A) the amount of gain with respect to an obligation which has not been recognized as of the close of such taxable year, multiplied by

(B) the maximum rate of tax in effect under section 1 or 11, whichever is appropriate, for such taxable year.

For purposes of applying the preceding sentence with respect to so much of the gain which, when recognized, will be treated as long-term capital gain, the maximum rate on net capital gain under section 1(h) or 1201 (whichever is appropriate) shall be taken into account.

(4) Applicable percentage.—For purposes of this subsection, the term "applicable percentage" means, with respect to obligations arising in any taxable year, the percentage determined by dividing—

(A) the portion of the aggregate face amount of such obligations outstanding as of the close of such taxable year in excess of $5,000,000, by

(B) the aggregate face amount of such obligations outstanding as of the close of such taxable year.

(5) Treatment as interest.—Any amount payable under this subsection shall be taken into account in computing the amount of any deduction allowable to the taxpayer for interest paid or accrued during the taxable year.

(6) Regulations.—The Secretary shall prescribe such regulations as may be necessary to carry out the provisions of this subsection including regulations providing for the application of this subsection in the case of contingent payments, short taxable years, and pass-thru entities.

(d) Pledges, etc., of installment obligations.—

(1) In general.—For purposes of section 453, if any indebtedness (hereinafter in this subsection referred to as ''secured indebtedness'') is secured by an installment obligation to which this section applies, the net proceeds of the secured indebtedness shall be treated as a payment received on such installment obligation as of the later of—

(A) the time the indebtedness becomes secured indebtedness, or

(B) the time the proceeds of such indebtedness are received by the taxpayer.

(2) Limitation based on total contract price.—The amount treated as received under paragraph (1) by reason of any secured indebtedness shall not exceed the excess (if any) of—

(A) the total contract price, over

(B) any portion of the total contract price received under the contract before the later of the times referred to in subparagraph (A) or (B) of paragraph (1) (including amounts previously treated as received under paragraph (1) but not including amounts not taken into account by reason of paragraph (3)).

(3) Later payments treated as receipt of tax paid amounts.—If any amount is treated as received under paragraph (1) with respect to any installment obligation, subsequent payments received on such obligation shall not be taken into account for purposes of section 453 to the extent that the aggregate of such subsequent payments does not exceed the aggregate amount treated as received under paragraph (1).

(4) Secured indebtedness.—For purposes of this subsection indebtedness is secured by an installment obligation to the extent that payment of principal or interest on such indebtedness is directly secured (under the terms of the indebtedness or any underlying arrangements) by any interest in such installment obligation. A payment shall be treated as directly secured by an interest in an installment obligation to the extent an arrangement allows the taxpayer to satisfy all or a portion of the indebtedness with the installment obligation.

(e) Regulations.—The Secretary shall prescribe such regulations as may be necessary to carry out the purposes of this section, including regulations—

(1) disallowing the use of the installment method in whole or in part for transactions in which the rules of this section otherwise would be avoided through the use of related persons, pass-thru entities, or intermediaries, and

(2) providing that the sale of an interest in a partnership or other pass-thru entity will be treated as a sale of the proportionate share of the assets of the partnership or other entity.

§ 453B. Gain or Loss on Disposition of Installment Obligations

(a) General Rule.—If an installment obligation is satisfied at other than its face value or distributed, transmitted, sold, or otherwise disposed of, gain or loss shall result to the extent of the difference between the basis of the obligation and—

(1) the amount realized, in the case of satisfaction at other than face value or a sale or exchange, or

(2) the fair market value of the obligation at the time of distribution, transmission, or disposition, in the case of the distribution, transmission, or disposition otherwise than by sale or exchange.

Any gain or loss so resulting shall be considered as resulting from the sale or exchange of the property in respect of which the installment obligation was received.

(b) Basis of obligation.—The basis of an installment obligation shall be the excess of the face value of the obligation over an amount equal to the income which would be returnable were the obligation satisfied in full.

(c) Special rule for transmission at death.—Except as provided in section 691 (relating to recipients of income in respect to decedents), this section shall not apply to the transmission of installment obligations at death.

(d) Exception for distributions to which section 337(a) applies.—Subsection (a) shall not apply to any distribution to which section 337(a) applies.

then no gain or loss with respect to the distribution of such obligation shall be recognized by the distributing corporation.

(e) Life insurance companies.—

(1) In general.—In the case of a disposition of an installment obligation by any person other than a life insurance company (as defined in section 816(a)) to such an insurance company or to a partnership of which such an insurance company is a partner, no provision of this subtitle providing for the nonrecognition of gain shall apply with respect to any gain resulting under subsection (a). If a corporation which is a life insurance company for the taxable year was (for the preceding taxable year) a corporation which was not a life insurance company, such corporation shall, for purposes of this subsection and subsection (a), be treated as having transferred to a life insurance company, on the last day of the preceding taxable year, all installment obligations which it held on such last day. A partnership of which a life insurance company becomes a partner shall, for purposes of this subsection and subsection (a), be treated as having transferred to a life insurance company, on the last day of the preceding taxable year of such partnership, all installment obligations which it holds at the time such insurance company becomes a partner.

(2) Special rule where life insurance company elects to treat income as not related to insurance business.—Paragraph (1) shall not apply to any transfer or deemed transfer of an installment obligation if the life insurance company elects (at such time and in such manner as the Secretary may by regulations prescribe) to determine its life insurance company taxable income—

(A) by returning the income on such installment obligation under the installment method prescribed in section 453, and

123

(B) as if such income were an item attributable to a noninsurance business (as defined in section 806(b)(3)).

(f) Obligation becomes unenforceable.—For purposes of this section, if any installment obligation is canceled or otherwise becomes unenforceable—

(1) the obligation shall be treated as if it were disposed of in a transaction other than a sale or exchange, and

(2) if the obligor and obligee are related persons (within the meaning of section 453(f)(1)), the fair market value of the obligation shall be treated as not less than its face amount.

(g) Transfers between spouses or incident to divorce.—In the case of any transfer described in subsection (a) of section 1041 (other than a transfer in trust)—

(1) subsection (a) of this section shall not apply, and

(2) the same tax treatment with respect to the transferred installment obligation shall apply to the transferee as would have applied to the transferor.

(h) Certain liquidating distributions by S corporations.—If—

(1) an installment obligation is distributed by an S corporation in a complete liquidation, and

(2) receipt of the obligation is not treated as payment for the stock by reason of section 453(h)(1), then, except for purposes of any tax imposed by subchapter S, no gain or loss with respect to the distribution of the obligation shall be recognized by the distributing corporation. Under regulations prescribed by the Secretary, the character of the gain or loss to the shareholder shall be determined in accordance with the principles of section 1366(b).

§ 465. Deductions Limited to Amount at Risk

(a) Limitation to amount at risk.—

(1) In general.—In the case of—

(A) an individual, and

(B) a C corporation with respect to which the stock ownership requirement of paragraph (2) of section 542(a) is met, engaged in an activity to which this section applies, any loss from such activity for the taxable year shall be allowed only to the extent of the aggregate amount with respect to which the taxpayer is at risk (within the meaning of subsection (b)) for such activity at the close of the taxable year.

(2) Deduction in succeeding year.—Any loss from an activity to which this section applies not allowed under this section for the taxable year shall be treated as a deduction allocable to such activity in the first succeeding taxable year.

(3) Special rules for applying paragraph (1)(B).—For purposes of paragraph (1)(B)—

(A) section 544(a)(2) shall be applied as if such section did not contain the phrase "or by or for his partner"; and

(B) sections 544(a)(4)(A) and 544(b)(1) shall be applied by substituting "the corporation meet the stock ownership requirements of section 542(a)(2)" for "the corporation a personal holding company".

(b) Amounts considered at risk.—

(1) In general.—For purposes of this section, a taxpayer shall be considered at risk for an activity with respect to amounts including—

(A) the amount of money and the adjusted basis of other property contributed by the taxpayer to the activity, and

(B) amounts borrowed with respect to such activity (as determined under paragraph (2)).

(2) Borrowed amounts.—For purposes of this section, a taxpayer shall be considered at risk with respect to amounts borrowed for use in an activity to the extent that he—

(A) is personally liable for the repayment of such amounts, or

(B) has pledged property, other than property used in such activity, as security for such borrowed amount (to the extent of the net fair market value of the taxpayer's interest in such property).

No property shall be taken into account as security if such property is directly or indirectly financed by indebtedness which is secured by property described in paragraph (1).

(3) Certain borrowed amounts excluded.—

(A) In general.—Except to the extent provided in regulations, for purposes of paragraph (1)(B), amounts borrowed shall not be considered to be at risk with respect to an activity if such amounts are borrowed from any person who has an interest in such activity or from a related person to a person (other than the taxpayer) having such an interest.

(B) Exceptions.—

(i) Interest as creditor.—Subparagraph (A) shall not apply to an interest as a creditor in the activity.

(ii) Interest as shareholder with respect to amounts borrowed by corporation.—In the case of amounts borrowed by a corporation from a shareholder, subparagraph (A) shall not apply to an interest as a shareholder.

(C) Related person.—For purposes of this subsection, a person (hereinafter in this paragraph referred to as the "related person") is related to any person if—

(i) the related person bears a relationship to such person specified in section 267(b) or section 707(b)(1), or

(ii) the related person and such person are engaged in trades or business under common control (within the meaning of subsections (a) and (b) of section 52).

For purposes of clause (i), in applying section 267(b) or 707(b)(1), "10 percent" shall be substituted for "50 percent."

(4) Exception.—Notwithstanding any other provision of this section, a taxpayer shall not be considered at risk with respect to amounts protected against loss through nonrecourse financing, guarantees, stop loss agreements, or other similar arrangements.

(5) Amounts at risk in subsequent years.—If in any taxable year the taxpayer has a loss from an activity to which subsection (a) applies, the amount with respect to which a taxpayer is considered to be at risk (within the meaning of subsection (b)) in subsequent

125

taxable years with respect to that activity shall be reduced by that portion of the loss which (after the application of subsection (a)) is allowable as a deduction.

(6) Qualified nonrecourse financing treated as amount at risk.—For purposes of this section—

(A) In general.—Notwithstanding any other provision of this subsection, in the case of an activity of holding real property, a taxpayer shall be considered at risk with respect to the taxpayer's share of any qualified nonrecourse financing which is secured by real property used in such activity.

(B) Qualified nonrecourse financing.—For purposes of this paragraph, the term "qualified nonrecourse financing" means any financing—

(i) which is borrowed by the taxpayer with respect to the activity of holding real property,

(ii) which is borrowed by the taxpayer from a qualified person or represents a loan from any Federal, State, or local government or instrumentality thereof, or is guaranteed by any Federal, State, or local government,

(iii) except to the extent provided in regulations, with respect to which no person is personally liable for repayment, and

(iv) which is not convertible debt.

(C) Special rule for partnerships.—In the case of a partnership, a partner's share of any qualified nonrecourse financing of such partnership shall be determined on the basis of the partner's share of liabilities of such partnership incurred in connection with such financing (within the meaning of section 752).

(D) Qualified person defined.—For purposes of this paragraph—

(i) In general.—The term "qualified person" has the meaning given such term by section 49(a)(1)(D)(iv).

(ii) Certain commercially reasonable financing from related persons.— For purposes of clause (i), section 49(a)(1)(D)(iv) shall be applied without regard to subclause (I) thereof (relating to financing from related persons) if the financing from the related person is commercially reasonable and on substantially the same terms as loans involving unrelated persons.

(E) Activity of holding real property.—For purposes of this paragraph—

(i) Incidental personal property and services.—The activity of holding real property includes the holding of personal property and the providing of services which are incidental to making real property available as living accommodations.

(ii) Mineral property.—The activity of holding real property shall not include the holding of mineral property.

(c) Activities to which section applies.—

(1) Types of activities.—This section applies to any taxpayer engaged in the activity of—

(A) holding, producing, or distributing motion picture films or video tapes,

(B) farming (as defined in section 464(e)),

(C) leasing any section 1245 property (as defined in section 1245(a)(3)),

(D) exploring for, or exploiting, oil and gas resources, or

(E) exploring for, or exploiting, geothermal deposits (as defined in section 613(e)(2)) as a trade or business or for the production of income.

(2) Separate activities.—For purposes of this section—

(A) In general.—Except as provided in subparagraph (B), a taxpayer's activity with respect to each—

    (i) film or video tape,

    (ii) section 1245 property which is leased or held for leasing,

    (iii) farm,

    (iv) oil and gas property (as defined under section 614), or

    (v) geothermal property (as defined under section 614), shall be treated as a separate activity.

(B) Aggregation rules.—

    (i) Special rule for leases of section 1245 property by partnerships or S corporations.—In the case of any partnership or S corporation, all activities with respect to section 1245 properties which—

        (I) are leased or held for lease, and

        (II) are placed in service in any taxable year of the partnership or S corporation, shall be treated as a single activity.

    (ii) Other aggregation rules.—Rules similar to the rules of subparagraphs (B) and (C) or paragraph (3) shall apply for purposes of this paragraph.

(3) Extension to other activities.—

(A) In general.—In the case of taxable years beginning after December 31, 1978, this section also applies to each activity—

    (i) engaged in by the taxpayer in carrying on a trade or business or for the production of income, and

    (ii) which is not described in paragraph (1).

(B) Aggregation of activities where taxpayer actively participates in management of trade or business.—Except as provided in subparagraph (C), for purposes of this section, activities described in subparagraph (A) which constitute a trade or business shall be treated as one activity if—

    (i) the taxpayer actively participates in the management of such trade or business, or

    (ii) such trade or business is carried on by a partnership or an S corporation and 65 percent or more of the losses for the taxable year is allocable to persons who actively participate in the management of the trade or business.

(C) Aggregation or separation of activities under regulations.—The Secretary shall prescribe regulations under which activities described in subparagraph (A) shall be aggregated or treated as separate activities.

(D) Application of subsection (b)(3).—In the case of an activity described in subparagraph (A), subsection (b)(3) shall apply only to the extent provided in regulations prescribed by the Secretary.

(4) Exclusion for certain equipment leasing by closely-held corporations.—

(A) In general.—In the case of a corporation described in subsection (a)(1)(B) actively engaged in equipment leasing—

(**i**) the activity of equipment leasing shall be treated as a separate activity, and

(**ii**) subsection (a) shall not apply to losses from such activity.

(B) 50–percent gross receipts test.—For purposes of subparagraph (A), a corporation shall not be considered to be actively engaged in equipment leasing unless 50 percent or more of the gross receipts of the corporation for the taxable year is attributable, under regulations prescribed by the Secretary, to equipment leasing.

(C) Component members of controlled group treated as a single corporation.—For purposes of subparagraph (A), the component members of a controlled group of corporations shall be treated as a single corporation.

(5) Waiver of controlled group rule where there is substantial leasing activity.—

(A) In general.—In the case of the component members of a qualified leasing group, paragraph (4) shall be applied—

(**i**) by substituting "80 percent" for "50 percent" in subparagraph (B) thereof, and

(**ii**) as if paragraph (4) did not include subparagraph (C) thereof.

(B) Qualified leasing group.—For purposes of this paragraph, the term "qualified leasing group" means a controlled group of corporations which, for the taxable year and each of the 2 immediately preceding taxable years, satisfied each of the following 3 requirements:

(**i**) **At least 3 employees.**—During the entire year, the group had at least 3 full-time employees substantially all of the services of whom were services directly related to the equipment leasing activity of the qualified leasing members.

(**ii**) **At least 5 separate leasing transactions.**—During the year, the qualified leasing members in the aggregate entered into at least 5 separate equipment leasing transactions.

(**iii**) **At least $1,000,000 equipment leasing receipts.**—During the year, the qualified leasing members in the aggregate had at least $1,000,000 in gross receipts from equipment leasing.

The term "qualified leasing group" does not include any controlled group of corporations to which, without regard to this paragraph, paragraph (4) applies.

(C) Qualified leasing member.—For purposes of this paragraph, a corporation shall be treated as a qualified leasing member for the taxable year only if for each of the taxable years referred to in subparagraph (B)—

(**i**) it is a component member of the controlled group of corporations, and

(ii) it meets the requirements of paragraph (4)(B) (as modified by subparagraph (A)(i) of this paragraph).

(6) Definitions relating to paragraphs (4) and (5).—For purposes of paragraphs (4) and (5)—

   (A) Equipment leasing.—The term "equipment leasing" means—

      (i) the leasing of equipment which is section 1245 property, and

      (ii) the purchasing, servicing, and selling of such equipment.

   (B) Leasing of master sound recordings, etc., excluded.—The term "equipment leasing" does not include the leasing of master sound recordings, and other similar contractual arrangements with respect to tangible or intangible assets associated with literary, artistic, or musical properties.

   (C) Controlled group of corporations; component member.—The terms "controlled group of corporations" and "component member" have the same meanings as when used in section 1563. The determination of the taxable years taken into account with respect to any controlled group of corporations shall be made in a manner consistent with the manner set forth in section 1563.

(7) Exclusion of active businesses of qualified C corporations.—

   (A) In general.—In the case of a taxpayer which is a qualified C corporation—

      (i) each qualifying business carried on by such taxpayer shall be treated as a separate activity, and

      (ii) subsection (a) shall not apply to losses from such business.

   (B) Qualified C corporation.—For purposes of subparagraph (A), the term "qualified C corporation" means any corporation described in subparagraph (B) of subsection (a)(1) which is not—

      (i) a personal holding company (as defined in section 542(a)), or

      (ii) a personal service corporation (as defined in section 269A(b) but determined by substituting "5 percent" for "10 percent" in section 269A(b)(2)).

   (C) Qualifying business.—For purposes of this paragraph, the term "qualifying business" means any active business if—

      (i) during the entire 12–month period ending on the last day of the taxable year, such corporation had at least 1 full-time employee substantially all the services of whom were in the active management of such business,

      (ii) during the entire 12–month period ending on the last day of the taxable year, such corporation had at least 3 full-time, nonowner employees substantially all of the services of whom were services directly related to such business,

      (iii) the amount of the deductions attributable to such business which are allowable to the taxpayer solely by reason of sections 162 and 404 for the taxable year exceeds 15 percent of the gross income from such business for such year, and

      (iv) such business is not an excluded business.

(D) Special rules for application of subparagraph (C).—

(i) Partnerships in which taxpayer is a qualified corporate partner.—In the case of an active business of a partnership, if—

(I) the taxpayer is a qualified corporate partner in the partnership, and

(II) during the entire 12–month period ending on the last day of the partnership's taxable year, there was at least 1 full-time employee of the partnership (or of a qualified corporate partner) substantially all the services of whom were in the active management of such business, then the taxpayer's proportionate share (determined on the basis of its profits interest) of the activities of the partnership in such business shall be treated as activities of the taxpayer (and clause (i) of subparagraph (C) shall not apply in determining whether such business is a qualifying business of the taxpayer).

(ii) Qualified corporate partner.—For purposes of clause (i), the term "qualified corporate partner" means any corporation if—

(I) such corporation is a general partner in the partnership,

(II) such corporation has an interest of 10 percent or more in the profits and losses of the partnership, and

(III) such corporation has contributed property to the partnership in an amount not less than the lesser of $500,000 or 10 percent of the net worth of the corporation.

For purposes of subclause (III), any contribution of property other than money shall be taken into account at its fair market value.

(iii) Deduction for owner employee compensation not taken into account.—For purposes of clause (iii) of subparagraph (C), there shall not be taken into account any deduction in respect of compensation for personal services rendered by any employee (other than a nonowner employee) of the taxpayer or any member of such employee's family (within the meaning of section 318(a)(1)).

(iv) Special rule for banks.—For purposes of clause (iii) of subparagraph (C), in the case of a bank (as defined in section 581) or a financial institution to which section 591 applies—

(I) gross income shall be determined without regard to the exclusion of interest from gross income under section 103, and

(II) in addition to the deductions described in such clause, there shall also be taken into account the amount of the deductions which are allowable for amounts paid or credited to the accounts of depositors or holders of accounts as dividends or interest on their deposits or withdrawable accounts under section 163 or 591.

(v) Special rule for life insurance companies.—

(I) In general.—Clause (iii) of subparagraph (C) shall not apply to any insurance business of a qualified life insurance company.

(II) Insurance business.—For purposes of subclause (I), the term "insurance business" means any business which is not a noninsurance business (within the meaning of section 806(b)(3)).

(III) Qualified life insurance company.—For purposes of subclause (I), the term "qualified life insurance company" means any company which would be a life insurance company as defined in section 816 if unearned premiums were not taken into account under subsections (a)(2) and (c)(2) of section 816.

(E) Definitions.—For purposes of this paragraph—

(i) Non-owner employee.—The term "non-owner employee" means any employee who does not own, at any time during the taxable year, more than 5 percent in value of the outstanding stock of the taxpayer. For purposes of the preceding sentence, section 318 shall apply, except that "5 percent" shall be substituted for "50 percent" in section 318(a)(2)(C).

(ii) Excluded business.—The term "excluded business" means—

(I) equipment leasing (as defined in paragraph (6)), and

(II) any business involving the use, exploitation, sale, lease, or other disposition of master sound recordings, motion picture films, video tapes, or tangible or intangible assets associated with literary, artistic, musical, or similar properties.

(iii) Special rules relating to communications industry, etc.—

(I) Business not excluded where taxpayer not completely at risk.—A business involving the use, exploitation, sale, lease, or other disposition of property described in subclause (II) of clause (ii) shall not constitute an excluded business by reason of such subclause if the taxpayer is at risk with respect to all amounts paid or incurred (or chargeable to capital account) in such business.

(II) Certain licensed businesses not excluded.—For purposes of subclause (II) of clause (ii), the provision of radio, television, cable television, or similar services pursuant to a license or franchise granted by the Federal Communications Commission or any other Federal, State, or local authority shall not constitute an excluded business by reason of such subclause.

(F) Affiliated group treated as 1 taxpayer.—For purposes of this paragraph—

(i) In general.—Except as provided in subparagraph (G), the component members of an affiliated group of corporations shall be treated as a single taxpayer.

(ii) Affiliated group of corporations.—The term "affiliated group of corporations" means an affiliated group (as defined in section 1504(a)) which files or is required to file consolidated income tax returns.

(iii) Component member.—The term "component member" means an includible corporation (as defined in section 1504) which is a member of the affiliated group.

(G) Loss of 1 member of affiliated group may not offset income of personal holding company or personal service corporation.—Nothing in this paragraph shall permit any loss of a member of an affiliated group to be used as an offset against the income of any other member of such group which is a personal holding company (as defined in section 542(a)) or a personal service corporation (as defined in section 269A(b) but determined by substituting "5 percent" for "10 percent" in section 269A(b)(2)).

(d) Definition of loss.—For purposes of this section, the term "loss" means the excess of the deductions allowable under this chapter for the taxable year (determined without regard to the first sentence of subsection (a)) and allocable to an activity to which this section applies over the income received or accrued by the taxpayer during the taxable year from such activity (determined without regard to subsection (e)(1)(A)).

(e) Recapture of losses where amount at risk is less than zero.—

(1) In general.—If zero exceeds the amount for which the taxpayer is at risk in any activity at the close of any taxable year—

    (A) the taxpayer shall include in his gross income for such taxable year (as income from such activity) an amount equal to such excess, and

    (B) an amount equal to the amount so included in gross income shall be treated as a deduction allocable to such activity for the first succeeding taxable year.

(2) Limitation.—The excess referred to in paragraph (1) shall not exceed—

    (A) the aggregate amount of the reductions required by subsection (b)(5) with respect to the activity by reason of losses for all prior taxable years beginning after December 31, 1978, reduced by

    (B) the amounts previously included in gross income with respect to such activity under this subsection.

§ 469.   Passive Activity Losses and Credits Limited

(a) Disallowance.—

(1) In general.—If for any taxable year the taxpayer is described in paragraph (2), neither—

    (A) the passive activity loss, nor

    (B) the passive activity credit, for the taxable year shall be allowed.

(2) Persons described.—The following are described in this paragraph:

    (A) any individual, estate, or trust,

    (B) any closely held C corporation, and

    (C) any personal service corporation.

(b) Disallowed loss or credit carried to next year.—Except as otherwise provided in this section, any loss or credit from an activity which is disallowed under subsection (a) shall be treated as a deduction or credit allocable to such activity in the next taxable year.

(c) Passive activity defined.—For purposes of this section—

(1) In general.—The term "passive activity" means any activity—

    (A) which involves the conduct of any trade or business, and

    (B) in which the taxpayer does not materially participate.

(2) Passive activity includes any rental activity.—Except as provided in paragraph (7), the term "passive activity" includes any rental activity.

(3) Working interests in oil and gas property.—

    (A) In general.—The term "passive activity" shall not include any working interest in any oil or gas property which the taxpayer holds directly or through an entity which does not limit the liability of the taxpayer with respect to such interest.

(B) Income in subsequent years.—If any taxpayer has any loss for any taxable year from a working interest in any oil or gas property which is treated as a loss which is not from a passive activity, then any net income from such property (or any property the basis of which is determined in whole or in part by reference to the basis of such property) for any succeeding taxable year shall be treated as income of the taxpayer which is not from a passive activity. If the preceding sentence applies to the net income from any property for any taxable year, any credits allowable under subpart B (other than section 27(a)) or D of part IV of subchapter A for such taxable year which are attributable to such property shall be treated as credits not from a passive activity to the extent the amount of such credits does not exceed the regular tax liability of the taxpayer for the taxable year which is allocable to such net income.

(4) Material participation not required for paragraphs (2) and (3).—Paragraphs (2) and (3) shall be applied without regard to whether or not the taxpayer materially participates in the activity.

(5) Trade or business includes research and experimentation activity.—For purposes of paragraph (1)(A), the term "trade or business" includes any activity involving research or experimentation (within the meaning of section 174).

(6) Activity in connection with trade or business or production of income.—To the extent provided in regulations, for purposes of paragraph (1)(A), the term "trade or business" includes—

(A) any activity in connection with a trade or business, or

(B) any activity with respect to which expenses are allowable as a deduction under section 212.

(7) Special rules for taxpayers in real property business.—

(A) In general.—If this paragraph applies to any taxpayer for a taxable year—

(i) paragraph (2) shall not apply to any rental real estate activity of such taxpayer for such taxable year, and

(ii) this section shall be applied as if each interest of the taxpayer in rental real estate were a separate activity.

Notwithstanding clause (ii), a taxpayer may elect to treat all interests in rental real estate as one activity. Nothing in the preceding provisions of this subparagraph shall be construed as affecting the determination of whether the taxpayer materially participates with respect to any interest in a limited partnership as a limited partner.

(B) Taxpayers to whom paragraph applies.—This paragraph shall apply to a taxpayer for a taxable year if—

(i) more than one-half of the personal services performed in trades or businesses by the taxpayer during such taxable year are performed in real property trades or businesses in which the taxpayer materially participates, and

(ii) such taxpayer performs more than 750 hours of services during the taxable year in real property trades or businesses in which the taxpayer materially participates.

In the case of a joint return, the requirements of the preceding sentence are satisfied if and only if either spouse separately satisfies such requirements. For purposes of the preceding sentence, activities in which a spouse materially participates shall be determined under subsection (h).

(C) Real property trade or business.—For purposes of this paragraph, the term "real property trade or business" means any real property development, redevelopment, construction, reconstruction, acquisition, conversion, rental, operation, management, leasing, or brokerage trade or business.

(D) Special rules for subparagraph (B).—

(i) Closely held C corporations.—In the case of a closely held C corporation, the requirements of subparagraph (B) shall be treated as met for any taxable year if more than 50 percent of the gross receipts of such corporation for such taxable year are derived from real property trades or businesses in which the corporation materially participates.

(ii) Personal services as an employee.—For purposes of subparagraph (B), personal services performed as an employee shall not be treated as performed in real property trades or businesses. The preceding sentence shall not apply if such employee is a 5–percent owner (as defined in section 416(i)(1)(B)) in the employer.

(d) Passive activity loss and credit defined.—For purposes of this section—

(1) Passive activity loss.—The term "passive activity loss" means the amount (if any) by which—

(A) the aggregate losses from all passive activities for the taxable year, exceed

(B) the aggregate income from all passive activities for such year.

(2) Passive activity credit.—The term "passive activity credit" means the amount (if any) by which—

(A) the sum of the credits from all passive activities allowable for the taxable year under—

(i) subpart D of part IV of subchapter A, or

(ii) subpart B (other than section 27(a)) of such part IV, exceeds

(B) the regular tax liability of the taxpayer for the taxable year allocable to all passive activities.

(e) Special rules for determining income or loss from a passive activity.—For purposes of this section—

(1) Certain income not treated as income from passive activity.—In determining the income or loss from any activity—

(A) In general.—There shall not be taken into account—

(i) any—

(I) gross income from interest, dividends, annuities, or royalties not derived in the ordinary course of a trade or business,

(II) expenses (other than interest) which are clearly and directly allocable to such gross income, and

(III) interest expense properly allocable to such gross income, and

(ii) gain or loss not derived in the ordinary course of a trade or business which is attributable to the disposition of property—

(I) producing income of a type described in clause (i), or

(II) held for investment.

For purposes of clause (ii), any interest in a passive activity shall not be treated as property held for investment.

(B) Return on working capital.—For purposes of subparagraph (A), any income, gain, or loss which is attributable to an investment of working capital shall be treated as not derived in the ordinary course of a trade or business.

(2) Passive losses of certain closely held corporations may offset active income.—

(A) In general.—If a closely held C corporation (other than a personal service corporation) has net active income for any taxable year, the passive activity loss of such taxpayer for such taxable year (determined without regard to this paragraph)—

(i) shall be allowable as a deduction against net active income, and

(ii) shall not be taken into account under subsection (a) to the extent so allowable as a deduction.

A similar rule shall apply in the case of any passive activity credit of the taxpayer.

(B) Net active income.—For purposes of this paragraph, the term "net active income" means the taxable income of the taxpayer for the taxable year determined without regard to—

(i) any income or loss from a passive activity, and

(ii) any item of gross income, expense, gain, or loss described in paragraph (1)(A).

(3) Compensation for personal services.—Earned income (within the meaning of section 911(d)(2)(A)) shall not be taken into account in computing the income or loss from a passive activity for any taxable year.

(4) Dividends reduced by dividends received deduction.—For purposes of paragraphs (1) and (2), income from dividends shall be reduced by the amount of any dividends received deduction under section 243, 244, or 245.

(f) Treatment of former passive activities.—For purposes of this section—

(1) In general.—If an activity is a former passive activity for any taxable year—

(A) any unused deduction allocable to such activity under subsection (b) shall be offset against the income from such activity for the taxable year,

(B) any unused credit allocable to such activity under subsection (b) shall be offset against the regular tax liability (computed after the application of paragraph (1)) allocable to such activity for the taxable year, and

(C) any such deduction or credit remaining after the application of subparagraphs (A) and (B) shall continue to be treated as arising from a passive activity.

(2) Change in status of closely held C corporation or personal service corporation.—If a taxpayer ceases for any taxable year to be a closely held Corporation or personal service corporation, this section shall continue to apply to losses and credits to which this section applied for any preceding taxable year in the same manner as if such taxpayer continued to be a closely held C corporation or personal service corporation, whichever is applicable.

(3) Former passive activity.—The term "former passive activity" means any activity which, with respect to the taxpayer—

(A) is not a passive activity for the taxable year, but

(B) was a passive activity for any prior taxable year.

(g) Dispositions of entire interest in passive activity.—If during the taxable year a taxpayer disposes of his entire interest in any passive activity (or former passive activity), the following rules shall apply:

(1) Fully taxable transaction.—

(A) In general.—If all gain or loss realized on such disposition is recognized, the excess of—

(i) any loss from such activity for such taxable year (determined after the application of subsection (b)), over

(ii) any net income or gain for such taxable year from all other passive activities (determined after the application of subsection (b)),

shall be treated as a loss which is not from a passive activity.

(B) Subparagraph (A) not to apply to disposition involving related party.—If the taxpayer and the person acquiring the interest bear a relationship to each other described in section 267(b) or section 707(b)(1), then subparagraph (A) shall not apply to any loss of the taxpayer until the taxable year in which such interest is acquired (in a transaction described in subparagraph (A)) by another person who does not bear such a relationship to the taxpayer.

(C) Income from prior years.—To the extent provided in regulations, income or gain from the activity for preceding taxable years shall be taken into account under subparagraph (A)(ii) for the taxable year to the extent necessary to prevent the avoidance of this section.

(2) Disposition by death.—If an interest in the activity is transferred by reason of the death of the taxpayer—

(A) paragraph (1)(A) shall apply to losses described in paragraph (1)(A) to the extent such losses are greater than the excess (if any) of—

(i) the basis of such property in the hands of the transferee, over

(ii) the adjusted basis of such property immediately before the death of the taxpayer, and

(B) any losses to the extent of the excess described in subparagraph (A) shall not be allowed as a deduction for any taxable year.

(3) Installment sale of entire interest.—In the case of an installment sale of an entire interest in an activity to which section 453 applies, paragraph (1) shall apply to the portion of such losses for each taxable year which bears the same ratio to all such losses as the gain recognized on such sale during such taxable year bears to the gross profit from such sale (realized or to be realized when payment is completed).

(h) Material participation defined.—For purposes of this section—

(1) In general.—A taxpayer shall be treated as materially participating in an activity only if the taxpayer is involved in the operations of the activity on a basis which is—

    (A) regular,

    (B) continuous, and

    (C) substantial.

(2) Interests in limited partnerships.—Except as provided in regulations, no interest in a limited partnership as a limited partner shall be treated as an interest with respect to which a taxpayer materially participates.

(3) Treatment of certain retired individuals and surviving spouses.—A taxpayer shall be treated as materially participating in any farming activity for a taxable year if paragraph (4) or (5) of section 2032A(b) would cause the requirements of section 2032A(b)(1)(C)(ii) to be met with respect to real property used in such activity if such taxpayer had died during the taxable year.

(4) Certain closely held C corporations and personal service corporations.—A closely held C corporation or personal service corporation shall be treated as materially participating in an activity only if—

    (A) 1 or more shareholders holding stock representing more than 50 percent (by value) of the outstanding stock of such corporation materially participate in such activity, or

    (B) in the case of a closely held C corporation (other than a personal service corporation), the requirements of section 465(c)(7)(C) (without regard to clause (iv)) are met with respect to such activity.

(5) Participation by spouse.—In determining whether a taxpayer materially participates, the participation of the spouse of the taxpayer shall be taken into account.

(i) $25,000 offset for rental real estate activities.—

(1) In general.—In the case of any natural person, subsection (a) shall not apply to that portion of the passive activity loss or the deduction equivalent (within the meaning of subsection (j)(5)) of the passive activity credit for any taxable year which is attributable to all rental real estate activities with respect to which such individual actively participated in such taxable year (and if any portion of such loss or credit arose in another taxable year, in such other taxable year).

(2) Dollar limitation.—The aggregate amount to which paragraph (1) applies for any taxable year shall not exceed $25,000.

(3) Phase-out of exemption.—

    (A) In general.—In the case of any taxpayer, the $25,000 amount under paragraph (2) shall be reduced (but not below zero) by 50 percent of the amount by which the adjusted gross income of the taxpayer for the taxable year exceeds $100,000.

    (B) Special phase-out of rehabilitation credit.—In the case of any portion of the passive activity credit for any taxable year which is attributable to the rehabilitation credit determined under section 47, subparagraph (A) shall be applied by substituting "$200,000" for "$100,000".

(C) Exception for commercial revitalization deduction.—Subparagraph (A) shall not apply to any portion of the passive activity loss for any taxable year which is attributable to the commercial revitalization deduction under section 1400I.

(D) Exception for low-income housing credit.—Subparagraph (A) shall not apply to any portion of the passive activity credit for any taxable year which is attributable to any credit determined under section 42.

(E) Ordering rules to reflect exceptions and separate phase-outs.—If subparagraph (B), (C), or (D) applies for a taxable year, paragraph (1) shall be applied—

 (i) first to the portion of the passive activity loss to which subparagraph (C) does not apply,

 (ii) second to the portion of such loss to which subparagraph (C) applies,

 (iii) third to the portion of the passive activity credit to which subparagraph (B) or (D) does not apply,

 (iv) fourth to the portion of such credit to which subparagraph (B) applies, and

 (v) then to the portion of such credit to which subparagraph (D) applies.

(F) Adjusted gross income.—For purposes of this paragraph, adjusted gross income shall be determined without regard to—

 (i) any amount includible in gross income under section 86,

 (ii) the amounts excludable from gross income under sections 135 and 137,

 (iii) the amounts allowable as a deduction under sections 199, 219, 221, and 222, and

 (iv) any passive activity loss or any loss allowable by reason of subsection (c)(7).

(4) Special rule for estates.—

(A) In general.—In the case of taxable years of an estate ending less than 2 years after the date of the death of the decedent, this subsection shall apply to all rental real estate activities with respect to which such decedent actively participated before his death.

(B) Reduction for surviving spouse's exemption.—For purposes of subparagraph (A), the $25,000 amount under paragraph (2) shall be reduced by the amount of the exemption under paragraph (1) (without regard to paragraph (3)) allowable to the surviving spouse of the decedent for the taxable year ending with or within the taxable year of the estate.

(5) Married individuals filing separately.—

(A) In general.—Except as provided in subparagraph (B), in the case of any married individual filing a separate return, this subsection shall be applied by substituting—

 (i) "$12,500" for "$25,000" each place it appears,

 (ii) "$50,000" for "$100,000" in paragraph (3)(A), and

 (iii) "$100,000" for "$200,000" in paragraph (3)(B).

(B) Taxpayers not living apart.—This subsection shall not apply to a taxpayer who—

(i) is a married individual filing a separate return for any taxable year, and

(ii) does not live apart from his spouse at all times during such taxable year.

(6) Active participation.—

(A) In general.—An individual shall not be treated as actively participating with respect to any interest in any rental real estate activity for any period if, at any time during such period, such interest (including any interest of the spouse of the individual) is less than 10 percent (by value) of all interests in such activity.

(B) No participation requirement for low-income housing, or rehabilitation credit, or commercial revitalization deduction.—**Paragraphs (1) and (4)(A)** shall be applied without regard to the active participation requirement in the case of—

(i) any credit determined under section 42 for any taxable year,

(ii) any rehabilitation credit determined under section 47, or.

(iii) any deduction under section 1400I (relating to commercial revitalization deduction).

(C) Interest as a limited partner.—Except as provided in regulations, no interest as a limited partner in a limited partnership shall be treated as an interest with respect to which the taxpayer actively participates.

(D) Participation by spouse.—In determining whether a taxpayer actively participates, the participation of the spouse of the taxpayer shall be taken into account.

(j) Other definitions and special rules.—For purposes of this section—

(1) Closely held C corporation.—The term "closely held C corporation" means any C corporation described in section 465(a)(1)(B).

(2) Personal service corporation.—The term "personal service corporation" has the meaning given such term by section 269A(b)(1), except that section 269A(b)(2) shall be applied—

(A) by substituting "any" for "more than 10 percent", and

(B) by substituting "any" for "50 percent or more in value" in section 318(a)(2)(C).

A corporation shall not be treated as a personal service corporation unless more than 10 percent of the stock (by value) in such corporation is held by employee-owners (within the meaning of section 269A(b)(2), as modified by the preceding sentence).

(3) Regular tax liability.—The term "regular tax liability" has the meaning given such term by section 26(b).

(4) Allocation of passive activity loss and credit.—The passive activity loss and the passive activity credit (and the $25,000 amount under subsection (i)) shall be allocated to activities, and within activities, on a pro rata basis in such manner as the Secretary may prescribe.

(5) Deduction equivalent.—The deduction equivalent of credits from a passive activity for any taxable year is the amount which (if allowed as a deduction) would reduce the regular tax liability for such taxable year by an amount equal to such credits.

(6) Special rule for gifts.—In the case of a disposition of any interest in a passive activity by gift—

(A) the basis of such interest immediately before the transfer shall be increased by the amount of any passive activity losses allocable to such interest with respect to which a deduction has not been allowed by reason of subsection (a), and

(B) such losses shall not be allowable as a deduction for any taxable year.

(7) Qualified residence interest.—The passive activity loss of a taxpayer shall be computed without regard to qualified residence interest (within the meaning of section 163(h)(3)).

(8) Rental activity.—The term "rental activity" means any activity where payments are principally for the use of tangible property.

(9) Election to increase basis of property by amount of disallowed credit.—For purposes of determining gain or loss from a disposition of any property to which subsection (g)(1) applies, the transferor may elect to increase the basis of such property immediately before the transfer by an amount equal to the portion of any unused credit allowable under this chapter which reduced the basis of such property for the taxable year in which such credit arose. If the taxpayer elects the application of this paragraph, such portion of the passive activity credit of such taxpayer shall not be allowed for any taxable year.

(10) Coordination with section 280A.—If a passive activity involves the use of a dwelling unit to which section 280A(c)(5) applies for any taxable year, any income, deduction, gain, or loss allocable to such use shall not be taken into account for purposes of this section for such taxable year.

(11) Aggregation of members of affiliated groups.—Except as provided in regulations, all members of an affiliated group which files a consolidated return shall be treated as 1 corporation.

(12) Special rule for distributions by estates or trusts.—If any interest in a passive activity is distributed by an estate or trust—

(A) the basis of such interest immediately before such distribution shall be increased by the amount of any passive activity losses allocable to such interest, and

(B) such losses shall not be allowable as a deduction for any taxable year.

(k) Separate application of section in case of publicly traded partnerships.—

(1) In general.—This section shall be applied separately with respect to items attributable to each publicly traded partnership (and subsection (i) shall not apply with respect to items attributable to any such partnership). The preceding sentence shall not apply to any credit determined under section 42, or any rehabilitation credit determined under section 47, attributable to a publicly traded partnership to the extent the amount of any such credits exceeds the regular tax liability attributable to income from such partnership.

(2) Publicly traded partnership.—For purposes of this section, the term "publicly traded partnership" means any partnership if—

(A) interests in such partnership are traded on an established securities market, or

(B) interests in such partnership are readily tradable on a secondary market (or the substantial equivalent thereof).

(3) Coordination with subsection (g).—For purposes of subsection (g), a taxpayer shall not be treated as having disposed of his entire interest in an activity of a publicly traded partnership until he disposes of his entire interest in such partnership.

(4) Application to regulated investment companies.—For purposes of this section, a regulated investment company (as defined in section 851) holding an interest in a qualified publicly traded partnership (as defined in section 851(h)) shall be treated as a taxpayer described in subsection (a)(2) with respect to items attributable to such interest.

(*l*) Regulations.—The Secretary shall prescribe such regulations as may be necessary or appropriate to carry out provisions of this section, including regulations—

(1) which specify what constitutes an activity, material participation, or active participation for purposes of this section,

(2) which provide that certain items of gross income will not be taken into account in determining income or loss from any activity (and the treatment of expenses allocable to such income),

(3) requiring net income or gain from a limited partnership or other passive activity to be treated as not from a passive activity,

(4) which provide for the determination of the allocation of interest expense for purposes of this section, and

(5) which deal with changes in marital status and changes between joint returns and separate returns.

(m) Phase-in of disallowance of losses and credits for interest held before date of enactment.—

(1) In general.—In the case of any passive activity loss or passive activity credit for any taxable year beginning in calendar years 1987 through 1990, subsection (a) shall not apply to the applicable percentage of that portion of such loss (or such credit) which is attributable to pre-enactment interests.

(2) Applicable percentage.—For purposes of this subsection, the applicable percentage shall be determined in accordance with the following table:

In the case of taxable years beginning in:	The applicable percentage is:
1987	65
1988	40
1989	20
1990	10.

(3) Portion of loss or credit attributable to pre-enactment interests.—For purposes of this subsection—

(A) In general.—The portion of the passive activity loss (or passive activity credit) for any taxable year which is attributable to pre-enactment interests is the lesser of—

(i) the amount of the passive activity loss (or passive activity credit) which is disallowed for the taxable year under subsection (a) (without regard to this subsection), or

(ii) the amount of the passive activity loss (or passive activity credit) which would be disallowed for the taxable year (without regard to this subsection and without regard to any amount allocable to an activity for the taxable year under subsection (b)) taking into account only pre-enactment interests.

(B) Pre-enactment interest.—

(i) In general.—The term "pre-enactment interest" means any interest in a passive activity held by a taxpayer on the date of the enactment of the Tax Reform Act of 1986, and at all times thereafter.

(ii) Binding contract exception.—For purposes of clause (i), any interest acquired after such date of enactment pursuant to a written binding contract in effect on such date, and at all times thereafter, shall be treated as held on such date.

(iii) Interest in activities.—The term "pre-enactment interest" shall not include an interest in a passive activity unless such activity was being conducted on such date of enactment. The preceding sentence shall not apply to an activity commencing after such date if—

(I) the property used in such activity is acquired pursuant to a written binding contract in effect on August 16, 1986, and at all times thereafter, or

(II) construction of property used in such activity began on or before August 16, 1986.

§ 528. Certain Homeowners Associations

(a) General rule.—A homeowners association (as defined in subsection (c)) shall be subject to taxation under this subtitle only to the extent provided in this section. A homeowners association shall be considered an organization exempt from income taxes for the purpose of any law which refers to organizations exempt from income taxes.

(b) Tax imposed.—A tax is hereby imposed for each taxable year on the homeowners association taxable income of every homeowners association. Such tax shall be equal to 30 percent of the homeowners association taxable income (32 percent of such income in the case of a timeshare association).

(c) Homeowners association defined.—For purposes of this section—

(1) Homeowners association.—The term "homeowners association" means an organization which is a condominium management association, a residential real estate management association, or a timeshare association if—

(A) such organization is organized and operated to provide for the acquisition, construction, management, maintenance, and care of association property,

(B) 60 percent or more of the gross income of such organization for the taxable year consists solely of amounts received as membership dues, fees, or assessments from—

(i) owners of residential units in the case of a condominium management association,

(ii) owners of residences or residential lots in the case of a residential real estate management association, or

(iii) owners of timeshare rights to use, or timeshare ownership interests in, association property in the case of a timeshare association,

(C) 90 percent or more of the expenditures of the organization for the taxable year are expenditures for the acquisition, construction, management, maintenance, and care of association property and, in the case of a timeshare association, for activities provided to or on behalf of members of the association,

(D) no part of the net earnings of such organization inures (other than by acquiring, constructing, or providing management, maintenance, and care of association property, and other than by a rebate of excess membership dues, fees, or assessments) to the benefit of any private shareholder or individual, and

(E) such organization elects (at such time and in such manner as the Secretary by regulations prescribes) to have this section apply for the taxable year.

(2) Condominium management association.—The term "condominium management association" means any organization meeting the requirement of subparagraph (A) of paragraph (1) with respect to a condominium project substantially all of the units of which are used by individuals for residences.

(3) Residential real estate management association.—The term "residential real estate management association" means any organization meeting the requirements of subparagraph (A) of paragraph (1) with respect to a subdivision, development, or similar area substantially all the lots or buildings of which may only be used by individuals for residences.

(4) Timeshare association.—The term "timeshare association" means any organization (other than a condominium management association) meeting the requirement of subparagraph (A) of paragraph (1) if any member thereof holds a timeshare right to use, or a timeshare ownership interest in, real property constituting association property.

(5) Association property.—The term "association property" means—

(A) property held by the organization,

(B) property commonly held by the members of the organization,

(C) property within the organization privately held by the members of the organization, and

(D) property owned by a governmental unit and used for the benefit of residents of such unit.

In the case of a timeshare association, such term includes property in which the timeshare association, or members of the association, have rights arising out of recorded easements, covenants, or other recorded instruments to use property related to the timeshare project.

(d) Homeowners association taxable income defined.—

(1) Taxable income defined.—For purposes of this section, the homeowners association taxable income of any organization for any taxable year is an amount equal to the excess (if any) of—

(A) the gross income for the taxable year (excluding any exempt function income), over

(B) the deductions allowed by this chapter which are directly connected with the production of the gross income (excluding exempt function income), computed with the modifications provided in paragraph (2).

(2) Modifications.—For purposes of this subsection—

(A) there shall be allowed a specific deduction of $100,

(B) no net operating loss deduction shall be allowed under section 172, and

(C) no deduction shall be allowed under part VIII of subchapter B (relating to special deductions for corporations).

(3) Exempt function income.—For purposes of this subsection, the term "exempt function income" means any amount received as membership dues, fees, or assessments from—

(A) owners of condominium housing units in the case of a condominium management association,

(B) owners of real property in the case of a residential real estate management association, or

(C) owners of timeshare rights to use, or timeshare ownership interests in, real property in the case of a timeshare association.

§ 1001. Determination of Amount of and Recognition of Gain or Loss

(a) Computation of gain or loss.—The gain from the sale or other disposition of property shall be the excess of the amount realized therefrom over the adjusted basis provided in section 1011 for determining gain, and the loss shall be the excess of the adjusted basis provided in such section for determining loss over the amount realized.

(b) Amount realized.—The amount realized from the sale or other disposition of property shall be the sum of any money received plus the fair market value of the property (other than money) received. In determining the amount realized—

(1) there shall not be taken into account any amount received as reimbursement for real property taxes which are treated under section 164(d) as imposed on the purchaser, and

(2) there shall be taken into account amounts representing real property taxes which are treated under section 164(d) as imposed on the taxpayer if such taxes are to be paid by the purchaser.

(c) Recognition of gain or loss.—Except as otherwise provided in this subtitle, the entire amount of the gain or loss, determined under this section, on the sale or exchange of property shall be recognized.

(d) Installment sales.—Nothing in this section shall be construed to prevent (in the case of property sold under contract providing for payment in installments) the taxation of that portion of any installment payment representing gain or profit in the year in which such payment is received.

(e) Certain term interests.—

(1) In general.—In determining gain or loss from the sale or other disposition of a term interest in property, that portion of the adjusted basis of such interest which is determined pursuant to section 1014, 1015, or 1041 (to the extent that such adjusted basis is a portion of the entire adjusted basis of the property) shall be disregarded.

(2) Term interest in property defined.—For purposes of paragraph (1), the term "term interest in property" means—

(A) a life interest in property,

(B) an interest in property for a term of years, or

(C) an income interest in a trust.

(3) Exception.—Paragraph (1) shall not apply to a sale or other disposition which is a part of a transaction in which the entire interest in property is transferred to any person or persons.

[(f) Repealed. Pub.L. 103–66, Title XIII, § 13213(a)(2)(E), Aug. 10, 1993, 107 Stat. 474]

§ 1011. Adjusted Basis for Determining Gain or Loss

(a) General rule.—The adjusted basis for determining the gain or loss from the sale or other disposition of property, whenever acquired, shall be the basis (determined under section 1012 or other applicable sections of this subchapter or subchapters C (relating to corporate distributions and adjustments), K (relating to partners and partnerships), and P (relating to capital gains and losses)), adjusted as provided in section 1016.

(b) Bargain sale to a charitable organization.—If a deduction is allowable under section 170 (relating to charitable contributions) by reason of a sale, then the adjusted basis for determining the gain from such sale shall be that portion of the adjusted basis which bears the same ratio to the adjusted basis as the amount realized bears to the fair market value of the property.

§ 1012. Basis of Property—Cost

The basis of property shall be the cost of such property, except as otherwise provided in this subchapter and subchapters C (relating to corporate distributions and adjustments), K (relating to partners and partnerships), and P (relating to capital gains and losses). The cost of real property shall not include any amount in respect of real property taxes which are treated under section 164(d) as imposed on the taxpayer.

§ 1019. Property on Which Lessee Has Made Improvements

Neither the basis nor the adjusted basis of any portion of real property shall, in the case of the lessor of such property, be increased or diminished on account of income derived by the lessor in respect of such property and excludable from gross income under section 109 (relating to improvements by lessee on lessor's property). If an amount representing any part of the value of real property attributable to buildings erected or other improvements made by a lessee in respect of such property was included in gross income of the lessor for any taxable year beginning before January 1, 1942, the basis of each portion of such property shall be properly adjusted for the amount so included in gross income.

§ 1031. Exchange of Property Held for Productive Use or Investment

(a) Nonrecognition of gain or loss from exchanges solely in kind.—

(1) In general.—No gain or loss shall be recognized on the exchange of property held for productive use in a trade or business or for investment if such property is exchanged solely for property of like kind which is to be held either for productive use in a trade or business or for investment.

(2) Exception.—This subsection shall not apply to any exchange of—

(A) stock in trade or other property held primarily for sale,

(B) stocks, bonds, or notes,

(C) other securities or evidences of indebtedness or interest,

(D) interests in a partnership,

(E) certificates of trust or beneficial interests, or

(F) choses in action.

For purposes of this section, an interest in a partnership which has in effect a valid election under section 761(a) to be excluded from the application of all of subchapter K shall be treated as an interest in each of the assets of such partnership and not as an interest in a partnership.

(3) Requirement that property be identified and that exchange be completed not more than 180 days after transfer of exchanged property.—**For purposes of** this subsection, any property received by the taxpayer shall be treated as property which is not like-kind property if—

(A) such property is not identified as property to be received in the exchange on or before the day which is 45 days after the date on which the taxpayer transfers the property relinquished in the exchange, or

(B) such property is received after the earlier of—

(i) the day which is 180 days after the date on which the taxpayer transfers the property relinquished in the exchange, or

(ii) the due date (determined with regard to extension) for the transferor's return of the tax imposed by this chapter for the taxable year in which the transfer of the relinquished property occurs.

(b) Gain from exchanges not solely in kind.—If an exchange would be within the provisions of subsection (a), of section 1035(a), of section 1036(a), or of section 1037(a), if it were not for the fact that the property received in exchange consists not only of property permitted by such provisions to be received without the recognition of gain, but also of other property or money, then the gain, if any, to the recipient shall be recognized, but in an amount not in excess of the sum of such money and the fair market value of such other property.

(c) Loss from exchanges not solely in kind.—If an exchange would be within the provisions of subsection (a), of section 1035(a), of section 1036(a), or of section 1037(a), if it were not for the fact that the property received in exchange consists not only of property permitted by such provisions to be received without the recognition of gain or loss, but also of other property or money, then no loss from the exchange shall be recognized.

(**d**) **Basis.**—If property was acquired on an exchange described in this section, section 1035(a), section 1036(a), or section 1037(a), then the basis shall be the same as that of the property exchanged, decreased in the amount of any money received by the taxpayer and increased in the amount of gain or decreased in the amount of loss to the taxpayer that was recognized on such exchange. If the property so acquired consisted in part of the type of property permitted by this section, section 1035(a), section 1036(a), or section 1037(a), to be received without the recognition of gain or loss, and in part of other property, the basis provided in this subsection shall be allocated between the properties (other than money) received, and for the purpose of the allocation there shall be assigned to such other property an amount equivalent to its fair market value at the date of the exchange. For purposes of this section, section 1035(a), and section 1036(a), where as part of the consideration to the taxpayer another party to the exchange assumed (as determined under section 357(d)) a liability of the taxpayer, such assumption shall be considered as money received by the taxpayer on the exchange.

(**e**) **Exchanges of livestock of different sexes.**—For purposes of this section, livestock of different sexes are not property of a like kind.

(**f**) **Special rules for exchanges between related persons.**—

(**1**) **In general.**—If—

(**A**) a taxpayer exchanges property with a related person,

(**B**) there is nonrecognition of gain or loss to the taxpayer under this section with respect to the exchange of such property (determined without regard to this subsection), and

(**C**) before the date 2 years after the date of the last transfer which was part of such exchange—

(**i**) the related person disposes of such property, or

(**ii**) the taxpayer disposes of the property received in the exchange from the related person which was of like kind to the property transferred by the taxpayer, there shall be no nonrecognition of gain or loss under this section to the taxpayer with respect to such exchange; except that any gain or loss recognized by the taxpayer by reason of this subsection shall be taken into account as of the date on which the disposition referred to in subparagraph (C) occurs.

(**2**) **Certain dispositions not taken into account.**—For purposes of paragraph (1)(C), there shall not be taken into account any disposition—

(**A**) after the earlier of the death of the taxpayer or the death of the related person,

(**B**) in a compulsory or involuntary conversion (within the meaning of section 1033) if the exchange occurred before the threat or imminence of such conversion, or

(**C**) with respect to which it is established to the satisfaction of the Secretary that neither the exchange nor such disposition had as one of its principal purposes the avoidance of Federal income tax.

(**3**) **Related person.**—For purposes of this subsection, the term "related person" means any person bearing a relationship to the taxpayer described in section 267(b) or 707(b)(1).

(**4**) **Treatment of certain transactions.**—This section shall not apply to any exchange which is part of a transaction (or series of transactions) structured to avoid the purposes of this subsection.

(g) Special rule where substantial diminution of risk.—

(1) In general.—If paragraph (2) applies to any property for any period, the running of the period set forth in subsection (f)(1)(C) with respect to such property shall be suspended during such period.

(2) Property to which subsection applies.—This paragraph shall apply to any property for any period during which the holder's risk of loss with respect to the property is substantially diminished by—

(A) the holding of a put with respect to such property,

(B) the holding by another person of a right to acquire such property, or

(C) a short sale or any other transaction.

(h) Special rules for foreign real and personal property.—For purposes of this section-

(1) Real property.—Real property located in the United States and real property located outside the United States are not property of a like kind.

(2) Personal property.—

(A) In general.—Personal property used predominantly within the United States and personal property used predominantly outside the United States are not property of a like kind.

(B) Predominant use.—Except as provided in subparagraphs (C) and (D), the predominant use of any property shall be determined based on—

(i) in the case of the property relinquished in the exchange, the 2–year period ending on the date of such relinquishment, and

(ii) in the case of the property acquired in the exchange, the 2–year period beginning on the date of such acquisition.

(C) Property held for less than 2 years.—Except in the case of an exchange which is part of a transaction (or series of transactions) structured to avoid the purposes of this subsection—

(i) only the periods the property was held by the person relinquishing the property (or any related person) shall be taken into account under subparagraph (B)(i), and

(ii) only the periods the property was held by the person acquiring the property (or any related person) shall be taken into account under subparagraph (B)(ii).

(D) Special rule for certain property.—Property described in any subparagraph of section 168(g)(4) shall be treated as used predominantly in the United States.

(i) Special rules for mutual ditch, reservoir, or irrigation company stock—For purposes of subsection (a)(2)(B), the term "stocks" shall not include shares in a mutual ditch, reservoir, or irrigation company if at the time of the exchange—

(1) the mutual ditch, reservoir, or irrigation company is an organization described in section 501(c)(12)(A) (determined without regard to the percentage of its income that is collected from its members for the purpose of meeting losses and expenses), and

148

(2) the shares in such company have been recognized by the highest court of the State in which such company was organized or by applicable State statute as constituting or representing real property or an interest in real property.

§ 1221. Capital Asset Defined

(a) In general.—For purposes of this subtitle, the term "capital asset" means property held by the taxpayer (whether or not connected with his trade or business), but does not include—

(1) stock in trade of the taxpayer or other property of a kind which would properly be included in the inventory of the taxpayer if on hand at the close of the taxable year, or property held by the taxpayer primarily for sale to customers in the ordinary course of his trade or business;

(2) property, used in his trade or business, of a character which is subject to the allowance for depreciation provided in section 167, or real property used in his trade or business;

(3) a copyright, a literary, musical, or artistic composition, a letter or memorandum, or similar property, held by—

    (A) a taxpayer whose personal efforts created such property,

    (B) in the case of a letter, memorandum, or similar property, a taxpayer for whom such property was prepared or produced, or

    (C) a taxpayer in whose hands the basis of such property is determined, for purposes of determining gain from a sale or exchange, in whole or part by reference to the basis of such property in the hands of a taxpayer described in subparagraph (A) or (B);

(4) accounts or notes receivable acquired in the ordinary course of trade or business for services rendered or from the sale of property described in paragraph (1);

(5) a publication of the United States Government (including the Congressional Record) which is received from the United States Government or any agency thereof, other than by purchase at the price at which it is offered for sale to the public, and which is held by—

    (A) a taxpayer who so received such publication, or

    (B) a taxpayer in whose hands the basis of such publication is determined, for purposes of determining gain from a sale or exchange, in whole or in part by reference to the basis of such publication in the hands of a taxpayer described in subparagraph (A);

(6) any commodities derivative financial instrument held by a commodities derivatives dealer, unless—

    (A) it is established to the satisfaction of the Secretary that such instrument has no connection to the activities of such dealer as a dealer, and

    (B) such instrument is clearly identified in such dealer's records as being described in subparagraph (A) before the close of the day on which it was acquired, originated, or entered into (or such other time as the Secretary may by regulations prescribe);

(7) any hedging transaction which is clearly identified as such before the close of the day on which it was acquired, originated, or entered into (or such other time as the Secretary may by regulations prescribe); or

(8) supplies of a type regularly used or consumed by the taxpayer in the ordinary course of a trade or business of the taxpayer.

(b) Definitions and special rules.—

(1) Commodities derivative financial instruments.—For purposes of subsection (a)(6)—

(A) Commodities derivatives dealer.—The term "commodities derivatives dealer" means a person which regularly offers to enter into, assume, offset, assign, or terminate positions in commodities derivative financial instruments with customers in the ordinary course of a trade or business.

(B) Commodities derivative financial instrument.—

(i) In general.—The term "commodities derivative financial instrument" means any contract or financial instrument with respect to commodities (other than a share of stock in a corporation, a beneficial interest in a partnership or trust, a note, bond, debenture, or other evidence of indebtedness, or a section 1256 contract (as defined in section 1256(b))), the value or settlement price of which is calculated by or determined by reference to a specified index.

(ii) Specified index.—The term "specified index" means any one or more or any combination of—

(I) a fixed rate, price, or amount, or

(II) a variable rate, price, or amount, which is based on any current, objectively determinable financial or economic information with respect to commodities which is not within the control of any of the parties to the contract or instrument and is not unique to any of the parties' circumstances.

(2) Hedging transaction.—

(A) In general.—For purposes of this section, the term "hedging transaction" means any transaction entered into by the taxpayer in the normal course of the taxpayer's trade or business primarily—

(i) to manage risk of price changes or currency fluctuations with respect to ordinary property which is held or to be held by the taxpayer,

(ii) to manage risk of interest rate or price changes or currency fluctuations with respect to borrowings made or to be made, or ordinary obligations incurred or to be incurred, by the taxpayer, or

(iii) to manage such other risks as the Secretary may prescribe in regulations.

(B) Treatment of nonidentification or improper identification of hedging transactions.—**Notwithstanding subsection (a)(7), the Secretary shall** prescribe regulations to properly characterize any income, gain, expense, or loss arising from a transaction—

(i) which is a hedging transaction but which was not identified as such in accordance with subsection (a)(7), or

(ii) which was so identified but is not a hedging transaction.

150

(3) Sale or exchange of self-created musical works.—At the election of the taxpayer, paragraphs (1) and (3) of subsection (a) shall not apply to musical compositions or copyrights in musical works sold or exchanged by a taxpayer described in subsection (a)(3).

(4) Regulations.—The Secretary shall prescribe such regulations as are appropriate to carry out the purposes of paragraph (6) and (7) of subsection (a) in the case of transactions involving related parties.

§ 1231. Property Used in the Trade or Business and Involuntary Conversions

(a) General rule.—

(1) Gains exceed losses.—If—

(A) the section 1231 gains for any taxable year, exceed

(B) the section 1231 losses for such taxable year, such gains and losses shall be treated as long-term capital gains or long-term capital losses, as the case may be.

(2) Gains do not exceed losses.—If—

(A) the section 1231 gains for any taxable year, do not exceed

(B) the section 1231 losses for such taxable year, such gains and losses shall not be treated as gains and losses from sales or exchanges of capital assets.

(3) Section 1231 gains and losses.—For purposes of this subsection—

(A) Section 1231 gain.—The term "section 1231 gain" means—

(i) any recognized gain on the sale or exchange of property used in the trade or business, and

(ii) any recognized gain from the compulsory or involuntary conversion (as a result of destruction in whole or in part, theft or seizure, or an exercise of the power of requisition or condemnation or the threat or imminence thereof) into other property or money of—

(I) property used in the trade or business, or

(II) any capital asset which is held for more than 1 year and is held in connection with a trade or business or a transaction entered into for profit.

(B) Section 1231 loss.—The term "section 1231 loss" means any recognized loss from a sale or exchange or conversion described in subparagraph (A).

(4) Special rules.—For purposes of this subsection—

(A) In determining under this subsection whether gains exceed losses—

(i) the section 1231 gains shall be included only if and to the extent taken into account in computing gross income, and

(ii) the section 1231 losses shall be included only if and to the extent taken into account in computing taxable income, except that section 1211 shall not apply.

(B) Losses (including losses not compensated for by insurance or otherwise) on the destruction, in whole or in part, theft or seizure, or requisition or condemnation of—

(i) property used in the trade or business, or

(ii) capital assets which are held for more than 1 year and are held in connection with a trade or business or a transaction entered into for profit, shall be treated as losses from a compulsory or involuntary conversion.

(C) In the case of any involuntary conversion (subject to the provisions of this subsection but for this sentence) arising from fire, storm, shipwreck, or other casualty, or from theft, of any—

(i) property used in the trade or business, or

(ii) any capital asset which is held for more than 1 year and is held in connection with a trade or business or a transaction entered into for profit, this subsection shall not apply to such conversion (whether resulting in gain or loss) if during the taxable year the recognized losses from such conversions exceed the recognized gains from such conversions.

(b) Definition of property used in the trade or business.—For purposes of this section—

(1) General rule.—The term "property used in the trade or business" means property used in the trade or business, of a character which is subject to the allowance for depreciation provided in section 167, held for more than 1 year, and real property used in the trade or business, held for more than 1 year, which is not—

(A) property of a kind which would properly be includible in the inventory of the taxpayer if on hand at the close of the taxable year,

(B) property held by the taxpayer primarily for sale to customers in the ordinary course of his trade or business,

(C) a copyright, a literary, musical, or artistic composition, a letter or memorandum, or similar property, held by a taxpayer described in paragraph (3) of section 1221(a), or

(D) a publication of the United States Government (including the Congressional Record) which is received from the United States Government, or any agency thereof, other than by purchase at the price at which it is offered for sale to the public, and which is held by a taxpayer described in paragraph (5) of section 1221(a).

(2) Timber, coal, or domestic iron ore.—Such term includes timber, coal, and iron ore with respect to which section 631 applies.

(3) Livestock.—Such term includes—

(A) cattle and horses, regardless of age, held by the taxpayer for draft, breeding, dairy, or sporting purposes, and held by him for 24 months or more from the date of acquisition, and

(B) other livestock, regardless of age, held by the taxpayer for draft, breeding, dairy, or sporting purposes, and held by him for 12 months or more from the date of acquisition.

Such term does not include poultry.

(4) Unharvested crop.—In the case of an unharvested crop on land used in the trade or business and held for more than 1 year, if the crop and the land are sold or exchanged (or compulsorily or involuntarily converted) at the same time and to the same person, the crop shall be considered as "property used in the trade or business."

(c) Recapture of net ordinary losses.—

(1) In general.—The net section 1231 gain for any taxable year shall be treated as ordinary income to the extent such gain does not exceed the non-recaptured net section 1231 losses.

(2) Non-recaptured net section 1231 losses.—For purposes of this subsection, the term "non-recaptured net section 1231 losses" means the excess of—

(A) the aggregate amount of the net section 1231 losses for the 5 most recent preceding taxable years beginning after December 31, 1981, over

(B) the portion of such losses taken into account under paragraph (1) for such preceding taxable years.

(3) Net section 1231 gain.—For purposes of this subsection, the term "net section 1231 gain" means the excess of—

(A) the section 1231 gains, over

(B) the section 1231 losses.

(4) Net section 1231 loss.—For purposes of this subsection, the term "net section 1231 loss" means the excess of—

(A) the section 1231 losses, over

(B) the section 1231 gains.

(5) Special rules.—For purposes of determining the amount of the net section 1231 gain or loss for any taxable year, the rules of paragraph (4) of subsection (a) shall apply.

§ 1237. Real Property Subdivided for Sale

(a) General.—Any lot or parcel which is part of a tract of real property in the hands of a taxpayer other than a C corporation shall not be deemed to be held primarily for sale to customers in the ordinary course of trade or business at the time of sale solely because of the taxpayer having subdivided such tract for purposes of sale or because of any activity incident to such subdivision or sale, if—

(1) such tract, or any lot or parcel thereof, had not previously been held by such taxpayer primarily for sale to customers in the ordinary course of trade or business (unless such tract at such previous time would have been covered by this section) and, in the same taxable year in which the sale occurs, such taxpayer does not so hold any other real property; and

(2) no substantial improvement that substantially enhances the value of the lot or parcel sold is made by the taxpayer on such tract while held by the taxpayer or is made pursuant to a contract of sale entered into between the taxpayer and the buyer. For purposes of this paragraph, an improvement shall be deemed to be made by the taxpayer if such improvement was made by—

(A) the taxpayer or members of his family (as defined in section 267(c)(4)), by a corporation controlled by the taxpayer an S corporation which included the taxpayer as a shareholder, or by a partnership which included the taxpayer as a partner; or

(B) a lessee, but only if the improvement constitutes income to the taxpayer; or

(C) Federal, State, or local government, or political subdivision thereof, but only if the improvement constitutes an addition to basis for the taxpayer; and

(3) such lot or parcel, except in the case of real property acquired by inheritance or devise, is held by the taxpayer for a period of 5 years.

(b) Special rules for application of section.—

(1) Gains.—If more than 5 lots or parcels contained in the same tract of real property are sold or exchanged, gain from any sale or exchange (which occurs in or after the taxable year in which the sixth lot or parcel is sold or exchanged) of any lot or parcel which comes within the provisions of paragraphs (1), (2) and (3) of subsection (a) of this section shall be deemed to be gain from the sale of property held primarily for sale to customers in the ordinary course of the trade or business to the extent of 5 percent of the selling price.

(2) Expenditures of sale.—For the purpose of computing gain under paragraph (1) of this subsection, expenditures incurred in connection with the sale or exchange of any lot or parcel shall neither be allowed as a deduction in computing taxable income, nor treated as reducing the amount realized on such sale or exchange; but so much of such expenditures as does not exceed the portion of gain deemed under paragraph (1) of this subsection to be gain from the sale of property held primarily for sale to customers in the ordinary course of trade or business shall be so allowed as a deduction, and the remainder, if any, shall be treated as reducing the amount realized on such sale or exchange.

(3) Necessary improvements.—No improvement shall be deemed a substantial improvement for purposes of subsection (a) if the lot or parcel is held by the taxpayer for a period of 10 years and if—

(A) such improvement is the building or installation of water, sewer, or drainage facilities or roads (if such improvement would except for this paragraph constitute a substantial improvement);

(B) it is shown to the satisfaction of the Secretary that the lot or parcel, the value of which was substantially enhanced by such improvement, would not have been marketable at the prevailing local price for similar building sites without such improvements; and

(C) the taxpayer elects, in accordance with regulations prescribed by the Secretary, to make no adjustment to basis of the lot or parcel, or of any other property owned by the taxpayer, on account of the expenditures for such improvements. Such election shall not make any item deductible which would not otherwise be deductible.

(c) Tract defined.—For purposes of this section, the term "tract of real property" means a single piece of real property, except that 2 or more pieces of real property shall be considered a tract if at any time they were contiguous in the hands of the taxpayer or if they would be contiguous except for the interposition of a road, street, railroad, stream, or similar property. If, following the sale or exchange of any lot or parcel from a tract of real property, no further sales or exchanges of any other lots or parcels from the remainder of such tract are made for a period of 5 years, such remainder shall be deemed a tract.

10. BANKRUPTCY CODE

11 U.S.C.A.

§ 361. Adequate protection

When adequate protection is required under section 362, 363, or 364 of this title of an interest of an entity in property, such adequate protection may be provided by—

(1) requiring the trustee to make a cash payment or periodic cash payments to such entity, to the extent that the stay under section 362 of this title, use, sale, or lease under section 363 of this title, or any grant of a lien under section 364 of this title results in a decrease in the value of such entity's interest in such property;

(2) providing to such entity an additional or replacement lien to the extent that such stay, use, sale, lease, or grant results in a decrease in the value of such entity's interest in such property; or

(3) granting such other relief, other than entitling such entity to compensation allowable under section 503(b)(1) of this title as an administrative expense, as will result in the realization by such entity of the indubitable equivalent of such entity's interest in such property.

§ 362. Automatic stay

(a) Except as provided in subsection (b) of this section, a petition filed under section 301, 302, or 303 of this title, or an application filed under section 5(a)(3) of the Securities Investor Protection Act of 1970, operates as a stay, applicable to all entities, of—

(1) the commencement or continuation, including the issuance or employment of process, of a judicial, administrative, or other action or proceeding against the debtor that was or could have been commenced before the commencement of the case under this title, or to recover a claim against the debtor that arose before the commencement of the case under this title;

(2) the enforcement, against the debtor or against property of the estate, of a judgment obtained before the commencement of the case under this title;

(3) any act to obtain possession of property of the estate or of property from the estate or to exercise control over property of the estate;

(4) any act to create, perfect, or enforce any lien against property of the estate;

(5) any act to create, perfect, or enforce against property of the debtor any lien to the extent that such lien secures a claim that arose before the commencement of the case under this title;

(6) any act to collect, assess, or recover a claim against the debtor that arose before the commencement of the case under this title;

(7) the setoff of any debt owing to the debtor that arose before the commencement of the case under this title against any claim against the debtor; and

(8) the commencement or continuation of a proceeding before the United States Tax Court concerning a corporate debtor's tax liability for a taxable period the bankruptcy court may determine or concerning the tax liability of a debtor who is an individual for a taxable period ending before the date of the order for relief under this title.

(b) The filing of a petition under section 301, 302, or 303 of this title, or of an application under section 5(a)(3) of the Securities Investor Protection Act of 1970, does not operate as a stay—

(1) under subsection (a) of this section, of the commencement or continuation of a criminal action or proceeding against the debtor;

(2) under subsection (a)—

(A) of the commencement or continuation of a civil action or proceeding—

(i) for the establishment of paternity;

(ii) for the establishment or modification of an order for domestic support obligations;

(iii) concerning child custody or visitation;

(iv) for the dissolution of a marriage, except to the extent that such proceeding seeks to determine the division of property that is property of the estate; or

(v) regarding domestic violence;

(B) of the collection of a domestic support obligation from property that is not property of the estate;

(C) with respect to the withholding of income that is property of the estate or property of the debtor for payment of a domestic support obligation under a judicial or administrative order or a statute;

(D) of the withholding, suspension, or restriction of a driver's license, a professional or occupational license, or a recreational license, under State law, as specified in section 466(a)(16) of the Social Security Act;

(E) of the reporting of overdue support owed by a parent to any consumer reporting agency as specified in section 466(a)(7) of the Social Security Act;

(F) of the interception of a tax refund, as specified in sections 464 and 466(a)(3) of the Social Security Act or under an analogous State law; or

(G) of the enforcement of a medical obligation, as specified under title IV of the Social Security Act;

(3) under subsection (a) of this section, of any act to perfect, or to maintain or continue the perfection of, an interest in property to the extent that the trustee's rights and powers are subject to such perfection under section 546(b) of this title or to the extent that such act is accomplished within the period provided under section 547(e)(2)(A) of this title;

(4) under paragraph (1), (2), (3), or (6) of subsection (a) of this section, of the commencement or continuation of an action or proceeding by a governmental unit or any organization exercising authority under the Convention on the Prohibition of the Development, Production, Stockpiling and Use of Chemical Weapons and on Their Destruction, opened for signature on January 13, 1993, to enforce such governmental unit's or organization's police and regulatory power, including the enforcement of a judgment other than a money

156

judgment, obtained in an action or proceeding by the governmental unit to enforce such governmental unit's or organization's police or regulatory power;

[(5) Repealed. Pub.L. 105–277, Div. I, Title VI, § 603(1), Oct. 21, 1998, 112 Stat. 2681–886]

(6) under subsection (a) of this section, of the exercise by a commodity broker, forward contract merchant, stockbroker, financial institution, financial participant, or securities clearing agency of any contractual right (as defined in section 555 or 556) under any security agreement or arrangement or other credit enhancement forming a part of or related to any commodity contract, forward contract or securities contract, or of any contractual right (as defined in section 555 or 556) to offset or net out any termination value, payment amount, or other transfer obligation arising under or in connection with 1 or more such contracts, including any master agreement for such contracts;

(7) under subsection (a) of this section, of the exercise by a repo participant or financial participant of any contractual right (as defined in section 559) under any security agreement or arrangement or other credit enhancement forming a part of or related to any repurchase agreement, or of any contractual right (as defined in section 559) to offset or net out any termination value, payment amount, or other transfer obligation arising under or in connection with 1 or more such agreements, including any master agreement for such agreements;

(8) under subsection (a) of this section, of the commencement of any action by the Secretary of Housing and Urban Development to foreclose a mortgage or deed of trust in any case in which the mortgage or deed of trust held by the Secretary is insured or was formerly insured under the National Housing Act and covers property, or combinations of property, consisting of five or more living units;

(9) under subsection (a), of—

(A) an audit by a governmental unit to determine tax liability;

(B) the issuance to the debtor by a governmental unit of a notice of tax deficiency;

(C) a demand for tax returns; or

(D) the making of an assessment for any tax and issuance of a notice and demand for payment of such an assessment (but any tax lien that would otherwise attach to property of the estate by reason of such an assessment shall not take effect unless such tax is a debt of the debtor that will not be discharged in the case and such property or its proceeds are transferred out of the estate to, or otherwise revested in, the debtor).

(10) under subsection (a) of this section, of any act by a lessor to the debtor under a lease of nonresidential real property that has terminated by the expiration of the stated term of the lease before the commencement of or during a case under this title to obtain possession of such property;

(11) under subsection (a) of this section, of the presentment of a negotiable instrument and the giving of notice of and protesting dishonor of such an instrument;

(12) under subsection (a) of this section, after the date which is 90 days after the filing of such petition, of the commencement or continuation, and conclusion to the entry of final judgment, of an action which involves a debtor subject to reorganization pursuant to chapter 11 of this title and which was brought by the Secretary of Transportation under section

157

31325 of title 46 (including distribution of any proceeds of sale) to foreclose a preferred ship or fleet mortgage, or a security interest in or relating to a vessel or vessel under construction, held by the Secretary of Transportation under chapter 537 of title 46 or section 109(h) of title 49, or under applicable State law;

(13) under subsection (a) of this section, after the date which is 90 days after the filing of such petition, of the commencement or continuation, and conclusion to the entry of final judgment, of an action which involves a debtor subject to reorganization pursuant to chapter 11 of this title and which was brought by the Secretary of Commerce under section 31325 of title 46 (including distribution of any proceeds of sale) to foreclose a preferred ship or fleet mortgage in a vessel or a mortgage, deed of trust, or other security interest in a fishing facility held by the Secretary of Commerce under chapter 537 of title 46;

(14) under subsection (a) of this section, of any action by an accrediting agency regarding the accreditation status of the debtor as an educational institution;

(15) under subsection (a) of this section, of any action by a State licensing body regarding the licensure of the debtor as an educational institution;

(16) under subsection (a) of this section, of any action by a guaranty agency, as defined in section 435(j) of the Higher Education Act of 1965 or the Secretary of Education regarding the eligibility of the debtor to participate in programs authorized under such Act;

(17) under subsection (a) of this section, of the exercise by a swap participant or financial participant of any contractual right (as defined in section 560) under any security agreement or arrangement or other credit enhancement forming a part of or related to any swap agreement, or of any contractual right (as defined in section 560) to offset or net out any termination value, payment amount, or other transfer obligation arising under or in connection with 1 or more such agreements, including any master agreement for such agreements;

(18) under subsection (a) of the creation or perfection of a statutory lien for an ad valorem property tax, or a special tax or special assessment on real property whether or not ad valorem, imposed by a governmental unit, if such tax or assessment comes due after the date of the filing of the petition;

(19) under subsection (a), of withholding of income from a debtor's wages and collection of amounts withheld, under the debtor's agreement authorizing that withholding and collection for the benefit of a pension, profit-sharing, stock bonus, or other plan established under section 401, 403, 408, 408A, 414, 457, or 501(c) of the Internal Revenue Code of 1986, that is sponsored by the employer of the debtor, or an affiliate, successor, or predecessor of such employer—

(A) to the extent that the amounts withheld and collected are used solely for payments relating to a loan from a plan under section 408(b)(1) of the Employee Retirement Income Security Act of 1974 or is subject to section 72(p) of the Internal Revenue Code of 1986; or

(B) a loan from a thrift savings plan permitted under subchapter III of chapter 84 of title 5, that satisfies the requirements of section 8433(g) of such title;

but nothing in this paragraph may be construed to provide that any loan made under a governmental plan under section 414(d), or a contract or account under section 403(b), of the Internal Revenue Code of 1986 constitutes a claim or a debt under this title;

(20) under subsection (a), of any act to enforce any lien against or security interest in real property following entry of the order under subsection (d)(4) as to such real property in any prior case under this title, for a period of 2 years after the date of the entry of such an order, except that the debtor, in a subsequent case under this title, may move for relief from such order based upon changed circumstances or for other good cause shown, after notice and a hearing;

(21) under subsection (a), of any act to enforce any lien against or security interest in real property—

    (A) if the debtor is ineligible under section 109(g) to be a debtor in a case under this title; or

    (B) if the case under this title was filed in violation of a bankruptcy court order in a prior case under this title prohibiting the debtor from being a debtor in another case under this title;

(22) subject to subsection (*l*), under subsection (a)(3), of the continuation of any eviction, unlawful detainer action, or similar proceeding by a lessor against a debtor involving residential property in which the debtor resides as a tenant under a lease or rental agreement and with respect to which the lessor has obtained before the date of the filing of the bankruptcy petition, a judgment for possession of such property against the debtor;

(23) subject to subsection (m), under subsection (a)(3), of an eviction action that seeks possession of the residential property in which the debtor resides as a tenant under a lease or rental agreement based on endangerment of such property or the illegal use of controlled substances on such property, but only if the lessor files with the court, and serves upon the debtor, a certification under penalty of perjury that such an eviction action has been filed, or that the debtor, during the 30–day period preceding the date of the filing of the certification, has endangered property or illegally used or allowed to be used a controlled substance on the property;

(24) under subsection (a), of any transfer that is not avoidable under section 544 and that is not avoidable under section 549;

(25) under subsection (a), of—

    (A) the commencement or continuation of an investigation or action by a securities self regulatory organization to enforce such organization's regulatory power;

    (B) the enforcement of an order or decision, other than for monetary sanctions, obtained in an action by such securities self regulatory organization to enforce such organization's regulatory power; or

    (C) any act taken by such securities self regulatory organization to delist, delete, or refuse to permit quotation of any stock that does not meet applicable regulatory requirements;

(26) under subsection (a), of the setoff under applicable nonbankruptcy law of an income tax refund, by a governmental unit, with respect to a taxable period that ended before the date of the order for relief against an income tax liability for a taxable period that also ended before the date of the order for relief, except that in any case in which the setoff of an income tax refund is not permitted under applicable nonbankruptcy law because of a pending action to determine the amount or legality of a tax liability, the governmental unit may hold the refund pending the resolution of the action, unless the court, on the motion of

the trustee and after notice and a hearing, grants the taxing authority adequate protection (within the meaning of section 361) for the secured claim of such authority in the setoff under section 506(a);

(27) under subsection (a) of this section, of the exercise by a master netting agreement participant of any contractual right (as defined in section 555, 556, 559, or 560) under any security agreement or arrangement or other credit enhancement forming a part of or related to any master netting agreement, or of any contractual right (as defined in section 555, 556, 559, or 560) to offset or net out any termination value, payment amount, or other transfer obligation arising under or in connection with 1 or more such master netting agreements to the extent that such participant is eligible to exercise such rights under paragraph (6), (7), or (17) for each individual contract covered by the master netting agreement in issue; and

(28) under subsection (a), of the exclusion by the Secretary of Health and Human Services of the debtor from participation in the medicare program or any other Federal health care program (as defined in section 1128B(f) of the Social Security Act pursuant to title XI or XVIII of such Act).

The provisions of paragraphs (12) and (13) of this subsection shall apply with respect to any such petition filed on or before December 31, 1989.

(c) Except as provided in subsections (d), (e), (f), and (h) of this section—

(1) the stay of an act against property of the estate under subsection (a) of this section continues until such property is no longer property of the estate;

(2) the stay of any other act under subsection (a) of this section continues until the earliest of—

(A) the time the case is closed;

(B) the time the case is dismissed; or

(C) if the case is a case under chapter 7 of this title concerning an individual or a case under chapter 9, 11, 12, or 13 of this title, the time a discharge is granted or denied;

(3) if a single or joint case is filed by or against debtor who is an individual in a case under chapter 7, 11, or 13, and if a single or joint case of the debtor was pending within the preceding 1–year period but was dismissed, other than a case refiled under a chapter other than chapter 7 after dismissal under section 707(b)—

(A) the stay under subsection (a) with respect to any action taken with respect to a debt or property securing such debt or with respect to any lease shall terminate with respect to the debtor on the 30th day after the filing of the later case;

(B) on the motion of a party in interest for continuation of the automatic stay and upon notice and a hearing, the court may extend the stay in particular cases as to any or all creditors (subject to such conditions or limitations as the court may then impose) after notice and a hearing completed before the expiration of the 30–day period only if the party in interest demonstrates that the filing of the later case is in good faith as to the creditors to be stayed; and

(C) for purposes of subparagraph (B), a case is presumptively filed not in good faith (but such presumption may be rebutted by clear and convincing evidence to the contrary)—

(i) as to all creditors, if—

(I) more than 1 previous case under any of chapters 7, 11, and 13 in which the individual was a debtor was pending within the preceding 1–year period;

(II) a previous case under any of chapters 7, 11, and 13 in which the individual was a debtor was dismissed within such 1–year period, after the debtor failed to—

(aa) file or amend the petition or other documents as required by this title or the court without substantial excuse (but mere inadvertence or negligence shall not be a substantial excuse unless the dismissal was caused by the negligence of the debtor's attorney);

(bb) provide adequate protection as ordered by the court; or

(cc) perform the terms of a plan confirmed by the court; or

(III) there has not been a substantial change in the financial or personal affairs of the debtor since the dismissal of the next most previous case under chapter 7, 11, or 13 or any other reason to conclude that the later case will be concluded—

(aa) if a case under chapter 7, with a discharge; or

(bb) if a case under chapter 11 or 13, with a confirmed plan that will be fully performed; and

(ii) as to any creditor that commenced an action under subsection (d) in a previous case in which the individual was a debtor if, as of the date of dismissal of such case, that action was still pending or had been resolved by terminating, conditioning, or limiting the stay as to actions of such creditor; and

(4)(A)(i) if a single or joint case is filed by or against a debtor who is an individual under this title, and if 2 or more single or joint cases of the debtor were pending within the previous year but were dismissed, other than a case refiled under section 707(b), the stay under subsection (a) shall not go into effect upon the filing of the later case; and

(ii) on request of a party in interest, the court shall promptly enter an order confirming that no stay is in effect;

(B) if, within 30 days after the filing of the later case, a party in interest requests the court may order the stay to take effect in the case as to any or all creditors (subject to such conditions or limitations as the court may impose), after notice and a hearing, only if the party in interest demonstrates that the filing of the later case is in good faith as to the creditors to be stayed;

(C) a stay imposed under subparagraph (B) shall be effective on the date of the entry of the order allowing the stay to go into effect; and

(D) for purposes of subparagraph (B), a case is presumptively filed not in good faith (but such presumption may be rebutted by clear and convincing evidence to the contrary)—

(i) as to all creditors if—

(I) 2 or more previous cases under this title in which the individual was a debtor were pending within the 1–year period;

(II) a previous case under this title in which the individual was a debtor was dismissed within the time period stated in this paragraph after the debtor failed to file or amend the petition or other documents as required by this title or the court

161

without substantial excuse (but mere inadvertence or negligence shall not be substantial excuse unless the dismissal was caused by the negligence of the debtor's attorney), failed to provide adequate protection as ordered by the court, or failed to perform the terms of a plan confirmed by the court; or

    (III) there has not been a substantial change in the financial or personal affairs of the debtor since the dismissal of the next most previous case under this title, or any other reason to conclude that the later case will not be concluded, if a case under chapter 7, with a discharge, and if a case under chapter 11 or 13, with a confirmed plan that will be fully performed; or

    (ii) as to any creditor that commenced an action under subsection (d) in a previous case in which the individual was a debtor if, as of the date of dismissal of such case, such action was still pending or had been resolved by terminating, conditioning, or limiting the stay as to such action of such creditor.

(d) On request of a party in interest and after notice and a hearing, the court shall grant relief from the stay provided under subsection (a) of this section, such as by terminating, annulling, modifying, or conditioning such stay—

(1) for cause, including the lack of adequate protection of an interest in property of such party in interest;

(2) with respect to a stay of an act against property under subsection (a) of this section, if—

    (A) the debtor does not have an equity in such property; and

    (B) such property is not necessary to an effective reorganization;

(3) with respect to a stay of an act against single asset real estate under subsection (a), by a creditor whose claim is secured by an interest in such real estate, unless, not later than the date that is 90 days after the entry of the order for relief (or such later date as the court may determine for cause by order entered within that 90–day period) or 30 days after the court determines that the debtor is subject to this paragraph, whichever is later—

    (A) the debtor has filed a plan of reorganization that has a reasonable possibility of being confirmed within a reasonable time; or

    (B) the debtor has commenced monthly payments that—

        (i) may, in the debtor's sole discretion, notwithstanding section 363(c)(2), be made from rents or other income generated before, on, or after the date of the commencement of the case by or from the property to each creditor whose claim is secured by such real estate (other than a claim secured by a judgment lien or by an unmatured statutory lien); and

        (ii) are in an amount equal to interest at the then applicable nondefault contract rate of interest on the value of the creditor's interest in the real estate; or

(4) with respect to a stay of an act against real property under subsection (a), by a creditor whose claim is secured by an interest in such real property, if the court finds that the filing of the petition was part of a scheme to delay, hinder, and defraud creditors that involved either—

    (A) transfer of all or part ownership of, or other interest in, such real property without the consent of the secured creditor or court approval; or

(B) multiple bankruptcy filings affecting such real property.

If recorded in compliance with applicable State laws governing notices of interests or liens in real property, an order entered under paragraph (4) shall be binding in any other case under this title purporting to affect such real property filed not later than 2 years after the date of the entry of such order by the court, except that a debtor in a subsequent case under this title may move for relief from such order based upon changed circumstances or for good cause shown, after notice and a hearing. Any Federal, State, or local governmental unit that accepts notices of interests or liens in real property shall accept any certified copy of an order described in this subsection for indexing and recording.

(e)(1) Thirty days after a request under subsection (d) of this section for relief from the stay of any act against property of the estate under subsection (a) of this section, such stay is terminated with respect to the party in interest making such request, unless the court, after notice and a hearing, orders such stay continued in effect pending the conclusion of, or as a result of, a final hearing and determination under subsection (d) of this section. A hearing under this subsection may be a preliminary hearing, or may be consolidated with the final hearing under subsection (d) of this section. The court shall order such stay continued in effect pending the conclusion of the final hearing under subsection (d) of this section if there is a reasonable likelihood that the party opposing relief from such stay will prevail at the conclusion of such final hearing. If the hearing under this subsection is a preliminary hearing, then such final hearing shall be concluded not later than thirty days after the conclusion of such preliminary hearing, unless the 30–day period is extended with the consent of the parties in interest or for a specific time which the court finds is required by compelling circumstances.

(2) Notwithstanding paragraph (1), in a case under chapter 7, 11, or 13 in which the debtor is an individual, the stay under subsection (a) shall terminate on the date that is 60 days after a request is made by a party in interest under subsection (d), unless—

(A) a final decision is rendered by the court during the 60–day period beginning on the date of the request; or

(B) such 60–day period is extended—

(i) by agreement of all parties in interest; or

(ii) by the court for such specific period of time as the court finds is required for good cause, as described in findings made by the court.

(f) Upon request of a party in interest, the court, with or without a hearing, shall grant such relief from the stay provided under subsection (a) of this section as is necessary to prevent irreparable damage to the interest of an entity in property, if such interest will suffer such damage before there is an opportunity for notice and a hearing under subsection (d) or (e) of this section.

(g) In any hearing under subsection (d) or (e) of this section concerning relief from the stay of any act under subsection (a) of this section—

(1) the party requesting such relief has the burden of proof on the issue of the debtor's equity in property; and

(2) the party opposing such relief has the burden of proof on all other issues.

(h)(1) In a case in which the debtor is an individual, the stay provided by subsection (a) is terminated with respect to personal property of the estate or of the debtor securing in whole or in part a claim, or subject to an unexpired lease, and such personal property shall no longer be property of the estate if the debtor fails within the applicable time set by section 521(a)(2)—

(A) to file timely any statement of intention required under section 521(a)(2) with respect to such personal property or to indicate in such statement that the debtor will either surrender such personal property or retain it and, if retaining such personal property, either redeem such personal property pursuant to section 722, enter into an agreement of the kind specified in section 524(c) applicable to the debt secured by such personal property, or assume such unexpired lease pursuant to section 365(p) if the trustee does not do so, as applicable; and

(B) to take timely the action specified in such statement, as it may be amended before expiration of the period for taking action, unless such statement specifies the debtor's intention to reaffirm such debt on the original contract terms and the creditor refuses to agree to the reaffirmation on such terms.

(2) Paragraph (1) does not apply if the court determines, on the motion of the trustee filed before the expiration of the applicable time set by section 521(a)(2), after notice and a hearing, that such personal property is of consequential value or benefit to the estate, and orders appropriate adequate protection of the creditor's interest, and orders the debtor to deliver any collateral in the debtor's possession to the trustee. If the court does not so determine, the stay provided by subsection (a) shall terminate upon the conclusion of the hearing on the motion.

(i) If a case commenced under chapter 7, 11, or 13 is dismissed due to the creation of a debt repayment plan, for purposes of subsection (c)(3), any subsequent case commenced by the debtor under any such chapter shall not be presumed to be filed not in good faith.

(j) On request of a party in interest, the court shall issue an order under subsection (c) confirming that the automatic stay has been terminated.

(k)(1) Except as provided in paragraph (2), an individual injured by any willful violation of a stay provided by this section shall recover actual damages, including costs and attorneys' fees, and, in appropriate circumstances, may recover punitive damages.

(2) If such violation is based on an action taken by an entity in the good faith belief that subsection (h) applies to the debtor, the recovery under paragraph (1) of this subsection against such entity shall be limited to actual damages.

(*l*)(1) Except as otherwise provided in this subsection, subsection (b) (22) shall apply on the date that is 30 days after the date on which the bankruptcy petition is filed, if the debtor files with the petition and serves upon the lessor a certification under penalty of perjury that—

(A) under nonbankruptcy law applicable in the jurisdiction, there are circumstances under which the debtor would be permitted to cure the entire monetary default that gave rise to the judgment for possession, after that judgment for possession was entered; and

(B) the debtor (or an adult dependent of the debtor) has deposited with the clerk of the court, any rent that would become due during the 30–day period after the filing of the bankruptcy petition.

(2) If, within the 30–day period after the filing of the bankruptcy petition, the debtor (or an adult dependent of the debtor) complies with paragraph (1) and files with the court and serves upon the lessor a further certification under penalty of perjury that the debtor (or an adult dependent of the debtor) has cured, under nonbankrupcty [FN1] law applicable in the jurisdiction, the entire monetary default that gave rise to the judgment under which possession is sought by the lessor, subsection (b)(22) shall not apply, unless ordered to apply by the court under paragraph (3).

(3)(A) If the lessor files an objection to any certification filed by the debtor under paragraph (1) or (2), and serves such objection upon the debtor, the court shall hold a hearing within 10 days after the filing and service of such objection to determine if the certification filed by the debtor under paragraph (1) or (2) is true.

(B) If the court upholds the objection of the lessor filed under subparagraph (A)—

(i) subsection (b)(22) shall apply immediately and relief from the stay provided under subsection (a)(3) shall not be required to enable the lessor to complete the process to recover full possession of the property; and

(ii) the clerk of the court shall immediately serve upon the lessor and the debtor a certified copy of the court's order upholding the lessor's objection.

(4) If a debtor, in accordance with paragraph (5), indicates on the petition that there was a judgment for possession of the residential rental property in which the debtor resides and does not file a certification under paragraph (1) or (2)—

(A) subsection (b)(22) shall apply immediately upon failure to file such certification, and relief from the stay provided under subsection (a)(3) shall not be required to enable the lessor to complete the process to recover full possession of the property; and

(B) the clerk of the court shall immediately serve upon the lessor and the debtor a certified copy of the docket indicating the absence of a filed certification and the applicability of the exception to the stay under subsection (b)(22).

(5)(A) Where a judgment for possession of residential property in which the debtor resides as a tenant under a lease or rental agreement has been obtained by the lessor, the debtor shall so indicate on the bankruptcy petition and shall provide the name and address of the lessor that obtained that pre-petition judgment on the petition and on any certification filed under this subsection.

(B) The form of certification filed with the petition, as specified in this subsection, shall provide for the debtor to certify, and the debtor shall certify—

(i) whether a judgment for possession of residential rental housing in which the debtor resides has been obtained against the debtor before the date of the filing of the petition; and

(ii) whether the debtor is claiming under paragraph (1) that under nonbankruptcy law applicable in the jurisdiction, there are circumstances under which the debtor would be permitted to cure the entire monetary default that gave rise to the judgment for possession, after that judgment of possession was entered, and has made the appropriate deposit with the court.

(C) The standard forms (electronic and otherwise) used in a bankruptcy proceeding shall be amended to reflect the requirements of this subsection.

(D) The clerk of the court shall arrange for the prompt transmittal of the rent deposited in accordance with paragraph (1)(B) to the lessor.

(m)(1) Except as otherwise provided in this subsection, subsection (b) (23) shall apply on the date that is 15 days after the date on which the lessor files and serves a certification described in subsection (b)(23).

(2)(A) If the debtor files with the court an objection to the truth or legal sufficiency of the certification described in subsection (b)(23) and serves such objection upon the lessor, subsection (b)(23) shall not apply, unless ordered to apply by the court under this subsection.

(B) If the debtor files and serves the objection under subparagraph (A), the court shall hold a hearing within 10 days after the filing and service of such objection to determine if the situation giving rise to the lessor's certification under paragraph (1) existed or has been remedied.

(C) If the debtor can demonstrate to the satisfaction of the court that the situation giving rise to the lessor's certification under paragraph (1) did not exist or has been remedied, the stay provided under subsection (a)(3) shall remain in effect until the termination of the stay under this section.

(D) If the debtor cannot demonstrate to the satisfaction of the court that the situation giving rise to the lessor's certification under paragraph (1) did not exist or has been remedied—

(i) relief from the stay provided under subsection (a)(3) shall not be required to enable the lessor to proceed with the eviction; and

(ii) the clerk of the court shall immediately serve upon the lessor and the debtor a certified copy of the court's order upholding the lessor's certification.

(3) If the debtor fails to file, within 15 days, an objection under paragraph (2)(A)—

(A) subsection (b)(23) shall apply immediately upon such failure and relief from the stay provided under subsection (a)(3) shall not be required to enable the lessor to complete the process to recover full possession of the property; and

(B) the clerk of the court shall immediately serve upon the lessor and the debtor a certified copy of the docket indicating such failure.

(n)(1) Except as provided in paragraph (2), subsection (a) does not apply in a case in which the debtor—

(A) is a debtor in a small business case pending at the time the petition is filed;

(B) was a debtor in a small business case that was dismissed for any reason by an order that became final in the 2–year period ending on the date of the order for relief entered with respect to the petition;

(C) was a debtor in a small business case in which a plan was confirmed in the 2–year period ending on the date of the order for relief entered with respect to the petition; or

(D) is an entity that has acquired substantially all of the assets or business of a small business debtor described in subparagraph (A), (B), or (C), unless such entity establishes by a preponderance of the evidence that such entity acquired substantially all of the assets or business of such small business debtor in good faith and not for the purpose of evading this paragraph.

(2) Paragraph (1) does not apply—

(A) to an involuntary case involving no collusion by the debtor with creditors; or

(B) to the filing of a petition if—

(i) the debtor proves by a preponderance of the evidence that the filing of the petition resulted from circumstances beyond the control of the debtor not foreseeable at the time the case then pending was filed; and

(ii) it is more likely than not that the court will confirm a feasible plan, but not a liquidating plan, within a reasonable period of time.

(*o*) The exercise of rights not subject to the stay arising under subsection (a) pursuant to paragraph (6), (7), (17), or (27) of subsection (b) shall not be stayed by any order of a court or administrative agency in any proceeding under this title.

§ 363. Use, sale, or lease of property

(a) In this section, "cash collateral" means cash, negotiable instruments, documents of title, securities, deposit accounts, or other cash equivalents whenever acquired in which the estate and an entity other than the estate have an interest and includes the proceeds, products, offspring, rents, or profits of property and the fees, charges, accounts or other payments for the use or occupancy of rooms and other public facilities in hotels, motels, or other lodging properties subject to a security interest as provided in section 552(b) of this title, whether existing before or after the commencement of a case under this title.

(b)(1) The trustee, after notice and a hearing, may use, sell, or lease, other than in the ordinary course of business, property of the estate, except that if the debtor in connection with offering a product or a service discloses to an individual a policy prohibiting the transfer of personally identifiable information about individuals to persons that are not affiliated with the debtor and if such policy is in effect on the date of the commencement of the case, then the trustee may not sell or lease personally identifiable information to any person unless—

(A) such sale or such lease is consistent with such policy; or

(B) after appointment of a consumer privacy ombudsman in accordance with section 332, and after notice and a hearing, the court approves such sale or such lease—

(i) giving due consideration to the facts, circumstances, and conditions of such sale or such lease; and

(ii) finding that no showing was made that such sale or such lease would violate applicable nonbankruptcy law.

(2) If notification is required under subsection (a) of section 7A of the Clayton Act in the case of a transaction under this subsection, then—

(A) notwithstanding subsection (a) of such section, the notification required by such subsection to be given by the debtor shall be given by the trustee; and

(B) notwithstanding subsection (b) of such section, the required waiting period shall end on the 15th day after the date of the receipt, by the Federal Trade Commission and the Assistant Attorney General in charge of the Antitrust Division of the Department of Justice, of the notification required under such subsection (a), unless such waiting period is extended—

(i) pursuant to subsection (e)(2) of such section, in the same manner as such subsection (e)(2) applies to a cash tender offer;

(ii) pursuant to subsection (g)(2) of such section; or

(iii) by the court after notice and a hearing.

(c)(1) If the business of the debtor is authorized to be operated under section 721, 1108, 1203, 1204, or 1304 of this title and unless the court orders otherwise, the trustee may enter into transactions, including the sale or lease of property of the estate, in the ordinary course of business, without notice or a hearing, and may use property of the estate in the ordinary course of business without notice or a hearing.

(2) The trustee may not use, sell, or lease cash collateral under paragraph (1) of this subsection unless—

(A) each entity that has an interest in such cash collateral consents; or

(B) the court, after notice and a hearing, authorizes such use, sale, or lease in accordance with the provisions of this section.

(3) Any hearing under paragraph (2)(B) of this subsection may be a preliminary hearing or may be consolidated with a hearing under subsection (e) of this section, but shall be scheduled in accordance with the needs of the debtor. If the hearing under paragraph (2)(B) of this subsection is a preliminary hearing, the court may authorize such use, sale, or lease only if there is a reasonable likelihood that the trustee will prevail at the final hearing under subsection (e) of this section. The court shall act promptly on any request for authorization under paragraph (2)(B) of this subsection.

(4) Except as provided in paragraph (2) of this subsection, the trustee shall segregate and account for any cash collateral in the trustee's possession, custody, or control.

(d) The trustee may use, sell, or lease property under subsection (b) or (c) of this section only—

(1) in accordance with applicable nonbankruptcy law that governs the transfer of property by a corporation or trust that is not a moneyed, business, or commercial corporation or trust; and

(2) to the extent not inconsistent with any relief granted under subsection (c), (d), (e), or (f) of section 362.

(e) Notwithstanding any other provision of this section, at any time, on request of an entity that has an interest in property used, sold, or leased, or proposed to be used, sold, or leased, by the trustee, the court, with or without a hearing, shall prohibit or condition such use, sale, or lease as is necessary to provide adequate protection of such interest. This subsection also applies to property that is subject to any unexpired lease of personal property (to the exclusion of such property being subject to an order to grant relief from the stay under section 362).

(f) The trustee may sell property under subsection (b) or (c) of this section free and clear of any interest in such property of an entity other than the estate, only if—

(1) applicable nonbankruptcy law permits sale of such property free and clear of such interest;

(2) such entity consents;

(3) such interest is a lien and the price at which such property is to be sold is greater than the aggregate value of all liens on such property;

(4) such interest is in bona fide dispute; or

(5) such entity could be compelled, in a legal or equitable proceeding, to accept a money satisfaction of such interest.

(g) Notwithstanding subsection (f) of this section, the trustee may sell property under subsection (b) or (c) of this section free and clear of any vested or contingent right in the nature of dower or curtesy.

(h) Notwithstanding subsection (f) of this section, the trustee may sell both the estate's interest, under subsection (b) or (c) of this section, and the interest of any co-owner in property in which the debtor had, at the time of the commencement of the case, an undivided interest as a tenant in common, joint tenant, or tenant by the entirety, only if—

(1) partition in kind of such property among the estate and such co-owners is impracticable;

(2) sale of the estate's undivided interest in such property would realize significantly less for the estate than sale of such property free of the interests of such co-owners;

(3) the benefit to the estate of a sale of such property free of the interests of co-owners outweighs the detriment, if any, to such co-owners; and

(4) such property is not used in the production, transmission, or distribution, for sale, of electric energy or of natural or synthetic gas for heat, light, or power.

(i) Before the consummation of a sale of property to which subsection (g) or (h) of this section applies, or of property of the estate that was community property of the debtor and the debtor's spouse immediately before the commencement of the case, the debtor's spouse, or a co-owner of such property, as the case may be, may purchase such property at the price at which such sale is to be consummated.

(j) After a sale of property to which subsection (g) or (h) of this section applies, the trustee shall distribute to the debtor's spouse or the co-owners of such property, as the case may be, and to the estate, the proceeds of such sale, less the costs and expenses, not including any compensation of the trustee, of such sale, according to the interests of such spouse or co-owners, and of the estate.

(k) At a sale under subsection (b) of this section of property that is subject to a lien that secures an allowed claim, unless the court for cause orders otherwise the holder of such claim may bid at such sale, and, if the holder of such claim purchases such property, such holder may offset such claim against the purchase price of such property.

(l) Subject to the provisions of section 365, the trustee may use, sell, or lease property under subsection (b) or (c) of this section, or a plan under chapter 11, 12, or 13 of this title may provide for the use, sale, or lease of property, notwithstanding any provision in a contract, a lease, or applicable law that is conditioned on the insolvency or financial condition of the debtor, on the commencement of a case under this title concerning the debtor, or on the appointment of or the taking possession by a trustee in a case under this title or a custodian, and that effects, or gives an option to effect, a forfeiture, modification, or termination of the debtor's interest in such property.

(m) The reversal or modification on appeal of an authorization under subsection (b) or (c) of this section of a sale or lease of property does not affect the validity of a sale or lease under such authorization to an entity that purchased or leased such property in good faith, whether or not such entity knew of the pendency of the appeal, unless such authorization and such sale or lease were stayed pending appeal.

(n) The trustee may avoid a sale under this section if the sale price was controlled by an agreement among potential bidders at such sale, or may recover from a party to such agreement any amount by which the value of the property sold exceeds the price at which such sale was consummated, and may recover any costs, attorneys' fees, or expenses incurred in avoiding such sale or recovering such amount. In addition to any recovery under the preceding sentence, the court may grant judgment for punitive damages in favor of the estate and against any such party that entered into such an agreement in willful disregard of this subsection.

(o) Notwithstanding subsection (f), if a person purchases any interest in a consumer credit transaction that is subject to the Truth in Lending Act or any interest in a consumer credit contract (as defined in section 433.1 of title 16 of the Code of Federal Regulations (January 1, 2004), as amended from time to time), and if such interest is purchased through a sale under this section, then such person shall remain subject to all claims and defenses that are related to such consumer credit transaction or such consumer credit contract, to the same extent as such person would be subject to such claims and defenses of the consumer had such interest been purchased at a sale not under this section.

(p) In any hearing under this section—

(1) the trustee has the burden of proof on the issue of adequate protection; and

(2) the entity asserting an interest in property has the burden of proof on the issue of the validity, priority, or extent of such interest.

§ 364. Obtaining credit

(a) If the trustee is authorized to operate the business of the debtor under section 721, 1108, 1203, 1204, or 1304 of this title, unless the court orders otherwise, the trustee may obtain unsecured credit and incur unsecured debt in the ordinary course of business allowable under section 503(b)(1) of this title as an administrative expense.

(b) The court, after notice and a hearing, may authorize the trustee to obtain unsecured credit or to incur unsecured debt other than under subsection (a) of this section, allowable under section 503(b)(1) of this title as an administrative expense.

(c) If the trustee is unable to obtain unsecured credit allowable under section 503(b)(1) of this title as an administrative expense, the court, after notice and a hearing, may authorize the obtaining of credit or the incurring of debt—

(1) with priority over any or all administrative expenses of the kind specified in section 503(b) or 507(b) of this title;

(2) secured by a lien on property of the estate that is not otherwise subject to a lien; or

(3) secured by a junior lien on property of the estate that is subject to a lien.

(d)(1) The court, after notice and a hearing, may authorize the obtaining of credit or the incurring of debt secured by a senior or equal lien on property of the estate that is subject to a lien only if—

(A) the trustee is unable to obtain such credit otherwise; and

(B) there is adequate protection of the interest of the holder of the lien on the property of the estate on which such senior or equal lien is proposed to be granted.

(2) In any hearing under this subsection, the trustee has the burden of proof on the issue of adequate protection.

(e) The reversal or modification on appeal of an authorization under this section to obtain credit or incur debt, or of a grant under this section of a priority or a lien, does not affect the validity of any debt so incurred, or any priority or lien so granted, to an entity that extended such credit in good faith, whether or not such entity knew of the pendency of the appeal, unless such authorization and the incurring of such debt, or the granting of such priority or lien, were stayed pending appeal.

(f) Except with respect to an entity that is an underwriter as defined in section 1145(b) of this title, section 5 of the Securities Act of 1933, the Trust Indenture Act of 1939, and any State or local law requiring registration for offer or sale of a security or registration or licensing of an issuer of, underwriter of, or broker or dealer in, a security does not apply to the offer or sale under this section of a security that is not an equity security.

§ 365. Executory contracts and unexpired leases

(a) Except as provided in sections 765 and 766 of this title and in subsections (b), (c), and (d) of this section, the trustee, subject to the court's approval, may assume or reject any executory contract or unexpired lease of the debtor.

(b)(1) If there has been a default in an executory contract or unexpired lease of the debtor, the trustee may not assume such contract or lease unless, at the time of assumption of such contract or lease, the trustee—

(A) cures, or provides adequate assurance that the trustee will promptly cure, such default other than a default that is a breach of a provision relating to the satisfaction of any provision (other than a penalty rate or penalty provision) relating to a default arising from any failure to perform nonmonetary obligations under an unexpired lease of real property, if it is impossible for the trustee to cure such default by performing nonmonetary acts at and after the time of assumption, except that if such default arises from a failure to operate in accordance with a nonresidential real property lease, then such default shall be cured by performance at and after the time of assumption in accordance with such lease, and pecuniary losses resulting from such default shall be compensated in accordance with the provisions of this paragraph;

(B) compensates, or provides adequate assurance that the trustee will promptly compensate, a party other than the debtor to such contract or lease, for any actual pecuniary loss to such party resulting from such default; and

(C) provides adequate assurance of future performance under such contract or lease.

(2) Paragraph (1) of this subsection does not apply to a default that is a breach of a provision relating to—

(A) the insolvency or financial condition of the debtor at any time before the closing of the case;

(B) the commencement of a case under this title;

(C) the appointment of or taking possession by a trustee in a case under this title or a custodian before such commencement; or

(D) the satisfaction of any penalty rate or penalty provision relating to a default arising from any failure by the debtor to perform nonmonetary obligations under the executory contract or unexpired lease.

(3) For the purposes of paragraph (1) of this subsection and paragraph (2)(B) of subsection (f), adequate assurance of future performance of a lease of real property in a shopping center includes adequate assurance—

(A) of the source of rent and other consideration due under such lease, and in the case of an assignment, that the financial condition and operating performance of the proposed assignee and its guarantors, if any, shall be similar to the financial condition and operating performance of the debtor and its guarantors, if any, as of the time the debtor became the lessee under the lease;

(B) that any percentage rent due under such lease will not decline substantially;

(C) that assumption or assignment of such lease is subject to all the provisions thereof, including (but not limited to) provisions such as a radius, location, use, or exclusivity provision, and will not breach any such provision contained in any other lease, financing agreement, or master agreement relating to such shopping center; and

(D) that assumption or assignment of such lease will not disrupt any tenant mix or balance in such shopping center.

(4) Notwithstanding any other provision of this section, if there has been a default in an unexpired lease of the debtor, other than a default of a kind specified in paragraph (2) of this subsection, the trustee may not require a lessor to provide services or supplies incidental to such lease before assumption of such lease unless the lessor is compensated under the terms of such lease for any services and supplies provided under such lease before assumption of such lease.

(c) The trustee may not assume or assign any executory contract or unexpired lease of the debtor, whether or not such contract or lease prohibits or restricts assignment of rights or delegation of duties, if—

(1)(A) applicable law excuses a party, other than the debtor, to such contract or lease from accepting performance from or rendering performance to an entity other than the debtor or the debtor in possession, whether or not such contract or lease prohibits or restricts assignment of rights or delegation of duties; and

(B) such party does not consent to such assumption or assignment; or

(2) such contract is a contract to make a loan, or extend other debt financing or financial accommodations, to or for the benefit of the debtor, or to issue a security of the debtor; or

(3) such lease is of nonresidential real property and has been terminated under applicable nonbankruptcy law prior to the order for relief.

[(4) Repealed. Pub.L. 109–8, Title III, § 328(a)(2)(C), Apr. 20, 2005, 119 Stat. 100] (d)(1) In a case under chapter 7 of this title, if the trustee does not assume or reject an executory contract or unexpired lease of residential real property or of personal property of the debtor within 60 days after the order for relief, or within such additional time as the court, for cause, within such 60–day period, fixes, then such contract or lease is deemed rejected.

(2) In a case under chapter 9, 11, 12, or 13 of this title, the trustee may assume or reject an executory contract or unexpired lease of residential real property or of personal property of the debtor at any time before the confirmation of a plan but the court, on the request of any party to such contract or lease, may order the trustee to determine within a specified period of time whether to assume or reject such contract or lease.

(3) The trustee shall timely perform all the obligations of the debtor, except those specified in section 365(b)(2), arising from and after the order for relief under any unexpired lease of nonresidential real property, until such lease is assumed or rejected, notwithstanding section 503(b)(1) of this title. The court may extend, for cause, the time for performance of any such obligation that arises within 60 days after the date of the order for relief, but the time for performance shall not be extended beyond such 60–day period. This subsection shall not be deemed to affect the trustee's obligations under the provisions of subsection (b) or (f) of this section. Acceptance of any such performance does not constitute waiver or relinquishment of the lessor's rights under such lease or under this title.

(4)(A) Subject to subparagraph (B), an unexpired lease of nonresidential real property under which the debtor is the lessee shall be deemed rejected, and the trustee shall immediately surrender that nonresidential real property to the lessor, if the trustee does not assume or reject the unexpired lease by the earlier of—

> (i) the date that is 120 days after the date of the order for relief; or

> (ii) the date of the entry of an order confirming a plan.

(B)(i) The court may extend the period determined under subparagraph (A), prior to the expiration of the 120–day period, for 90 days on the motion of the trustee or lessor for cause.

> (ii) If the court grants an extension under clause (i), the court may grant a subsequent extension only upon prior written consent of the lessor in each instance.

(5) The trustee shall timely perform all of the obligations of the debtor, except those specified in section 365(b)(2), first arising from or after 60 days after the order for relief in a case under chapter 11 of this title under an unexpired lease of personal property (other than personal property leased to an individual primarily for personal, family, or household purposes), until such lease is assumed or rejected notwithstanding section 503(b)(1) of this title, unless the court, after notice and a hearing and based on the equities of the case, orders otherwise with respect to the obligations or timely performance thereof. This subsection shall not be deemed to affect the trustee's obligations under the provisions of subsection (b) or (f). Acceptance of any such performance does not constitute waiver or relinquishment of the lessor's rights under such lease or under this title.

[(6) to (9) Repealed. Pub.L. 109–8, Title III, § 328(a)(3)(A), Apr. 20, 2005, 119 Stat. 100]

[(10) Redesignated (5)]

(e)(1) Notwithstanding a provision in an executory contract or unexpired lease, or in applicable law, an executory contract or unexpired lease of the debtor may not be terminated or modified, and any right or obligation under such contract or lease may not be terminated or modified, at any time after the commencement of the case solely because of a provision in such contract or lease that is conditioned on—

(A) the insolvency or financial condition of the debtor at any time before the closing of the case;

(B) the commencement of a case under this title; or

(C) the appointment of or taking possession by a trustee in a case under this title or a custodian before such commencement.

(2) Paragraph (1) of this subsection does not apply to an executory contract or unexpired lease of the debtor, whether or not such contract or lease prohibits or restricts assignment of rights or delegation of duties, if—

(A)(i) applicable law excuses a party, other than the debtor, to such contract or lease from accepting performance from or rendering performance to the trustee or to an assignee of such contract or lease, whether or not such contract or lease prohibits or restricts assignment of rights or delegation of duties; and

(ii) such party does not consent to such assumption or assignment; or

(B) such contract is a contract to make a loan, or extend other debt financing or financial accommodations, to or for the benefit of the debtor, or to issue a security of the debtor.

(f)(1) Except as provided in subsections (b) and (c) of this section, notwithstanding a provision in an executory contract or unexpired lease of the debtor, or in applicable law, that prohibits, restricts, or conditions the assignment of such contract or lease, the trustee may assign such contract or lease under paragraph (2) of this subsection.

(2) The trustee may assign an executory contract or unexpired lease of the debtor only if—

(A) the trustee assumes such contract or lease in accordance with the provisions of this section; and

(B) adequate assurance of future performance by the assignee of such contract or lease is provided, whether or not there has been a default in such contract or lease.

(3) Notwithstanding a provision in an executory contract or unexpired lease of the debtor, or in applicable law that terminates or modifies, or permits a party other than the debtor to terminate or modify, such contract or lease or a right or obligation under such contract or lease on account of an assignment of such contract or lease, such contract, lease, right, or obligation may not be terminated or modified under such provision because of the assumption or assignment of such contract or lease by the trustee.

(g) Except as provided in subsections (h)(2) and (i)(2) of this section, the rejection of an executory contract or unexpired lease of the debtor constitutes a breach of such contract or lease—

(1) if such contract or lease has not been assumed under this section or under a plan confirmed under chapter 9, 11, 12, or 13 of this title, immediately before the date of the filing of the petition; or

174

(2) if such contract or lease has been assumed under this section or under a plan confirmed under chapter 9, 11, 12, or 13 of this title—

(A) if before such rejection the case has not been converted under section 1112, 1208, or 1307 of this title, at the time of such rejection; or

(B) if before such rejection the case has been converted under section 1112, 1208, or 1307 of this title—

(i) immediately before the date of such conversion, if such contract or lease was assumed before such conversion; or

(ii) at the time of such rejection, if such contract or lease was assumed after such conversion.

(h)(1)(A) If the trustee rejects an unexpired lease of real property under which the debtor is the lessor and—

(i) if the rejection by the trustee amounts to such a breach as would entitle the lessee to treat such lease as terminated by virtue of its terms, applicable nonbankruptcy law, or any agreement made by the lessee, then the lessee under such lease may treat such lease as terminated by the rejection; or

(ii) if the term of such lease has commenced, the lessee may retain its rights under such lease (including rights such as those relating to the amount and timing of payment of rent and other amounts payable by the lessee and any right of use, possession, quiet enjoyment, subletting, assignment, or hypothecation) that are in or appurtenant to the real property for the balance of the term of such lease and for any renewal or extension of such rights to the extent that such rights are enforceable under applicable nonbankruptcy law.

(B) If the lessee retains its rights under subparagraph (A)(ii), the lessee may offset against the rent reserved under such lease for the balance of the term after the date of the rejection of such lease and for the term of any renewal or extension of such lease, the value of any damage caused by the nonperformance after the date of such rejection, of any obligation of the debtor under such lease, but the lessee shall not have any other right against the estate or the debtor on account of any damage occurring after such date caused by such nonperformance.

(C) The rejection of a lease of real property in a shopping center with respect to which the lessee elects to retain its rights under subparagraph (A)(ii) does not affect the enforceability under applicable nonbankruptcy law of any provision in the lease pertaining to radius, location, use, exclusivity, or tenant mix or balance.

(D) In this paragraph, "lessee" includes any successor, assign, or mortgagee permitted under the terms of such lease.

(2)(A) If the trustee rejects a timeshare interest under a timeshare plan under which the debtor is the timeshare interest seller and—

(i) if the rejection amounts to such a breach as would entitle the timeshare interest purchaser to treat the timeshare plan as terminated under its terms, applicable nonbankruptcy law, or any agreement made by timeshare interest purchaser, the timeshare interest purchaser under the timeshare plan may treat the timeshare plan as terminated by such rejection; or

(ii) if the term of such timeshare interest has commenced, then the timeshare interest purchaser may retain its rights in such timeshare interest for the balance of such term and for any term of renewal or extension of such timeshare interest to the extent that such rights are enforceable under applicable nonbankruptcy law.

(B) If the timeshare interest purchaser retains its rights under subparagraph (A), such timeshare interest purchaser may offset against the moneys due for such timeshare interest for the balance of the term after the date of the rejection of such timeshare interest, and the term of any renewal or extension of such timeshare interest, the value of any damage caused by the nonperformance after the date of such rejection, of any obligation of the debtor under such timeshare plan, but the timeshare interest purchaser shall not have any right against the estate or the debtor on account of any damage occurring after such date caused by such nonperformance.

(i)(1) If the trustee rejects an executory contract of the debtor for the sale of real property or for the sale of a timeshare interest under a timeshare plan, under which the purchaser is in possession, such purchaser may treat such contract as terminated, or, in the alternative, may remain in possession of such real property or timeshare interest.

(2) If such purchaser remains in possession—

(A) such purchaser shall continue to make all payments due under such contract, but may,[1] offset against such payments any damages occurring after the date of the rejection of such contract caused by the nonperformance of any obligation of the debtor after such date, but such purchaser does not have any rights against the estate on account of any damages arising after such date from such rejection, other than such offset; and

(B) the trustee shall deliver title to such purchaser in accordance with the provisions of such contract, but is relieved of all other obligations to perform under such contract.

(j) A purchaser that treats an executory contract as terminated under subsection (i) of this section, or a party whose executory contract to purchase real property from the debtor is rejected and under which such party is not in possession, has a lien on the interest of the debtor in such property for the recovery of any portion of the purchase price that such purchaser or party has paid.

(k) Assignment by the trustee to an entity of a contract or lease assumed under this section relieves the trustee and the estate from any liability for any breach of such contract or lease occurring after such assignment.

(l) If an unexpired lease under which the debtor is the lessee is assigned pursuant to this section, the lessor of the property may require a deposit or other security for the performance of the debtor's obligations under the lease substantially the same as would have been required by the landlord upon the initial leasing to a similar tenant.

(m) For purposes of this section 365 and sections 541(b)(2) and 362(b)(10), leases of real property shall include any rental agreement to use real property.

(n)(1) If the trustee rejects an executory contract under which the debtor is a licensor of a right to intellectual property, the licensee under such contract may elect—

(A) to treat such contract as terminated by such rejection if such rejection by the trustee amounts to such a breach as would entitle the licensee to treat such contract as

---

1. So in original. The comma probably should not appear.

terminated by virtue of its own terms, applicable nonbankruptcy law, or an agreement made by the licensee with another entity; or

(B) to retain its rights (including a right to enforce any exclusivity provision of such contract, but excluding any other right under applicable nonbankruptcy law to specific performance of such contract) under such contract and under any agreement supplementary to such contract, to such intellectual property (including any embodiment of such intellectual property to the extent protected by applicable nonbankruptcy law), as such rights existed immediately before the case commenced, for—

(i) the duration of such contract; and

(ii) any period for which such contract may be extended by the licensee as of right under applicable nonbankruptcy law.

(2) If the licensee elects to retain its rights, as described in paragraph (1)(B) of this subsection, under such contract—

(A) the trustee shall allow the licensee to exercise such rights;

(B) the licensee shall make all royalty payments due under such contract for the duration of such contract and for any period described in paragraph (1)(B) of this subsection for which the licensee extends such contract; and

(C) the licensee shall be deemed to waive—

(i) any right of setoff it may have with respect to such contract under this title or applicable nonbankruptcy law; and

(ii) any claim allowable under section 503(b) of this title arising from the performance of such contract.

(3) If the licensee elects to retain its rights, as described in paragraph (1)(B) of this subsection, then on the written request of the licensee the trustee shall—

(A) to the extent provided in such contract, or any agreement supplementary to such contract, provide to the licensee any intellectual property (including such embodiment) held by the trustee; and

(B) not interfere with the rights of the licensee as provided in such contract, or any agreement supplementary to such contract, to such intellectual property (including such embodiment) including any right to obtain such intellectual property (or such embodiment) from another entity.

(4) Unless and until the trustee rejects such contract, on the written request of the licensee the trustee shall—

(A) to the extent provided in such contract or any agreement supplementary to such contract—

(i) perform such contract; or

(ii) provide to the licensee such intellectual property (including any embodiment of such intellectual property to the extent protected by applicable nonbankruptcy law) held by the trustee; and

(B) not interfere with the rights of the licensee as provided in such contract, or any agreement supplementary to such contract, to such intellectual property (including such embodiment), including any right to obtain such intellectual property (or such embodiment) from another entity.

(*o*) In a case under chapter 11 of this title, the trustee shall be deemed to have assumed (consistent with the debtor's other obligations under section 507), and shall immediately cure any deficit under, any commitment by the debtor to a Federal depository institutions regulatory agency (or predecessor to such agency) to maintain the capital of an insured depository institution, and any claim for a subsequent breach of the obligations thereunder shall be entitled to priority under section 507. This subsection shall not extend any commitment that would otherwise be terminated by any act of such an agency.

(p)(1) If a lease of personal property is rejected or not timely assumed by the trustee under subsection (d), the leased property is no longer property of the estate and the stay under section 362(a) is automatically terminated.

(2)(A) If the debtor in a case under chapter 7 is an individual, the debtor may notify the creditor in writing that the debtor desires to assume the lease. Upon being so notified, the creditor may, at its option, notify the debtor that it is willing to have the lease assumed by the debtor and may condition such assumption on cure of any outstanding default on terms set by the contract.

(B) If, not later than 30 days after notice is provided under subparagraph (A), the debtor notifies the lessor in writing that the lease is assumed, the liability under the lease will be assumed by the debtor and not by the estate.

(C) The stay under section 362 and the injunction under section 524(a) (2) shall not be violated by notification of the debtor and negotiation of cure under this subsection.

(3) In a case under chapter 11 in which the debtor is an individual and in a case under chapter 13, if the debtor is the lessee with respect to personal property and the lease is not assumed in the plan confirmed by the court, the lease is deemed rejected as of the conclusion of the hearing on confirmation. If the lease is rejected, the stay under section 362 and any stay under section 1301 is automatically terminated with respect to the property subject to the lease.

§ 548. Fraudulent transfers and obligations

(a)(1) The trustee may avoid any transfer of an interest of the debtor in property, or any obligation incurred by the debtor, that was made or incurred on or within one year before the date of the filing of the petition, if the debtor voluntarily or involuntarily—

(A) made such transfer or incurred such obligation with actual intent to hinder, delay, or defraud any entity to which the debtor was or became, on or after the date that such transfer was made or such obligation was incurred, indebted; or

(B)(i) received less than a reasonably equivalent value in exchange for such transfer or obligation; and

(ii)(I) was insolvent on the date that such transfer was made or such obligation was incurred, or became insolvent as a result of such transfer or obligation;

(II) was engaged in business or a transaction, or was about to engage in business or a transaction, for which any property remaining with the debtor was an unreasonably small capital; or

(III) intended to incur, or believed that the debtor would incur, debts that would be beyond the debtor's ability to pay as such debts matured.

(2) A transfer of a charitable contribution to a qualified religious or charitable entity or organization shall not be considered to be a transfer covered under paragraph (1)(B) in any case in which.—

(A) the amount of that contribution does not exceed 15 percent of the gross annual income of the debtor for the year in which the transfer of the contribution is made; or

(B) the contribution made by a debtor exceeded the percentage amount of gross annual income specified in subparagraph (A), if the transfer was consistent with the practices of the debtor in making charitable contributions.

(b) The trustee of a partnership debtor may avoid any transfer of an interest of the debtor in property, or any obligation incurred by the debtor, that was made or incurred on or within one year before the date of the filing of the petition, to a general partner in the debtor, if the debtor was insolvent on the date such transfer was made or such obligation was incurred, or became insolvent as a result of such transfer or obligation.

(c) Except to the extent that a transfer or obligation voidable under this section is voidable under section 544, 545, or 547 of this title, a transferee or obligee of such a transfer or obligation that takes for value and in good faith has a lien on or may retain any interest transferred or may enforce any obligation incurred, as the case may be, to the extent that such transferee or obligee gave value to the debtor in exchange for such transfer or obligation.

(d)(1) For the purposes of this section, a transfer is made when such transfer is so perfected that a bona fide purchaser from the debtor against whom applicable law permits such transfer to be perfected cannot acquire an interest in the property transferred that is superior to the interest in such property of the transferee, but if such transfer is not so perfected before the commencement of the case, such transfer is made immediately before the date of the filing of the petition.

(2) In this section—

(A) "value" means property, or satisfaction or securing of a present or antecedent debt of the debtor, but does not include an unperformed promise to furnish support to the debtor or to a relative of the debtor;

(B) a commodity broker, forward contract merchant, stockbroker, financial institution, or securities clearing agency that receives a margin payment, as defined in section 101, 741, or 761 of this title, or settlement payment, as defined in section 101 or 741 of this title, takes for value to the extent of such payment;

(C) a repo participant that receives a margin payment, as defined in section 741 or 761 of this title, or settlement payment, as defined in section 741 of this title, in connection with a repurchase agreement, takes for value to the extent of such payment; and

(D) a swap participant that receives a transfer in connection with a swap agreement takes for value to the extent of such transfer.

179

(3) In this section, the term "charitable contribution" means a charitable contribution, as that term is defined in section 170(c) of the Internal Revenue Code of 1986, if that contribution—

(A) is made by a natural person; and

(B) consists of.—

(i) a financial instrument (as that term is defined in section 731(c)(2)(C) of the Internal Revenue Code of 1986); or

(ii) cash.

(4) In this section, the term "qualified religious or charitable entity or organization" means—

(A) an entity described in section 170(c)(1) of the Internal Revenue Code of 1986; or

(B) an entity or organization described in section 170(c)(2) of the Internal Revenue Code of 1986.

§ 1101. Definitions for this chapter

In this chapter—

(1) "debtor in possession" means debtor except when a person that has qualified under section 322 of this title is serving as trustee in the case;

(2) "substantial consummation" means—

(A) transfer of all or substantially all of the property proposed by the plan to be transferred;

(B) assumption by the debtor or by the successor to the debtor under the plan of the business or of the management of all or substantially all of the property dealt with by the plan; and

(C) commencement of distribution under the plan.

§ 1106. Duties of trustee and examiner

(a) A trustee shall—

(1) perform the duties of the trustee, as specified in paragraphs (2), (5), (7), (8), (9), (10), (11), and (12) of section 704;

(2) if the debtor has not done so, file the list, schedule, and statement required under section 521(1) of this title;

(3) except to the extent that the court orders otherwise, investigate the acts, conduct, assets, liabilities, and financial condition of the debtor, the operation of the debtor's business and the desirability of the continuance of such business, and any other matter relevant to the case or to the formulation of a plan;

(4) as soon as practicable—

(A) file a statement of any investigation conducted under paragraph (3) of this subsection, including any fact ascertained pertaining to fraud, dishonesty, incompetence, misconduct, mismanagement, or irregularity in the management of the affairs of the debtor, or to a cause of action available to the estate; and

(B) transmit a copy or a summary of any such statement to any creditors' committee or equity security holders' committee, to any indenture trustee, and to such other entity as the court designates;

(5) as soon as practicable, file a plan under section 1121 of this title, file a report of why the trustee will not file a plan, or recommend conversion of the case to a case under chapter 7, 12, or 13 of this title or dismissal of the case;

(6) for any year for which the debtor has not filed a tax return required by law, furnish, without personal liability, such information as may be required by the governmental unit with which such tax return was to be filed, in light of the condition of the debtor's books and records and the availability of such information;

(7) after confirmation of a plan, file such reports as are necessary or as the court orders; and

(8) if with respect to the debtor there is a claim for a domestic support obligation, provide the applicable notice specified in subsection (c).

(b) An examiner appointed under section 1104(d) of this title shall perform the duties specified in paragraphs (3) and (4) of subsection (a) of this section, and, except to the extent that the court orders otherwise, any other duties of the trustee that the court orders the debtor in possession not to perform.

(c)(1) In a case described in subsection (a)(8) to which subsection (a)(8) applies, the trustee shall—

(A)(i) provide written notice to the holder of the claim described in subsection (a)(8) of such claim and of the right of such holder to use the services of the State child support enforcement agency established under sections 464 and 466 of the Social Security Act for the State in which such holder resides, for assistance in collecting child support during and after the case under this title; and

(ii) include in the notice required by clause (i) the address and telephone number of such State child support enforcement agency;

(B)(i) provide written notice to such State child support enforcement agency of such claim; and

(ii) include in the notice required by clause (i) the name, address, and telephone number of such holder; and

(C) at such time as the debtor is granted a discharge under section 1141, provide written notice to such holder and to such State child support enforcement agency of—

(i) the granting of the discharge;

(ii) the last recent known address of the debtor;

(iii) the last recent known name and address of the debtor's employer; and

(iv) the name of each creditor that holds a claim that—

(I) is not discharged under paragraph (2), (4), or (14A) of section 523(a); or

(II) was reaffirmed by the debtor under section 524(c).

181

(2)(A) The holder of a claim described in subsection (a)(8) or the State child enforcement support agency of the State in which such holder resides may request from a creditor described in paragraph (1)(C)(iv) the last known address of the debtor.

(B) Notwithstanding any other provision of law, a creditor that makes a disclosure of a last known address of a debtor in connection with a request made under subparagraph (A) shall not be liable by reason of making such disclosure.

§ 1107.   Rights, powers, and duties of debtor in possession

(a) Subject to any limitations on a trustee serving in a case under this chapter, and to such limitations or conditions as the court prescribes, a debtor in possession shall have all the rights, other than the right to compensation under section 330 of this title, and powers, and shall perform all the functions and duties, except the duties specified in sections 1106(a)(2), (3), and (4) of this title, of a trustee serving in a case under this chapter.

(b) Notwithstanding section 327(a) of this title, a person is not disqualified for employment under section 327 of this title by a debtor in possession solely because of such person's employment by or representation of the debtor before the commencement of the case.

§ 1111.   Claims and interests

(a) A proof of claim or interest is deemed filed under section 501 of this title for any claim or interest that appears in the schedules filed under section 521(1) or 1106(a)(2) of this title, except a claim or interest that is scheduled as disputed, contingent, or unliquidated.

(b)(1)(A) A claim secured by a lien on property of the estate shall be allowed or disallowed under section 502 of this title the same as if the holder of such claim had recourse against the debtor on account of such claim, whether or not such holder has such recourse, unless—

(i) the class of which such claim is a part elects, by at least two-thirds in amount and more than half in number of allowed claims of such class, application of paragraph (2) of this subsection; or

(ii) such holder does not have such recourse and such property is sold under section 363 of this title or is to be sold under the plan.

(B) A class of claims may not elect application of paragraph (2) of this subsection if—

(i) the interest on account of such claims of the holders of such claims in such property is of inconsequential value; or

(ii) the holder of a claim of such class has recourse against the debtor on account of such claim and such property is sold under section 363 of this title or is to be sold under the plan.

(2) If such an election is made, then notwithstanding section 506(a) of this title, such claim is a secured claim to the extent that such claim is allowed.

§ 1121.   Who may file a plan

(a) The debtor may file a plan with a petition commencing a voluntary case, or at any time in a voluntary case or an involuntary case.

(b) Except as otherwise provided in this section, only the debtor may file a plan until after 120 days after the date of the order for relief under this chapter.

(c) Any party in interest, including the debtor, the trustee, a creditors' committee, an equity security holders' committee, a creditor, an equity security holder, or any indenture trustee, may file a plan if and only if—

(1) a trustee has been appointed under this chapter;

(2) the debtor has not filed a plan before 120 days after the date of the order for relief under this chapter; or

(3) the debtor has not filed a plan that has been accepted, before 180 days after the date of the order for relief under this chapter, by each class of claims or interests that is impaired under the plan.

(d) On request of a party in interest made within the respective periods specified in subsections (b) and (c) of this section and after notice and a hearing, the court may for cause reduce or increase the 120–day period or the 180–day period referred to in this section.

(e) In a case in which the debtor is a small business and elects to be considered a small business—

(1) only the debtor may file a plan until after 100 days after the date of the order for relief under this chapter;

(2) all plans shall be filed within 160 days after the date of the order for relief; and

(3) on request of a party in interest made within the respective periods specified in paragraphs (1) and (2) and after notice and a hearing, the court may—

(A) reduce the 100–day period or the 160–day period specified in paragraph (1) or (2) for cause; and

(B) increase the 100–day period specified in paragraph (1) if the debtor shows that the need for an increase is caused by circumstances for which the debtor should not be held accountable.

§ 1122. Classification of claims or interests

(a) Except as provided in subsection (b) of this section, a plan may place a claim or an interest in a particular class only if such claim or interest is substantially similar to the other claims or interests of such class.

(b) A plan may designate a separate class of claims consisting only of every unsecured claim that is less than or reduced to an amount that the court approves as reasonable and necessary for administrative convenience.

§ 1123. Contents of plan

(a) Notwithstanding any otherwise applicable nonbankruptcy law, a plan shall—

(1) designate, subject to section 1122 of this title, classes of claims, other than claims of a kind specified in section 507(a)(2), 507(a)(3), or 507(a)(8) of this title and classes of interests;

(2) specify any class of claims or interests that is not impaired under the plan;

(3) specify the treatment of any class of claims or interests that is impaired under the plan;

183

(4) provide the same treatment for each claim or interest of a particular class, unless the holder of a particular claim or interest agrees to a less favorable treatment of such particular claim or interest;

(5) provide adequate means for the plan's implementation, such as—

(A) retention by the debtor of all or any part of the property of the estate;

(B) transfer of all or any part of the property of the estate to one or more entities, whether organized before or after the confirmation of such plan;

(C) merger or consolidation of the debtor with one or more persons;

(D) sale of all or any part of the property of the estate, either subject to or free of any lien, or the distribution of all or any part of the property of the estate among those having an interest in such property of the estate;

(E) satisfaction or modification of any lien;

(F) cancellation or modification of any indenture or similar instrument;

(G) curing or waiving of any default;

(H) extension of a maturity date or a change in an interest rate or other term of outstanding securities;

(I) amendment of the debtor's charter; or

(J) issuance of securities of the debtor, or of any entity referred to in subparagraph (B) or (C) of this paragraph, for cash, for property, for existing securities, or in exchange for claims or interests, or for any other appropriate purpose;

(6) provide for the inclusion in the charter of the debtor, if the debtor is a corporation, or of any corporation referred to in paragraph (5)(B) or (5)(C) of this subsection, of a provision prohibiting the issuance of nonvoting equity securities, and providing, as to the several classes of securities possessing voting power, an appropriate distribution of such power among such classes, including, in the case of any class of equity securities having a preference over another class of equity securities with respect to dividends, adequate provisions for the election of directors representing such preferred class in the event of default in the payment of such dividends;

(7) contain only provisions that are consistent with the interests of creditors and equity security holders and with public policy with respect to the manner of selection of any officer, director, or trustee under the plan and any successor to such officer, director, or trustee; and

(8) in a case in which the debtor is an individual, provide for the payment to creditors under the plan of all or such portion of earnings from personal services performed by the debtor after the commencement of the case or other future income of the debtor as is necessary for the execution of the plan.

(b) Subject to subsection (a) of this section, a plan may—

(1) impair or leave unimpaired any class of claims, secured or unsecured, or of interests;

(2) subject to section 365 of this title, provide for the assumption, rejection, or assignment of any executory contract or unexpired lease of the debtor not previously rejected under such section;

(3) provide for—

(A) the settlement or adjustment of any claim or interest belonging to the debtor or to the estate; or

(B) the retention and enforcement by the debtor, by the trustee, or by a representative of the estate appointed for such purpose, of any such claim or interest;

(4) provide for the sale of all or substantially all of the property of the estate, and the distribution of the proceeds of such sale among holders of claims or interests; and

(5) include any other appropriate provision not inconsistent with the applicable provisions of this title.

(c) In a case concerning an individual, a plan proposed by an entity other than the debtor may not provide for the use, sale, or lease of property exempted under section 522 of this title, unless the debtor consents to such use, sale, or lease.

(d) Notwithstanding subsection (a) of this section and sections 506(b), 1129(a)(7), and 1129(b) of this title, if it is proposed in a plan to cure a default the amount necessary to cure the default shall be determined in accordance with the underlying agreement and applicable nonbankruptcy law.

§ 1124. Impairment of claims or interests

Except as provided in section 1123(a)(4) of this title, a class of claims or interests is impaired under a plan unless, with respect to each claim or interest of such class, the plan—

(1) leaves unaltered the legal, equitable, and contractual rights to which such claim or interest entitles the holder of such claim or interest;

(2) notwithstanding any contractual provision or applicable law that entitles the holder of such claim or interest to demand or receive accelerated payment of such claim or interest after the occurrence of a default—

(A) cures any such default that occurred before or after the commencement of the case under this title, other than a default of a kind specified in section 365(b)(2) of this title or a kind that section 365(b)(2) expressly does not require to be cured;

(B) reinstates the maturity of such claim or interest as such maturity existed before such default;

(C) compensates the holder of such claim or interest for any damages incurred as a result of any reasonable reliance by such holder on such contractual provision or such applicable law;

(D) if such claim or such interest arises from any failure to perform a nonmonetary obligation, other than a default arising from failure to operate a nonresidential real property lease subject to section 365(b)(1)(A), compensates the holder of such claim or such interest (other than the debtor or an insider) for any actual pecuniary loss incurred by such holder as a result of such failure; and

(E) does not otherwise alter the legal, equitable, or contractual rights to which such claim or interest entitles the holder of such claim or interest; or

[(3) Repealed, Pub. L. 103–394, Title II, § 213(d)(3), Oct. 22, 1994, 108 Stat. 4126].

§ 1129.   Confirmation of plan

(a) The court shall confirm a plan only if all of the following requirements are met:

(1) The plan complies with the applicable provisions of this title.

(2) The proponent of the plan complies with the applicable provisions of this title.

(3) The plan has been proposed in good faith and not by any means forbidden by law.

(4) Any payment made or to be made by the proponent, by the debtor, or by a person issuing securities or acquiring property under the plan, for services or for costs and expenses in or in connection with the case, or in connection with the plan and incident to the case, has been approved by, or is subject to the approval of, the court as reasonable.

(5)(A)(i) The proponent of the plan has disclosed the identity and affiliations of any individual proposed to serve, after confirmation of the plan, as a director, officer, or voting trustee of the debtor, an affiliate of the debtor participating in a joint plan with the debtor, or a successor to the debtor under the plan; and

(ii) the appointment to, or continuance in, such office of such individual, is consistent with the interests of creditors and equity security holders and with public policy; and

(B) the proponent of the plan has disclosed the identity of any insider that will be employed or retained by the reorganized debtor, and the nature of any compensation for such insider.

(6) Any governmental regulatory commission with jurisdiction, after confirmation of the plan, over the rates of the debtor has approved any rate change provided for in the plan, or such rate change is expressly conditioned on such approval.

(7) With respect to each impaired class of claims or interests—

(A) each holder of a claim or interest of such class—

(i) has accepted the plan; or

(ii) will receive or retain under the plan on account of such claim or interest property of a value, as of the effective date of the plan, that is not less than the amount that such holder would so receive or retain if the debtor were liquidated under chapter 7 of this title on such date; or

(B) if section 1111(b)(2) of this title applies to the claims of such class, each holder of a claim of such class will receive or retain under the plan on account of such claim property of a value, as of the effective date of the plan, that is not less than the value of such holder's interest in the estate's interest in the property that secures such claims.

(8) With respect to each class of claims or interests—

(A) such class has accepted the plan; or

(B) such class is not impaired under the plan.

(9) Except to the extent that the holder of a particular claim has agreed to a different treatment of such claim, the plan provides that—

(A) with respect to a claim of a kind specified in section 507(a)(2) or 507(a)(3) of this title, on the effective date of the plan, the holder of such claim will receive on account of such claim cash equal to the allowed amount of such claim;

(B) with respect to a class of claims of a kind specified in section 507(a)(1), 507(a)(4), 507(a)(5), 507(a)(6), or 507(a)(7) of this title, each holder of a claim of such class will receive—

(i) if such class has accepted the plan, deferred cash payments of a value, as of the effective date of the plan, equal to the allowed amount of such claim; or

(ii) if such class has not accepted the plan, cash on the effective date of the plan equal to the allowed amount of such claim;

(C) with respect to a claim of a kind specified in section 507(a)(8) of this title, the holder of such claim will receive on account of such claim regular installment payments in cash—

(i) of a total value, as of the effective date of the plan, equal to the allowed amount of such claim;

(ii) over a period ending not later than 5 years after the date of the order for relief under section 301, 302, or 303; and

(iii) in a manner not less favorable than the most favored nonpriority unsecured claim provided for by the plan (other than cash payments made to a class of creditors under section 1122(b)); and

(D) with respect to a secured claim which would otherwise meet the description of an unsecured claim of a governmental unit under section 507(a)(8), but for the secured status of that claim, the holder of that claim will receive on account of that claim, cash payments, in the same manner and over the same period, as prescribed in subparagraph (C).

(10) If a class of claims is impaired under the plan, at least one class of claims that is impaired under the plan has accepted the plan, determined without including any acceptance of the plan by any insider.

(11) Confirmation of the plan is not likely to be followed by the liquidation, or the need for further financial reorganization, of the debtor or any successor to the debtor under the plan, unless such liquidation or reorganization is proposed in the plan.

(12) All fees payable under section 1930 of title 28, as determined by the court at the hearing on confirmation of the plan, have been paid or the plan provides for the payment of all such fees on the effective date of the plan.

(13) The plan provides for the continuation after its effective date of payment of all retiree benefits, as that term is defined in section 1114 of this title, at the level established pursuant to subsection (e)(1)(B) or (g) of section 1114 of this title, at any time prior to confirmation of the plan, for the duration of the period the debtor has obligated itself to provide such benefits.

(14) If the debtor is required by a judicial or administrative order, or by statute, to pay a domestic support obligation, the debtor has paid all amounts payable under such order or such statute for such obligation that first become payable after the date of the filing of the petition.

(15) In a case in which the debtor is an individual and in which the holder of an allowed unsecured claim objects to the confirmation of the plan—

(A) the value, as of the effective date of the plan, of the property to be distributed under the plan on account of such claim is not less than the amount of such claim; or

(B) the value of the property to be distributed under the plan is not less than the projected disposable income of the debtor (as defined in section 1325(b)(2)) to be received during the 5–year period beginning on the date that the first payment is due under the plan, or during the period for which the plan provides payments, whichever is longer.

(16) All transfers of property of the plan shall be made in accordance with any applicable provisions of nonbankruptcy law that govern the transfer of property by a corporation or trust that is not a moneyed, business, or commercial corporation or trust.

(b)(1) Notwithstanding section 510(a) of this title, if all of the applicable requirements of subsection (a) of this section other than paragraph (8) are met with respect to a plan, the court, on request of the proponent of the plan, shall confirm the plan notwithstanding the requirements of such paragraph if the plan does not discriminate unfairly, and is fair and equitable, with respect to each class of claims or interests that is impaired under, and has not accepted, the plan.

(2) For the purpose of this subsection, the condition that a plan be fair and equitable with respect to a class includes the following requirements:

(A) With respect to a class of secured claims, the plan provides—

(i)(I) that the holders of such claims retain the liens securing such claims, whether the property subject to such liens is retained by the debtor or transferred to another entity, to the extent of the allowed amount of such claims; and

(II) that each holder of a claim of such class receive on account of such claim deferred cash payments totaling at least the allowed amount of such claim, of a value, as of the effective date of the plan, of at least the value of such holder's interest in the estate's interest in such property;

(ii) for the sale, subject to section 363(k) of this title, of any property that is subject to the liens securing such claims, free and clear of such liens, with such liens to attach to the proceeds of such sale, and the treatment of such liens on proceeds under clause (i) or (iii) of this subparagraph; or

(iii) for the realization by such holders of the indubitable equivalent of such claims.

(B) With respect to a class of unsecured claims—

(i) the plan provides that each holder of a claim of such class receive or retain on account of such claim property of a value, as of the effective date of the plan, equal to the allowed amount of such claim; or

(ii) the holder of any claim or interest that is junior to the claims of such class will not receive or retain under the plan on account of such junior claim or interest any property, except that in a case in which the debtor is an individual, the debtor may retain property included in the estate under section 1115, subject to the requirements of subsection (a)(14) of this section.

(C) With respect to a class of interests—

(i) the plan provides that each holder of an interest of such class receive or retain on account of such interest property of a value, as of the effective date of the plan, equal to the greatest of the allowed amount of any fixed liquidation preference to which such holder is entitled, any fixed redemption price to which such holder is entitled, or the value of such interest; or

(ii) the holder of any interest that is junior to the interests of such class will not receive or retain under the plan on account of such junior interest any property.

(c) Notwithstanding subsections (a) and (b) of this section and except as provided in section 1127(b) of this title, the court may confirm only one plan, unless the order of confirmation in the case has been revoked under section 1144 of this title. If the requirements of subsections (a) and (b) of this section are met with respect to more than one plan, the court shall consider the preferences of creditors and equity security holders in determining which plan to confirm.

(d) Notwithstanding any other provision of this section, on request of a party in interest that is a governmental unit, the court may not confirm a plan if the principal purpose of the plan is the avoidance of taxes or the avoidance of the application of section 5 of the Securities Act of 1933. In any hearing under this subsection, the governmental unit has the burden of proof on the issue of avoidance.

(e) In a small business case, the court shall confirm a plan that complies with the applicable provisions of this title and that is filed in accordance with section 1121(e) not later than 45 days after the plan is filed unless the time for confirmation is extended in accordance with section 1121(e)(3).

11. ENVIRONMENTAL REGULATIONS AFFECTING REAL ESTATE

a. COMPREHENSIVE ENVIRONMENTAL RESPONSE, COMPENSATION, AND LIABILITY ACT ("CERCLA")

---

42 U.S.C.A.

§ 9601. Definitions

For purpose of this subchapter—

(1) The term "act of God" means an unanticipated grave natural disaster or other natural phenomenon of an exceptional, inevitable, and irresistible character, the effects of which could not have been prevented or avoided by the exercise of due care or foresight.

(2) The term "Administrator" means the Administrator of the United States Environmental Protection Agency.

(3) The term "barrel" means forty-two United States gallons at sixty degrees Fahrenheit.

(4) The term "claim" means a demand in writing for a sum certain.

(5) The term "claimant" means any person who presents a claim for compensation under this chapter.

(6) The term "damages" means damages for injury or loss of natural resources as set forth in section 9607(a) or 9611(b) of this title.

(7) The term "drinking water supply" means any raw or finished water source that is or may be used by a public water system (as defined in the Safe Drinking Water Act [42 U.S.C.A. § 300f et seq.]) or as drinking water by one or more individuals.

(8) The term "environment" means (A) the navigable waters, the waters of the contiguous zone, and the ocean waters of which the natural resources are under the exclusive management authority of the United States under the Magnuson–Stevens Fishery Conservation and Management Act [16 U.S.C.A. § 1801 et seq.], and (B) any other surface water, ground water, drinking water supply, land surface or subsurface strata, or ambient air within the United States or under the jurisdiction of the United States.

(9) The term "facility" means (A) any building, structure, installation, equipment, pipe or pipeline (including any pipe into a sewer or publicly owned treatment works), well, pit, pond, lagoon, impoundment, ditch, landfill, storage container, motor vehicle, rolling stock, or aircraft, or (B) any site or area where a hazardous substance has been deposited, stored, disposed of, or placed, or otherwise come to be located; but does not include any consumer product in consumer use or any vessel.

(10) The term "federally permitted release" means (A) discharges in compliance with a permit under section 1342 of Title 33, (B) discharges resulting from circumstances identified and reviewed and made part of the public record with respect to a permit issued or modified under section 1342 of Title 33 and subject to a condition of such permit, (C) continuous or anticipated intermittent discharges from a point source, identified in a permit or permit application under section 1342 of Title 33, which are caused by events occurring within the scope of relevant operating or treatment systems, (D) discharges in compliance with a legally enforceable permit under section 1344 of Title 33, (E) releases in compliance with a legally enforceable final permit issued pursuant to section 3005(a) through (d) of the Solid Waste Disposal Act [42 U.S.C.A. § 6925(a) to (d)] from a hazardous waste treatment, storage, or disposal facility when such permit specifically identifies the hazardous substances and makes such substances subject to a standard of practice, control procedure or bioassay limitation or condition, or other control on the hazardous substances in such releases, (F) any release in compliance with a legally enforceable permit issued under section 1412 of Title 33 of[1] section 1413 of Title 33, (G) any injection of fluids authorized under Federal underground injection control programs or State programs submitted for Federal approval (and not disapproved by the Administrator of the Environmental Protection Agency) pursuant to part C of the Safe Drinking Water Act [42 U.S.C.A. § 300h et seq.], (H) any emission into the air subject to a permit or control regulation under section 111 [42 U.S.C.A. § 7411], section 112 [42 U.S.C.A. § 7412], Title I part C [42 U.S.C.A. § 7470 et seq.], Title I part D [42 U.S.C.A. § 7501 et seq.], or State implementation plans submitted in accordance with section 110 of the Clean Air Act [42 U.S.C.A. § 7410] (and not disapproved by the Administrator of the Environmental Protection Agency), including any schedule or waiver granted, promulgated, or approved under these sections, (I) any injection of fluids or other materials authorized under applicable State law (i) for the purpose of stimulating or treating wells for the production of crude oil, natural gas, or water, (ii) for the purpose of secondary, tertiary, or other enhanced recovery of crude oil or natural gas, or (iii) which are brought to the surface in conjunction with the production of crude oil or natural gas and which are reinjected, (J) the introduction of any pollutant into a publicly owned treatment works when such pollutant is specified in and in compliance with applicable pretreatment standards of section 1317(b) or (c) of Title 33 and enforceable requirements in a pretreatment program submitted by a State or municipality for Federal approval under section 1342 of Title 33, and (K) any release of source, special nuclear, or byproduct material, as those terms are defined in the Atomic Energy Act of 1954 [42 U.S.C.A. § 2011 et seq.], in compliance with a legally enforceable license, permit, regulation, or order issued pursuant to the Atomic Energy Act of 1954.

(11) The term "Fund" or "Trust Fund" means the Hazardous Substance Superfund established by section 9507 of Title 26.

(12) The term "ground water" means water in a saturated zone or stratum beneath the surface of land or water.

(13) The term "guarantor" means any person, other than the owner or operator, who provides evidence of financial responsibility for an owner or operator under this chapter.

(14) The term "hazardous substance" means (A) any substance designated pursuant to section 1321(b)(2)(A) of Title 33, (B) any element, compound, mixture, solution, or substance designated pursuant to section 9602 of this title, (C) any hazardous waste having the characteristics identified under or listed pursuant to section 3001 of the Solid Waste Disposal Act [42 U.S.C.A. § 6921] (but not including any waste the regulation of which under the Solid Waste Disposal Act [42 U.S.C.A. § 6901 et seq.] has been suspended by Act of Congress), (D) any toxic pollutant listed under section 1317(a) of Title 33, (E) any

---

1. So in original. Probably should be "or".

hazardous air pollutant listed under section 112 of the Clean Air Act [42 U.S.C.A. § 7412], and (F) any imminently hazardous chemical substance or mixture with respect to which the Administrator has taken action pursuant to section 2606 of Title 15. The term does not include petroleum, including crude oil or any fraction thereof which is not otherwise specifically listed or designated as a hazardous substance under subparagraphs (A) through (F) of this paragraph, and the term does not include natural gas, natural gas liquids, liquefied natural gas, or synthetic gas usable for fuel (or mixtures of natural gas and such synthetic gas).

(15) The term "navigable waters" or "navigable waters of the United States" means the waters of the United States, including the territorial seas.

(16) The term "natural resources" means land, fish, wildlife, biota, air, water, ground water, drinking water supplies, and other such resources belonging to, managed by, held in trust by, appertaining to, or otherwise controlled by the United States (including the resources of the fishery conservation zone established by the Magnuson–Stevens Fishery Conservation and Management Act [16 U.S.C.A. § 1801 et seq.]) any State or local government, any foreign government, any Indian tribe, or, if such resources are subject to a trust restriction on alienation, any member of an Indian tribe.

(17) The term "offshore facility" means any facility of any kind located in, on, or under, any of the navigable waters of the United States, and any facility of any kind which is subject to the jurisdiction of the United States and is located in, on, or under any other waters, other than a vessel or a public vessel.

(18) The term "onshore facility" means any facility (including, but not limited to, motor vehicles and rolling stock) of any kind located in, on, or under, any land or nonnavigable waters within the United States.

(19) The term "otherwise subject to the jurisdiction of the United States" means subject to the jurisdiction of the United States by virtue of United States citizenship, United States vessel documentation or numbering, or as provided by international agreement to which the United States is a party.

(20)(A) The term "owner or operator" means (i) in the case of a vessel, any person owning, operating, or chartering by demise, such vessel, (ii) in the case of an onshore facility or an offshore facility, any person owning or operating such facility, and (iii) in the case of any facility, title or control of which was conveyed due to bankruptcy, foreclosure, tax delinquency, abandonment, or similar means to a unit of State or local government, any person who owned, operated, or otherwise controlled activities at such facility immediately beforehand. Such term does not include a person, who, without participating in the management of a vessel or facility, holds indicia of ownership primarily to protect his security interest in the vessel or facility.

(B) In the case of a hazardous substance which has been accepted for transportation by a common or contract carrier and except as provided in section 9607(a)(3) or (4) of this title, (i) the term "owner or operator" shall mean such common carrier or other bona fide for hire carrier acting as an independent contractor during such transportation, (ii) the shipper of such hazardous substance shall not be considered to have caused or contributed to any release during such transportation which resulted solely from circumstances or conditions beyond his control.

(C) In the case of a hazardous substance which has been delivered by a common or contract carrier to a disposal or treatment facility and except as provided in section 9607(a)(3) or (4) of this title, (i) the term "owner or operator" shall not include such common or contract carrier, and (ii) such common or contract carrier shall not be considered to have caused or contributed to any release at such disposal or treatment facility resulting from circumstances or conditions beyond its control.

(D) The term "owner or operator" does not include a unit of State or local government which acquired ownership or control involuntarily through bankruptcy, tax delinquency, abandonment, or other circumstances in which the government involuntarily acquires title by virtue of its function as sovereign. The exclusion provided under this paragraph shall not apply to any State or local government which has caused or contributed to the release or threatened release of a hazardous substance from the facility, and such a State or local government shall be subject to the provisions of this chapter in the same manner and to the same extent, both procedurally and substantively, as any nongovernmental entity, including liability under section 9607 of this title.

(E) Exclusion of lenders not participants in management

    (i) Indicia of ownership to protect security

The term "owner or operator" does not include a person that is a lender that, without participating in the management of a vessel or facility, holds indicia of ownership primarily to protect the security interest of the person in the vessel or facility.

    (ii) Foreclosure

The term "owner or operator" does not include a person that is a lender that did not participate in management of a vessel or facility prior to foreclosure, notwithstanding that the person—

    (I) forecloses on the vessel or facility; and

    (II) after foreclosure, sells, re-leases (in the case of a lease finance transaction), or liquidates the vessel or facility, maintains business activities, winds up operations, undertakes a response action under section 9607(d)(1) of this title or under the direction of an on-scene coordinator appointed under the National Contingency Plan, with respect to the vessel or facility, or takes any other measure to preserve, protect, or prepare the vessel or facility prior to sale or disposition, if the person seeks to sell, re-lease (in the case of a lease finance transaction), or otherwise divest the person of the vessel or facility at the earliest practicable, commercially reasonable time, on commercially reasonable terms, taking into account market conditions and legal and regulatory requirements.

(F) Participation in management

For purposes of subparagraph (E)—

    (i) the term "participate in management"—

    (I) means actually participating in the management or operational affairs of a vessel or facility; and

    (II) does not include merely having the capacity to influence, or the unexercised right to control, vessel or facility operations;

193

(ii) a person that is a lender and that holds indicia of ownership primarily to protect a security interest in a vessel or facility shall be considered to participate in management only if, while the borrower is still in possession of the vessel or facility encumbered by the security interest, the person—

(I) exercises decisionmaking control over the environmental compliance related to the vessel or facility, such that the person has undertaken responsibility for the hazardous substance handling or disposal practices related to the vessel or facility; or

(II) exercises control at a level comparable to that of a manager of the vessel or facility, such that the person has assumed or manifested responsibility—

(aa) for the overall management of the vessel or facility encompassing day-to-day decisionmaking with respect to environmental compliance; or

(bb) over all or substantially all of the operational functions (as distinguished from financial or administrative functions) of the vessel or facility other than the function of environmental compliance;

(iii) the term "participate in management" does not include performing an act or failing to act prior to the time at which a security interest is created in a vessel or facility; and

(iv) the term "participate in management" does not include—

(I) holding a security interest or abandoning or releasing a security interest;

(II) including in the terms of an extension of credit, or in a contract or security agreement relating to the extension, a covenant, warranty, or other term or condition that relates to environmental compliance;

(III) monitoring or enforcing the terms and conditions of the extension of credit or security interest;

(IV) monitoring or undertaking 1 or more inspections of the vessel or facility;

(V) requiring a response action or other lawful means of addressing the release or threatened release of a hazardous substance in connection with the vessel or facility prior to, during, or on the expiration of the term of the extension of credit;

(VI) providing financial or other advice or counseling in an effort to mitigate, prevent, or cure default or diminution in the value of the vessel or facility;

(VII) restructuring, renegotiating, or otherwise agreeing to alter the terms and conditions of the extension of credit or security interest, exercising forbearance;

(VIII) exercising other remedies that may be available under applicable law for the breach of a term or condition of the extension of credit or security agreement; or

(IX) conducting a response action under section 9607(d) of this title or under the direction of an on-scene coordinator appointed under the National Contingency Plan,

if the actions do not rise to the level of participating in management (within the meaning of clauses (i) and (ii)).

(G) Other terms

As used in this chapter:

(i) Extension of credit

The term "extension of credit" includes a lease finance transaction—

(I) in which the lessor does not initially select the leased vessel or facility and does not during the lease term control the daily operations or maintenance of the vessel or facility; or

(II) that conforms with regulations issued by the appropriate Federal banking agency or the appropriate State bank supervisor (as those terms are defined in section 1813 of Title 12)[2] or with regulations issued by the National Credit Union Administration Board, as appropriate.

(ii) Financial or administrative function

The term "financial or administrative function" includes a function such as that of a credit manager, accounts payable officer, accounts receivable officer, personnel manager, comptroller, or chief financial officer, or a similar function.

(iii) Foreclosure; foreclose

The terms "foreclosure" and "foreclose" mean, respectively, acquiring, and to acquire, a vessel or facility through—

(I)(aa) purchase at sale under a judgment or decree, power of sale, or nonjudicial foreclosure sale;

(bb) a deed in lieu of foreclosure, or similar conveyance from a trustee; or

(cc) repossession,

if the vessel or facility was security for an extension of credit previously contracted;

(II) conveyance pursuant to an extension of credit previously contracted, including the termination of a lease agreement; or

(III) any other formal or informal manner by which the person acquires, for subsequent disposition, title to or possession of a vessel or facility in order to protect the security interest of the person.

(iv) Lender

The term "lender" means—

(I) an insured depository institution (as defined in section 1813 of Title 12);

(II) an insured credit union (as defined in section 1752 of Title 12);

(III) a bank or association chartered under the Farm Credit Act of 1971 (12 U.S.C. 2001 et seq.);

(IV) a leasing or trust company that is an affiliate of an insured depository institution;

---

2. So in original. Probably should be followed by a closing parenthesis.

(V) any person (including a successor or assignee of any such person) that makes a bona fide extension of credit to or takes or acquires a security interest from a nonaffiliated person;

(VI) the Federal National Mortgage Association, the Federal Home Loan Mortgage Corporation, the Federal Agricultural Mortgage Corporation, or any other entity that in a bona fide manner buys or sells loans or interests in loans;

(VII) a person that insures or guarantees against a default in the repayment of an extension of credit, or acts as a surety with respect to an extension of credit, to a nonaffiliated person; and

(VIII) a person that provides title insurance and that acquires a vessel or facility as a result of assignment or conveyance in the course of underwriting claims and claims settlement.

(v) Operational function

The term "operational function" includes a function such as that of a facility or plant manager, operations manager, chief operating officer, or chief executive officer.

(vi) Security interest

The term "security interest" includes a right under a mortgage, deed of trust, assignment, judgment lien, pledge, security agreement, factoring agreement, or lease and any other right accruing to a person to secure the repayment of money, the performance of a duty, or any other obligation by a nonaffiliated person.

(21) The term "person" means an individual, firm, corporation, association, partnership, consortium, joint venture, commercial entity, United States Government, State, municipality, commission, political subdivision of a State, or any interstate body.

(22) The term "release" means any spilling, leaking, pumping, pouring, emitting, emptying, discharging, injecting, escaping, leaching, dumping, or disposing into the environment (including the abandonment or discarding of barrels, containers, and other closed receptacles containing any hazardous substance or pollutant or contaminant), but excludes (A) any release which results in exposure to persons solely within a workplace, with respect to a claim which such persons may assert against the employer of such persons, (B) emissions from the engine exhaust of a motor vehicle, rolling stock, aircraft, vessel, or pipeline pumping station engine, (C) release of source, byproduct, or special nuclear material from a nuclear incident, as those terms are defined in the Atomic Energy Act of 1954 [42 U.S.C.A. § 2011 et seq.], if such release is subject to requirements with respect to financial protection established by the Nuclear Regulatory Commission under section 170 of such Act [42 U.S.C.A. § 2210], or, for the purposes of section 9604 of this title or any other response action, any release of source byproduct, or special nuclear material from any processing site designated under section 7912(a)(1) or 7942(a) of this title, and (D) the normal application of fertilizer.

(23) The terms "remove" or "removal" means[3] the cleanup or removal of released hazardous substances from the environment, such actions as may be necessary taken in the event of the threat of release of hazardous substances into the environment, such actions as may be necessary to monitor, assess, and evaluate the release or threat of release of

---

3. So in original. Probably should be "mean".

hazardous substances, the disposal of removed material, or the taking of such other actions as may be necessary to prevent, minimize, or mitigate damage to the public health or welfare or to the environment, which may otherwise result from a release or threat of release. The term includes, in addition, without being limited to, security fencing or other measures to limit access, provision of alternative water supplies, temporary evacuation and housing of threatened individuals not otherwise provided for, action taken under section 9604(b) of this title, and any emergency assistance which may be provided under the Disaster Relief and Emergency Assistance Act [42 U.S.C.A. § 5121 et seq.].

(24) The terms "remedy" or "remedial action" means[4] those actions consistent with permanent remedy taken instead of or in addition to removal actions in the event of a release or threatened release of a hazardous substance into the environment, to prevent or minimize the release of hazardous substances so that they do not migrate to cause substantial danger to present or future public health or welfare or the environment. The term includes, but is not limited to, such actions at the location of the release as storage, confinement, perimeter protection using dikes, trenches, or ditches, clay cover, neutralization, cleanup of released hazardous substances and associated contaminated materials, recycling or reuse, diversion, destruction, segregation of reactive wastes, dredging or excavations, repair or replacement of leaking containers, collection of leachate and runoff, onsite treatment or incineration, provision of alternative water supplies, and any monitoring reasonably required to assure that such actions protect the public health and welfare and the environment. The term includes the costs of permanent relocation of residents and businesses and community facilities where the President determines that, alone or in combination with other measures, such relocation is more cost-effective than and environmentally preferable to the transportation, storage, treatment, destruction, or secure disposition offsite of hazardous substances, or may otherwise be necessary to protect the public health or welfare; the term includes offsite transport and offsite storage, treatment, destruction, or secure disposition of hazardous substances and associated contaminated materials.

(25) The terms "respond" or "response" means[5] remove, removal, remedy, and remedial action;,[6] all such terms (including the terms "removal" and "remedial action") include enforcement activities related thereto.

(26) The terms "transport" or "transportation" means[7] the movement of a hazardous substance by any mode, including a hazardous liquid pipeline facility (as defined in section 60101(a) of Title 49), and in the case of a hazardous substance which has been accepted for transportation by a common or contract carrier, the term "transport" or "transportation" shall include any stoppage in transit which is temporary, incidental to the transportation movement, and at the ordinary operating convenience of a common or contract carrier, and any such stoppage shall be considered as a continuity of movement and not as the storage of a hazardous substance.

(27) The terms "United States" and "State" include the several States of the United States, the District of Columbia, the Commonwealth of Puerto Rico, Guam, American

---

4. So in original. Probably should be "mean".

5. So in original. Probably should be "mean".

6. So in original.

7. So in original. Probably should be "mean".

Samoa, the United States Virgin Islands, the Commonwealth of the Northern Marianas, and any other territory or possession over which the United States has jurisdiction.

(28) The term "vessel" means every description of watercraft or other artificial contrivance used, or capable of being used, as a means of transportation on water.

(29) The terms "disposal", "hazardous waste", and "treatment" shall have the meaning provided in section 1004 of the Solid Waste Disposal Act [42 U.S.C.A. § 6903].

(30) The terms "territorial sea" and "contiguous zone" shall have the meaning provided in section 1362 of Title 33.

(31) The term "national contingency plan" means the national contingency plan published under section 1321(c) of Title 33 or revised pursuant to section 9605 of this title.

(32) The terms "liable" or "liability" under this subchapter shall be construed to be the standard of liability which obtains under section 1321 of Title 33.

(33) The term "pollutant or contaminant" shall include, but not be limited to, any element, substance, compound, or mixture, including disease-causing agents, which after release into the environment and upon exposure, ingestion, inhalation, or assimilation into any organism, either directly from the environment or indirectly by ingestion through food chains, will or may reasonably be anticipated to cause death, disease, behavioral abnormalities, cancer, genetic mutation, physiological malfunctions (including malfunctions in reproduction) or physical deformations, in such organisms or their offspring; except that the term "pollutant or contaminant" shall not include petroleum, including crude oil or any fraction thereof which is not otherwise specifically listed or designated as a hazardous substance under subparagraphs (A) through (F) of paragraph (14) and shall not include natural gas, liquefied natural gas, or synthetic gas of pipeline quality (or mixtures of natural gas and such synthetic gas).

(34) The term "alternative water supplies" includes, but is not limited to, drinking water and household water supplies.

(35)(A) The term "contractual relationship", for the purpose of section 9607(b)(3) of this title, includes, but is not limited to, land contracts, deeds, easements, leases, or other instruments transferring title or possession, unless the real property on which the facility concerned is located was acquired by the defendant after the disposal or placement of the hazardous substance on, in, or at the facility, and one or more of the circumstances described in clause (i), (ii), or (iii) is also established by the defendant by a preponderance of the evidence:

> **(i)** At the time the defendant acquired the facility the defendant did not know and had no reason to know that any hazardous substance which is the subject of the release or threatened release was disposed of on, in, or at the facility.

> **(ii)** The defendant is a government entity which acquired the facility by escheat, or through any other involuntary transfer or acquisition, or through the exercise of eminent domain authority by purchase or condemnation.

> **(iii)** The defendant acquired the facility by inheritance or bequest.

In addition to establishing the foregoing, the defendant must establish that the defendant has satisfied the requirements of section 9607(b)(3)(a) and (b) of this title, provides full cooperation, assistance, and facility access to the persons that are authorized to conduct response actions at the facility (including the cooperation and access necessary for the installation, integrity, operation, and maintenance of any complete or partial response action at the facility), is in compliance with any land use restrictions established or relied on in connection with the response action at a facility, and does not impede the effectiveness or integrity of any institutional control employed at the facility in connection with a response action.

(B) Reason to know

(i) All appropriate inquiries

To establish that the defendant had no reason to know of the matter described in subparagraph (A)(i), the defendant must demonstrate to a court that—

(I) on or before the date on which the defendant acquired the facility, the defendant carried out all appropriate inquiries, as provided in clauses (ii) and (iv), into the previous ownership and uses of the facility in accordance with generally accepted good commercial and customary standards and practices; and

(II) the defendant took reasonable steps to—

(aa) stop any continuing release;

(bb) prevent any threatened future release; and

(cc) prevent or limit any human, environmental, or natural resource exposure to any previously released hazardous substance.

(ii) Standards and practices

Not later than 2 years after January 11, 2002, the Administrator shall by regulation establish standards and practices for the purpose of satisfying the requirement to carry out all appropriate inquiries under clause (i).

(iii) Criteria

In promulgating regulations that establish the standards and practices referred to in clause (ii), the Administrator shall include each of the following:

(I) The results of an inquiry by an environmental professional.

(II) Interviews with past and present owners, operators, and occupants of the facility for the purpose of gathering information regarding the potential for contamination at the facility.

(III) Reviews of historical sources, such as chain of title documents, aerial photographs, building department records, and land use records, to determine previous uses and occupancies of the real property since the property was first developed.

(IV) Searches for recorded environmental cleanup liens against the facility that are filed under Federal, State, or local law.

(V) Reviews of Federal, State, and local government records, waste disposal records, underground storage tank records, and hazardous waste handling, generation, treatment, disposal, and spill records, concerning contamination at or near the facility.

(VI) Visual inspections of the facility and of adjoining properties.

(VII) Specialized knowledge or experience on the part of the defendant.

(VIII) The relationship of the purchase price to the value of the property, if the property was not contaminated.

(IX) Commonly known or reasonably ascertainable information about the property.

(X) The degree of obviousness of the presence or likely presence of contamination at the property, and the ability to detect the contamination by appropriate investigation.

(iv) Interim standards and practices

(I) Property purchased before May 31, 1997

With respect to property purchased before May 31, 1997, in making a determination with respect to a defendant described in clause (i), a court shall take into account—

(aa) any specialized knowledge or experience on the part of the defendant;

(bb) the relationship of the purchase price to the value of the property, if the property was not contaminated;

(cc) commonly known or reasonably ascertainable information about the property;

(dd) the obviousness of the presence or likely presence of contamination at the property; and

(ee) the ability of the defendant to detect the contamination by appropriate inspection.

(II) Property purchased on or after May 31, 1997

With respect to property purchased on or after May 31, 1997, and until the Administrator promulgates the regulations described in clause (ii), the procedures of the American Society for Testing and Materials, including the document known as "Standard E1527–97", entitled "Standard Practice for Environmental Site Assessment: Phase 1 Environmental Site Assessment Process", shall satisfy the requirements in clause (i).

(v) Site inspection and title search

In the case of property for residential use or other similar use purchased by a nongovernmental or noncommercial entity, a facility inspection and title search that reveal no basis for further investigation shall be considered to satisfy the requirements of this subparagraph.

(C) Nothing in this paragraph or in section 9607(b)(3) of this title shall diminish the liability of any previous owner or operator of such facility who would otherwise be liable under this chapter. Notwithstanding this paragraph, if the defendant obtained actual knowledge of the release or threatened release of a hazardous substance at such facility when the defendant owned the real property and then subsequently transferred ownership of the property to another person without disclosing such knowledge, such defendant shall be treated as liable under section 9607(a)(1) of this title and no defense under section 9607(b)(3) of this title shall be available to such defendant.

(D) Nothing in this paragraph shall affect the liability under this chapter of a defendant who, by any act or omission, caused or contributed to the release or threatened release of a hazardous substance which is the subject of the action relating to the facility.

(36) The term "Indian tribe" means any Indian tribe, band, nation, or other organized group or community, including any Alaska Native village but not including any Alaska Native regional or village corporation, which is recognized as eligible for the special programs and services provided by the United States to Indians because of their status as Indians.

(37)(A) The term "service station dealer" means any person—

    (i) who owns or operates a motor vehicle service station, filling station, garage, or similar retail establishment engaged in the business of selling, repairing, or servicing motor vehicles, where a significant percentage of the gross revenue of the establishment is derived from the fueling, repairing, or servicing of motor vehicles, and

    (ii) who accepts for collection, accumulation, and delivery to an oil recycling facility, recycled oil that (I) has been removed from the engine of a light duty motor vehicle or household appliances by the owner of such vehicle or appliances, and (II) is presented, by such owner, to such person for collection, accumulation, and delivery to an oil recycling facility.

    (B) For purposes of section 9614(c) of this title, the term "service station dealer" shall, notwithstanding the provisions of subparagraph (A), include any government agency that establishes a facility solely for the purpose of accepting recycled oil that satisfies the criteria set forth in subclauses (I) and (II) of subparagraph (A)(ii), and, with respect to recycled oil that satisfies the criteria set forth in subclauses (I) and (II), owners or operators of refuse collection services who are compelled by State law to collect, accumulate, and deliver such oil to an oil recycling facility.

    (C) The President shall promulgate regulations regarding the determination of what constitutes a significant percentage of the gross revenues of an establishment for purposes of this paragraph.

(38) The term "incineration vessel" means any vessel which carries hazardous substances for the purpose of incineration of such substances, so long as such substances or residues of such substances are on board.

(39) Brownfield site

    (A) In general

The term "brownfield site" means real property, the expansion, redevelopment, or reuse of which may be complicated by the presence or potential presence of a hazardous substance, pollutant, or contaminant.

    (B) Exclusions

The term "brownfield site" does not include—

    (i) a facility that is the subject of a planned or ongoing removal action under this subchapter;

    (ii) a facility that is listed on the National Priorities List or is proposed for listing;

    (iii) a facility that is the subject of a unilateral administrative order, a court order, an administrative order on consent or judicial consent decree that has been issued to or entered into by the parties under this chapter;

201

(iv) a facility that is the subject of a unilateral administrative order, a court order, an administrative order on consent or judicial consent decree that has been issued to or entered into by the parties, or a facility to which a permit has been issued by the United States or an authorized State under the Solid Waste Disposal Act (42 U.S.C. 6901 et seq.), the Federal Water Pollution Control Act (33 U.S.C. 1321), the Toxic Substances Control Act (15 U.S.C. 2601 et seq.), or the Safe Drinking Water Act (42 U.S.C. 300f et seq.);

(v) a facility that—

(I) is subject to corrective action under section 3004(u) or 3008(h) of the Solid Waste Disposal Act (42 U.S.C. 6924(u), 6928(h)); and

(II) to which a corrective action permit or order has been issued or modified to require the implementation of corrective measures;

(vi) a land disposal unit with respect to which—

(I) a closure notification under subtitle C of the Solid Waste Disposal Act (42 U.S.C. 6921 et seq.) has been submitted; and

(II) closure requirements have been specified in a closure plan or permit;

(vii) a facility that is subject to the jurisdiction, custody, or control of a department, agency, or instrumentality of the United States, except for land held in trust by the United States for an Indian tribe;

(viii) a portion of a facility—

(I) at which there has been a release of polychlorinated biphenyls; and

(II) that is subject to remediation under the Toxic Substances Control Act (15 U.S.C. 2601 et seq.); or

(ix) a portion of a facility, for which portion, assistance for response activity has been obtained under subtitle I of the Solid Waste Disposal Act (42 U.S.C. 6991 et seq.) from the Leaking Underground Storage Tank Trust Fund established under section 9508 of Title 26.

(C) Site-by-site determinations

Notwithstanding subparagraph (B) and on a site-by-site basis, the President may authorize financial assistance under section 9604(k) of this title to an eligible entity at a site included in clause (i), (iv), (v), (vi), (viii), or (ix) of subparagraph (B) if the President finds that financial assistance will protect human health and the environment, and either promote economic development or enable the creation of, preservation of, or addition to parks, greenways, undeveloped property, other recreational property, or other property used for nonprofit purposes.

(D) Additional areas

For the purposes of section 9604(k) of this title, the term ''brownfield site'' includes a site that—

(i) meets the definition of ''brownfield site'' under subparagraphs (A) through (C); and

(ii)(I) is contaminated by a controlled substance (as defined in section 802 of Title 21);

(II)(aa) is contaminated by petroleum or a petroleum product excluded from the definition of "hazardous substance" under this section; and

(bb) is a site determined by the Administrator or the State, as appropriate, to be—

(AA) of relatively low risk, as compared with other petroleum-only sites in the State; and

(BB) a site for which there is no viable responsible party and which will be assessed, investigated, or cleaned up by a person that is not potentially liable for cleaning up the site; and

(cc) is not subject to any order issued under section 6991b(h) of this title; or

(III) is mine-scarred land.

(40) Bona fide prospective purchaser

The term "bona fide prospective purchaser" means a person (or a tenant of a person) that acquires ownership of a facility after the date of the enactment of this paragraph and that establishes each of the following by a preponderance of the evidence:

(A) Disposal prior to acquisition

All disposal of hazardous substances at the facility occurred before the person acquired the facility.

(B) Inquiries

(i) In general

The person made all appropriate inquiries into the previous ownership and uses of the facility in accordance with generally accepted good commercial and customary standards and practices in accordance with clauses (ii) and (iii).

(ii) Standards and practices

The standards and practices referred to in clauses (ii) and (iv) of paragraph (35)(B) of this section shall be considered to satisfy the requirements of this subparagraph.

(iii) Residential use

In the case of property in residential or other similar use at the time of purchase by a nongovernmental or noncommercial entity, a facility inspection and title search that reveal no basis for further investigation shall be considered to satisfy the requirements of this subparagraph.

(C) Notices

The person provides all legally required notices with respect to the discovery or release of any hazardous substances at the facility.

(D) Care

The person exercises appropriate care with respect to hazardous substances found at the facility by taking reasonable steps to—

(i) stop any continuing release;

(ii) prevent any threatened future release; and

(iii) prevent or limit human, environmental, or natural resource exposure to any previously released hazardous substance.

(E) Cooperation, assistance, and access

The person provides full cooperation, assistance, and access to persons that are authorized to conduct response actions or natural resource restoration at a vessel or facility (including the cooperation and access necessary for the installation, integrity, operation, and maintenance of any complete or partial response actions or natural resource restoration at the vessel or facility).

(F) Institutional control

The person—

(i) is in compliance with any land use restrictions established or relied on in connection with the response action at a vessel or facility; and

(ii) does not impede the effectiveness or integrity of any institutional control employed at the vessel or facility in connection with a response action.

(G) Requests; subpoenas

The person complies with any request for information or administrative subpoena issued by the President under this chapter.

(H) No affiliation

The person is not—

(i) potentially liable, or affiliated with any other person that is potentially liable, for response costs at a facility through—

(I) any direct or indirect familial relationship; or

(II) any contractual, corporate, or financial relationship (other than a contractual, corporate, or financial relationship that is created by the instruments by which title to the facility is conveyed or financed or by a contract for the sale of goods or services); or

(ii) the result of a reorganization of a business entity that was potentially liable.

(41) Eligible response site

(A) In general

The term "eligible response site" means a site that meets the definition of a brownfield site in subparagraphs (A) and (B) of paragraph (39) of this section, as modified by subparagraphs (B) and (C) of this paragraph.

(B) Inclusions

The term "eligible response site" includes—

(i) notwithstanding paragraph (39)(B)(ix) of this section, a portion of a facility, for which portion assistance for response activity has been obtained under subtitle I of the Solid Waste Disposal Act (42 U.S.C. 6991 et seq.) from the Leaking Underground Storage Tank Trust Fund established under section 9508 of Title 26; or

(ii) a site for which, notwithstanding the exclusions provided in subparagraph (C) or paragraph (39)(B) of this section, the President determines, on a site-by-site basis and after consultation with the State, that limitations on enforcement under section 9628 of this title at sites specified in clause (iv), (v), (vi) or (viii) of paragraph (39)(B) of this section would be appropriate and will—

(I) protect human health and the environment; and

(II) promote economic development or facilitate the creation of, preservation of, or addition to a park, a greenway, undeveloped property, recreational property, or other property used for nonprofit purposes.

(C) Exclusions

The term "eligible response site" does not include—

(i) a facility for which the President—

(I) conducts or has conducted a preliminary assessment or site inspection; and

(II) after consultation with the State, determines or has determined that the site obtains a preliminary score sufficient for possible listing on the National Priorities List, or that the site otherwise qualifies for listing on the National Priorities List; unless the President has made a determination that no further Federal action will be taken; or

(ii) facilities that the President determines warrant particular consideration as identified by regulation, such as sites posing a threat to a sole-source drinking water aquifer or a sensitive ecosystem.

§ 9607. Liability

(a) Covered persons; scope; recoverable costs and damages; interest rate; "comparable maturity" date

Notwithstanding any other provision or rule of law, and subject only to the defenses set forth in subsection (b) of this section—

(1) the owner and operator of a vessel or a facility,

(2) any person who at the time of disposal of any hazardous substance owned or operated any facility at which such hazardous substances were disposed of,

(3) any person who by contract, agreement, or otherwise arranged for disposal or treatment, or arranged with a transporter for transport for disposal or treatment, of hazardous substances owned or possessed by such person, by any other party or entity, at any facility or incineration vessel owned or operated by another party or entity and containing such hazardous substances, and

(4) any person who accepts or accepted any hazardous substances for transport to disposal or treatment facilities, incineration vessels or sites selected by such person, from which there is a release, or a threatened release which causes the incurrence of response costs, of a hazardous substance, shall be liable for—

(A) all costs of removal or remedial action incurred by the United States Government or a State or an Indian tribe not inconsistent with the national contingency plan;

(B) any other necessary costs of response incurred by any other person consistent with the national contingency plan;

(C) damages for injury to, destruction of, or loss of natural resources, including the reasonable costs of assessing such injury, destruction, or loss resulting from such a release; and

(D) the costs of any health assessment or health effects study carried out under section 9604(i) of this title.

The amounts recoverable in an action under this section shall include interest on the amounts recoverable under subparagraphs (A) through (D). Such interest shall accrue from the later of (i) the date payment of a specified amount is demanded in writing, or (ii) the date of the expenditure concerned. The rate of interest on the outstanding unpaid balance of the amounts recoverable under this section shall be the same rate as is specified for interest on investments of the Hazardous Substance Superfund established under subchapter A of chapter 98 of Title 26. For purposes of applying such amendments to interest under this subsection, the term "comparable maturity" shall be determined with reference to the date on which interest accruing under this subsection commences.

(b) Defenses

There shall be no liability under subsection (a) of this section for a person otherwise liable who can establish by a preponderance of the evidence that the release or threat of release of a hazardous substance and the damages resulting therefrom were caused solely by—

(1) an act of God;

(2) an act of war;

(3) an act or omission of a third party other than an employee or agent of the defendant, or than one whose act or omission occurs in connection with a contractual relationship, existing directly or indirectly, with the defendant (except where the sole contractual arrangement arises from a published tariff and acceptance for carriage by a common carrier by rail), if the defendant establishes by a preponderance of the evidence that (a) he exercised due care with respect to the hazardous substance concerned, taking into consideration the characteristics of such hazardous substance, in light of all relevant facts and circumstances, and (b) he took precautions against foreseeable acts or omissions of any such third party and the consequences that could foreseeably result from such acts or omissions; or

(4) any combination of the foregoing paragraphs.

(c) Determination of amounts

(1) Except as provided in paragraph (2) of this subsection, the liability under this section of an owner or operator or other responsible person for each release of a hazardous substance or incident involving release of a hazardous substance shall not exceed—

(A) for any vessel, other than an incineration vessel, which carries any hazardous substance as cargo or residue, $300 per gross ton, or $5,000,000, whichever is greater;

(B) for any other vessel, other than an incineration vessel, $300 per gross ton, or $500,000, whichever is greater;

(C) for any motor vehicle, aircraft, hazardous liquid pipeline facility (as defined in section 60101(a) of Title 49), or rolling stock, $50,000,000 or such lesser amount as the President shall establish by regulation, but in no event less than $5,000,000 (or, for releases of hazardous substances as defined in section 9601(14)(A) of this title into the

206

navigable waters, $8,000,000). Such regulations shall take into account the size, type, location, storage, and handling capacity and other matters relating to the likelihood of release in each such class and to the economic impact of such limits on each such class; or

(D) for any incineration vessel or any facility other than those specified in subparagraph (C) of this paragraph, the total of all costs of response plus $50,000,000 for any damages under this subchapter.

(2) Notwithstanding the limitations in paragraph (1) of this subsection, the liability of an owner or operator or other responsible person under this section shall be the full and total costs of response and damages, if (A)(i) the release or threat of release of a hazardous substance was the result of willful misconduct or willful negligence within the privity or knowledge of such person, or (ii) the primary cause of the release was a violation (within the privity or knowledge of such person) of applicable safety, construction, or operating standards or regulations; or (B) such person fails or refuses to provide all reasonable cooperation and assistance requested by a responsible public official in connection with response activities under the national contingency plan with respect to regulated carriers subject to the provisions of Title 49 or vessels subject to the provisions of Title 33, 46, or 46 Appendix, subparagraph (A)(ii) of this paragraph shall be deemed to refer to Federal standards or regulations.

(3) If any person who is liable for a release or threat of release of a hazardous substance fails without sufficient cause to properly provide removal or remedial action upon order of the President pursuant to section 9604 or 9606 of this title, such person may be liable to the United States for punitive damages in an amount at least equal to, and not more than three times, the amount of any costs incurred by the Fund as a result of such failure to take proper action. The President is authorized to commence a civil action against any such person to recover the punitive damages, which shall be in addition to any costs recovered from such person pursuant to section 9612(c) of this title. Any moneys received by the United States pursuant to this subsection shall be deposited in the Fund.

(d) Rendering care or advice

(1) In general

Except as provided in paragraph (2), no person shall be liable under this subchapter for costs or damages as a result of actions taken or omitted in the course of rendering care, assistance, or advice in accordance with the National Contingency Plan ("NCP") or at the direction of an onscene coordinator appointed under such plan, with respect to an incident creating a danger to public health or welfare or the environment as a result of any releases of a hazardous substance or the threat thereof. This paragraph shall not preclude liability for costs or damages as the result of negligence on the part of such person.

(2) State and local governments

No State or local government shall be liable under this subchapter for costs or damages as a result of actions taken in response to an emergency created by the release or threatened release of a hazardous substance generated by or from a facility owned by another person. This paragraph shall not preclude liability for costs or damages as a result of gross negligence or intentional misconduct by the State or local government. For the purpose of the preceding sentence, reckless, willful, or wanton misconduct shall constitute gross negligence.

(3) Savings provision

This subsection shall not alter the liability of any person covered by the provisions of paragraph (1), (2), (3), or (4) of subsection (a) of this section with respect to the release or threatened release concerned.

(e) Indemnification, hold harmless, etc., agreements or conveyances; subrogation rights

(1) No indemnification, hold harmless, or similar agreement or conveyance shall be effective to transfer from the owner or operator of any vessel or facility or from any person who may be liable for a release or threat of release under this section, to any other person the liability imposed under this section. Nothing in this subsection shall bar any agreement to insure, hold harmless, or indemnify a party to such agreement for any liability under this section.

(2) Nothing in this subchapter, including the provisions of paragraph (1) of this subsection, shall bar a cause of action that an owner or operator or any other person subject to liability under this section, or a guarantor, has or would have, by reason of subrogation or otherwise against any person.

(f) Natural resources liability; designation of public trustees of natural resources

(1) Natural resources liability

In the case of an injury to, destruction of, or loss of natural resources under subparagraph (C) of subsection (a) of this section liability shall be to the United States Government and to any State for natural resources within the State or belonging to, managed by, controlled by, or appertaining to such State and to any Indian tribe for natural resources belonging to, managed by, controlled by, or appertaining to such tribe, or held in trust for the benefit of such tribe, or belonging to a member of such tribe if such resources are subject to a trust restriction on alienation: *Provided, however,* That no liability to the United States or State or Indian tribe shall be imposed under subparagraph (C) of subsection (a) of this section, where the party sought to be charged has demonstrated that the damages to natural resources complained of were specifically identified as an irreversible and irretrievable commitment of natural resources in an environmental impact statement, or other comparable environment analysis, and the decision to grant a permit or license authorizes such commitment of natural resources, and the facility or project was otherwise operating within the terms of its permit or license, so long as, in the case of damages to an Indian tribe occurring pursuant to a Federal permit or license, the issuance of that permit or license was not inconsistent with the fiduciary duty of the United States with respect to such Indian tribe. The President, or the authorized representative of any State, shall act on behalf of the public as trustee of such natural resources to recover for such damages. Sums recovered by the United States Government as trustee under this subsection shall be retained by the trustee, without further appropriation, for use only to restore, replace, or acquire the equivalent of such natural resources. Sums recovered by a State as trustee under this subsection shall be available for use only to restore, replace, or acquire the equivalent of such natural resources by the State. The measure of damages in any action under subparagraph (C) of subsection (a) of this section shall not be limited by the sums which can be used to restore or replace such resources. There shall be no double recovery under this chapter for natural resource damages, including the costs of damage assessment or restoration, rehabilitation, or acquisition for the same release and natural resource. There shall be no recovery under the authority of subparagraph (C) of subsection (a) of this section where such damages and the release of a hazardous substance from which such damages resulted have occurred wholly before December 11, 1980.

(2) Designation of Federal and State officials

(A) Federal

The President shall designate in the National Contingency Plan published under section 9605 of this title the Federal officials who shall act on behalf of the public as trustees for natural resources under this chapter and section 1321 of Title 33. Such officials shall assess damages for injury to, destruction of, or loss of natural resources for purposes of this chapter and such section 1321 of Title 33 for those resources under their trusteeship and may, upon request of and reimbursement from a State and at the Federal officials' discretion, assess damages for those natural resources under the State's trusteeship.

(B) State

The Governor of each State shall designate State officials who may act on behalf of the public as trustees for natural resources under this chapter and section 1321 of Title 33 and shall notify the President of such designations. Such State officials shall assess damages to natural resources for the purposes of this chapter and such section 1321 of Title 33 for those natural resources under their trusteeship.

(C) Rebuttable presumption

Any determination or assessment of damages to natural resources for the purposes of this chapter and section 1321 of Title 33 made by a Federal or State trustee in accordance with the regulations promulgated under section 9651(c) of this title shall have the force and effect of a rebuttable presumption on behalf of the trustee in any administrative or judicial proceeding under this chapter or section 1321 of Title 33.

(g) Federal agencies

For provisions relating to Federal agencies, see section 9620 of this title.

(h) Owner or operator of vessel

The owner or operator of a vessel shall be liable in accordance with this section, under maritime tort law, and as provided under section 9614 of this title notwithstanding any provision of the Act of March 3, 1851 (46 U.S.C. 183ff) or the absence of any physical damage to the proprietary interest of the claimant.

(i) Application of a registered pesticide product

No person (including the United States or any State or Indian tribe) may recover under the authority of this section for any response costs or damages resulting from the application of a pesticide product registered under the Federal Insecticide, Fungicide, and Rodenticide Act [7 U.S.C.A. § 136 et seq.]. Nothing in this paragraph shall affect or modify in any way the obligations or liability of any person under any other provision of State or Federal law, including common law, for damages, injury, or loss resulting from a release of any hazardous substance or for removal or remedial action or the costs of removal or remedial action of such hazardous substance.

(j) Obligations or liability pursuant to federally permitted release

Recovery by any person (including the United States or any State or Indian tribe) for response costs or damages resulting from a federally permitted release shall be pursuant to existing law in lieu of this section. Nothing in this paragraph shall affect or modify in any way the obligations or liability of any person under any other provision of State or Federal law, including common law, for damages, injury, or loss resulting from a release of any hazardous substance or for removal or remedial action or the costs of removal or remedial action of such hazardous substance. In addition, costs of response incurred by the Federal Government in connection with a discharge specified in section 9601(10)(B) or (C) of this title shall be recoverable in an action brought under section 1319(b) of Title 33.

(k) Transfer to, and assumption by, Post–Closure Liability Fund of liability of owner or operator of hazardous waste disposal facility in receipt of permit under applicable solid waste disposal law; time, criteria applicable, procedures, etc.; monitoring costs; reports

(1) The liability established by this section or any other law for the owner or operator of a hazardous waste disposal facility which has received a permit under subtitle C of the Solid Waste Disposal Act [42 U.S.C.A. § 6921 et seq.], shall be transferred to and assumed by the Post-closure Liability Fund established by section 9641 of this title when—

> **(A)** such facility and the owner and operator thereof has complied with the requirements of subtitle C of the Solid Waste Disposal Act [42 U.S.C.A. § 6921 et seq.] and regulations issued thereunder, which may affect the performance of such facility after closure; and

> **(B)** such facility has been closed in accordance with such regulations and the conditions of such permit, and such facility and the surrounding area have been monitored as required by such regulations and permit conditions for a period not to exceed five years after closure to demonstrate that there is no substantial likelihood that any migration offsite or release from confinement of any hazardous substance or other risk to public health or welfare will occur.

(2) Such transfer of liability shall be effective ninety days after the owner or operator of such facility notifies the Administrator of the Environmental Protection Agency (and the State where it has an authorized program under section 3006(b) of the Solid Waste Disposal Act [42 U.S.C.A. § 6926(b)]) that the conditions imposed by this subsection have been satisfied. If within such ninety-day period the Administrator of the Environmental Protection Agency or such State determines that any such facility has not complied with all the conditions imposed by this subsection or that insufficient information has been provided to demonstrate such compliance, the Administrator or such State shall so notify the owner and operator of such facility and the administrator of the Fund established by section 9641 of this title, and the owner and operator of such facility shall continue to be liable with respect to such facility under this section and other law until such time as the Administrator and such State determines that such facility has complied with all conditions imposed by this subsection. A determination by the Administrator or such State that a facility has not complied with all conditions imposed by this subsection or that insufficient information has been supplied to demonstrate compliance, shall be a final administrative action for purposes of judicial review. A request for additional information shall state in specific terms the data required.

(3) In addition to the assumption of liability of owners and operators under paragraph (1) of this subsection, the Post-closure Liability Fund established by section 9641 of this title may be used to pay costs of monitoring and care and maintenance of a site incurred by other persons after the period of monitoring required by regulations under subtitle C of the Solid Waste Disposal Act [42 U.S.C.A. § 6921 et seq.] for hazardous waste disposal facilities meeting the conditions of paragraph (1) of this subsection.

(4)(A) Not later than one year after December 11, 1980, the Secretary of the Treasury shall conduct a study and shall submit a report thereon to the Congress on the feasibility of establishing or qualifying an optional system of private insurance for postclosure financial responsibility for hazardous waste disposal facilities to which this subsection applies. Such study shall include a specification of adequate and realistic minimum standards to assure that any such privately placed insurance will carry out the purposes of this subsection in a reliable, enforceable, and practical manner. Such a study shall include an examination of the public and private incentives, programs, and actions necessary to make privately placed insurance a practical and effective option to the financing system for the Post-closure Liability Fund provided in subchapter II of this chapter.

(B) Not later than eighteen months after December 11, 1980, and after a public hearing, the President shall by rule determine whether or not it is feasible to establish or qualify an optional system of private insurance for postclosure financial responsibility for hazardous waste disposal facilities to which this subsection applies. If the President determines the establishment or qualification of such a system would be infeasible, he shall promptly publish an explanation of the reasons for such a determination. If the President determines the establishment or qualification of such a system would be feasible, he shall promptly publish notice of such determination. Not later than six months after an affirmative determination under the preceding sentence and after a public hearing, the President shall by rule promulgate adequate and realistic minimum standards which must be met by any such privately placed insurance, taking into account the purposes of this chapter and this subsection. Such rules shall also specify reasonably expeditious procedures by which privately placed insurance plans can qualify as meeting such minimum standards.

(C) In the event any privately placed insurance plan qualifies under subparagraph (B), any person enrolled in, and complying with the terms of, such plan shall be excluded from the provisions of paragraphs (1), (2), and (3) of this subsection and exempt from the requirements to pay any tax or fee to the Post-closure Liability Fund under subchapter II of this chapter.

(D) The President may issue such rules and take such other actions as are necessary to effectuate the purposes of this paragraph.

(5) Suspension of liability transfer

Notwithstanding paragraphs (1), (2), (3), and (4) of this subsection and subsection (j) of section 9611 of this title, no liability shall be transferred to or assumed by the Post–Closure Liability Trust Fund established by section 9641 of this title prior to completion of the study required under paragraph (6) of this subsection, transmission of a report of such study to both Houses of Congress, and authorization of such a transfer or assumption by Act of Congress following receipt of such study and report.

(6) Study of options for post-closure program

(A) Study

The Comptroller General shall conduct a study of options for a program for the management of the liabilities associated with hazardous waste treatment, storage, and disposal sites after their closure which complements the policies set forth in the Hazardous and Solid Waste Amendments of 1984 and assures the protection of human health and the environment.

(B) Program elements

The program referred to in subparagraph (A) shall be designed to assure each of the following:

    (i) Incentives are created and maintained for the safe management and disposal of hazardous wastes so as to assure protection of human health and the environment.

    (ii) Members of the public will have reasonable confidence that hazardous wastes will be managed and disposed of safely and that resources will be available to address any problems that may arise and to cover costs of long-term monitoring, care, and maintenance of such sites.

    (iii) Persons who are or seek to become owners and operators of hazardous waste disposal facilities will be able to manage their potential future liabilities and to attract the investment capital necessary to build, operate, and close such facilities in a manner which assures protection of human health and the environment.

(C) Assessments

The study under this paragraph shall include assessments of treatment, storage, and disposal facilities which have been or are likely to be issued a permit under section 3005 of the Solid Waste Disposal Act [42 U.S.C.A. § 6925] and the likelihood of future insolvency on the part of owners and operators of such facilities. Separate assessments shall be made for different classes of facilities and for different classes of land disposal facilities and shall include but not be limited to—

    (i) the current and future financial capabilities of facility owners and operators;

    (ii) the current and future costs associated with facilities, including the costs of routine monitoring and maintenance, compliance monitoring, corrective action, natural resource damages, and liability for damages to third parties; and

    (iii) the availability of mechanisms by which owners and operators of such facilities can assure that current and future costs, including post-closure costs, will be financed.

(D) Procedures

In carrying out the responsibilities of this paragraph, the Comptroller General shall consult with the Administrator, the Secretary of Commerce, the Secretary of the Treasury, and the heads of other appropriate Federal agencies.

(E) Consideration of options

In conducting the study under this paragraph, the Comptroller General shall consider various mechanisms and combinations of mechanisms to complement the policies set forth in the Hazardous and Solid Waste Amendments of 1984 to serve the purposes set forth in subparagraph (B) and to assure that the current and future costs associated with hazardous waste facilities, including post-closure costs, will be adequately financed and, to the greatest extent possible, borne by the owners and operators of such facilities. Mechanisms to be considered include, but are not limited to—

(i) revisions to closure, post-closure, and financial responsibility requirements under subtitles C and I of the Solid Waste Disposal Act [42 U.S.C.A. §§ 6921 et seq. and 6991 et seq.];

(ii) voluntary risk pooling by owners and operators;

(iii) legislation to require risk pooling by owners and operators;

(iv) modification of the Post–Closure Liability Trust Fund previously established by section 9641 of this title, and the conditions for transfer of liability under this subsection, including limiting the transfer of some or all liability under this subsection only in the case of insolvency of owners and operators;

(v) private insurance;

(vi) insurance provided by the Federal Government;

(vii) coinsurance, reinsurance, or pooled-risk insurance, whether provided by the private sector or provided or assisted by the Federal Government; and

(viii) creation of a new program to be administered by a new or existing Federal agency or by a federally chartered corporation.

(F) Recommendations

The Comptroller General shall consider options for funding any program under this section and shall, to the extent necessary, make recommendations to the appropriate committees of Congress for additional authority to implement such program.

(*l*) Federal lien

(1) In general

All costs and damages for which a person is liable to the United States under subsection (a) of this section (other than the owner or operator of a vessel under paragraph (1) of subsection (a) of this section) shall constitute a lien in favor of the United States upon all real property and rights to such property which—

(A) belong to such person; and

(B) are subject to or affected by a removal or remedial action.

(2) Duration

The lien imposed by this subsection shall arise at the later of the following:

(A) The time costs are first incurred by the United States with respect to a response action under this chapter.

(B) The time that the person referred to in paragraph (1) is provided (by certified or registered mail) written notice of potential liability.

Such lien shall continue until the liability for the costs (or a judgment against the person arising out of such liability) is satisfied or becomes unenforceable through operation of the statute of limitations provided in section 9613 of this title.

213

(3) Notice and validity

The lien imposed by this subsection shall be subject to the rights of any purchaser, holder of a security interest, or judgment lien creditor whose interest is perfected under applicable State law before notice of the lien has been filed in the appropriate office within the State (or county or other governmental subdivision), as designated by State law, in which the real property subject to the lien is located. Any such purchaser, holder of a security interest, or judgment lien creditor shall be afforded the same protections against the lien imposed by this subsection as are afforded under State law against a judgment lien which arises out of an unsecured obligation and which arises as of the time of the filing of the notice of the lien imposed by this subsection. If the State has not by law designated one office for the receipt of such notices of liens, the notice shall be filed in the office of the clerk of the United States district court for the district in which the real property is located. For purposes of this subsection, the terms "purchaser" and "security interest" shall have the definitions provided under section 6323(h) of Title 26.

(4) Action in rem

The costs constituting the lien may be recovered in an action in rem in the United States district court for the district in which the removal or remedial action is occurring or has occurred. Nothing in this subsection shall affect the right of the United States to bring an action against any person to recover all costs and damages for which such person is liable under subsection (a) of this section.

(m) Maritime lien

All costs and damages for which the owner or operator of a vessel is liable under subsection (a)(1) of this section with respect to a release or threatened release from such vessel shall constitute a maritime lien in favor of the United States on such vessel. Such costs may be recovered in an action in rem in the district court of the United States for the district in which the vessel may be found. Nothing in this subsection shall affect the right of the United States to bring an action against the owner or operator of such vessel in any court of competent jurisdiction to recover such costs.

(n) Liability of fiduciaries

(1) In general

The liability of a fiduciary under any provision of this chapter for the release or threatened release of a hazardous substance at, from, or in connection with a vessel or facility held in a fiduciary capacity shall not exceed the assets held in the fiduciary capacity.

(2) Exclusion

Paragraph (1) does not apply to the extent that a person is liable under this chapter independently of the person's ownership of a vessel or facility as a fiduciary or actions taken in a fiduciary capacity.

(3) Limitation

Paragraphs (1) and (4) do not limit the liability pertaining to a release or threatened release of a hazardous substance if negligence of a fiduciary causes or contributes to the release or threatened release.

(4) Safe harbor

A fiduciary shall not be liable in its personal capacity under this chapter for—

(A) undertaking or directing another person to undertake a response action under subsection (d)(1) of this section or under the direction of an on scene coordinator designated under the National Contingency Plan;

(B) undertaking or directing another person to undertake any other lawful means of addressing a hazardous substance in connection with the vessel or facility;

(C) terminating the fiduciary relationship;

(D) including in the terms of the fiduciary agreement a covenant, warranty, or other term or condition that relates to compliance with an environmental law, or monitoring, modifying or enforcing the term or condition;

(E) monitoring or undertaking 1 or more inspections of the vessel or facility;

(F) providing financial or other advice or counseling to other parties to the fiduciary relationship, including the settlor or beneficiary;

(G) restructuring, renegotiating, or otherwise altering the terms and conditions of the fiduciary relationship;

(H) administering, as a fiduciary, a vessel or facility that was contaminated before the fiduciary relationship began; or

(I) declining to take any of the actions described in subparagraphs (B) through (H).

(5) Definitions

As used in this chapter:

(A) Fiduciary

The term "fiduciary"—

    (i) means a person acting for the benefit of another party as a bona fide—

        (I) trustee;

        (II) executor;

        (III) administrator;

        (IV) custodian;

        (V) guardian of estates or guardian ad litem;

        (VI) receiver;

        (VII) conservator;

        (VIII) committee of estates of incapacitated persons;

        (IX) personal representative;

        (X) trustee (including a successor to a trustee) under an indenture agreement, trust agreement, lease, or similar financing agreement, for debt securities, certificates of interest or certificates of participation in debt securities, or other forms of indebtedness as to which the trustee is not, in the capacity of trustee, the lender; or

        (XI) representative in any other capacity that the Administrator, after providing public notice, determines to be similar to the capacities described in subclauses (I) through (X); and

215

(ii) does not include—

(I) a person that is acting as a fiduciary with respect to a trust or other fiduciary estate that was organized for the primary purpose of, or is engaged in, actively carrying on a trade or business for profit, unless the trust or other fiduciary estate was created as part of, or to facilitate, 1 or more estate plans or because of the incapacity of a natural person; or

(II) a person that acquires ownership or control of a vessel or facility with the objective purpose of avoiding liability of the person or of any other person.

(B) Fiduciary capacity

The term "fiduciary capacity" means the capacity of a person in holding title to a vessel or facility, or otherwise having control of or an interest in the vessel or facility, pursuant to the exercise of the responsibilities of the person as a fiduciary.

(6) Savings clause

Nothing in this subsection—

(A) affects the rights or immunities or other defenses that are available under this chapter or other law that is applicable to a person subject to this subsection; or

(B) creates any liability for a person or a private right of action against a fiduciary or any other person.

(7) No effect on certain persons

Nothing in this subsection applies to a person if the person—

(A)(i) acts in a capacity other than that of a fiduciary or in a beneficiary capacity; and

(ii) in that capacity, directly or indirectly benefits from a trust or fiduciary relationship; or

(B)(i) is a beneficiary and a fiduciary with respect to the same fiduciary estate; and

(ii) as a fiduciary, receives benefits that exceed customary or reasonable compensation, and incidental benefits, permitted under other applicable law.

(8) Limitation

This subsection does not preclude a claim under this chapter against—

(A) the assets of the estate or trust administered by the fiduciary; or

(B) a nonemployee agent or independent contractor retained by a fiduciary.

(o) De micromis exemption

(1) In general

Except as provided in paragraph (2), a person shall not be liable, with respect to response costs at a facility on the National Priorities List, under this chapter if liability is based solely on paragraph (3) or (4) of subsection (a), and the person, except as provided in paragraph (4) of this subsection, can demonstrate that—

(A) the total amount of the material containing hazardous substances that the person arranged for disposal or treatment of, arranged with a transporter for transport for disposal or treatment of, or accepted for transport for disposal or treatment, at the facility was less than 110 gallons of liquid materials or less than 200 pounds of solid materials (or such greater or lesser amounts as the Administrator may determine by regulation); and

(B) all or part of the disposal, treatment, or transport concerned occurred before April 1, 2001.

(2) Exceptions

Paragraph (1) shall not apply in a case in which—

(A) the President determines that—

(i) the materials containing hazardous substances referred to in paragraph (1) have contributed significantly or could contribute significantly, either individually or in the aggregate, to the cost of the response action or natural resource restoration with respect to the facility; or

(ii) the person has failed to comply with an information request or administrative subpoena issued by the President under this chapter or has impeded or is impeding, through action or inaction, the performance of a response action or natural resource restoration with respect to the facility; or

(B) a person has been convicted of a criminal violation for the conduct to which the exemption would apply, and that conviction has not been vitiated on appeal or otherwise.

(3) No judicial review

A determination by the President under paragraph (2)(A) shall not be subject to judicial review.

(4) NonGovernmental third-party contribution actions

In the case of a contribution action, with respect to response costs at a facility on the National Priorities List, brought by a party, other than a Federal, State, or local government, under this chapter, the burden of proof shall be on the party bringing the action to demonstrate that the conditions described in paragraph (1)(A) and (B) of this subsection are not met.

(p) Municipal solid waste exemption

(1) In general

Except as provided in paragraph (2) of this subsection, a person shall not be liable, with respect to response costs at a facility on the National Priorities List, under paragraph (3) of subsection (a) of this section for municipal solid waste disposed of at a facility if the person, except as provided in paragraph (5) of this subsection, can demonstrate that the person is—

(A) an owner, operator, or lessee of residential property from which all of the person's municipal solid waste was generated with respect to the facility;

(B) a business entity (including a parent, subsidiary, or affiliate of the entity) that, during its 3 taxable years preceding the date of transmittal of written notification from the President of its potential liability under this section, employed on average not more than 100 full-time individuals, or the equivalent thereof, and that is a small business concern (within the meaning of the Small Business Act (15 U.S.C. 631 et seq.)) from which was generated all of the municipal solid waste attributable to the entity with respect to the facility; or

(C) an organization described in section 501(c)(3) of Title 26 and exempt from tax under section 501(a) of Title 26 that, during its taxable year preceding the date of transmittal of written notification from the President of its potential liability under this section, employed not more than 100 paid individuals at the location from which was generated all of the municipal solid waste attributable to the organization with respect to the facility.

For purposes of this subsection, the term "affiliate" has the meaning of that term provided in the definition of "small business concern" in regulations promulgated by the Small Business Administration in accordance with the Small Business Act (15 U.S.C. 631 et seq.).

(2) Exception

Paragraph (1) shall not apply in a case in which the President determines that—

(A) the municipal solid waste referred to in paragraph (1) has contributed significantly or could contribute significantly, either individually or in the aggregate, to the cost of the response action or natural resource restoration with respect to the facility;

(B) the person has failed to comply with an information request or administrative subpoena issued by the President under this chapter; or

(C) the person has impeded or is impeding, through action or inaction, the performance of a response action or natural resource restoration with respect to the facility.

(3) No judicial review

A determination by the President under paragraph (2) shall not be subject to judicial review.

(4) Definition of municipal solid waste

(A) In general

For purposes of this subsection, the term "municipal solid waste" means waste material—

(i) generated by a household (including a single or multifamily residence); and

(ii) generated by a commercial, industrial, or institutional entity, to the extent that the waste material—

(I) is essentially the same as waste normally generated by a household;

(II) is collected and disposed of with other municipal solid waste as part of normal municipal solid waste collection services; and

(III) contains a relative quantity of hazardous substances no greater than the relative quantity of hazardous substances contained in waste material generated by a typical single-family household.

(B) Examples

Examples of municipal solid waste under subparagraph (A) include food and yard waste, paper, clothing, appliances, consumer product packaging, disposable diapers, office supplies, cosmetics, glass and metal food containers, elementary or secondary school science laboratory waste, and household hazardous waste.

(C) Exclusions

The term "municipal solid waste" does not include—

(i) combustion ash generated by resource recovery facilities or municipal incinerators; or

(ii) waste material from manufacturing or processing operations (including pollution control operations) that is not essentially the same as waste normally generated by households.

(5) Burden of proof

In the case of an action, with respect to response costs at a facility on the National Priorities List, brought under this section or section 9613 of this title by—

(A) a party, other than a Federal, State, or local government, with respect to municipal solid waste disposed of on or after April 1, 2001; or

(B) any party with respect to municipal solid waste disposed of before April 1, 2001, the burden of proof shall be on the party bringing the action to demonstrate that the conditions described in paragraphs (1) and (4) for exemption for entities and organizations described in paragraph (1)(B) and (C) are not met.

(6) Certain actions not permitted

No contribution action may be brought by a party, other than a Federal, State, or local government, under this chapter with respect to circumstances described in paragraph (1)(A).

(7) Costs and fees

A nongovernmental entity that commences, after the date of the enactment of this subsection, a contribution action under this chapter shall be liable to the defendant for all reasonable costs of defending the action, including all reasonable attorney's fees and expert witness fees, if the defendant is not liable for contribution based on an exemption under this subsection or subsection (*o*) of this section.

(q) Contiguous properties

(1) Not considered to be an owner or operator

(A) In general

A person that owns real property that is contiguous to or otherwise similarly situated with respect to, and that is or may be contaminated by a release or threatened release of a hazardous substance from, real property that is not owned by that person shall not be considered to be an owner or operator of a vessel or facility under paragraph (1) or (2) of subsection (a) solely by reason of the contamination if—

(i) the person did not cause, contribute, or consent to the release or threatened release;

(ii) the person is not—

(I) potentially liable, or affiliated with any other person that is potentially liable, for response costs at a facility through any direct or indirect familial relationship or any contractual, corporate, or financial relationship (other than a contractual, corporate, or financial relationship that is created by a contract for the sale of goods or services); or

(II) the result of a reorganization of a business entity that was potentially liable;

(iii) the person takes reasonable steps to—

(I) stop any continuing release;

(II) prevent any threatened future release; and

(III) prevent or limit human, environmental, or natural resource exposure to any hazardous substance released on or from property owned by that person;

(iv) the person provides full cooperation, assistance, and access to persons that are authorized to conduct response actions or natural resource restoration at the vessel or facility from which there has been a release or threatened release (including the cooperation and access necessary for the installation, integrity, operation, and maintenance of any complete or partial response action or natural resource restoration at the vessel or facility);

(v) the person—

(I) is in compliance with any land use restrictions established or relied on in connection with the response action at the facility; and

(II) does not impede the effectiveness or integrity of any institutional control employed in connection with a response action;

(vi) the person is in compliance with any request for information or administrative subpoena issued by the President under this chapter;

(vii) the person provides all legally required notices with respect to the discovery or release of any hazardous substances at the facility; and

(viii) At the time at which the person acquired the property, the person

(I) conducted all appropriate inquiry within the meaning of section 9601(35)(B) of this title with respect to the property; and

(II) did not know or have reason to know that the property was or could be contaminated by a release or threatened release of one or more hazardous substances from other real property not owned or operated by the person.

(B) Demonstration

To qualify as a person described in subparagraph (A), a person must establish by a preponderance of the evidence that the conditions in clauses (i) through (viii) of subparagraph (A) have been met.

(C) Bona fide prospective purchaser

Any person that does not qualify as a person described in this paragraph because the person had, or had reason to have, knowledge specified in subparagraph (A)(viii) at the time of acquisition of the real property may qualify as a bona fide prospective purchaser under section 9601(40) of this title if the person is otherwise described in that section.

(D) Ground water

With respect to a hazardous substance from one or more sources that are not on the property of a person that is a contiguous property owner that enters ground water beneath the property of the person solely as a result of subsurface migration in an aquifer, subparagraph (A)(iii) shall not require the person to conduct ground water investigations or to install ground water remediation systems, except in accordance with the policy of the Environmental Protection Agency concerning owners of property containing contaminated aquifers, dated May 24, 1995.

(2) Effect of law

With respect to a person described in this subsection, nothing in this subsection—

(A) limits any defense to liability that may be available to the person under any other provision of law; or

(B) imposes liability on the person that is not otherwise imposed by subsection (a) of this section.

(3) Assurances

The Administrator may—

(A) issue an assurance that no enforcement action under this chapter will be initiated against a person described in paragraph (1); and

(B) grant a person described in paragraph (1) protection against a cost recovery or contribution action under section 9613(f) of this title.

(r) Prospective purchaser and windfall lien

(1) Limitation on liability

Notwithstanding subsection (a)(1) of this section, a bona fide prospective purchaser whose potential liability for a release or threatened release is based solely on the purchaser's being considered to be an owner or operator of a facility shall not be liable as long as the bona fide prospective purchaser does not impede the performance of a response action or natural resource restoration.

(2) Lien

If there are unrecovered response costs incurred by the United States at a facility for which an owner of the facility is not liable by reason of paragraph (1), and if each of the conditions described in paragraph (3) is met, the United States shall have a lien on the facility, or may by agreement with the owner, obtain from the owner a lien on any other property or other assurance of payment satisfactory to the Administrator, for the unrecovered response costs.

(3) Conditions

The conditions referred to in paragraph (2) are the following:

(A) Response action

A 1response action for which there are unrecovered costs of the United States is carried out at the facility.

(B) Fair market value

The response action increases the fair market value of the facility above the fair market value of the facility that existed before the response action was initiated.

(4) Amount; duration

A lien under paragraph (2)—

221

(A) shall be in an amount not to exceed the increase in fair market value of the property attributable to the response action at the time of a sale or other disposition of the property;

(B) shall arise at the time at which costs are first incurred by the United States with respect to a response action at the facility;

(C) shall be subject to the requirements of subsection (*l*)(3); and

(D) shall continue until the earlier of—

(i) satisfaction of the lien by sale or other means; or

(ii) notwithstanding any statute of limitations under section 9613 of this tile, recovery of all response costs incurred at the facility.

§ 9613. Civil Proceedings

. . .

(f) Contribution

(1) Contribution

Any person may seek contribution from any other person who is liable or potentially liable under section 9607(a) of this title, during or following any civil action under section 9606 of this title or under section 9607(a) of this title. Such claims shall be brought in accordance with this section and the Federal Rules of Civil Procedure, and shall be governed by Federal law. In resolving contribution claims, the court may allocate response costs among liable parties using such equitable factors as the court determines are appropriate. Nothing in this subsection shall diminish the right of any person to bring an action for contribution in the absence of a civil action under section 9606 or section 9607 of this title.

. . .

———

b. "ALL APPROPRIATE INQUIRY" RULE

40 CODE OF FEDERAL REGULATIONS

§ 312.10 Definitions.

(a) Terms used in this part and not defined below, but defined in either CERCLA or 40 CFR part 300 (the National Oil and Hazardous Substances Pollution Contingency Plan) shall have the definitions provided in CERCLA or 40 CFR part 300.

(b) When used in this part, the following terms have the meanings provided as follows:

Abandoned property means: property that can be presumed to be deserted, or an intent to relinquish possession or control can be inferred from the general disrepair or lack of activity thereon such that a reasonable person could believe that there was an intent on the part of the current owner to surrender rights to the property.

Adjoining properties means: any real property or properties the border of which is (are) shared in part or in whole with that of the subject property, or that would be shared in part or in whole with that of the subject property but for a street, road, or other public thoroughfare separating the properties.

Data gap means: a lack of or inability to obtain information required by the standards and practices listed in subpart C of this part despite good faith efforts by the environmental professional or persons identified under § 312.1(b), as appropriate, to gather such information pursuant to §§ 312.20(e)(1) and 312.20(e)(2).

Date of acquisition or purchase date means: the date on which a person acquires title to the property.

Environmental Professional means:

(1) a person who possesses sufficient specific education, training, and experience necessary to exercise professional judgment to develop opinions and conclusions regarding conditions indicative of releases or threatened releases (see § 312.1(c)) on, at, in, or to a property, sufficient to meet the objectives and performance factors in § 312.20(e) and (f).

(2) Such a person must:

(i) Hold a current Professional Engineer's or Professional Geologist's license or registration from a state, tribe, or U.S. territory (or the Commonwealth of Puerto Rico) and have the equivalent of three (3) years of full-time relevant experience; or

(ii) Be licensed or certified by the federal government, a state, tribe, or U.S. territory (or the Commonwealth of Puerto Rico) to perform environmental inquiries as defined in § 312.21 and have the equivalent of three (3) years of full-time relevant experience; or

(iii) Have a Baccalaureate or higher degree from an accredited institution of higher education in a discipline of engineering or science and the equivalent of five (5) years of full-time relevant experience; or

(iv) Have the equivalent of ten (10) years of full-time relevant experience.

(3) An environmental professional should remain current in his or her field through participation in continuing education or other activities.

(4) The definition of environmental professional provided above does not preempt state professional licensing or registration requirements such as those for a professional geologist, engineer, or site remediation professional. Before commencing work, a person should determine the applicability of state professional licensing or registration laws to the activities to be undertaken as part of the inquiry identified in § 312.21(b).

(5) A person who does not qualify as an environmental professional under the foregoing definition may assist in the conduct of all appropriate inquiries in accordance with this part if such person is under the supervision or responsible charge of a person meeting the definition of an environmental professional provided above when conducting such activities.

Relevant experience, as used in the definition of environmental professional in this section, means: participation in the performance of all appropriate inquiries investigations, environmental site assessments, or other site investigations that may include environmental analyses, investigations, and remediation which involve the understanding of surface and subsurface environmental conditions and the processes used to evaluate these conditions and for which professional judgment was used to develop opinions regarding conditions indicative of releases or threatened releases (see § 312.1(c)) to the subject property.

Good faith means: the absence of any intention to seek an unfair advantage or to defraud another party; an honest and sincere intention to fulfill one's obligations in the conduct or transaction concerned.

Institutional controls means: non-engineered instruments, such as administrative and/or legal controls, that help to minimize the potential for human exposure to contamination and/or protect the integrity of a remedy.

§ 312.11 References.

The following industry standards may be used to comply with the requirements set forth in §§ 312.23 through 312.31:

(a) The procedures of ASTM International Standard E1527–05 entitled "Standard Practice for Environmental Site Assessments: Phase I Environmental Site Assessment Process."

(b) The procedures of ASTM International Standard E2247–08 entitled "Standard Practice for Environmental Site Assessments: Phase I Environmental Site Assessment Process for Forestland or Rural Property." This standard is available from ASTM International at http://www.astm.org, 1–610–832–9585.

§ 312.20 All appropriate inquiries.

(a) "All appropriate inquiries" pursuant to CERCLA section 101(35)(B) must be conducted within one year prior to the date of acquisition of the subject property and must include:

(1) An inquiry by an environmental professional (as defined in § 312.10), as provided in § 312.21;

(2) The collection of information pursuant to § 312.22 by persons identified under § 312.1(b); and

(3) Searches for recorded environmental cleanup liens, as required in § 312.25.

(b) Notwithstanding paragraph (a) of this section, the following components of the all appropriate inquiries must be conducted or updated within 180 days of and prior to the date of acquisition of the subject property:

(1) Interviews with past and present owners, operators, and occupants (see § 312.23);

(2) Searches for recorded environmental cleanup liens (see § 312.25);

(3) Reviews of federal, tribal, state, and local government records (see § 312.26);

(4) Visual inspections of the facility and of adjoining properties (see § 312.27); and

(5) The declaration by the environmental professional (see § 312.21(d)).

(c) All appropriate inquiries may include the results of and information contained in an inquiry previously conducted by, or on the behalf of, persons identified under § 312.1(b) and who are responsible for the inquiries for the subject property, provided:

(1) Such information was collected during the conduct of all appropriate inquiries in compliance with the requirements of CERCLA sections 101(35)(B), 101(40)(B) and 107(q)(A)(viii);

(2) Such information was collected or updated within one year prior to the date of acquisition of the subject property;

(3) Notwithstanding paragraph (b)(2) of this section, the following components of the inquiries were conducted or updated within 180 days of and prior to the date of acquisition of the subject property:

(i) Interviews with past and present owners, operators, and occupants (see § 312.23);

(ii) Searches for recorded environmental cleanup liens (see § 312.25);

(iii) Reviews of federal, tribal, state, and local government records (see § 312.26);

(iv) Visual inspections of the facility and of adjoining properties (see § 312.27); and

(v) The declaration by the environmental professional (see § 312.21(d)).

(4) Previously collected information is updated to include relevant changes in the conditions of the property and specialized knowledge, as outlined in § 312.28, of the persons conducting the all appropriate inquiries for the subject property, including persons identified in § 312.1(b) and the environmental professional, defined in § 312.10.

(d) All appropriate inquiries can include the results of report(s) specified in § 312.21(c), that have been prepared by or for other persons, provided that:

(1) The report(s) meets the objectives and performance factors of this regulation, as specified in paragraphs (e) and (f) of this section; and

(2) The person specified in § 312.1(b) and seeking to use the previously collected information reviews the information and conducts the additional inquiries pursuant to §§ 312.28, 312.29 and 312.30 and the all appropriate inquiries are updated in paragraph (b)(3) of this section, as necessary.

(e) Objectives. The standards and practices set forth in this part for All Appropriate Inquiries are intended to result in the identification of conditions indicative of releases and threatened releases of hazardous substances on, at, in, or to the subject property.

(1) In performing the all appropriate inquiries, as defined in this section and provided in the standards and practices set forth this subpart, the persons identified under § 312.1(b)(1) and the environmental professional, as defined in § 312.10, must seek to identify through the conduct of the standards and practices set forth in this subpart, the following types of information about the subject property:

(i) Current and past property uses and occupancies;

(ii) Current and past uses of hazardous substances;

(iii) Waste management and disposal activities that could have caused releases or threatened releases of hazardous substances;

(iv) Current and past corrective actions and response activities undertaken to address past and on-going releases of hazardous substances;

(v) Engineering controls;

(vi) Institutional controls; and

(vii) Properties adjoining or located nearby the subject property that have environmental conditions that could have resulted in conditions indicative of releases or threatened releases of hazardous substances to the subject property.

(2) In the case of persons identified in § 312.1(b)(2), the standards and practices for All Appropriate Inquiries set forth in this part are intended to result in the identification of conditions indicative of releases and threatened releases of hazardous substances, pollutants, contaminants, petroleum and petroleum products, and controlled substances (as defined in 21 U.S.C. 802) on, at, in, or to the subject property. In performing the all appropriate inquiries, as defined in this section and provided in the standards and practices set forth in this subpart, the persons identified under § 312.1(b) and the environmental professional, as defined in § 312.10, must seek to identify through the conduct of the standards and practices set forth in this subpart, the following types of information about the subject property:

(i) Current and past property uses and occupancies;

(ii) Current and past uses of hazardous substances, pollutants, contaminants, petroleum and petroleum products, and controlled substances (as defined in 21 U.S.C. 802);

(iii) Waste management and disposal activities;

(iv) Current and past corrective actions and response activities undertaken to address past and on-going releases of hazardous substances pollutants, contaminants, petroleum and petroleum products, and controlled substances (as defined in 21 U.S.C. 802);

(v) Engineering controls;

(vi) Institutional controls; and

(vii) Properties adjoining or located nearby the subject property that have environmental conditions that could have resulted in conditions indicative of releases or threatened releases of hazardous substances, pollutants, contaminants, petroleum and petroleum products, and controlled substances (as defined in 21 U.S.C. 802) to the subject property.

(f) Performance factors. In performing each of the standards and practices set forth in this subpart and to meet the objectives stated in paragraph (e) of this section, the persons identified under § 312.1(b) or the environmental professional as defined in § 312.10 (as appropriate to the particular standard and practice) must seek to:

(1) Gather the information that is required for each standard and practice listed in this subpart that is publicly available, obtainable from its source within reasonable time and cost constraints, and which can practicably be reviewed; and

(2) Review and evaluate the thoroughness and reliability of the information gathered in complying with each standard and practice listed in this subpart taking into account information gathered in the course of complying with the other standards and practices of this subpart.

(g) To the extent there are data gaps (as defined in § 312.10) in the information developed as part of the inquiries in paragraph (e) of this section that affect the ability of persons (including the environmental professional) conducting the all appropriate inquiries to identify conditions indicative of releases or threatened releases in each area of inquiry under each standard and practice such persons should identify such data gaps, identify the sources of information consulted to address such data gaps, and comment upon the significance of such data gaps with regard to the ability to identify conditions indicative of releases or threatened releases of hazardous substances [and in the case of persons identified in § 312.1(b)(2), hazardous substances, pollutants, contaminants, petroleum and petroleum products, and controlled substances (as defined in 21 U.S.C. 802)] on, at, in, or to the subject property. Sampling and analysis may be conducted to develop information to address data gaps.

(h) Releases and threatened releases identified as part of the all appropriate inquiries should be noted in the report of the inquiries. These standards and practices however are not intended to require the identification in the written report prepared pursuant to § 312.21(c) of quantities or amounts, either individually or in the aggregate, of hazardous substances pollutants, contaminants, petroleum and petroleum products, and controlled substances (as defined in 21 U.S.C. 802) that because of said quantities and amounts, generally would not pose a threat to human health or the environment.

§ 312.21 Results of inquiry by an environmental professional.

(a) Persons identified under § 312.1(b) must undertake an inquiry, as defined in paragraph (b) of this section, by an environmental professional, or conducted under the supervision or responsible charge of, an environmental professional, as defined in § 312.10. Such inquiry is hereafter referred to as "the inquiry of the environmental professional."

(b) The inquiry of the environmental professional must include the requirements set forth in §§ 312.23 (interviews with past and present owners * * *), 312.24 (reviews of historical sources * * *), 312.26 (reviews of government records), 312.27 (visual inspections), 312.30 (commonly known or reasonably ascertainable information), and 312.31 (degree of obviousness of the presence * * * and the ability to detect the contamination * * *). In addition, the inquiry should take into account information provided to the environmental professional as a result of the additional inquiries conducted by persons identified in § 312.1(b) and in accordance with the requirements of § 312.22.

(c) The results of the inquiry by an environmental professional must be documented in a written report that, at a minimum, includes the following:

(1) An opinion as to whether the inquiry has identified conditions indicative of releases or threatened releases of hazardous substances [and in the case of inquiries conducted for persons identified in § 312.1(b)(2) conditions indicative of releases and threatened releases of pollutants, contaminants, petroleum and petroleum products, and controlled substances (as defined in 21 U.S.C. 802)] on, at, in, or to the subject property;

(2) An identification of data gaps (as defined in § 312.10) in the information developed as part of the inquiry that affect the ability of the environmental professional to identify conditions indicative of releases or threatened releases of hazardous substances [and in the case of inquiries conducted for persons identified in § 312.1(b)(2) conditions indicative of releases and threatened releases of pollutants, contaminants, petroleum and

227

petroleum products, and controlled substances (as defined in 21 U.S.C. 802)] on, at, in, or to the subject property and comments regarding the significance of such data gaps on the environmental professional's ability to provide an opinion as to whether the inquiry has identified conditions indicative of releases or threatened releases on, at, in, or to the subject property. If there are data gaps such that the environmental professional cannot reach an opinion regarding the identification of conditions indicative of releases and threatened releases, such data gaps must be noted in the environmental professional's opinion in paragraph (c)(1) of this section; and

(3) The qualifications of the environmental professional(s).

(d) The environmental professional must place the following statements in the written document identified in paragraph (c) of this section and sign the document:

"[I, We] declare that, to the best of [my, our] professional knowledge and belief, [I, we] meet the definition of Environmental Professional as defined in § 312.10 of this part."

"[I, We] have the specific qualifications based on education, training, and experience to assess a property of the nature, history, and setting of the subject property. [I, We] have developed and performed the all appropriate inquiries in conformance with the standards and practices set forth in 40 CFR Part 312."

§ 312.22 Additional inquiries.

(a) Persons identified under § 312.1(b) must conduct the inquiries listed in paragraphs (a)(1) through (a)(4) below and may provide the information associated with such inquiries to the environmental professional responsible for conducting the activities listed in § 312.21:

(1) As required by § 312.25 and if not otherwise obtained by the environmental professional, environmental cleanup liens against the subject property that are filed or recorded under federal, tribal, state, or local law;

(2) As required by § 312.28, specialized knowledge or experience of the person identified in § 312.1(b);

(3) As required by § 312.29, the relationship of the purchase price to the fair market value of the subject property, if the property was not contaminated; and

(4) As required by § 312.30, and if not otherwise obtained by the environmental professional, commonly known or reasonably ascertainable information about the subject property.

§ 312.23 Interviews with past and present owners, operators, and occupants.

(a) Interviews with owners, operators, and occupants of the subject property must be conducted for the purposes of achieving the objectives and performance factors of § 312.20(e) and (f).

(b) The inquiry of the environmental professional must include interviewing the current owner and occupant of the subject property. If the property has multiple occupants, the inquiry of the environmental professional shall include interviewing major occupants, as well as those occupants likely to use, store, treat, handle or dispose of hazardous substances [and in the case of inquiries conducted for persons identified in § 312.1(b)(2) pollutants,

228

contaminants, petroleum and petroleum products, and controlled substances (as defined in 21 U.S.C. 802)], or those who have likely done so in the past.

(c) The inquiry of the environmental professional also must include, to the extent necessary to achieve the objectives and performance factors of § 312.20(e) and (f), interviewing one or more of the following persons:

(1) Current and past facility managers with relevant knowledge of uses and physical characteristics of the property;

(2) Past owners, occupants, or operators of the subject property; or

(3) Employees of current and past occupants of the subject property.

(d) In the case of inquiries conducted at "abandoned properties," as defined in § 312.10, where there is evidence of potential unauthorized uses of the subject property or evidence of uncontrolled access to the subject property, the environmental professional's inquiry must include interviewing one or more (as necessary) owners or occupants of neighboring or nearby properties from which it appears possible to have observed uses of, or releases at, such abandoned properties for the purpose of gathering information necessary to achieve the objectives and performance factors of § 312.20(e) and (f).

§ 312.24 Reviews of historical sources of information.

(a) Historical documents and records must be reviewed for the purposes of achieving the objectives and performance factors of § 312.20(e) and (f). Historical documents and records may include, but are not limited to, aerial photographs, fire insurance maps, building department records, chain of title documents, and land use records.

(b) Historical documents and records reviewed must cover a period of time as far back in the history of the subject property as it can be shown that the property contained structures or from the time the property was first used for residential, agricultural, commercial, industrial, or governmental purposes. For the purpose of achieving the objectives and performance factors of § 312.20(e) and (f), the environmental professional may exercise professional judgment in context of the facts available at the time of the inquiry as to how far back in time it is necessary to search historical records.

§ 312.25 Searches for recorded environmental cleanup liens.

(a) All appropriate inquiries must include a search for the existence of environmental cleanup liens against the subject property that are filed or recorded under federal, tribal, state, or local law.

(b) All information collected regarding the existence of such environmental cleanup liens associated with the subject property by persons to whom this part is applicable per § 312.1(b) and not by an environmental professional, may be provided to the environmental professional or retained by the applicable party.

§ 312.26 Reviews of Federal, State, Tribal, and local government records.

(a) Federal, tribal, state, and local government records or data bases of government records of the subject property and adjoining properties must be reviewed for the purposes of achieving the objectives and performance factors of § 312.20(e) and (f).

(b) With regard to the subject property, the review of federal, tribal, and state government records or data bases of such government records and local government records and data bases of such records should include:

(1) Records of reported releases or threatened releases, including site investigation reports for the subject property;

(2) Records of activities, conditions, or incidents likely to cause or contribute to releases or threatened releases as defined in § 312.1(c), including landfill and other disposal unit location records and permits, storage tank records and permits, hazardous waste handler and generator records and permits, federal, tribal and state government listings of sites identified as priority cleanup sites, and spill reporting records;

(3) CERCLIS records;

(4) Public health records;

(5) Emergency Response Notification System records;

(6) Registries or publicly available lists of engineering controls; and

(7) Registries or publicly available lists of institutional controls, including environmental land use restrictions, applicable to the subject property.

(c) With regard to nearby or adjoining properties, the review of federal, tribal, state, and local government records or databases of government records should include the identification of the following:

(1) Properties for which there are government records of reported releases or threatened releases. Such records or databases containing such records and the associated distances from the subject property for which such information should be searched include the following:

(i) Records of NPL sites or tribal-and state-equivalent sites (one mile);

(ii) RCRA facilities subject to corrective action (one mile);

(iii) Records of federally-registered, or state-permitted or registered, hazardous waste sites identified for investigation or remediation, such as sites enrolled in state and tribal voluntary cleanup programs and tribal-and state-listed brownfields sites (one-half mile);

(iv) Records of leaking underground storage tanks (one-half mile); and

(2) Properties that previously were identified or regulated by a government entity due to environmental concerns at the property. Such records or databases containing such records and the associated distances from the subject property for which such information should be searched include the following:

(i) Records of delisted NPL sites (one-half mile);

(ii) Registries or publicly available lists of engineering controls (one-half mile); and

(iii) Records of former CERCLIS sites with no further remedial action notices (one-half mile).

(3) Properties for which there are records of federally-permitted, tribal-permitted or registered, or state-permitted or registered waste management activities. Such records or data bases that may contain such records include the following:

(i) Records of RCRA small quantity and large quantity generators (adjoining properties);

(ii) Records of federally-permitted, tribal-permitted, or state-permitted (or registered) landfills and solid waste management facilities (one-half mile); and

(iii) Records of registered storage tanks (adjoining property).

(4) A review of additional government records with regard to sites identified under paragraphs (c)(1) through (c)(3) of this section may be necessary in the judgment of the environmental professional for the purpose of achieving the objectives and performance factors of § 312.20(e) and (f).

(d) The search distance from the subject property boundary for reviewing government records or databases of government records listed in paragraph (c) of this section may be modified based upon the professional judgment of the environmental professional. The rationale for such modifications must be documented by the environmental professional. The environmental professional may consider one or more of the following factors in determining an alternate appropriate search distance:

(1) The nature and extent of a release;

(2) Geologic, hydrogeologic, or topographic conditions of the subject property and surrounding environment;

(3) Land use or development densities;

(4) The property type;

(5) Existing or past uses of surrounding properties;

(6) Potential migration pathways (e.g., groundwater flow direction, prevalent wind direction); or

(7) Other relevant factors.

§ 312.27 Visual inspections of the facility and of adjoining properties.

(a) For the purpose of achieving the objectives and performance factors of § 312.20(e) and (f), the inquiry of the environmental professional must include:

(1) A visual on-site inspection of the subject property and facilities and improvements on the subject property, including a visual inspection of the areas where hazardous substances may be or may have been used, stored, treated, handled, or disposed. Physical limitations to the visual inspection must be noted.

(2) A visual inspection of adjoining properties, from the subject property line, public rights-of-way, or other vantage point (e.g., aerial photography), including a visual inspection of areas where hazardous substances may be or may have been stored, treated, handled or disposed. Physical limitations to the inspection of adjacent properties must be noted.

(b) Persons conducting site characterization and assessments using a grant awarded under CERCLA section 104(k)(2)(B) must include in the inquiries referenced in § 312.27(a) visual inspections of areas where hazardous substances, and may include, as applicable per the terms and conditions of the grant or cooperative agreement, pollutants and contaminants, petroleum and petroleum products, and controlled substances as defined in 21 U.S.C. 802 may be or may have been used, stored, treated, handled or disposed at the subject property and adjoining properties.

(c) Except as noted in this subsection, a visual on-site inspection of the subject property must be conducted. In the unusual circumstance where an on-site visual inspection of the subject property cannot be performed because of physical limitations, remote and inaccessible location, or other inability to obtain access to the property, provided good faith (as defined in § 312.10) efforts have been taken to obtain such access, an on-site inspection will not be required. The mere refusal of a voluntary seller to provide access to the subject property does not constitute an unusual circumstance. In such unusual circumstances, the inquiry of the environmental professional must include:

(1) Visually inspecting the subject property via another method (such as aerial imagery for large properties), or visually inspecting the subject property from the nearest accessible vantage point (such as the property line or public road for small properties);

(2) Documentation of efforts undertaken to obtain access and an explanation of why such efforts were unsuccessful; and

(3) Documentation of other sources of information regarding releases or threatened releases at the subject property that were consulted in accordance with § 312.20(e). Such documentation should include comments by the environmental professional on the significance of the failure to conduct a visual on-site inspection of the subject property with regard to the ability to identify conditions indicative of releases or threatened releases on, at, in, or to the subject property, if any.

§ 312.28   Specialized knowledge or experience on the part of the defendant.

(a) Persons to whom this part is applicable per § 312.1(b) must take into account, their specialized knowledge of the subject property, the area surrounding the subject property, the conditions of adjoining properties, and any other experience relevant to the inquiry, for the purpose of identifying conditions indicative of releases or threatened releases at the subject property, as defined in § 312.1(c).

(b) All appropriate inquiries, as outlined in § 312.20, are not complete unless the results of the inquiries take into account the relevant and applicable specialized knowledge and experience of the persons responsible for undertaking the inquiry (as described in § 312.1(b)).

§ 312.29   The relationship of the purchase price to the value of the property, if the property was not contaminated.

(a) Persons to whom this part is applicable per § 312.1(b) must consider whether the purchase price of the subject property reasonably reflects the fair market value of the property, if the property were not contaminated.

(b) Persons who conclude that the purchase price of the subject property does not reasonably reflect the fair market value of that property, if the property were not contaminated, must consider whether or not the differential in purchase price and fair market value is due to the presence of releases or threatened releases of hazardous substances.

(c) Persons conducting site characterization and assessments with the use of a grant awarded under CERCLA section 104(k)(2)(B) and who know that the purchase price of the subject property does not reasonably reflect the fair market value of that property, if the property were not contaminated, must consider whether or not the differential in purchase price and fair market value is due to the presence of releases or threatened releases of hazardous substances, pollutants, contaminants, petroleum and petroleum products, or controlled substances as defined in 21 U.S.C. 802.

§ 312.30 Commonly known or reasonably ascertainable information about the property.

(a) Throughout the inquiries, persons to whom this part is applicable per § 312.1(b) and environmental professionals conducting the inquiry must take into account commonly known or reasonably ascertainable information within the local community about the subject property and consider such information when seeking to identify conditions indicative of releases or threatened releases, as set forth in § 312.1(c), at the subject property.

(b) Commonly known information may include information obtained by the person to whom this part applies in § 312.1(b) or by the environmental professional about releases or threatened releases at the subject property that is incidental to the information obtained during the inquiry of the environmental professional.

(c) To the extent necessary to achieve the objectives and performance factors of § 312.20(e) and (f), persons to whom this part is applicable per § 312.1(b) and the environmental professional must gather information from varied sources whose input either individually or taken together may provide commonly known or reasonably ascertainable information about the subject property; the environmental professional may refer to one or more of the following sources of information:

(1) Current owners or occupants of neighboring properties or properties adjacent to the subject property;

(2) Local and state government officials who may have knowledge of, or information related to, the subject property;

(3) Others with knowledge of the subject property; and

(4) Other sources of information (e.g., newspapers, Web sites, community organizations, local libraries and historical societies).

§ 312.31 The degree of obviousness of the presence or likely presence of contamination at the property, and the ability to detect the contamination by appropriate investigation.

(a) Persons to whom this part is applicable per § 312.1(b) and environmental professionals conducting an inquiry of a property on behalf of such persons must take into account the information collected under § 312.23 through 312.30 in considering the degree of obviousness of the presence of releases or threatened releases at the subject property.

(b) Persons to whom this part is applicable per § 312.1(b) and environmental professionals conducting an inquiry of a property on behalf of such persons must take into account the information collected under § 312.23 through 312.30 in considering the ability to detect contamination by appropriate investigation. The inquiry of the environmental professional should include an opinion regarding additional appropriate investigation, if any.

B. FORMS

1. BROKER'S LISTING AGREEMENT*

CALIFORNIA ASSOCIATION OF REALTORS®

RESIDENTIAL LISTING AGREEMENT
(Exclusive Authorization and Right to Sell)
(C.A.R. Form RLA, Revised 4/07)

a1. EXCLUSIVE RIGHT TO SELL: _____ ("Seller")
hereby employs and grants _____ ("Broker")
beginning (date) _____ and ending at 11:59 P.M. on (date) _____ ("Listing Period")
the exclusive and irrevocable right to sell or exchange the real property in the City of _____,
County of _____, Assessor's Parcel No. _____,
California, described as: _____ ("Property").

2. ITEMS EXCLUDED AND INCLUDED: Unless otherwise specified in a real estate purchase agreement, all fixtures and fittings that are attached to the Property are included, and personal property items are excluded, from the purchase price.
ADDITIONAL ITEMS EXCLUDED: _____
ADDITIONAL ITEMS INCLUDED: _____
Seller intends that the above items be excluded or included in offering the Property for sale, but understands that: **(i)** the purchase agreement supersedes any intention expressed above and will ultimately determine which items are excluded and included in the sale; and **(ii)** Broker is not responsible for and does not guarantee that the above exclusions and/or inclusions will be in the purchase agreement.

3. LISTING PRICE AND TERMS:
    A. The listing price shall be: _____
    _____ Dollars ($ _____).
    B. Additional Terms: _____

4. COMPENSATION TO BROKER:
Notice: The amount or rate of real estate commissions is not fixed by law. They are set by each Broker individually and may be negotiable between Seller and Broker (real estate commissions include all compensation and fees to Broker).
    A. Seller agrees to pay to Broker as compensation for services irrespective of agency relationship(s), either ☐ _____ percent of the listing price (or if a purchase agreement is entered into, of the purchase price), or ☐ $ _____,
    AND _____, as follows:
        (1) If during the Listing Period, or any extension, Broker, Seller, cooperating broker, or any other person procures a buyer(s) who offers to purchase the Property on the above price and terms, or on any price and terms acceptable to Seller. (Broker is entitled to compensation whether any escrow resulting from such offer closes during or after the expiration of the Listing Period.)
    OR (2) If within _____ calendar days **(a)** after the end of the Listing Period or any extension; or **(b)** after any cancellation of this Agreement, unless otherwise agreed, Seller enters into a contract to sell, convey, lease or otherwise transfer the Property to anyone ("Prospective Buyer") or that person's related entity: **(i)** who physically entered and was shown the Property during the Listing Period or any extension by Broker or a cooperating broker; or **(ii)** for whom Broker or any cooperating broker submitted to Seller a signed, written offer to acquire, lease, exchange or obtain an option on the Property. Seller, however, shall have no obligation to Broker under paragraph 4A(2) unless, not later than **3 calendar days** after the end of the Listing Period or any extension or cancellation, Broker has given Seller a written notice of the names of such Prospective Buyers.
    OR (3) If, without Broker's prior written consent, the Property is withdrawn from sale, conveyed, leased, rented, otherwise transferred, or made unmarketable by a voluntary act of Seller during the Listing Period, or any extension.
    B. If completion of the sale is prevented by a party to the transaction other than Seller, then compensation due under paragraph 4A shall be payable only if and when Seller collects damages by suit, arbitration, settlement or otherwise, and then in an amount equal to the lesser of one-half of the damages recovered or the above compensation, after first deducting title and escrow expenses and the expenses of collection, if any.
    C. In addition, Seller agrees to pay Broker: _____
    D. Seller has been advised of Broker's policy regarding cooperation with, and the amount of compensation offered to, other brokers.
        (1) Broker is authorized to cooperate with and compensate brokers participating through the multiple listing service(s) ("MLS") by offering MLS brokers either ☐ _____ percent of the purchase price, or ☐ $ _____.
        (2) Broker is authorized to cooperate with and compensate brokers operating outside the MLS as per Broker's policy.
    E. Seller hereby irrevocably assigns to Broker the above compensation from Seller's funds and proceeds in escrow. Broker may submit this Agreement, as instructions to compensate Broker pursuant to paragraph 4A, to any escrow regarding the Property involving Seller and a buyer, Prospective Buyer or other transferee.

* Reprinted with permission, California Association of Realtors ®. Endorsement not implied.

F. **(1)** Seller represents that Seller has not previously entered into a listing agreement with another broker regarding the Property, unless specified as follows: _____.

(2) Seller warrants that Seller has no obligation to pay compensation to any other broker regarding the Property unless the Property is transferred to any of the following individuals or entities: _____

_____.

(3) If the Property is sold to anyone listed above during the time Seller is obligated to compensate another broker: **(I)** Broker is not entitled to compensation under this Agreement; and **(II)** Broker is not obligated to represent Seller in such transaction.

RLA REVISED 4/07 (PAGE 1 OF 3)   Print Date

Seller acknowledges receipt of a copy of this page.
Seller's Initials (_____)(_____)

Reviewed by _____ Date _____

RESIDENTIAL LISTING AGREEMENT - EXCLUSIVE (RLA PAGE 1 OF 3)

Property Address: _____ Date: _____

5. **OWNERSHIP, TITLE AND AUTHORITY:** Seller warrants that: **(i)** Seller is the owner of the Property; **(ii)** no other persons or entities have title to the Property; and **(iii)** Seller has the authority to both execute this Agreement and sell the Property. Exceptions to ownership, title and authority are as follows: _____.

6. **MULTIPLE LISTING SERVICE:** All terms of the transaction, including financing, if applicable, will be provided to the selected MLS for publication, dissemination and use by persons and entities on terms approved by the MLS. Seller authorizes Broker to comply with all applicable MLS rules. MLS rules allow MLS data to be made available by the MLS to additional Internet sites unless Broker gives the MLS instructions to the contrary. MLS rules generally provide that residential real property and vacant lot listings be submitted to the MLS within 48 hours or some other period of time after all necessary signatures have been obtained on the listing agreement. However, Broker will not have to submit this listing to the MLS if, within that time, Broker submits to the MLS a form signed by Seller (C.A.R. Form SEL or the locally required form) instructing Broker to withhold the listing from the MLS. Information about this listing will be provided to the MLS of Broker's selection unless a form instructing Broker to withhold the listing from the MLS is attached to this listing Agreement.

7. **SELLER REPRESENTATIONS:** Seller represents that, unless otherwise specified in writing, Seller is unaware of: **(i)** any Notice of Default recorded against the Property; **(ii)** any delinquent amounts due under any loan secured by, or other obligation affecting, the Property; **(iii)** any bankruptcy, insolvency or similar proceeding affecting the Property; **(iv)** any litigation, arbitration, administrative action, government investigation or other pending or threatened action that affects or may affect the Property or Seller's ability to transfer it; and **(v)** any current, pending or proposed special assessments affecting the Property. Seller shall promptly notify Broker in writing if Seller becomes aware of any of these items during the Listing Period or any extension thereof.

8. **BROKER'S AND SELLER'S DUTIES:** Broker agrees to exercise reasonable effort and due diligence to achieve the purposes of this Agreement. Unless Seller gives Broker written instructions to the contrary, Broker is authorized to order reports and disclosures as appropriate or necessary and advertise and market the Property by any method and in any medium selected by Broker, including MLS and the Internet, and, to the extent permitted by these media, control the dissemination of the information submitted to any medium. Seller agrees to consider offers presented by Broker, and to act in good faith to accomplish the sale of the Property by, among other things, making the Property available for showing at reasonable times and referring to Broker all inquiries of any party interested in the Property. Seller is responsible for determining at what price to list and sell the Property. **Seller further agrees to indemnify, defend and hold Broker harmless from all claims, disputes, litigation, judgments and attorney fees arising from any incorrect information supplied by Seller, or from any material facts that Seller knows but fails to disclose.**

9. **DEPOSIT:** Broker is authorized to accept and hold on Seller's behalf any deposits to be applied toward the purchase price.

10. **AGENCY RELATIONSHIPS:**
    A. **Disclosure:** If the Property includes residential property with one-to-four dwelling units, Seller shall receive a "Disclosure Regarding Agency Relationships" form prior to entering into this Agreement.
    B. **Seller Representation:** Broker shall represent Seller in any resulting transaction, except as specified in paragraph 4F.
    C. **Possible Dual Agency With Buyer:** Depending upon the circumstances, it may be necessary or appropriate for Broker to act as an agent for both Seller and buyer, exchange party, or one or more additional parties ("Buyer"). Broker shall, as soon as practicable, disclose to Seller any election to act as a dual agent representing both Seller and Buyer. If a Buyer is procured directly by Broker or an associate-licensee in Broker's firm, Seller hereby consents to Broker acting as a dual agent for Seller and such Buyer. In the event of an exchange, Seller hereby consents to Broker collecting compensation from additional parties for services rendered, provided there is disclosure to all parties of such agency and compensation. Seller understands and agrees that: **(i)** Broker, without the prior written consent of Seller, will not disclose to Buyer that Seller is willing to sell the Property at a price less than the listing price; **(ii)** Broker, without the prior written consent of Buyer, will not disclose to Seller that Buyer is willing to pay a price greater than the offered price; and **(iii)** except for (i) and (ii) above, a dual agent is obligated to disclose known facts materially affecting the value or desirability of the Property to both parties.
    D. **Other Sellers:** Seller understands that Broker may have or obtain listings on other properties, and that potential buyers may consider, make offers on, or purchase through Broker, property the same as or similar to Seller's Property. Seller consents to Broker's representation of sellers and buyers of other properties before, during and after the end of this Agreement.
    E. **Confirmation:** If the Property includes residential property with one-to-four dwelling units, Broker shall confirm the agency relationship described above, or as modified, in writing, prior to or concurrent with Seller's execution of a purchase agreement.

11. **SECURITY AND INSURANCE:** Broker is not responsible for loss of or damage to personal or real property, or person, whether attributable to use of a keysafe/lockbox, a showing of the Property, or otherwise. Third parties, including, but not limited to, appraisers, inspectors, brokers and prospective buyers, may have access to, and take videos and photographs of, the interior of the Property. Seller agrees: **(i)** to take reasonable precautions to safeguard and protect valuables that might be accessible during showings of the Property; and **(ii)** to obtain insurance to protect against these risks. Broker does not maintain insurance to protect Seller.

12. **KEYSAFE/LOCKBOX:** A keysafe/lockbox is designed to hold a key to the Property to permit access to the Property by Broker, cooperating brokers, MLS participants, their authorized licensees and representatives, authorized inspectors, and accompanied prospective buyers. Broker, cooperating brokers, MLS and Associations/Boards of REALTORS® are **not** insurers against injury, theft, loss, vandalism or damage attributed to the use of a keysafe/lockbox. Seller does (or if checked ☐ does not) authorize Broker to install a keysafe/lockbox. If Seller does not occupy the Property, Seller shall be responsible for obtaining occupant(s)' written permission for use of a keysafe/lockbox.

13. **SIGN:** Seller does (or if checked ☐ does not) authorize Broker to install a FOR SALE/SOLD sign on the Property.

14. **EQUAL HOUSING OPPORTUNITY:** The Property is offered in compliance with federal, state and local anti-discrimination laws.

15. **ATTORNEY FEES:** In any action, proceeding or arbitration between Seller and Broker regarding the obligation to pay compensation under this Agreement, the prevailing Seller or Broker shall be entitled to reasonable attorney fees and costs from the non-prevailing Seller or Broker, except as provided in paragraph 19A.

16. **ADDITIONAL TERMS:** _____
_____
_____

Seller acknowledges receipt of a copy of this page.
Seller's Initials (_____)(_____)

RLA REVISED 4/07 (PAGE 2 OF 3)

| Reviewed by _____ Date _____ |

EQUAL HOUSING OPPORTUNITY

RESIDENTIAL LISTING AGREEMENT - EXCLUSIVE (RLA PAGE 2 OF 3)

Property Address: _____ Date: _____

17. **MANAGEMENT APPROVAL:** If an associate-licensee in Broker's office (salesperson or broker-associate) enters into this Agreement on Broker's behalf, and Broker or Manager does not approve of its terms, Broker or Manager has the right to cancel this Agreement, in writing, within **5 Days** After its execution.

18. **SUCCESSORS AND ASSIGNS:** This Agreement shall be binding upon Seller and Seller's successors and assigns.

19. **DISPUTE RESOLUTION:**

   A. **MEDIATION:** Seller and Broker agree to mediate any dispute or claim arising between them out of this Agreement, or any resulting transaction, before resorting to arbitration or court action, subject to paragraph 19B(2) below. Paragraph 19B(2) below applies whether or not the arbitration provision is initialed. Mediation fees, if any, shall be divided equally among the parties involved. If, for any dispute or claim to which this paragraph applies, any party commences an action without first attempting to resolve the matter through mediation, or refuses to mediate after a request has been made, then that party shall not be entitled to recover attorney fees, even if they would otherwise be available to that party in any such action. THIS MEDIATION PROVISION APPLIES WHETHER OR NOT THE ARBITRATION PROVISION IS INITIALED.

   B. **ARBITRATION OF DISPUTES: (1)** Seller and Broker agree that any dispute or claim in law or equity arising between them regarding the obligation to pay compensation under this Agreement, which is not settled through mediation, shall be decided by neutral, binding arbitration, including and subject to paragraph 19B(2) below. The arbitrator shall be a retired judge or justice, or an attorney with at least 5 years of residential real estate law experience, unless the parties mutually agree to a different arbitrator, who shall render an award in accordance with substantive California law. The parties shall have the right to discovery in accordance with California Code of Civil Procedure §1283.05. In all other respects, the arbitration shall be conducted in accordance with Title 9 of Part III of the California Code of Civil Procedure. Judgment upon the award of the arbitrator(s) may be entered in any court having jurisdiction. Interpretation of this agreement to arbitrate shall be governed by the Federal Arbitration Act.
   (2) EXCLUSIONS FROM MEDIATION AND ARBITRATION: The following matters are excluded from mediation and arbitration: (i) a judicial or non-judicial foreclosure or other action or proceeding to enforce a deed of trust, mortgage, or installment land sale contract as defined in California Civil Code §2985; (ii) an unlawful detainer action; (iii) the filing or enforcement of a mechanic's lien; and (iv) any matter that is within the jurisdiction of a probate, small claims, or bankruptcy court. The filing of a court action to enable the recording of a notice of pending action, for order of attachment, receivership, injunction, or other provisional remedies, shall not constitute a waiver of the mediation and arbitration provisions.

   > **"NOTICE: BY INITIALING IN THE SPACE BELOW YOU ARE AGREEING TO HAVE ANY DISPUTE ARISING OUT OF THE MATTERS INCLUDED IN THE 'ARBITRATION OF DISPUTES' PROVISION DECIDED BY NEUTRAL ARBITRATION AS PROVIDED BY CALIFORNIA LAW AND YOU ARE GIVING UP ANY RIGHTS YOU MIGHT POSSESS TO HAVE THE DISPUTE LITIGATED IN A COURT OR JURY TRIAL. BY INITIALING IN THE SPACE BELOW YOU ARE GIVING UP YOUR JUDICIAL RIGHTS TO DISCOVERY AND APPEAL, UNLESS THOSE RIGHTS ARE SPECIFICALLY INCLUDED IN THE 'ARBITRATION OF DISPUTES' PROVISION. IF YOU REFUSE TO SUBMIT TO ARBITRATION AFTER AGREEING TO THIS PROVISION, YOU MAY BE COMPELLED TO ARBITRATE UNDER THE AUTHORITY OF THE CALIFORNIA CODE OF CIVIL PROCEDURE. YOUR AGREEMENT TO THIS ARBITRATION PROVISION IS VOLUNTARY."**

   > **"WE HAVE READ AND UNDERSTAND THE FOREGOING AND AGREE TO SUBMIT DISPUTES ARISING OUT OF THE MATTERS INCLUDED IN THE 'ARBITRATION OF DISPUTES' PROVISION TO NEUTRAL ARBITRATION."**

Seller's Initials _____/_____	Broker's Initials _____/_____

20. **ENTIRE AGREEMENT:** All prior discussions, negotiations and agreements between the parties concerning the subject matter of this Agreement are superseded by this Agreement, which constitutes the entire contract and a complete and exclusive expression of their agreement, and may not be contradicted by evidence of any prior agreement or contemporaneous oral agreement. If any provision of this Agreement is held to be ineffective or invalid, the remaining provisions will nevertheless be given full force and effect. This Agreement and any supplement, addendum or modification, including any photocopy or facsimile, may be executed in counterparts.

By signing below, Seller acknowledges that Seller has read, understands, received a copy of and agrees to the terms of this Agreement.

Seller _____ Date _____

Address _____ City _____ State _____ Zip _____

Telephone _____ Fax _____ E-mail _____

BROKER'S LISTING AGREEMENT

Seller _____ Date _____

Address _____ City _____ State _____ Zip _____

Telephone _____ Fax _____ E-mail _____

Real Estate Broker (Firm) _____ DRE Lic. # _____

By (Agent) _____ DRE Lic. # _____ Date _____

Address _____ City _____ State _____ Zip _____

Telephone _____ Fax _____ E-mail _____

THIS FORM HAS BEEN APPROVED BY THE CALIFORNIA ASSOCIATION OF REALTORS® (C.A.R.). NO REPRESENTATION IS MADE AS TO THE LEGAL VALIDITY OR ADEQUACY OF ANY PROVISION IN ANY SPECIFIC TRANSACTION. A REAL ESTATE BROKER IS THE PERSON QUALIFIED TO ADVISE ON REAL ESTATE TRANSACTIONS. IF YOU DESIRE LEGAL OR TAX ADVICE, CONSULT AN APPROPRIATE PROFESSIONAL.
This form is available for use by the entire real estate industry. It is not intended to identify the user as a REALTOR®. REALTOR® is a registered collective membership mark which may be used only by members of the NATIONAL ASSOCIATION OF REALTORS® who subscribe to its Code of Ethics.

Published and Distributed by:
REAL ESTATE BUSINESS SERVICES, INC.
a subsidiary of the California Association of REALTORS®
525 South Virgil Avenue, Los Angeles, California 90020

Reviewed by _____ Date _____

EQUAL HOUSING
OPPORTUNITY

RLA REVISED 4/07 (PAGE 3 OF 3)

RESIDENTIAL LISTING AGREEMENT - EXCLUSIVE (RLA PAGE 3 OF 3)

239

2. DEPOSIT RECEIPT FORM*

CALIFORNIA
ASSOCIATION
OF REALTORS ®

CALIFORNIA
RESIDENTIAL PURCHASE AGREEMENT
AND JOINT ESCROW INSTRUCTIONS
For Use With Single Family Residential Property — Attached or Detached
(C.A.R. Form RPA-CA, Revised 11/07)

Date _____, at _____, California.
1. **OFFER:**
   A. **THIS IS AN OFFER FROM** _____ ("Buyer").
   B. **THE REAL PROPERTY TO BE ACQUIRED** is described as _____
   _____, Assessor's Parcel No. _____, situated in
   _____, County of _____, California, ("Property").
   C. **THE PURCHASE PRICE** offered is _____
   _____ Dollars $ _____.
   D. **CLOSE OF ESCROW** shall occur on _____ (date)(or ☐ _____ **Days** After Acceptance).
2. **FINANCE TERMS:** Obtaining the loans below **is a contingency** of this Agreement unless: **(i)** either 2K or 2L is checked below; or **(ii)** otherwise agreed in writing. Buyer shall act diligently and in good faith to obtain the designated loans. Obtaining deposit, down payment and closing costs **is not a contingency.** Buyer represents that funds will be good when deposited with Escrow Holder.
   A. **INITIAL DEPOSIT:** Buyer has given a deposit in the amount of . . . .$ _____
   to the agent submitting the offer (or to ☐ _____), by personal check
   (or ☐ _____), made payable to _____,
   which shall be held uncashed until Acceptance and then deposited within **3 business days** after
   Acceptance (or ☐ _____), with
   Escrow Holder, (or ☐ into Broker's trust account).
   B. **INCREASED DEPOSIT:** Buyer shall deposit with Escrow Holder an increased deposit in the amount of . . . .$ _____
   within _____ **Days** After Acceptance, or ☐ _____.
   C. **FIRST LOAN IN THE AMOUNT OF** . . . .$ _____
   (1) NEW First Deed of Trust in favor of lender, encumbering the Property, securing a note payable at
   maximum interest of _____ % fixed rate, or _____ % initial adjustable rate with a maximum
   interest rate of _____ %, balance due in _____ years, amortized over _____ years. Buyer
   shall pay loan fees/points not to exceed _____ . (These terms apply whether the designated loan
   is conventional, FHA or VA.)
   (2) ☐ FHA ☐ VA: (The following terms only apply to the FHA or VA loan that is checked.)
   Seller shall pay _____ % discount points. Seller shall pay other fees not allowed to be paid by Buyer,
   ☐ not to exceed $_____ . Seller shall pay the cost of lender required Repairs (including
   those for wood destroying pest) not otherwise provided for in this Agreement, ☐ not to exceed $
   _____ . (Actual loan amount may increase if mortgage insurance premiums, funding fees or
   closing costs are financed.)
   D. **ADDITIONAL FINANCING TERMS:** ☐ Seller financing, (C.A.R. Form SFA); ☐ secondary financing, ...$ _____
   (C.A.R. Form PAA, paragraph 4A); ☐ assumed financing (C.A.R. Form PAA, paragraph 4B)
   _____
   _____
   E. **BALANCE OF PURCHASE PRICE** (not including costs of obtaining loans and other closing costs) in the amount of . . .$ _____
   to be deposited with Escrow Holder within sufficient time to close escrow.
   F. **PURCHASE PRICE (TOTAL):** . . . .$ _____
   G. **LOAN APPLICATIONS:** Within **7 (or** ☐ _____ **) Days** After Acceptance, Buyer shall provide Seller a letter from lender or mortgage loan broker stating that, based on a review of Buyer's written application and credit report, Buyer is prequalified or preapproved for the NEW loan specified in 2C above.
   H. **VERIFICATION OF DOWN PAYMENT AND CLOSING COSTS:** Buyer (or Buyer's lender or loan broker pursuant to 2G) shall, within **7 (or** ☐ _____ **) Days** After Acceptance, provide Seller written verification of Buyer's down payment and closing costs.
   I. **LOAN CONTINGENCY REMOVAL: (i)** Within **17 (or** ☐ _____ **) Days** After Acceptance, Buyer shall, as specified in paragraph 14, remove the loan contingency or cancel this Agreement; OR **(ii)** (if checked) ☐ the loan contingency shall remain in effect until the designated loans are funded.
   J. **APPRAISAL CONTINGENCY AND REMOVAL:** This Agreement is (**OR**, if checked, ☐ is NOT) contingent upon the Property appraising at no less than the specified purchase price. If there is a loan contingency, at the time the loan contingency is removed (or, if checked, ☐ within **17 (or** _____ **) Days** After Acceptance), Buyer shall, as specified in paragraph 14B(3), remove the appraisal contingency or cancel this Agreement. If there is no loan contingency, Buyer shall, as specified in paragraph 14B(3), remove the appraisal contingency within **17 (or** _____ **) Days** After Acceptance.

* Reprinted with permission, California Association of
Realtors ®. Endorsement not implied.
240

K. ☐ **NO LOAN CONTINGENCY** (If checked): Obtaining any loan in paragraphs 2C, 2D or elsewhere in this Agreement is NOT a contingency of this Agreement. If Buyer does not obtain the loan and as a result Buyer does not purchase the Property, Seller may be entitled to Buyer's deposit or other legal remedies.

L. ☐ **ALL CASH OFFER** (If checked): No loan is needed to purchase the Property. Buyer shall, within **7 (or** ☐ _____ **) Days** After Acceptance, provide Seller written verification of sufficient funds to close this transaction.

3. **CLOSING AND OCCUPANCY:**

A. Buyer intends (or ☐ does not intend) to occupy the Property as Buyer's primary residence.

B. **Seller-occupied or vacant property:** Occupancy shall be delivered to Buyer at _____ AM/PM, ☐ on the date of Close Of Escrow; ☐ on _____; or ☐ no later than _____ **Days** After Close Of Escrow. (C.A.R. Form PAA, paragraph 2.) If transfer of title and occupancy do not occur at the same time, Buyer and Seller are advised to: **(i)** enter into a written occupancy agreement; and **(ii)** consult with their insurance and legal advisors.

RPA-CA REVISED 11/07 (PAGE 1 OF 8) Print Date

Buyer's Initials (_____)(_____)
Seller's Initials (_____)(_____)

Reviewed by _____ Date _____

CALIFORNIA RESIDENTIAL PURCHASE AGREEMENT (RPA-CA PAGE 1 OF 8)

Property Address: _____ Date: _____

   C. **Tenant-occupied property: (i) Property shall be vacant** at least **5** (or ☐ _____) **Days** Prior to Close Of Escrow, unless otherwise agreed in writing. **Note to Seller: If you are unable to deliver Property vacant in accordance with rent control and other applicable Law, you may be in breach of this Agreement.**

   OR (ii) (if checked) ☐ **Tenant to remain in possession.** The attached addendum is incorporated into this Agreement (C.A.R. Form PAA, paragraph 3.);

   OR (iii) (if checked) ☐ **This Agreement is contingent** upon Buyer and Seller entering into a written agreement regarding occupancy of the Property within the time specified in paragraph 14B(1). If no written agreement is reached within this time, either Buyer or Seller may cancel this Agreement in writing.

   D. At Close Of Escrow, Seller assigns to Buyer any assignable warranty rights for items included in the sale and shall provide any available Copies of such warranties. Brokers cannot and will not determine the assignability of any warranties.

   E. At Close Of Escrow, unless otherwise agreed in writing, Seller shall provide keys and/or means to operate all locks, mailboxes, security systems, alarms and garage door openers. If Property is a condominium or located in a common interest subdivision, Buyer may be required to pay a deposit to the Homeowners' Association ("HOA") to obtain keys to accessible HOA facilities.

4. ALLOCATION OF COSTS (If checked)**:** Unless otherwise specified here, this paragraph only determines who is to pay for the report, inspection, test or service mentioned. If not specified here or elsewhere in this Agreement, the determination of who is to pay for any work recommended or identified by any such report, inspection, test or service shall be by the method specified in paragraph 14B(2).

   A. WOOD DESTROYING PEST INSPECTION:

     (1) ☐ Buyer ☐ Seller shall pay for an inspection and report for wood destroying pests and organisms ("Report") which shall be prepared by _____, a registered structural pest control company. The Report shall cover the accessible areas of the main building and attached structures and, if checked: ☐ detached garages and carports, ☐ detached decks, ☐ the following other structures or areas _____. The Report shall not include roof coverings. If Property is a condominium or located in a common interest subdivision, the Report shall include only the separate interest and any exclusive-use areas being transferred and shall not include common areas, unless otherwise agreed. Water tests of shower pans on upper level units may not be performed without consent of the owners of property below the shower.

   OR (2) ☐ **(If checked)** The attached addendum (C.A.R. Form WPA) regarding wood destroying pest inspection and allocation of cost is incorporated into this Agreement.

   B. OTHER INSPECTIONS AND REPORTS:

     (1) ☐ Buyer ☐ Seller shall pay to have septic or private sewage disposal systems inspected _____.

     (2) ☐ Buyer ☐ Seller shall pay to have domestic wells tested for water potability and productivity _____.

     (3) ☐ Buyer ☐ Seller shall pay for a natural hazard zone disclosure report prepared by _____.

     (4) ☐ Buyer ☐ Seller shall pay for the following inspection or report _____.

     (5) ☐ Buyer ☐ Seller shall pay for the following inspection or report _____.

   C. GOVERNMENT REQUIREMENTS AND RETROFIT:

     (1) ☐ Buyer ☐ Seller shall pay for smoke detector installation and/or water heater bracing, if required by Law. Prior to Close Of Escrow, Seller shall provide Buyer a written statement of compliance in accordance with state and local Law, unless exempt.

     (2) ☐ Buyer ☐ Seller shall pay the cost of compliance with any other minimum mandatory government retrofit standards, inspections and reports if required as a condition of closing escrow under any Law. _____.

   D. ESCROW AND TITLE:

     (1) ☐ Buyer ☐ Seller shall pay escrow fee _____

      Escrow Holder shall be _____

     (2) ☐ Buyer ☐ Seller shall pay for **owner's** title insurance policy specified in paragraph 12E _____

      Owner's title policy to be issued by _____

      (Buyer shall pay for any title insurance policy insuring Buyer's **lender**, unless otherwise agreed in writing.)

   E. OTHER COSTS:

     (1) ☐ Buyer ☐ Seller shall pay County transfer tax or transfer fee _____.

     (2) ☐ Buyer ☐ Seller shall pay City transfer tax or transfer fee _____.

     (3) ☐ Buyer ☐ Seller shall pay HOA transfer fee _____.

     (4) ☐ Buyer ☐ Seller shall pay HOA document preparation fees _____.

     (5) ☐ Buyer ☐ Seller shall pay the cost, not to exceed $ _____, of a one-year home warranty plan, issued by _____

      with the following optional coverage: _____.

     (6) ☐ Buyer ☐ Seller shall pay for _____.

     (7) ☐ Buyer ☐ Seller shall pay for _____.

5. STATUTORY DISCLOSURES (INCLUDING LEAD-BASED PAINT HAZARD DISCLOSURES) AND CANCELLATION RIGHTS:

A. **(1)** Seller shall, within the time specified in paragraph 14A, deliver to Buyer, if required by Law: **(i)** Federal Lead-Based Paint Disclosures and pamphlet ("Lead Disclosures"); and **(ii)** disclosures or notices required by sections 1102 et. seq. and 1103 et. seq. of the California Civil Code ("Statutory Disclosures"). Statutory Disclosures include, but are not limited to, a Real Estate Transfer Disclosure Statement ("TDS"), Natural Hazard Disclosure Statement ("NHD"), notice or actual knowledge of release of illegal controlled substance, notice of special tax and/or assessments (or, if allowed, substantially equivalent notice regarding the Mello-Roos Community Facilities Act and Improvement Bond Act of 1915) and, if Seller has actual knowledge, of industrial use and military ordinance location disclosure (C.A.R. Form SSD).

(2) Buyer shall, within the time specified in paragraph 14B(1), return Signed Copies of the Statutory and Lead Disclosures to Seller.

(3) In the event Seller, prior to Close Of Escrow, becomes aware of adverse conditions materially affecting the Property, or any material inaccuracy in disclosures, information or representations previously provided to Buyer of which Buyer is otherwise unaware, Seller shall promptly provide a subsequent or amended disclosure or notice, in writing, covering those items. **However, a subsequent or amended disclosure shall not be required for conditions and material inaccuracies disclosed in reports ordered and paid for by Buyer.**

Buyer's Initials (_____)(_____)
Seller's Initials (_____)(_____)

Reviewed by _____ Date _____

CALIFORNIA RESIDENTIAL PURCHASE AGREEMENT (RPA-CA PAGE 2 OF 8)

243

Property Address: _____ Date: _____

(4) If any disclosure or notice specified in 5A(1), or subsequent or amended disclosure or notice is delivered to Buyer after the offer is Signed, Buyer shall have the right to cancel this Agreement within **3 Days** After delivery in person, or **5 Days** After delivery by deposit in the mail, by giving written notice of cancellation to Seller or Seller's agent. (Lead Disclosures sent by mail must be sent certified mail or better.)

(5) Note to Buyer and Seller: Waiver of Statutory and Lead Disclosures is prohibited by Law.

B. NATURAL AND ENVIRONMENTAL HAZARDS: Within the time specified in paragraph 14A, Seller shall, if required by Law: **(i)** deliver to Buyer earthquake guides (and questionnaire) and environmental hazards booklet; **(ii)** even if exempt from the obligation to provide a NHD, disclose if the Property is located in a Special Flood Hazard Area; Potential Flooding (Inundation) Area; Very High Fire Hazard Zone; State Fire Responsibility Area; Earthquake Fault Zone; Seismic Hazard Zone; and **(iii)** disclose any other zone as required by Law and provide any other information required for those zones.

C. MEGAN'S LAW DATABASE DISCLOSURE: Notice: Pursuant to Section 290.46 of the Penal Code, information about specified registered sex offenders is made available to the public via an Internet Web site maintained by the Department of Justice at www.meganslaw.ca.gov. Depending on an offender's criminal history, this information will include either the address at which the offender resides or the community of residence and ZIP Code in which he or she resides. (Neither Seller nor Brokers are required to check this website. If Buyer wants further information, Broker recommends that Buyer obtain information from this website during Buyer's inspection contingency period. Brokers do not have expertise in this area.)

6. CONDOMINIUM/PLANNED UNIT DEVELOPMENT DISCLOSURES:

A. SELLER HAS: 7 (or ☐ _____) Days After Acceptance to disclose to Buyer whether the Property is a condominium, or is located in a planned unit development or other common interest subdivision (C.A.R. Form SSD).

B. If the Property is a condominium or is located in a planned unit development or other common interest subdivision, Seller has **3 (or ☐ _____) Days** After Acceptance to request from the HOA (C.A.R. Form HOA): **(i)** Copies of any documents required by Law; **(ii)** disclosure of any pending or anticipated claim or litigation by or against the HOA; **(iii)** a statement containing the location and number of designated parking and storage spaces; **(iv)** Copies of the most recent 12 months of HOA minutes for regular and special meetings; and **(v)** the names and contact information of all HOAs governing the Property (collectively, "CI Disclosures"). Seller shall itemize and deliver to Buyer all CI Disclosures received from the HOA and any CI Disclosures in Seller's possession. Buyer's approval of CI Disclosures is a contingency of this Agreement as specified in paragraph 14B(3).

7. CONDITIONS AFFECTING PROPERTY:

A. Unless otherwise agreed: **(i) the Property is sold (a) in its PRESENT physical condition as of the date of Acceptance and (b) subject to Buyer's Investigation rights; (ii)** the Property, including pool, spa, landscaping and grounds, is to be maintained in substantially the same condition as on the date of Acceptance; and **(iii)** all debris and personal property not included in the sale shall be removed by Close Of Escrow.

B. SELLER SHALL, within the time specified in paragraph 14A, DISCLOSE KNOWN MATERIAL FACTS AND DEFECTS affecting the Property, including known insurance claims within the past five years, AND MAKE OTHER DISCLOSURES REQUIRED BY LAW (C.A.R. Form SSD).

C. NOTE TO BUYER: You are strongly advised to conduct investigations of the entire Property in order to determine its present condition since Seller may not be aware of all defects affecting the Property or other factors that you consider important. Property improvements may not be built according to code, in compliance with current Law, or have had permits issued.

D. NOTE TO SELLER: Buyer has the right to inspect the Property and, as specified in paragraph 14B, based upon information discovered in those inspections: (i) cancel this Agreement; or (ii) request that you make Repairs or take other action.

8. ITEMS INCLUDED AND EXCLUDED:

A. NOTE TO BUYER AND SELLER: Items listed as included or excluded in the MLS, flyers or marketing materials are **not** included in the purchase price or excluded from the sale unless specified in 8B or C.

B. ITEMS INCLUDED IN SALE:

(1) All EXISTING fixtures and fittings that are attached to the Property;

(2) Existing electrical, mechanical, lighting, plumbing and heating fixtures, ceiling fans, fireplace inserts, gas logs and grates, solar systems, built-in appliances, window and door screens, awnings, shutters, window coverings, attached floor coverings, television antennas, satellite dishes, private integrated telephone systems, air coolers/conditioners, pool/spa equipment, garage door openers/remote controls, mailbox, in-ground landscaping, trees/shrubs, water softeners, water purifiers, security systems/alarms; and

(3) The following items: _____
_____

(4) Seller represents that all items included in the purchase price, unless otherwise specified, are owned by Seller.

(5) All items included shall be transferred free of liens and without Seller warranty.

C. ITEMS EXCLUDED FROM SALE: _____
_____

9. BUYER'S INVESTIGATION OF PROPERTY AND MATTERS AFFECTING PROPERTY:

    A. Buyer's acceptance of the condition of, and any other matter affecting the Property, is a contingency of this Agreement as specified in this paragraph and paragraph 14B. Within the time specified in paragraph 14B(1), Buyer shall have the right, at Buyer's expense unless otherwise agreed, to conduct inspections, investigations, tests, surveys and other studies ("Buyer Investigations"), including, but not limited to, the right to: **(i)** inspect for lead-based paint and other lead-based paint hazards; **(ii)** inspect for wood destroying pests and organisms; **(iii)** review the registered sex offender database; **(iv)** confirm the insurability of Buyer and the Property; and **(v)** satisfy Buyer as to any matter specified in the attached Buyer's Inspection Advisory (C.A.R. Form BIA). Without Seller's prior written consent, Buyer shall neither make nor cause to be made: **(i)** invasive or destructive Buyer Investigations; or **(ii)** inspections by any governmental building or zoning inspector or government employee, unless required by Law.

    B. Buyer shall complete Buyer Investigations and, as specified in paragraph 14B, remove the contingency or cancel this Agreement. Buyer shall give Seller, at no cost, complete Copies of all Buyer Investigation reports obtained by Buyer. Seller shall make the Property available for all Buyer Investigations. Seller shall have water, gas, electricity and all operable pilot lights on for Buyer's Investigations and through the date possession is made available to Buyer.

Buyer's Initials (_____)(_____)
Seller's Initials (_____)(_____)

Reviewed by _____ Date _____

RPA-CA REVISED 11/07 (PAGE 3 OF 8)

CALIFORNIA RESIDENTIAL PURCHASE AGREEMENT (RPA-CA PAGE 3 OF 8)

Property Address: _____ Date: _____

10. REPAIRS: Repairs shall be completed prior to final verification of condition unless otherwise agreed in writing. Repairs to be performed at Seller's expense may be performed by Seller or through others, provided that the work complies with applicable Law, including governmental permit, inspection and approval requirements. Repairs shall be performed in a good, skillful manner with materials of quality and appearance comparable to existing materials. It is understood that exact restoration of appearance or cosmetic items following all Repairs may not be possible. Seller shall: **(i)** obtain receipts for Repairs performed by others; **(ii)** prepare a written statement indicating the Repairs performed by Seller and the date of such Repairs; and **(iii)** provide Copies of receipts and statements to Buyer prior to final verification of condition.

11. BUYER INDEMNITY AND SELLER PROTECTION FOR ENTRY UPON PROPERTY: Buyer shall: **(i)** keep the Property free and clear of liens; **(ii)** repair all damage arising from Buyer Investigations; and **(iii)** indemnify and hold Seller harmless from all resulting liability, claims, demands, damages and costs. Buyer shall carry, or Buyer shall require anyone acting on Buyer's behalf to carry, policies of liability, workers' compensation and other applicable insurance, defending and protecting Seller from liability for any injuries to persons or property occurring during any Buyer Investigations or work done on the Property at Buyer's direction prior to Close Of Escrow. Seller is advised that certain protections may be afforded Seller by recording a "Notice of Non-responsibility" (C.A.R. Form NNR) for Buyer Investigations and work done on the Property at Buyer's direction. Buyer's obligations under this paragraph shall survive the termination of this Agreement.

12. TITLE AND VESTING:
    A. Within the time specified in paragraph 14, Buyer shall be provided a current preliminary (title) report, which is only an offer by the title insurer to issue a policy of title insurance and may not contain every item affecting title. Buyer's review of the preliminary report and any other matters which may affect title are a contingency of this Agreement as specified in paragraph 14B.
    B. Title is taken in its present condition subject to all encumbrances, easements, covenants, conditions, restrictions, rights and other matters, whether of record or not, as of the date of Acceptance except: **(i)** monetary liens of record unless Buyer is assuming those obligations or taking the Property subject to those obligations; and **(ii)** those matters which Seller has agreed to remove in writing.
    C. Within the time specified in paragraph 14A, Seller has a duty to disclose to Buyer all matters known to Seller affecting title, whether of record or not.
    D. At Close Of Escrow, Buyer shall receive a grant deed conveying title (or, for stock cooperative or long-term lease, an assignment of stock certificate or of Seller's leasehold interest), including oil, mineral and water rights if currently owned by Seller. Title shall vest as designated in Buyer's supplemental escrow instructions. THE MANNER OF TAKING TITLE MAY HAVE SIGNIFICANT LEGAL AND TAX CONSEQUENCES. CONSULT AN APPROPRIATE PROFESSIONAL.
    E. Buyer shall receive a CLTA/ALTA Homeowner's Policy of Title Insurance. A title company, at Buyer's request, can provide information about the availability, desirability, coverage, and cost of various title insurance coverages and endorsements. If Buyer desires title coverage other than that required by this paragraph, Buyer shall instruct Escrow Holder in writing and pay any increase in cost.

13. SALE OF BUYER'S PROPERTY:
    A. This Agreement is NOT contingent upon the sale of any property owned by Buyer.
OR B. ☐ (If checked): The attached addendum (C.A.R. Form COP) regarding the contingency for the sale of property owned by Buyer is incorporated into this Agreement.

14. TIME PERIODS; REMOVAL OF CONTINGENCIES; CANCELLATION RIGHTS: The following time periods may only be extended, altered, modified or changed by mutual written agreement. Any removal of contingencies or cancellation under this paragraph must be in writing (C.A.R. Form CR).
    A. SELLER HAS: 7 (or ☐ _____) Days After Acceptance to deliver to Buyer all reports, disclosures and information for which Seller is responsible under paragraphs 4, 5A and B, 6A, 7B and 12.
    B. (1) BUYER HAS: 17 (or ☐ _____) Days After Acceptance, unless otherwise agreed in writing, to:
        (i) complete all Buyer Investigations; approve all disclosures, reports and other applicable information, which Buyer receives from Seller; and approve all matters affecting the Property (including lead-based paint and lead-based paint hazards as well as other information specified in paragraph 5 and insurability of Buyer and the Property); and
        (ii) return to Seller Signed Copies of Statutory and Lead Disclosures delivered by Seller in accordance with paragraph 5A.
      (2) Within the time specified in 14B(1), Buyer may request that Seller make repairs or take any other action regarding the Property (C.A.R. Form RR). Seller has no obligation to agree to or respond to Buyer's requests.
      (3) By the end of the time specified in 14B(1) (or 2I for loan contingency or 2J for appraisal contingency), Buyer shall, in writing, remove the applicable contingency (C.A.R. Form CR) or cancel this Agreement. However, if **(i)** government-mandated inspections/reports required as a condition of closing; or **(ii)** Common Interest Disclosures pursuant to paragraph 6B are not made within the time specified in 14A, then Buyer has **5 (or ☐ _____) Days** After receipt of any such items, or the time specified in 14B(1), whichever is later, to remove the applicable contingency or cancel this Agreement in writing.
    C. CONTINUATION OF CONTINGENCY OR CONTRACTUAL OBLIGATION; SELLER RIGHT TO CANCEL:
      (1) Seller right to Cancel; Buyer Contingencies: Seller, after first giving Buyer a Notice to Buyer to Perform (as specified below), may cancel this Agreement in writing and authorize return of Buyer's deposit if, by the time specified in this Agreement, Buyer does not remove in writing the applicable contingency or cancel this Agreement. Once all contingencies have been removed, failure of either Buyer or Seller to close escrow on time may be a breach of this Agreement.

246

(2) Continuation of Contingency: Even after the expiration of the time specified in 14B, Buyer retains the right to make requests to Seller, remove in writing the applicable contingency or cancel this Agreement until Seller cancels pursuant to 14C(1). Once Seller receives Buyer's written removal of all contingencies, Seller may not cancel this Agreement pursuant to 14C(1).

(3) Seller right to Cancel; Buyer Contract Obligations: Seller, after first giving Buyer a Notice to Buyer to Perform (as specified below), may cancel this Agreement in writing and authorize return of Buyer's deposit for any of the following reasons: **(i)** if Buyer fails to deposit funds as required by 2A or 2B; **(ii)** if the funds deposited pursuant to 2A or 2B are not good when deposited; **(iii)** if Buyer fails to provide a letter as required by 2G; **(iv)** if Buyer fails to provide verification as required by 2H or 2L; **(v)** if Seller reasonably disapproves of the verification provided by 2H or 2L; **(vi)** if Buyer fails to return Statutory and Lead Disclosures as required by paragraph 5A(2); or **(vii)** if Buyer fails to sign or initial a separate liquidated damage form for an increased deposit as required by paragraph 16. **Seller is not required to give Buyer a Notice to Perform regarding Close of Escrow.**

(4) Notice To Buyer To Perform: The Notice to Buyer to Perform (C.A.R. Form NBP) shall: **(i)** be in writing; **(ii)** be signed by Seller; and **(iii)** give Buyer at least **24** (or ☐ _____) hours (or until the time specified in the applicable paragraph, whichever occurs last) to take the applicable action. A Notice to Buyer to Perform may not be given any earlier than **2 Days** Prior to the expiration of the applicable time for Buyer to remove a contingency or cancel this Agreement or meet a 14C(3) obligation.

Buyer's Initials (_____)(_____)
Seller's Initials (_____)(_____)

Reviewed by _____ Date _____

RPA-CA REVISED 11/07 (PAGE 4 OF 8)

EQUAL HOUSING OPPORTUNITY

CALIFORNIA RESIDENTIAL PURCHASE AGREEMENT (RPA-CA PAGE 4 OF 8)

247

Property Address: _____ Date: _____

   D. **EFFECT OF BUYER'S REMOVAL OF CONTINGENCIES :** If Buyer removes, in writing, any contingency or cancellation rights, unless otherwise specified in a separate written agreement between Buyer and Seller, Buyer shall conclusively be deemed to have: **(i)** completed all Buyer Investigations, and review of reports and other applicable information and disclosures pertaining to that contingency or cancellation right; **(ii)** elected to proceed with the transaction; and **(iii)** assumed all liability, responsibility and expense for Repairs or corrections pertaining to that contingency or cancellation right, or for inability to obtain financing.

   E. **EFFECT OF CANCELLATION ON DEPOSITS:** If Buyer or Seller gives written notice of cancellation pursuant to rights duly exercised under the terms of this Agreement, Buyer and Seller agree to Sign mutual instructions to cancel the sale and escrow and release deposits to the party entitled to the funds, less fees and costs incurred by that party. Fees and costs may be payable to service providers and vendors for services and products provided during escrow. **Release of funds will require mutual Signed release instructions from Buyer and Seller, judicial decision or arbitration award. A party may be subject to a civil penalty of up to $1,000 for refusal to sign such instructions if no good faith dispute exists as to who is entitled to the deposited funds (Civil Code §1057.3).**

15. FINAL VERIFICATION OF CONDITION: Buyer shall have the right to make a final inspection of the Property within **5 (or _____) Days** Prior to Close Of Escrow, NOT AS A CONTINGENCY OF THE SALE, but solely to confirm: **(i)** the Property is maintained pursuant to paragraph 7A; **(ii)** Repairs have been completed as agreed; and **(iii)** Seller has complied with Seller's other obligations under this Agreement.

16. LIQUIDATED DAMAGES: If Buyer fails to complete this purchase because of Buyer's default, Seller shall retain, as liquidated damages, the deposit actually paid. If the Property is a dwelling with no more than four units, one of which Buyer intends to occupy, then the amount retained shall be no more than 3% of the purchase price. Any excess shall be returned to Buyer. Release of funds will require mutual, Signed release instructions from both Buyer and Seller, judicial decision or arbitration award.
    BUYER AND SELLER SHALL SIGN A SEPARATE LIQUIDATED DAMAGES PROVISION FOR ANY INCREASED DEPOSIT. (C.A.R. FORM RID)

Buyer's Initials _____/_____	Seller's Initials _____/_____

17. DISPUTE RESOLUTION:

   A. **MEDIATION:** Buyer and Seller agree to mediate any dispute or claim arising between them out of this Agreement, or any resulting transaction, before resorting to arbitration or court action. Paragraphs 17B(2) and (3) below apply to mediation whether or not the Arbitration provision is initialed. Mediation fees, if any, shall be divided equally among the parties involved. If, for any dispute or claim to which this paragraph applies, any party commences an action without first attempting to resolve the matter through mediation, or refuses to mediate after a request has been made, then that party shall not be entitled to recover attorney fees, even if they would otherwise be available to that party in any such action. THIS MEDIATION PROVISION APPLIES WHETHER OR NOT THE ARBITRATION PROVISION IS INITIALED.

   B. **ARBITRATION OF DISPUTES: (1) Buyer and Seller agree that any dispute or claim in Law or equity arising between them out of this Agreement or any resulting transaction, which is not settled through mediation, shall be decided by neutral, binding arbitration, including and subject to paragraphs 17B(2) and (3) below. The arbitrator shall be a retired judge or justice, or an attorney with at least 5 years of residential real estate Law experience, unless the parties mutually agree to a different arbitrator, who shall render an award in accordance with substantive California Law. The parties shall have the right to discovery in accordance with California Code of Civil Procedure §1283.05. In all other respects, the arbitration shall be conducted in accordance with Title 9 of Part III of the California Code of Civil Procedure. Judgment upon the award of the arbitrator(s) may be entered into any court having jurisdiction. Interpretation of this agreement to arbitrate shall be governed by the Federal Arbitration Act.**
    (2) EXCLUSIONS FROM MEDIATION AND ARBITRATION: The following matters are excluded from mediation and arbitration: (i) a judicial or non-judicial foreclosure or other action or proceeding to enforce a deed of trust, mortgage or installment land sale contract as defined in California Civil Code §2985; (ii) an unlawful detainer action; (iii) the filing or enforcement of a mechanic's lien; and (iv) any matter that is within the jurisdiction of a probate, small claims or bankruptcy court. The filing of a court action to enable the recording of a notice of pending action, for order of attachment, receivership, injunction, or other provisional remedies, shall not constitute a waiver of the mediation and arbitration provisions.
    (3) BROKERS: Buyer and Seller agree to mediate and arbitrate disputes or claims involving either or both Brokers, consistent with 17A and B, provided either or both Brokers shall have agreed to such mediation or arbitration prior to, or within a reasonable time after, the dispute or claim is presented to Brokers. Any election by either or both Brokers to participate in mediation or arbitration shall not result in Brokers being deemed parties to the Agreement.

248

"NOTICE: BY INITIALING IN THE SPACE BELOW YOU ARE AGREEING TO HAVE ANY DISPUTE ARISING OUT OF THE MATTERS INCLUDED IN THE 'ARBITRATION OF DISPUTES' PROVISION DECIDED BY NEUTRAL ARBITRATION AS PROVIDED BY CALIFORNIA LAW AND YOU ARE GIVING UP ANY RIGHTS YOU MIGHT POSSESS TO HAVE THE DISPUTE LITIGATED IN A COURT OR JURY TRIAL. BY INITIALING IN THE SPACE BELOW YOU ARE GIVING UP YOUR JUDICIAL RIGHTS TO DISCOVERY AND APPEAL, UNLESS THOSE RIGHTS ARE SPECIFICALLY INCLUDED IN THE 'ARBITRATION OF DISPUTES' PROVISION. IF YOU REFUSE TO SUBMIT TO ARBITRATION AFTER AGREEING TO THIS PROVISION, YOU MAY BE COMPELLED TO ARBITRATE UNDER THE AUTHORITY OF THE CALIFORNIA CODE OF CIVIL PROCEDURE. YOUR AGREEMENT TO THIS ARBITRATION PROVISION IS VOLUNTARY."

"WE HAVE READ AND UNDERSTAND THE FOREGOING AND AGREE TO SUBMIT DISPUTES ARISING OUT OF THE MATTERS INCLUDED IN THE 'ARBITRATION OF DISPUTES' PROVISION TO NEUTRAL ARBITRATION."

Buyer's Initials _____ / _____   Seller's Initials _____ / _____

Buyer's Initials (_____)(_____)
Seller's Initials (_____)(_____)

Reviewed by _____ Date _____

EQUAL HOUSING OPPORTUNITY

RPA-CA REVISED 11/07 (PAGE 5 OF 8)

CALIFORNIA RESIDENTIAL PURCHASE AGREEMENT (RPA-CA PAGE 5 OF 8)

Property Address: _____ Date: _____

18. **PRORATIONS OF PROPERTY TAXES AND OTHER ITEMS:** Unless otherwise agreed in writing, the following items shall be PAID CURRENT and prorated between Buyer and Seller as of Close Of Escrow: real property taxes and assessments, interest, rents, HOA regular, special, and emergency dues and assessments imposed prior to Close Of Escrow, premiums on insurance assumed by Buyer, payments on bonds and assessments assumed by Buyer, and payments on Mello-Roos and other Special Assessment District bonds and assessments that are now a lien. The following items shall be assumed by Buyer WITHOUT CREDIT toward the purchase price: prorated payments on Mello-Roos and other Special Assessment District bonds and assessments and HOA special assessments that are now a lien but not yet due. Property will be reassessed upon change of ownership. Any supplemental tax bills shall be paid as follows: **(i)** for periods after Close Of Escrow, by Buyer; and **(ii)** for periods prior to Close Of Escrow, by Seller. TAX BILLS ISSUED AFTER CLOSE OF ESCROW SHALL BE HANDLED DIRECTLY BETWEEN BUYER AND SELLER. Prorations shall be made based on a 30-day month.

19. **WITHHOLDING TAXES:** Seller and Buyer agree to execute any instrument, affidavit, statement or instruction reasonably necessary to comply with federal (FIRPTA) and California withholding Law, if required (C.A.R. Forms AS and AB).

20. **MULTIPLE LISTING SERVICE ("MLS"):** Brokers are authorized to report to the MLS a pending sale and, upon Close Of Escrow, the terms of this transaction to be published and disseminated to persons and entities authorized to use the information on terms approved by the MLS.

21. **EQUAL HOUSING OPPORTUNITY:** The Property is sold in compliance with federal, state and local anti-discrimination Laws.

22. **ATTORNEY FEES:** In any action, proceeding, or arbitration between Buyer and Seller arising out of this Agreement, the prevailing Buyer or Seller shall be entitled to reasonable attorney fees and costs from the non-prevailing Buyer or Seller, except as provided in paragraph 17A.

23. **SELECTION OF SERVICE PROVIDERS:** If Brokers refer Buyer or Seller to persons, vendors, or service or product providers ("Providers"), Brokers do not guarantee the performance of any Providers. Buyer and Seller may select ANY Providers of their own choosing.

24. **TIME OF ESSENCE; ENTIRE CONTRACT; CHANGES:** Time is of the essence. All understandings between the parties are incorporated in this Agreement. Its terms are intended by the parties as a final, complete and exclusive expression of their Agreement with respect to its subject matter, and may not be contradicted by evidence of any prior agreement or contemporaneous oral agreement. If any provision of this Agreement is held to be ineffective or invalid, the remaining provisions will nevertheless be given full force and effect. **Neither this Agreement nor any provision in it may be extended, amended, modified, altered or changed, except in writing Signed by Buyer and Seller.**

25. **OTHER TERMS AND CONDITIONS,** including attached supplements:
    A. ☑ Buyer's Inspection Advisory (C.A.R. Form BIA)
    B. ☐ Purchase Agreement Addendum (C.A.R. Form PAA paragraph numbers: _____) _____
    C. ☐ Statewide Buyer and Seller Advisory (C.A.R. Form SBSA)
    D. ☐ Seller shall provide Buyer with a completed Seller Property Questionnaire (C.A.R. form SPQ) within the time specified in paragraph 14A
    E. _____
    _____

26. **DEFINITIONS:** As used in this Agreement:
    A. **"Acceptance"** means the time the offer or final counter offer is accepted in writing by a party and is delivered to and personally received by the other party or that party's authorized agent in accordance with the terms of this offer or a final counter offer.
    B. **"Agreement"** means the terms and conditions of this accepted California Residential Purchase Agreement and any accepted counter offers and addenda.
    C. **"C.A.R. Form"** means the specific form referenced or another comparable form agreed to by the parties.
    D. **"Close Of Escrow"** means the date the grant deed, or other evidence of transfer of title, is recorded. If the scheduled close of escrow falls on a Saturday, Sunday or legal holiday, then close of escrow shall be the next business day after the scheduled close of escrow date.
    E. **"Copy"** means copy by any means including photocopy, NCR, facsimile and electronic.
    F. **"Days"** means calendar days, unless otherwise required by Law.
    G. **"Days After"** means the specified number of calendar days after the occurrence of the event specified, not counting the calendar date on which the specified event occurs, and ending at 11:59PM on the final day.

H. **"Days Prior"** means the specified number of calendar days before the occurrence of the event specified, not counting the calendar date on which the specified event is scheduled to occur.

I. **"Electronic Copy" or "Electronic Signature"** means, as applicable, an electronic copy or signature complying with California Law. Buyer and Seller agree that electronic means will not be used by either party to modify or alter the content or integrity of this Agreement without the knowledge and consent of the other.

J. **"Law"** means any law, code, statute, ordinance, regulation, rule or order, which is adopted by a controlling city, county, state or federal legislative, judicial or executive body or agency.

K. **"Notice to Buyer to Perform"** means a document (C.A.R. Form NBP), which shall be in writing and Signed by Seller and shall give Buyer at least 24 hours **(or as otherwise specified in paragraph 14C(4))** to remove a contingency or perform as applicable.

L. **"Repairs"** means any repairs (including pest control), alterations, replacements, modifications or retrofitting of the Property provided for under this Agreement.

M. **"Signed"** means either a handwritten or electronic signature on an original document, Copy or any counterpart.

N. **Singular and Plural** terms each include the other, when appropriate.

Buyer's Initials (_____)(_____)
Seller's Initials (_____)(_____)

Reviewed by _____ Date _____

RPA-CA REVISED 11/07 (PAGE 6 OF 8)

EQUAL HOUSING OPPORTUNITY

CALIFORNIA RESIDENTIAL PURCHASE AGREEMENT (RPA-CA PAGE 6 OF 8)

Property Address: _____ Date: _____

27. AGENCY:

    A. DISCLOSURE: Buyer and Seller each acknowledge prior receipt of C.A.R. Form AD "Disclosure Regarding Real Estate Agency Relationships."

    B. POTENTIALLY COMPETING BUYERS AND SELLERS: Buyer and Seller each acknowledge receipt of a disclosure of the possibility of multiple representation by the Broker representing that principal. This disclosure may be part of a listing agreement, buyer-broker agreement or separate document (C.A.R. Form DA). Buyer understands that Broker representing Buyer may also represent other potential buyers, who may consider, make offers on or ultimately acquire the Property. Seller understands that Broker representing Seller may also represent other sellers with competing properties of interest to this Buyer.

    C. CONFIRMATION: The following agency relationships are hereby confirmed for this transaction:
Listing Agent _____ (Print Firm Name) is the agent of (check one): ☐ the Seller exclusively; or ☐ both the Buyer and Seller.
Selling Agent _____ (Print Firm Name) (if not same as Listing Agent) is the agent of (check one): ☐ the Buyer exclusively; or ☐ the Seller exclusively; or ☐ both the Buyer and Seller. Real Estate Brokers are not parties to the Agreement between Buyer and Seller.

28. JOINT ESCROW INSTRUCTIONS TO ESCROW HOLDER:

    A. The following paragraphs, or applicable portions thereof, of this Agreement constitute the joint escrow instructions of Buyer and Seller to Escrow Holder, which Escrow Holder is to use along with any related counter offers and addenda, and any additional mutual instructions to close the escrow: 1, 2, 4, 12, 13B, 14E, 18, 19, 24, 25B and 25D, 26, 28, 29, 32A, 33 and paragraph D of the section titled Real Estate Brokers on page 8. If a Copy of the separate compensation agreement(s) provided for in paragraph 29 or 32A, or paragraph D of the section titled Real Estate Brokers on page 8 is deposited with Escrow Holder by Broker, Escrow Holder shall accept such agreement(s) and pay out from Buyer's or Seller's funds, or both, as applicable, the Broker's compensation provided for in such agreement(s). The terms and conditions of this Agreement not set forth in the specified paragraphs are additional matters for the information of Escrow Holder, but about which Escrow Holder need not be concerned. Buyer and Seller will receive Escrow Holder's general provisions directly from Escrow Holder and will execute such provisions upon Escrow Holder's request. To the extent the general provisions are inconsistent or conflict with this Agreement, the general provisions will control as to the duties and obligations of Escrow Holder only. Buyer and Seller will execute additional instructions, documents and forms provided by Escrow Holder that are reasonably necessary to close the escrow.

    B. A Copy of this Agreement shall be delivered to Escrow Holder within **3** business days after Acceptance (or ☐ _____). Buyer and Seller authorize Escrow Holder to accept and rely on Copies and Signatures as defined in this Agreement as originals, to open escrow and for other purposes of escrow. The validity of this Agreement as between Buyer and Seller is not affected by whether or when Escrow Holder Signs this Agreement.

    C. Brokers are a party to the escrow for the sole purpose of compensation pursuant to paragraphs 29, 32A and paragraph D of the section titled Real Estate Brokers on page 8. Buyer and Seller irrevocably assign to Brokers compensation specified in paragraphs 29 and 32A, respectively, and irrevocably instruct Escrow Holder to disburse those funds to Brokers at Close Of Escrow or pursuant to any other mutually executed cancellation agreement. Compensation instructions can be amended or revoked only with the written consent of Brokers. Escrow Holder shall immediately notify Brokers: **(i)** if Buyer's initial or any additional deposit is not made pursuant to this Agreement, or is not good at time of deposit with Escrow Holder; or **(ii)** if Buyer and Seller instruct Escrow Holder to cancel escrow.

    D. A Copy of any amendment that affects any paragraph of this Agreement for which Escrow Holder is responsible shall be delivered to Escrow Holder within **2** business days after mutual execution of the amendment.

29. BROKER COMPENSATION FROM BUYER: If applicable, upon Close Of Escrow, **Buyer** agrees to pay compensation to Broker as specified in a separate written agreement between Buyer and Broker.

30. TERMS AND CONDITIONS OF OFFER:
This is an offer to purchase the Property on the above terms and conditions. All paragraphs with spaces for initials by Buyer and Seller are incorporated in this Agreement only if initialed by all parties. If at least one but not all parties initial, a counter offer is required until agreement is reached. Seller has the right to continue to offer the Property for sale and to accept any other offer at any time prior to notification of Acceptance. Buyer has read and acknowledges receipt of a Copy of the offer and agrees to the above confirmation of agency relationships. If this offer is accepted and Buyer subsequently defaults, Buyer may be responsible for payment of Brokers' compensation. This Agreement and any supplement, addendum or modification, including any Copy, may be Signed in two or more counterparts, all of which shall constitute one and the same writing.

RPA-CA REVISED 11/07 (PAGE 7 OF 8)

Buyer's Initials (_____)(_____)
Seller's Initials (_____)(_____)

| Reviewed by _____ Date _____ |

EQUAL HOUSING
OPPORTUNITY

CALIFORNIA RESIDENTIAL PURCHASE AGREEMENT (RPA-CA PAGE 7 OF 8)

Property Address: _____ Date: _____

31. EXPIRATION OF OFFER: This offer shall be deemed revoked and the deposit shall be returned unless the offer is Signed by Seller and a Copy of the Signed offer is personally received by Buyer, or by _____, who is authorized to receive it by 5:00 PM on the third Day after this offer is signed by Buyer (or, if checked, ☐ by _____ (date), at _____ AM/PM).

Date _____   Date _____

BUYER _____   BUYER _____

_____   _____
(Print name)   **(Print name)**

_____
(Address)

32. BROKER COMPENSATION FROM SELLER:
  A. Upon Close Of Escrow, **Seller** agrees to pay compensation to Broker as specified in a separate written agreement between Seller and Broker.
  B. If escrow does not close, compensation is payable as specified in that separate written agreement.
33. ACCEPTANCE OF OFFER: Seller warrants that Seller is the owner of the Property, or has the authority to execute this Agreement. Seller accepts the above offer, agrees to sell the Property on the above terms and conditions, and agrees to the above confirmation of agency relationships. Seller has read and acknowledges receipt of a Copy of this Agreement, and authorizes Broker to deliver a Signed Copy to Buyer.
  ☐ (If checked) **SUBJECT TO ATTACHED COUNTER OFFER, DATED** _____.

Date _____   Date _____

SELLER _____   SELLER _____

_____   _____
(Print name)   **(Print name)**

_____
(Address)

(____/____) **CONFIRMATION OF ACCEPTANCE:** A Copy of Signed Acceptance was personally received by Buyer or Buyer's authorized
(Initials)   agent on (date) _____ at _____ AM/PM. **A binding Agreement is created when a Copy of Signed Acceptance is personally received by Buyer or Buyer's authorized agent whether or not confirmed in this document. Completion of this confirmation is not legally required in order to create a binding Agreement; it is solely intended to evidence the date that Confirmation of Acceptance has occurred.**

REAL ESTATE BROKERS:
A. Real Estate Brokers are not parties to the Agreement between Buyer and Seller.
B. Agency relationships are confirmed as stated in paragraph 27.
C. If specified in paragraph 2A, Agent who submitted the offer for Buyer acknowledges receipt of deposit.
D. COOPERATING BROKER COMPENSATION: Listing Broker agrees to pay Cooperating Broker **(Selling Firm)** and Cooperating Broker agrees to accept, out of Listing Broker's proceeds in escrow: **(i)** the amount specified in the MLS, provided Cooperating Broker is a Participant of the MLS in which the Property is offered for sale or a reciprocal MLS; or **(ii)** ☐ (if checked) the amount specified in a separate written agreement (C.A.R. Form CBC) between Listing Broker and Cooperating Broker.

Real Estate Broker (Selling Firm) _____ DRE Lic. # _____
By _____ DRE Lic. # _____ Date _____
Address _____ City _____ State _____ Zip _____
Telephone _____ Fax _____ E-mail _____

Real Estate Broker (Listing Firm) _____ DRE Lic. # _____
By _____ DRE Lic. # _____ Date _____
Address _____ City _____ State _____ Zip _____
Telephone _____ Fax _____ E-mail _____

REAL ESTATE BROKERS:
A. **Real Estate Brokers are not parties to the Agreement between Buyer and Seller.**
B. **Agency relationships are confirmed as stated in paragraph 27.**
C. If specified in paragraph 2A, Agent who submitted the offer for Buyer acknowledges receipt of deposit.
D. **COOPERATING BROKER COMPENSATION:** Listing Broker agrees to pay Cooperating Broker **(Selling Firm)** and Cooperating Broker agrees to accept, out of Listing Broker's proceeds in escrow: **(i)** the amount specified in the MLS, provided Cooperating Broker is a Participant of the MLS in which the Property is offered for sale or a reciprocal MLS; or **(ii)** ☐ (if checked) the amount specified in a separate written agreement (C.A.R. Form CBC) between Listing Broker and Cooperating Broker.

Real Estate Broker (Selling Firm) _____ DRE Lic. # _____
By _____ DRE Lic. # _____ Date _____
Address _____ City _____ State _____ Zip _____
Telephone _____ Fax _____ E-mail _____

Real Estate Broker (Listing Firm) _____ DRE Lic. # _____
By _____ DRE Lic. # _____ Date _____
Address _____ City _____ State _____ Zip _____
Telephone _____ Fax _____ E-mail _____

ESCROW HOLDER ACKNOWLEDGMENT:
Escrow Holder acknowledges receipt of a Copy of this Agreement, (if checked, ☐ a deposit in the amount of $ _____), counter offer numbers _____ and _____, and agrees to act as Escrow Holder subject to paragraph 28 of this Agreement, any supplemental escrow instructions and the terms of Escrow Holder's general provisions.

Escrow Holder is advised that the date of Confirmation of Acceptance of the Agreement as between Buyer and Seller is _____

Escrow Holder _____ Escrow # _____
By _____ Date _____
Address _____
Phone/Fax/E-mail_____
Escrow Holder is licensed by the California Department of ☐ Corporations, ☐ Insurance, ☐ Real Estate. License # _____

(___ / ___) **REJECTION OF OFFER:** No counter offer is being made. This offer was reviewed and rejected by Seller on
(Seller's Initials) _____ (Date)

Reviewed by _____ Date _____

EQUAL HOUSING OPPORTUNITY

RPA-CA REVISED 11/07 (PAGE 8 OF 8)
CALIFORNIA RESIDENTIAL PURCHASE AGREEMENT (RPA-CA PAGE 8 OF 8)

3. CONTRACT OF SALE

NYSLTA Form 8041 (Rev. 11/78) — CONTRACT OF SALE — 5/88

WARNING:
NO REPRESENTATION IS MADE THAT THIS FORM OF CONTRACT FOR THE SALE AND PURCHASE OF REAL ESTATE COMPLIES WITH SECTION 5-702 OF THE GENERAL OBLIGATIONS LAW ("PLAIN ENGLISH"). CONSULT YOUR LAWYER BEFORE SIGNING IT.

NOTE: FIRE AND CASUALTY LOSSES:
This contract form does not provide for what happens in the event of fire or casualty loss before the title closing. Unless different provision is made in this contract, Section 5-1311 of the General Obligations Law will apply. One part of that law makes a purchaser responsible for fire and casualty loss upon taking of title to or possession of the premises.

DATE:

CONTRACT OF SALE made as of the   day of   , 19

BETWEEN

PARTIES:

Address:

hereinafter called "SELLER", who agrees to sell:

and

Address:

hereinafter called "PURCHASER" who agrees to buy the property, including all buildings and improvements thereon (the

PREMISES:

"PREMISES"), more fully described on a separate page marked "Schedule A," and also known as:

Street Address:

Tax Map Designation:

Together with SELLER'S interest, if any, in streets and unpaid awards as set forth in Paragraph 9.

PERSONAL PROPERTY:

The sale also includes all fixtures and articles of personal property attached to or used in connection with the PREMISES unless specifically excluded below. SELLER states that they are paid for and owned by SELLER free and clear of any lien other than the EXISTING MORTGAGE(S). They include but are not limited to plumbing, heating, lighting and cooking fixtures, bathroom and kitchen cabinets, mantels, door mirrors, venetian blinds, shades, screens, awnings, storm windows, window boxes, storm doors, mail boxes, weather vanes, flagpoles, pumps, shrubbery, fencing, outdoor statuary, tool sheds, dishwashers, washing machines, clothes dryers, garbage disposal units, ranges, refrigerators, freezers, air conditioning equipment and installations, and wall to wall carpeting.

Excluded from this sale are: Furniture and household furnishings,

256

1. **(a)** The purchase price is $

Payable as follows:

On the signing of this contract, by check subject to collection: $

By allowance for the principal amount still unpaid on EXISTING MORTGAGE(S): $

By a Purchase Money Note and Mortgage from PURCHASER (or assigns) to SELLER: $

BALANCE AT CLOSING:

(b) If this sale is subject to an EXISTING MORTGAGE, the Purchase Money Note and Mortgage will also provide that it will remain subject to the prior lien of any EXISTING MORTGAGE even though the EXISTING MORTGAGE is extended or modified in good faith. The Purchase Money Note and Mortgage shall be drawn on the standard form of New York Board of Title Underwriters by the attorney for SELLER, PURCHASER shall pay the mortgage recording tax, recording fees and the attorney's fee in the amount of $ for its preparation.

(c) If any required payments are made on an EXISTING MORTGAGE between now and CLOSING which reduce the unpaid principal amount of an EXISTING MORTGAGE below the amount shown in paragraph 2, then the balance of the price payable at CLOSING will be adjusted. SELLER agrees that the amount shown in Paragraph 2 is reasonably correct and that only payments required by the EXISTING MORTGAGE will be made.

(d) If there is a mortgage escrow account that is maintained for the purpose of paying taxes or insurance, etc. SELLER shall assign it to PURCHASER, if it can be assigned. In the event PURCHASER shall pay the amount in the escrow account to SELLER at CLOSING.

[G14201]

EXISTING MORTGAGES:

2. The PREMISES will be conveyed subject to the continuing lien of "EXISTING MORTGAGE(S)" as follows:

Mortgage now in the unpaid principal amount of $ and interest at the rate of   per cent per year, presently payable   in installments of $, which include principal, interest, and with any balance of principal being due and payable on

SELLER hereby states that no EXISTING MORTGAGE contains any provision that permits the holder of the mortgage to require its immediate payment in full or to change any other term thereof by reason of the fact of CLOSING.

ACCEPTABLE FUNDS:

3. All money payable under this contract, unless otherwise specified, shall be either:

a. Cash, but not over one thousand ($1,000.00) Dollars.
Good certified check of PURCHASER, or official check of any bank, trust company, or savings and loan association having a banking office in the State of New York, payable to the order of SELLER, or to the order of PURCHASER and duly endorsed by PURCHASER (if an individual) to the order of SELLER in the presence of SELLER or SELLER'S attorney.
c. Money other than the purchase price, payable to SELLER at CLOSING, may be by check of PURCHASER up to the amount of   (\$) dollars, or
d. As otherwise agreed to in writing by SELLER or SELLER'S attorney.

"SUBJECT TO" PROVISIONS:

4. The PREMISES are to be transferred subject to:

a. Laws and governmental regulations that affect the use and maintenance of the PREMISES, provided that they are not violated by the buildings and improvements erected on the PREMISES.
b. Consents for the erection of any structures on, under or above any streets on which the PREMISES abut.
c. Encroachments of stoops, areas, cellar steps, trim and cornices, if any, upon any street or highway.

TITLE COMPANY APPROVAL:

5. SELLER shall give and PURCHASER shall accept such title as
                                                                    , a member of The New York State Land Title Association will be willing to approve and insure in accordance with their standard form of title policy, subject only to the matters provided for in this contract.

CLOSING DEFINED AND FORM OF DEED:

6. "CLOSING" means the settlement of the obligations of SELLER and PURCHASER to each other under this contract, including the payment of the purchase price to SELLER, and the delivery to PURCHASER of a
                                        deed in proper statuary form for recording so as to transfer full ownership (fee simple title) to the PREMISES, free of all encumbrances except as herein stated. The deed will contain a convenant by the SELLER as required by Section 13 of the Lien Law.

If SELLER is a corporation, it will deliver to PURCHASER at the time of CLOSING (a) a resolution of its Board of Directors authorizing the sale and delivery of the deed, and (b) a certificate by the Secretary or Assistant Secretary of the corporation certifying such resolution and setting forth facts showing that the transfer is in conformity with the requirements of Section 909 of the Business Corporation Law. The deed in such case shall contain a recital sufficient to establish compliance with that section.

CLOSING DATE AND PLACE:

7. CLOSING will take place at the office of
      at   o'clock on   19

BROKER:

8. PURCHASER hereby states that PURCHASER has not dealt with any broker in connection with this sale other than

and SELLER agrees to pay the broker the commission earned thereby (pursuant to separate agreement).

STREETS AND ASSIGN-MENT OF UNPAID AWARDS:

9. This sale includes all of SELLER'S ownership and rights, if any, in any land lying in the bed of any street or highway, opened or proposed, in front of or adjoining the PREMISES to the center line thereof. It also includes any right of SELLER to any unpaid award by reason of any taking by condemnation and/or for any damage to the PREMISES by reason of change of grade of any street or highway. SELLER will deliver at no additional cost to PURCHASER, at CLOSING, or thereafter, on demand, any documents which PURCHASER may require to collect the award and damages.

MORTGAGEE'S CERTIFICATE LETTER AS TO EXISTING MORTGAGE(S):

10. SELLER agrees to deliver to PURCHASER at CLOSING a certificate dated not more than thirty (30) days before the CLOSING signed by the holder of each EXISTING MORTGAGE, in form for recording, certifying the amount of the unpaid principal and interest, date of maturity, and rate of interest.

SELLER shall pay the fees for recording such certificate. If the holder of a mortgage is a bank or other institution as defined in Section 274-a, Real Property Law, it may, instead of the certificate, furnish an unqualified letter dated not more than thirty (30) days before CLOSING containing the same information. SELLER hereby states that any EXISTING MORTGAGE will not be in default at the time of CLOSING.

COMPLIANCE WITH STATE AND MUNICIPAL DEPARTMENT VIOLATIONS AND ORDERS:

11. a. SELLER will comply with all notes or notices of violations of law or municipal ordinances, order or requirements noted in or issued by any governmental department having authority as to lands, housing, buildings, fire, health and labor conditions affecting the PREMISES at the date hereof. The PREMISES shall be transferred free of them at CLOSING and this provision shall survive CLOSING. SELLER shall furnish PURCHASER with any authorizations necessary to make the searches that could disclose these matters.

OMIT IF THE PROPERTY IS NOT IN THE CITY OF NEW YORK

b. All obligations affecting the PREMISES, incurred pursuant to the Administrative Code of the City of New York prior to closing and payable in money shall be discharged by SELLER at CLOSING. This provision shall survive CLOSING.

INSTALLMENT ASSESSMENT:

12. If at the time of CLOSING the PREMISES are affected by an assessment which is or may become payable in annual installments, and the first installment is then a lien, or has been paid, then for the purposes of this contract all the unpaid installments shall be considered due and are to be paid by SELLER at CLOSING.

[G14202]

259

APPORTION-MENTS:	13. The following are to apportioned as of midnight of the day before the day of CLOSING. (a) Rents as and when collected. (b) Interest on EXISTING MORTGAGE(S). (c) Premiums on existing transferrable insurance policies and renewals of those expiring prior to CLOSING. (d) Taxes, water charges and sewer rents, on the basis of the fiscal period for which assessed. (e) Fuel, if any. (f) Vault charges, if any. If CLOSING shall occur before a new tax rate is fixed, the apportionment of taxes shall be upon the basis of the old tax rate for the preceeding period applied to the latest assessed valuation. Any errors or omissions in computing apportionments at CLOSING shall be corrected. This provision shall survive CLOSING.
WATER METER READINGS:	14. If there be a water meter on the PREMISES, SELLER shall furnish a reading to a date not more than thirty (30) days before CLOSING date and the unfixed meter charge and sewer rent, if any, shall be apportioned on the basis of such last reading.
ALLOWANCE FOR UNPAID TAXES, ETC.:	15. SELLER has the option to credit PURCHASER as an adjustment of the purchase price with the amount of any unpaid taxes, assessments, water charges and sewer rents, together with any interest and penalties thereon to a date not less than five (5) business days after CLOSING, provided that official bills therefor computed to said date are produced at CLOSING.
USE OF PURCHASE PRICE TO PAY ENCUM-BRANCES:	16. If there is anything else affecting the sale which SELLER is obligated to pay and discharge at CLOSING, SELLER may use any portion of the balance of the purchase price to discharge it. As an alternative SELLER may deposit money with the title insurance company employed by PURCHASER and required by it to assure its discharge, but only if the title insurance company will insure PURCHASER'S title clear of the matter or insure against its enforcement out of the PREMISES. Upon request, made within a reasonable time before CLOSING, the PURCHASER agrees to provide separate certified checks as requested to assist in clearing up these matters.
AFFIDAVIT AS TO JUDGMENTS BANKRUPT-CIES:	17. If a title examination discloses judgments, bankruptcies or other returns against persons having names the same as or similar to that of SELLER, SELLER shall deliver a satisfactory detailed affidavit at CLOSING showing that they are not against SELLER.
DEED TRANSFER AND RECORDING TAXES:	18. At CLOSING, SELLER shall deliver a certified check payable to the order of the appropriate State, City or County officer in the amount of any applicable transfer and/or recording tax payable by reason of the delivery or recording of the deed, together with any required tax return. PURCHASER agrees to duly complete the tax return and to cause the check(s) and the tax return to be delivered to the appropriate officer promptly after CLOSING.
PURCHASER'S LIEN:	19. All money paid on account of this contract, and the reasonable expenses of examination of the title to the PREMISES and of any survey and survey inspection charges are hereby made liens on the PREMISES and collectable out of the PREMISES. Such liens shall not continue after default in performance of the contract by PURCHASER.
SELLER'S INABILITY TO CONVEY LIMITATION OF LIABILITY:	20. If SELLER is unable to transfer title to PURCHASER in accordance with this contract, SELLER'S sole liability shall be to refund all money paid on account of this contract, plus all charges made for: (i) examining the title, (ii) any appropriate additional searches made in accordance with this contract, and (iii) survey and survey inspection charges. Upon such refund and payment this contract shall be considered cancelled, and neither SELLER nor PURCHASER shall have any further rights against the other.
CONDITION OF PROPERTY:	21. PURCHASER has inspected the buildings on the PREMISES and the personal property included in this sale and is thoroughly acquainted with their condition. PURCHASER agrees to purchase them "as is" and in their present condition subject to reasonable use, wear, tear, and natural deterioration between now and CLOSING. PURCHASER shall have the right, after reasonable notice to SELLER, to inspect them before CLOSING.
ENTIRE AGREEMENT:	22. All prior understandings and agreements between SELLER and PURCHASER are merged in this contract. It completely expresses their full agreement. It has been entered into after full investigation, neither party relying upon any statements made by anyone else that is not set forth in this contract.
CHANGES MUST BE IN WRITING:	23. This contract may not be changed or cancelled except in writing: The contract shall also apply to and bind the distributees, heirs, executors, administrators, successors and assigns of the respective parties. Each of the parties hereby authorize their attorneys to agree in writing to any changes in dates and time periods provided for in this contract.

SINGULAR ALSO MEANS PLURAL:

24. Any singular word or term herein shall also be read as in the plural whenever the sense of this contract may require it.

In Presence Of:

_____

_____

_____

_____

OVER

[G14203]

STATE OF NEW YORK, COUNTY OF   **ss:**
On the   day of   19   , before me
personally came

to me known to be the individual   described in and who
executed the foregoing instrument, and acknowledged that
      executed the same.

STATE OF NEW YORK, COUNTY OF   **ss:**
On the   day of   19   , before me
personally came

to me known to be the individual   described in and who
executed the foregoing instrument, and acknowledged that
      executed the same.

STATE OF NEW YORK, COUNTY OF   **ss:**
On the   day of   19   , before me
personally came
to me known, who, being by me duly sworn, did depose and say
that   he resides at No.

that   he is the
of
                   , the corporation described
in and which executed the foregoing instrument; that   he
knows the seal of said corporation; that the seal affixed to said
instrument is such corporate seal; that it was so affixed by order of
the board of directors of said corporation, and that   he
signed h   name thereto by like order.

STATE OF NEW YORK, COUNTY OF   **ss:**
On the   day of   19   , before me
personally came
to me known and known to me to be a partner in

a partnership, and known to me to be the person described in and
who executed the foregoing instrument in the partnership name,
and said

duly acknowledged that he executed the foregoing instrument for
and on behalf of said partnership.

Closing the title under the within contract is hereby adjourned to   19   , at
o'clock, at   ; title to be closed and all adjustments to be made
as of   19
Dated,   19
For value received, the within contract and all the right, title and interest of the purchaser thereunder are hereby assigned, transferred and set over unto
and said assignee hereby assumes all obligations of the purchaser thereunder.
Dated,   19

_____
                                    Purchaser

_____
                     Assignee of Purchaser

Contract of Sale

ITLE NO. _____

          From:

          To:

PREMISES

Section
Block
Lot
County or Town
Street Numbered Address

Recorded At Request of
Fidelity National Title
RETURN BY MAIL TO:

                                  Zip No.

[G14204]

4. WARRANTY DEED WITH MORTGAGE AND LIEN COVENANT

This Indenture, Made the   day of
Nineteen hundred and

Between

part   of the first part, and

Witnesseth, that the part   of the first part, in consideration of
Dollars ($)
lawful money of the United States,
paid by the part   of the second part, do   hereby grant and release unto the
part   of the second part,   and assigns forever, all

This conveyance is made and accepted subject to an indebtedness secured by a
mortgage upon said premises held by

which said mortgage was recorded in the   County Clerk's office,
on the   day of   19   , in Liber
of Mortgages at page   , on which there is an unpaid principal of
Dollars,
($), with interest from   19   , at the rate
of   per cent per annum, which said mortgage debt the part   of the second
part hereby assume and agree to pay, as part of the purchase price of the above described premises,
and the part   of the second part hereby executed and acknowledged this Instrument as by
Law required.   (C839)

263

TOGETHER with the appurtenances and all the estate and rights of the part   of the first part in and to said premises.

TO HAVE AND TO HOLD the premises herein granted unto the part   of the second part, and assigns forever.

AND SAID

                                         covenant   as follows:

FIRST, That the part   of the second part shall quietly enjoy the said premises:

SECOND, That said

will forever WARRANT the title to said premises.

THIRD, Subject to the trust fund provisions of section thirteen of the lien law.

IN WITNESS WHEREOF, The parties hereto have hereunto set their hands and seals the day and year first above written.

IN PRESENCE OF

_____ (L.S.)

_____ (L.S.)

_____ (L.S.)

_____ (L.S.)

STATE OF NEW YORK   }   On this   day of
COUNTY OF   } ss.   nineteen hundred and
before me, the subscriber, personally appeared

to me personally known and known to me to be the same person   described in and who executed the within instrument, and   he   acknowledged to me that   he   executed the same.

_____

STATE OF NEW YORK   }   On this   day of
COUNTY OF   } ss.   nineteen hundred and
before me, the subscriber, personally appeared

to me personally known and known to me to be the same person   described in and who executed the within instrument, and   he   acknowledged to me that   he   executed the same.

_____

5. AMERICAN LAND TITLE ASSOCIATION OWNER'S POLICY

OWNER'S POLICY OF TITLE INSURANCE

Issued by
Blank Title Insurance Company

Any notice of claim and any other notice or statement in writing required to be given to the Company under this Policy must be given to the Company at the address shown in Section 18 of the Conditions.

COVERED RISKS

SUBJECT TO THE EXCLUSIONS FROM COVERAGE, THE EXCEPTIONS FROM COVERAGE CONTAINED IN SCHEDULE B, AND THE CONDITIONS, BLANK TITLE INSURANCE COMPANY, a Blank corporation (the "Company") insures, as of Date of Policy and, to the extent stated in Covered Risks 9 and 10, after Date of Policy, against loss or damage, not exceeding the Amount of Insurance, sustained or incurred by the Insured by reason of:

1. Title being vested other than as stated in Schedule A.

2. Any defect in or lien or encumbrance on the Title. This Covered Risk includes but is not limited to insurance against loss from

    (a) A defect in the Title caused by

        (i) forgery, fraud, undue influence, duress, incompetency, incapacity, or impersonation;

        (ii) failure of any person or Entity to have authorized a transfer or conveyance;

        (iii) a document affecting Title not properly created, executed, witnessed, sealed, acknowledged, notarized, or delivered;

        (iv) failure to perform those acts necessary to create a document by electronic means authorized by law;

        (v) a document executed under a falsified, expired, or otherwise invalid power of attorney;

        (vi) a document not properly filed, recorded, or indexed in the Public Records including failure to perform those acts by electronic means authorized by law; or

        (vii) a defective judicial or administrative proceeding.

    (b) The lien of real estate taxes or assessments imposed on the Title by a governmental authority due or payable, but unpaid.

    (c) Any encroachment, encumbrance, violation, variation, or adverse circumstance affecting the Title that would be disclosed by an accurate and complete land survey of the Land. The term "encroachment" includes encroachments of existing improvements located on the Land onto adjoining land, and encroachments onto the Land of existing improvements located on adjoining land.

3. Unmarketable Title.

4. No right of access to and from the Land.

5. The violation or enforcement of any law, ordinance, permit, or governmental regulation (including those relating to building and zoning) restricting, regulating, prohibiting, or relating to

(a) the occupancy, use, or enjoyment of the Land;

(b) the character, dimensions, or location of any improvement erected on the Land;

(c) the subdivision of land; or

(d) environmental protection

if a notice, describing any part of the Land, is recorded in the Public Records setting forth the violation or intention to enforce, but only to the extent of the violation or enforcement referred to in that notice.

6. An enforcement action based on the exercise of a governmental police power not covered by Covered Risk 5 if a notice of the enforcement action, describing any part of the Land, is recorded in the Public Records, but only to the extent of the enforcement referred to in that notice.

7. The exercise of the rights of eminent domain if a notice of the exercise, describing any part of the Land, is recorded in the Public Records.

8. Any taking by a governmental body that has occurred and is binding on the rights of a purchaser for value without Knowledge.

9. Title being vested other than as stated in Schedule A or being defective

(a) as a result of the avoidance in whole or in part, or from a court order providing an alternative remedy, of a transfer of all or any part of the title to or any interest in the Land occurring prior to the transaction vesting Title as shown in Schedule A because that prior transfer constituted a fraudulent or preferential transfer under federal bankruptcy, state insolvency, or similar creditors' rights laws; or

(b) because the instrument of transfer vesting Title as shown in Schedule A constitutes a preferential transfer under federal bankruptcy, state insolvency, or similar creditors' rights laws by reason of the failure of its recording in the Public Records

(i) to be timely, or

(ii) to impart notice of its existence to a purchaser for value or to a judgment or lien creditor.

10. Any defect in or lien or encumbrance on the Title or other matter included in Covered Risks 1 through 9 that has been created or attached or has been filed or recorded in the Public Records subsequent to Date of Policy and prior to the recording of the deed or other instrument of transfer in the Public Records that vests Title as shown in Schedule A.

The Company will also pay the costs, attorneys' fees, and expenses incurred in defense of any matter insured against by this Policy, but only to the extent provided in the Conditions.

[Witness clause optional]

BLANK TITLE INSURANCE COMPANY

BY: _____
PRESIDENT

BY: _____
SECRETARY

EXCLUSIONS FROM COVERAGE

The following matters are expressly excluded from the coverage of this policy, and the Company will not pay loss or damage, costs, attorneys' fees, or expenses that arise by reason of:

1. (a) Any law, ordinance, permit, or governmental regulation (including those relating to building and zoning) restricting, regulating, prohibiting, or relating to

    (i) the occupancy, use, or enjoyment of the Land;
    (ii) the character, dimensions, or location of any improvement erected on the Land;
    (iii) the subdivision of land; or
    (iv) environmental protection;
    or the effect of any violation of these laws, ordinances, or governmental regulations. This Exclusion 1(a) does not modify or limit the coverage provided under Covered Risk 5.

    (b) Any governmental police power. This Exclusion 1(b) does not modify or limit the coverage provided under Covered Risk 6.

2. Rights of eminent domain. This Exclusion does not modify or limit the coverage provided under Covered Risk 7 or 8.

3. Defects, liens, encumbrances, adverse claims, or other matters

    (a) created, suffered, assumed, or agreed to by the Insured Claimant;
    (b) not Known to the Company, not recorded in the Public Records at Date of Policy, but Known to the Insured Claimant and not disclosed in writing to the Company by the Insured Claimant prior to the date the Insured Claimant became an Insured under this policy;
    (c) resulting in no loss or damage to the Insured Claimant;
    (d) attaching or created subsequent to Date of Policy (however, this does not modify or limit the coverage provided under Covered Risk 9 and 10); or
    (e) resulting in loss or damage that would not have been sustained if the Insured Claimant had paid value for the Title.

4. Any claim, by reason of the operation of federal bankruptcy, state insolvency, or similar creditors' rights laws, that the transaction vesting the Title as shown in Schedule A, is

    (a) a fraudulent conveyance or fraudulent transfer; or
    (b) a preferential transfer for any reason not stated in Covered Risk 9 of this policy.

5. Any lien on the Title for real estate taxes or assessments imposed by governmental authority and created or attaching between Date of Policy and the date of recording of the deed or other instrument of transfer in the Public Records that vests Title as shown in Schedule A.

267

SCHEDULE A

Name and Address of Title Insurance Company:

[File No.:   ]   Policy No.:

Address Reference:

Amount of Insurance:$ [Premium: $]

Date of Policy: [at a.m./p.m.]

1. Name of Insured:

2. The estate or interest in the Land that is insured by this policy is:

3. Title is vested in:

4. The Land referred to in this policy is described as follows:

SCHEDULE B

[File No.   ]   Policy No.

EXCEPTIONS FROM COVERAGE

This policy does not insure against loss or damage, and the Company will not pay costs, attorneys' fees, or expenses that arise by reason of:

1.   [Policy may include regional exceptions if so desired by the issuing

2.   Company.]ᵃ

3.   [Variable exceptions such as taxes, easements, CC & R's, etc., shown here]

4.

---

a.   A sample of printed exceptions in a Schedule B reads as follows (Chicago Title Insurance Company, Schedule B, Form No. 1896 (Rev. 3/89). Copyright 1989, Chicago Title Insurance Company. Reprinted with permission.):

General Exceptions:

(1) Rights or claims of parties in possession not shown by the public records.

(2) Encroachments, overlaps, boundary line disputes, and any other matters which would be disclosed by an accurate survey and inspection of the premises.

(3) Easements or claims of easements not shown by the public records.

(4) Any lien, or right to a lien, for services, labor, or material heretofore or hereafter furnished, imposed by law and not shown by the public records.

(5) Taxes or special assessments which are not shown as existing liens by the public records.

Special Exceptions: The mortgage, if any, referred to in Item 4 of Schedule A, if this schedule is attached to an Owner's Policy.

(6) Taxes and assessments for the year ___ and subsequent years.

CONDITIONS

1. DEFINITION OF TERMS

The following terms when used in this policy mean:

(a) "Amount of Insurance": The amount stated in Schedule A, as may be increased or decreased by endorsement to this policy, increased by Section 8(b), or decreased by Sections 10 and 11 of these Conditions.

(b) "Date of Policy": The date designated as "Date of Policy" in Schedule A.

(c) "Entity": A corporation, partnership, trust, limited liability company, or other similar legal entity.

(d) "Insured": The Insured named in Schedule A.

   (i) the term "Insured" also includes

   (A) successors to the Title of the Insured by operation of law as distinguished from purchase, including heirs, devisees, survivors, personal representatives, or next of kin;

   (B) successors to an Insured by dissolution, merger, consolidation, distribution, or reorganization;

   (C) successors to an Insured by its conversion to another kind of Entity;

   (D) a grantee of an Insured under a deed delivered without payment of actual valuable consideration conveying the Title

      (1) if the stock, shares, memberships, or other equity interests of the grantee are wholly-owned by the named Insured,

      (2) if the grantee wholly owns the named Insured,

      (3) if the grantee is wholly-owned by an affiliated Entity of the named Insured, provided the affiliated Entity and the named Insured are both wholly-owned by the same person or Entity, or

      (4) if the grantee is a trustee or beneficiary of a trust created by a written instrument established by the Insured named in Schedule A for estate planning purposes.

   (ii) with regard to (A), (B), (C), and (D) reserving, however, all rights and defenses as to any successor that the Company would have had against any predecessor Insured.

(e) "Insured Claimant": An Insured claiming loss or damage.

(f) "Knowledge" or "Known": Actual knowledge, not constructive knowledge or notice that may be imputed to an Insured by reason of the Public Records or any other records that impart constructive notice of matters affecting the Title.

(g) "Land": The land described in Schedule A, and affixed improvements that by law constitute real property. The term "Land" does not include any property beyond the lines of the area described in Schedule A, nor any right, title, interest, estate, or easement in abutting streets, roads, avenues, alleys, lanes, ways, or waterways, but this does not modify or limit the extent that a right of access to and from the Land is insured by this policy.

(h) "Mortgage": Mortgage, deed of trust, trust deed, or other security instrument, including one evidenced by electronic means authorized by law.

(i) "Public Records": Records established under state statutes at Date of Policy for the purpose of imparting constructive notice of matters relating to real property to purchasers for value and without Knowledge. With respect to Covered Risk 5(d), "Public Records" shall also include environmental protection liens filed in the records of the clerk of the United States District Court for the district where the Land is located.

(j) "Title": The estate or interest described in Schedule A.

(k) "Unmarketable Title": Title affected by an alleged or apparent matter that would permit a prospective purchaser or lessee of the Title or lender on the Title to be released from the obligation to purchase, lease, or lend if there is a contractual condition requiring the delivery of marketable title.

2. CONTINUATION OF INSURANCE

The coverage of this policy shall continue in force as of Date of Policy in favor of an Insured, but only so long as the Insured retains an estate or interest in the Land, or holds an obligation secured by a purchase money Mortgage given by a purchaser from the Insured, or only so long as the Insured shall have liability by reason of warranties in any transfer or conveyance of the Title. This policy shall not continue in force in favor of any purchaser from the Insured of either (i) an estate or interest in the Land, or (ii) an obligation secured by a purchase money Mortgage given to the Insured.

3. NOTICE OF CLAIM TO BE GIVEN BY INSURED CLAIMANT

The Insured shall notify the Company promptly in writing (i) in case of any litigation as set forth in Section 5(a) of these Conditions, (ii) in case Knowledge shall come to an Insured hereunder of any claim of title or interest that is adverse to the Title, as insured, and that might cause loss or damage for which the Company may be liable by virtue of this policy, or (iii) if the Title, as insured, is rejected as Unmarketable Title. If the Company is prejudiced by the failure of the Insured Claimant to provide prompt notice, the Company's liability to the Insured Claimant under the policy shall be reduced to the extent of the prejudice.

4. PROOF OF LOSS

In the event the Company is unable to determine the amount of loss or damage, the Company may, at its option, require as a condition of payment that the Insured Claimant furnish a signed proof of loss. The proof of loss must describe the defect, lien, encumbrance, or other matter insured against by this policy that constitutes the basis of loss or damage and shall state, to the extent possible, the basis of calculating the amount of the loss or damage.

5. DEFENSE AND PROSECUTION OF ACTIONS

(a) Upon written request by the Insured, and subject to the options contained in Section 7 of these Conditions, the Company, at its own cost and without unreasonable delay, shall provide for the defense of an Insured in litigation in which any third party asserts a claim covered by this policy adverse to the Insured. This obligation is limited to only those stated causes of action alleging matters insured against by this policy. The Company shall have the right to select counsel of its choice (subject to the

271

right of the Insured to object for reasonable cause) to represent the Insured as to those stated causes of action. It shall not be liable for and will not pay the fees of any other counsel. The Company will not pay any fees, costs, or expenses incurred by the Insured in the defense of those causes of action that allege matters not insured against by this policy.

(b) The Company shall have the right, in addition to the options contained in Section 7 of these Conditions, at its own cost, to institute and prosecute any action or proceeding or to do any other act that in its opinion may be necessary or desirable to establish the Title, as insured, or to prevent or reduce loss or damage to the Insured. The Company may take any appropriate action under the terms of this policy, whether or not it shall be liable to the Insured. The exercise of these rights shall not be an admission of liability or waiver of any provision of this policy. If the Company exercises its rights under this subsection, it must do so diligently.

(c) Whenever the Company brings an action or asserts a defense as required or permitted by this policy, the Company may pursue the litigation to a final determination by a court of competent jurisdiction, and it expressly reserves the right, in its sole discretion, to appeal any adverse judgment or order.

6. DUTY OF INSURED CLAIMANT TO COOPERATE

(a) In all cases where this policy permits or requires the Company to prosecute or provide for the defense of any action or proceeding and any appeals, the Insured shall secure to the Company the right to so prosecute or provide defense in the action or proceeding, including the right to use, at its option, the name of the Insured for this purpose. Whenever requested by the Company, the Insured, at the Company's expense, shall give the Company all reasonable aid (i) in securing evidence, obtaining witnesses, prosecuting or defending the action or proceeding, or effecting settlement, and (ii) in any other lawful act that in the opinion of the Company may be necessary or desirable to establish the Title or any other matter as insured. If the Company is prejudiced by the failure of the Insured to furnish the required cooperation, the Company's obligations to the Insured under the policy shall terminate, including any liability or obligation to defend, prosecute, or continue any litigation, with regard to the matter or matters requiring such cooperation.

(b) The Company may reasonably require the Insured Claimant to submit to examination under oath by any authorized representative of the Company and to produce for examination, inspection, and copying, at such reasonable times and places as may be designated by the authorized representative of the Company, all records, in whatever medium maintained, including books, ledgers, checks, memoranda, correspondence, reports, e-mails, disks, tapes, and videos whether bearing a date before or after Date of Policy, that reasonably pertain to the loss or damage. Further, if requested by any authorized representative of the Company, the Insured Claimant shall grant its permission, in writing, for any authorized representative of the Company to examine, inspect, and copy all of these records in the custody or control of a third party that reasonably pertain to the loss or damage. All information designated as confidential by the Insured Claimant provided to the Company pursuant to this Section shall not be disclosed to others unless, in the reasonable judgment of the Company, it is necessary in the administration of the claim. Failure of the Insured Claimant to submit for examination under oath, produce any reasonably requested information, or grant permission to secure reasonably necessary information from third parties as required in this subsection, unless prohibited by law or governmental regulation, shall terminate any liability of the Company under this policy as to that claim.

7. OPTIONS TO PAY OR OTHERWISE SETTLE CLAIMS; TERMINATION OF LIABILITY

In case of a claim under this policy, the Company shall have the following additional options:

(a) To Pay or Tender Payment of the Amount of Insurance.

To pay or tender payment of the Amount of Insurance under this policy together with any costs, attorneys' fees, and expenses incurred by the Insured Claimant that were authorized by the Company up to the time of payment or tender of payment and that the Company is obligated to pay.

Upon the exercise by the Company of this option, all liability and obligations of the Company to the Insured under this policy, other than to make the payment required in this subsection, shall terminate, including any liability or obligation to defend, prosecute, or continue any litigation.

(b) To Pay or Otherwise Settle With Parties Other Than the Insured or With the Insured Claimant.

(i) to pay or otherwise settle with other parties for or in the name of an Insured Claimant any claim insured against under this policy. In addition, the Company will pay any costs, attorneys' fees, and expenses incurred by the Insured Claimant that were authorized by the Company up to the time of payment and that the Company is obligated to pay; or

(ii) to pay or otherwise settle with the Insured Claimant the loss or damage provided for under this policy, together with any costs, attorneys' fees, and expenses incurred by the Insured Claimant that were authorized by the Company up to the time of payment and that the Company is obligated to pay.

Upon the exercise by the Company of either of the options provided for in subsections (b)(i) or (ii), the Company's obligations to the Insured under this policy for the claimed loss or damage, other than the payments required to be made, shall terminate, including any liability or obligation to defend, prosecute, or continue any litigation.

8. DETERMINATION AND EXTENT OF LIABILITY

This policy is a contract of indemnity against actual monetary loss or damage sustained or incurred by the Insured Claimant who has suffered loss or damage by reason of matters insured against by this policy.

(a) The extent of liability of the Company for loss or damage under this policy shall not exceed the lesser of

(i) the Amount of Insurance; or

(ii) the difference between the value of the Title as insured and the value of the Title subject to the risk insured against by this policy.

273

(b) If the Company pursues its rights under Section 5 of these Conditions and is unsuccessful in establishing the Title, as insured,

    (i) the Amount of Insurance shall be increased by 10%, and

    (ii) the Insured Claimant shall have the right to have the loss or damage determined either as of the date the claim was made by the Insured Claimant or as of the date it is settled and paid.

(c) In addition to the extent of liability under (a) and (b), the Company will also pay those costs, attorneys' fees, and expenses incurred in accordance with Sections 5 and 7 of these Conditions.

9. LIMITATION OF LIABILITY

(a) If the Company establishes the Title, or removes the alleged defect, lien, or encumbrance, or cures the lack of a right of access to or from the Land, or cures the claim of Unmarketable Title, all as insured, in a reasonably diligent manner by any method, including litigation and the completion of any appeals, it shall have fully performed its obligations with respect to that matter and shall not be liable for any loss or damage caused to the Insured.

(b) In the event of any litigation, including litigation by the Company or with the Company's consent, the Company shall have no liability for loss or damage until there has been a final determination by a court of competent jurisdiction, and disposition of all appeals, adverse to the Title, as insured.

(c) The Company shall not be liable for loss or damage to the Insured for liability voluntarily assumed by the Insured in settling any claim or suit without the prior written consent of the Company.

10. REDUCTION OF INSURANCE; REDUCTION OR TERMINATION OF LIABILITY

All payments under this policy, except payments made for costs, attorneys' fees, and expenses, shall reduce the Amount of Insurance by the amount of the payment.

11. LIABILITY NONCUMULATIVE

The Amount of Insurance shall be reduced by any amount the Company pays under any policy insuring a Mortgage to which exception is taken in Schedule B or to which the Insured has agreed, assumed, or taken subject, or which is executed by an Insured after Date of Policy and which is a charge or lien on the Title, and the amount so paid shall be deemed a payment to the Insured under this policy.

12. PAYMENT OF LOSS

When liability and the extent of loss or damage have been definitely fixed in accordance with these Conditions, the payment shall be made within 30 days.

13. RIGHTS OF RECOVERY UPON PAYMENT OR SETTLEMENT

(a) Whenever the Company shall have settled and paid a claim under this policy, it shall be subrogated and entitled to the rights of the Insured Claimant in the Title and all other rights and remedies in respect to the claim that the Insured Claimant has against any person or property, to the extent of the amount of any loss, costs, attorneys' fees, and expenses paid by the Company. If requested by the Company, the

274

Insured Claimant shall execute documents to evidence the transfer to the Company of these rights and remedies. The Insured Claimant shall permit the Company to sue, compromise, or settle in the name of the Insured Claimant and to use the name of the Insured Claimant in any transaction or litigation involving these rights and remedies.

If a payment on account of a claim does not fully cover the loss of the Insured Claimant, the Company shall defer the exercise of its right to recover until after the Insured Claimant shall have recovered its loss.

(b) The Company's right of subrogation includes the rights of the Insured to indemnities, guaranties, other policies of insurance, or bonds, notwithstanding any terms or conditions contained in those instruments that address subrogation rights.

14. ARBITRATION

Either the Company or the Insured may demand that the claim or controversy shall be submitted to arbitration pursuant to the Title Insurance Arbitration Rules of the American Land Title Association ("Rules"). Except as provided in the Rules, there shall be no joinder or consolidation with claims or controversies of other persons. Arbitrable matters may include, but are not limited to, any controversy or claim between the Company and the Insured arising out of or relating to this policy, any service in connection with its issuance or the breach of a policy provision, or to any other controversy or claim arising out of the transaction giving rise to this policy. All arbitrable matters when the Amount of Insurance is $2,000,000 or less shall be arbitrated at the option of either the Company or the Insured. All arbitrable matters when the Amount of Insurance is in excess of $2,000,000 shall be arbitrated only when agreed to by both the Company and the Insured. Arbitration pursuant to this policy and under the Rules shall be binding upon the parties. Judgment upon the award rendered by the Arbitrator(s) may be entered in any court of competent jurisdiction.

15. LIABILITY LIMITED TO THIS POLICY; POLICY ENTIRE CONTRACT

(a) This policy together with all endorsements, if any, attached to it by the Company is the entire policy and contract between the Insured and the Company. In interpreting any provision of this policy, this policy shall be construed as a whole.

(b) Any claim of loss or damage that arises out of the status of the Title or by any action asserting such claim shall be restricted to this policy.

(c) Any amendment of or endorsement to this policy must be in writing and authenticated by an authorized person, or expressly incorporated by Schedule A of this policy.

(d) Each endorsement to this policy issued at any time is made a part of this policy and is subject to all of its terms and provisions. Except as the endorsement expressly states, it does not (i) modify any of the terms and provisions of the policy, (ii) modify any prior endorsement, (iii) extend the Date of Policy, or (iv) increase the Amount of Insurance.

16. SEVERABILITY

In the event any provision of this policy, in whole or in part, is held invalid or unenforceable under applicable law, the policy shall be deemed not to include that provision or such part held to be invalid, but all other provisions shall remain in full force and effect.

17. CHOICE OF LAW; FORUM

(a) Choice of Law: The Insured acknowledges the Company has underwritten the risks covered by this policy and determined the premium charged therefor in reliance upon the law affecting interests in real property and applicable to the interpretation, rights, remedies, or enforcement of policies of title insurance of the jurisdiction where the Land is located.

Therefore, the court or an arbitrator shall apply the law of the jurisdiction where the Land is located to determine the validity of claims against the Title that are adverse to the Insured and to interpret and enforce the terms of this policy. In neither case shall the court or arbitrator apply its conflicts of law principles to determine the applicable law.

(b) Choice of Forum: Any litigation or other proceeding brought by the Insured against the Company must be filed only in a state or federal court within the United States of America

or its territories having appropriate jurisdiction.

18. NOTICES, WHERE SENT

Any notice of claim and any other notice or statement in writing required to be given to the Company under this policy must be given to the Company at [fill in].

NOTE: Bracketed [ ] material optional

6. AMERICAN LAND TITLE ASSOCIATION LOAN POLICY

LOAN POLICY OF TITLE INSURANCE

Issued by

Blank Title Insurance Company

Any notice of claim and any other notice or statement in writing required to be given to the Company under this Policy must be given to the Company at the address shown in Section 17 of the Conditions.

COVERED RISKS

SUBJECT TO THE EXCLUSIONS FROM COVERAGE, THE EXCEPTIONS FROM COVERAGE CONTAINED IN SCHEDULE B, AND THE CONDITIONS, BLANK TITLE INSURANCE COMPANY, a Blank corporation (the "Company") insures as of Date of Policy and, to the extent stated in Covered Risks 11, 13, and 14, after Date of Policy, against loss or damage, not exceeding the Amount of Insurance, sustained or incurred by the Insured by reason of:

1. Title being vested other than as stated in Schedule A.
2. Any defect in or lien or encumbrance on the Title. This Covered Risk includes but is not limited to insurance against loss from

   (a) A defect in the Title caused by

       (i) forgery, fraud, undue influence, duress, incompetency, incapacity, or impersonation;

       (ii) failure of any person or Entity to have authorized a transfer or conveyance;

       (iii) a document affecting Title not properly created, executed, witnessed, sealed, acknowledged, notarized, or delivered;

       (iv) failure to perform those acts necessary to create a document by electronic means authorized by law;

       (v) a document executed under a falsified, expired, or otherwise invalid power of attorney;

       (vi) a document not properly filed, recorded, or indexed in the Public Records including failure to perform those acts by electronic means authorized by law; or

       (vii) a defective judicial or administrative proceeding.

   (b) The lien of real estate taxes or assessments imposed on the Title by a governmental authority due or payable, but unpaid.

   (c) Any encroachment, encumbrance, violation, variation, or adverse circumstance affecting the Title that would be disclosed by an accurate and complete land survey of the Land. The term "encroachment" includes encroachments of existing improvements located on the Land onto adjoining land, and encroachments onto the Land of existing improvements located on adjoining land.

3. Unmarketable Title.
4. No right of access to and from the Land.

5. The violation or enforcement of any law, ordinance, permit, or governmental regulation (including those relating to building and zoning) restricting, regulating, prohibiting, or relating to

(a) the occupancy, use, or enjoyment of the Land;

(b) the character, dimensions, or location of any improvement erected on the Land;

(c) the subdivision of land; or

(d) environmental protection

if a notice, describing any part of the Land, is recorded in the Public Records setting forth the violation or intention to enforce, but only to the extent of the violation or enforcement referred to in that notice.

6. An enforcement action based on the exercise of a governmental police power not covered by Covered Risk 5 if a notice of the enforcement action, describing any part of the Land, is recorded in the Public Records, but only to the extent of the enforcement referred to in that notice.

7. The exercise of the rights of eminent domain if a notice of the exercise, describing any part of the Land, is recorded in the Public Records.

8. Any taking by a governmental body that has occurred and is binding on the rights of a purchaser for value without Knowledge.

9. The invalidity or unenforceability of the lien of the Insured Mortgage upon the Title. This Covered Risk includes but is not limited to insurance against loss from any of the following impairing the lien of the Insured Mortgage

(a) forgery, fraud, undue influence, duress, incompetency, incapacity, or impersonation;

(b) failure of any person or Entity to have authorized a transfer or conveyance;

(c) the Insured Mortgage not being properly created, executed, witnessed, sealed, acknowledged, notarized, or delivered;

(d) failure to perform those acts necessary to create a document by electronic means authorized by law;

(e) a document executed under a falsified, expired, or otherwise invalid power of attorney;

(f) a document not properly filed, recorded, or indexed in the Public Records including failure to perform those acts by electronic means authorized by law; or

(g) a defective judicial or administrative proceeding.

10. The lack of priority of the lien of the Insured Mortgage upon the Title over any other lien or encumbrance.

11. The lack of priority of the lien of the Insured Mortgage upon the Title

(a) as security for each and every advance of proceeds of the loan secured by the Insured Mortgage over any statutory lien for services, labor, or material arising from construction of an improvement or work related to the Land when the improvement or work is either

(i) contracted for or commenced on or before Date of Policy; or

278

        (ii) contracted for, commenced, or continued after Date of Policy if the construction is financed, in whole or in part, by proceeds of the loan secured by the Insured Mortgage that the Insured has advanced or is obligated on Date of Policy to advance; and

    (b) over the lien of any assessments for street improvements under construction or completed at Date of Policy.

12.   The invalidity or unenforceability of any assignment of the Insured Mortgage, provided the assignment is shown in Schedule A, or the failure of the assignment shown in Schedule A to vest title to the Insured Mortgage in the named Insured assignee free and clear of all liens.

13.   The invalidity, unenforceability, lack of priority, or avoidance of the lien of the Insured Mortgage upon the Title

    (a) resulting from the avoidance in whole or in part, or from a court order providing an alternative remedy, of any transfer of all or any part of the title to or any interest in the Land occurring prior to the transaction creating the lien of the Insured Mortgage because that prior transfer constituted a fraudulent or preferential transfer under federal bankruptcy, state insolvency, or similar creditors' rights laws; or

    (b) because the Insured Mortgage constitutes a preferential transfer under federal bankruptcy, state insolvency, or similar creditors' rights laws by reason of the failure of its recording in the Public Records

        (i) to be timely, or

        (ii) to impart notice of its existence to a purchaser for value or to a judgment or lien creditor.

14.   Any defect in or lien or encumbrance on the Title or other matter included in Covered Risks 1 through 13 that has been created or attached or has been filed or recorded in the Public Records subsequent to Date of Policy and prior to the recording of the Insured Mortgage in the Public Records.

The Company will also pay the costs, attorneys' fees, and expenses incurred in defense of any matter insured against by this Policy, but only to the extent provided in the Conditions.

[Witness clause optional]

BLANK TITLE INSURANCE COMPANY

BY: _____

PRESIDENT

BY: _____

SECRETARY

EXCLUSIONS FROM COVERAGE

The following matters are expressly excluded from the coverage of this policy, and the Company will not pay loss or damage, costs, attorneys' fees, or expenses that arise by reason of:

1. (a) Any law, ordinance, permit, or governmental regulation (including those relating to building and zoning) restricting, regulating, prohibiting, or relating to

   (i) the occupancy, use, or enjoyment of the Land;
   (ii) the character, dimensions, or location of any improvement erected on the Land;
   (iii) the subdivision of land; or
   (iv) environmental protection;

   or the effect of any violation of these laws, ordinances, or governmental regulations. This Exclusion 1(a) does not modify or limit the coverage provided under Covered Risk 5.

   (b) Any governmental police power. This Exclusion 1(b) does not modify or limit the coverage provided under Covered Risk 6.

2. Rights of eminent domain. This Exclusion does not modify or limit the coverage provided under Covered Risk 7 or 8.

3. Defects, liens, encumbrances, adverse claims, or other matters

   (a) created, suffered, assumed, or agreed to by the Insured Claimant;

   (b) not Known to the Company, not recorded in the Public Records at Date of Policy, but Known to the Insured Claimant and not disclosed in writing to the Company by the Insured Claimant prior to the date the Insured Claimant became an Insured under this policy;

   (c) resulting in no loss or damage to the Insured Claimant;

   (d) attaching or created subsequent to Date of Policy (however, this does not modify or limit the coverage provided under Covered Risk 11, 13, or 14); or

   (e) resulting in loss or damage that would not have been sustained if the Insured Claimant had paid value for the Insured Mortgage.

4. Unenforceability of the lien of the Insured Mortgage because of the inability or failure of an Insured to comply with applicable doing-business laws of the state where the Land is situated.

5. Invalidity or unenforceability in whole or in part of the lien of the Insured Mortgage that arises out of the transaction evidenced by the Insured Mortgage and is based upon usury or any consumer credit protection or truth-in-lending law.

6. Any claim, by reason of the operation of federal bankruptcy, state insolvency, or similar creditors' rights laws, that the transaction creating the lien of the Insured Mortgage, is

   (a) a fraudulent conveyance or fraudulent transfer, or

   (b) a preferential transfer for any reason not stated in Covered Risk 13(b) of this policy.

280

7. Any lien on the Title for real estate taxes or assessments imposed by governmental authority and created or attaching between Date of Policy and the date of recording of the Insured Mortgage in the Public Records. This Exclusion does not modify or limit the coverage provided under Covered Risk 11(b).

SCHEDULE A

Name and Address of Title Insurance Company:

[File No.   ]   Policy No.:

Loan No.:

Address Reference:

Amount of Insurance: $ [Premium: $]

Date of Policy: [at a.m./p.m.]

1. Name of Insured:

2. The estate or interest in the Land that is encumbered by the Insured Mortgage is:

3. Title is vested in:

4. The Insured Mortgage and its assignments, if any, are described as follows:

5. The Land referred to in this policy is described as follows:

[6. This policy incorporates by reference those ALTA endorsements selected below:

    4–06   (Condominium)
    4.1–06
    5–06   (Planned Unit Development)
    5.1–06
    6–06   (Variable Rate)
    6.2–06   (Variable Rate—Negative Amortization)
    8.1–06   (Environmental Protection Lien) Paragraph b refers to the following state statute(s):
    9–06   (Restrictions, Encroachments, Minerals)
    13.1–06 (Leasehold Loan)
    14–06   Future Advance–Priority)
    14.1–06 (Future Advance–Knowledge)
    14.3–06 (Future Advance–Reverse Mortgage)
    22–06   (Location) The type of improvement is a _____, and the street address is as shown above.]

SCHEDULE B

[File No.   ]   Policy No.

EXCEPTIONS FROM COVERAGE

[Except as provided in Schedule B—Part II,] t[or T]his policy does not insure against loss or damage, and the Company will not pay costs, attorneys' fees, or expenses that arise by reason of:

[PART I

PART II

In addition to the matters set forth in Part I of this Schedule, the Title is subject to the following matters, and the Company insures against loss or damage sustained in the event that they are not subordinate to the lien of the Insured Mortgage:]

CONDITIONS

1. DEFINITION OF TERMS

The following terms when used in this policy mean:

(a) "Amount of Insurance": The amount stated in Schedule A, as may be increased or decreased by endorsement to this policy, increased by Section 8(b) or decreased by Section 10 of these Conditions.

(b) "Date of Policy": The date designated as "Date of Policy" in Schedule A.

(c) "Entity": A corporation, partnership, trust, limited liability company, or other similar legal entity.

(d) "Indebtedness": The obligation secured by the Insured Mortgage including one evidenced by electronic means authorized by law, and if that obligation is the payment of a debt, the Indebtedness is the sum of

  (i) the amount of the principal disbursed as of Date of Policy;
  (ii) the amount of the principal disbursed subsequent to Date of Policy;
  (iii) the construction loan advances made subsequent to Date of Policy for the purpose of financing in whole or in part the construction of an improvement to the Land or related to the Land that the Insured was and continued to be obligated to advance at Date of Policy and at the date of the advance;
  (iv) interest on the loan;
  (v) the prepayment premiums, exit fees, and other similar fees or penalties allowed by law;
  (vi) the expenses of foreclosure and any other costs of enforcement;
  (vii) the amounts advanced to assure compliance with laws or to protect the lien or the priority of the lien of the Insured Mortgage before the acquisition of the estate or interest in the Title;
  (viii) the amounts to pay taxes and insurance; and
  (ix) the reasonable amounts expended to prevent deterioration of improvements;

but the Indebtedness is reduced by the total of all payments and by any amount forgiven by an Insured.

(e) "Insured": The Insured named in Schedule A.

  (i) The term "Insured" also includes

    (A) the owner of the Indebtedness and each successor in ownership of the Indebtedness, whether the owner or successor owns the Indebtedness for its own account or as a trustee or other fiduciary, except a successor who is an obligor under the provisions of Section 12(c) of these Conditions;
    (B) the person or Entity who has "control" of the "transferable record," if the Indebtedness is evidenced by a "transferable record," as these terms are defined by applicable electronic transactions law;
    (C) successors to an Insured by dissolution, merger, consolidation, distribution, or reorganization;
    (D) successors to an Insured by its conversion to another kind of Entity;

(E) a grantee of an Insured under a deed delivered without payment of actual valuable consideration conveying the Title

    (1) if the stock, shares, memberships, or other equity interests of the grantee are wholly-owned by the named Insured,

    (2) if the grantee wholly owns the named Insured, or

    (3) if the grantee is wholly-owned by an affiliated Entity of the named Insured, provided the affiliated Entity and the named Insured are both wholly-owned by the same person or Entity;

(F) any government agency or instrumentality that is an insurer or guarantor under an insurance contract or guaranty insuring or guaranteeing the Indebtedness secured by the Insured Mortgage, or any part of it, whether named as an Insured or not;

(ii) With regard to (A), (B), (C), (D), and (E) reserving, however, all rights and defenses as to any successor that the Company would have had against any predecessor Insured, unless the successor acquired the Indebtedness as a purchaser for value without Knowledge of the asserted defect, lien, encumbrance, or other matter insured against by this policy.

(f) "Insured Claimant": An Insured claiming loss or damage.

(g) "Insured Mortgage": The Mortgage described in paragraph 4 of Schedule A.

(h) "Knowledge" or "Known": Actual knowledge, not constructive knowledge or notice that may be imputed to an Insured by reason of the Public Records or any other records that impart constructive notice of matters affecting the Title.

(i) "Land": The land described in Schedule A, and affixed improvements that by law constitute real property. The term "Land" does not include any property beyond the lines of the area described in Schedule A, nor any right, title, interest, estate, or easement in abutting streets, roads, avenues, alleys, lanes, ways, or waterways, but this does not modify or limit the extent that a right of access to and from the Land is insured by this policy.

(j) "Mortgage": Mortgage, deed of trust, trust deed, or other security instrument, including one evidenced by electronic means authorized by law.

(k) "Public Records": Records established under state statutes at Date of Policy for the purpose of imparting constructive notice of matters relating to real property to purchasers for value and without Knowledge. With respect to Covered Risk 5(d), "Public Records" shall also include environmental protection liens filed in the records of the clerk of the United States District Court for the district where the Land is located.

(*l*) "Title": The estate or interest described in Schedule A.

(m) "Unmarketable Title": Title affected by an alleged or apparent matter that would permit a prospective purchaser or lessee of the Title or lender on the Title or a prospective purchaser of the Insured Mortgage to be released from the obligation to purchase, lease, or lend if there is a contractual condition requiring the delivery of marketable title.

2. CONTINUATION OF INSURANCE

The coverage of this policy shall continue in force as of Date of Policy in favor of an Insured after acquisition of the Title by an Insured or after conveyance by an Insured, but only so long as the Insured retains an estate or interest in the Land, or holds an obligation secured by a purchase money Mortgage given by a purchaser from the Insured, or only so long as the Insured shall have liability by reason of warranties in any transfer or conveyance of the Title. This policy shall not continue in force in favor of any purchaser from the Insured of either (i) an estate or interest in the Land, or (ii) an obligation secured by a purchase money Mortgage given to the Insured.

3. NOTICE OF CLAIM TO BE GIVEN BY INSURED CLAIMANT

The Insured shall notify the Company promptly in writing (i) in case of any litigation as set forth in Section 5(a) of these Conditions, (ii) in case Knowledge shall come to an Insured of any claim of title or interest that is adverse to the Title or the lien of the Insured Mortgage, as insured, and that might cause loss or damage for which the Company may be liable by virtue of this policy, or (iii) if the Title or the lien of the Insured Mortgage, as insured, is rejected as Unmarketable Title. If the Company is prejudiced by the failure of the Insured Claimant to provide prompt notice, the Company's liability to the Insured Claimant under the policy shall be reduced to the extent of the prejudice.

4. PROOF OF LOSS

In the event the Company is unable to determine the amount of loss or damage, the Company may, at its option, require as a condition of payment that the Insured Claimant furnish a signed proof of loss. The proof of loss must describe the defect, lien, encumbrance, or other matter insured against by this policy that constitutes the basis of loss or damage and shall state, to the extent possible, the basis of calculating the amount of the loss or damage.

5. DEFENSE AND PROSECUTION OF ACTIONS

(a) Upon written request by the Insured, and subject to the options contained in Section 7 of these Conditions, the Company, at its own cost and without unreasonable delay, shall provide for the defense of an Insured in litigation in which any third party asserts a claim covered by this policy adverse to the Insured. This obligation is limited to only those stated causes of action alleging matters insured against by this policy. The Company shall have the right to select counsel of its choice (subject to the right of the Insured to object for reasonable cause) to represent the Insured as to those stated causes of action. It shall not be liable for and will not pay the fees of any other counsel. The Company will not pay any fees, costs, or expenses incurred by the Insured in the defense of those causes of action that allege matters not insured against by this policy.

(b) The Company shall have the right, in addition to the options contained in Section 7 of these Conditions, at its own cost, to institute and prosecute any action or proceeding or to do any other act that in its opinion may be necessary or desirable to establish the Title or the lien of the Insured Mortgage, as insured, or to prevent or reduce loss or damage to the Insured. The Company may take any appropriate action under the terms of this policy, whether or not it shall be liable to the Insured. The exercise of these rights shall not be an admission of liability or waiver of any provision of this policy. If the Company exercises its rights under this subsection, it must do so diligently.

(c) Whenever the Company brings an action or asserts a defense as required or permitted by this policy, the Company may pursue the litigation to a final determination by a court of competent jurisdiction, and it expressly reserves the right, in its sole discretion, to appeal any adverse judgment or order.

6. DUTY OF INSURED CLAIMANT TO COOPERATE

(a) In all cases where this policy permits or requires the Company to prosecute or provide for the defense of any action or proceeding and any appeals, the Insured shall secure to the Company the right to so prosecute or provide defense in the action or proceeding, including the right to use, at its option, the name of the Insured for this purpose.

Whenever requested by the Company, the Insured, at the Company's expense, shall give the Company all reasonable aid (i) in securing evidence, obtaining witnesses, prosecuting or defending the action or proceeding, or effecting settlement, and (ii) in any other lawful act that in the opinion of the Company may be necessary or desirable to establish the Title, the lien of the Insured Mortgage, or any other matter as insured. If the Company is prejudiced by the failure of the Insured to furnish the required cooperation, the Company's obligations to the Insured under the policy shall terminate, including any liability or obligation to defend, prosecute, or continue any litigation, with regard to the matter or matters requiring such cooperation.

(b) The Company may reasonably require the Insured Claimant to submit to examination under oath by any authorized representative of the Company and to produce for examination, inspection, and copying, at such reasonable times and places as may be designated by the authorized representative of the Company, all records, in whatever medium maintained, including books, ledgers, checks, memoranda, correspondence, reports, e-mails, disks, tapes, and videos whether bearing a date before or after Date of Policy, that reasonably pertain to the loss or damage. Further, if requested by any authorized representative of the Company, the Insured Claimant shall grant its permission, in writing, for any authorized representative of the Company to examine, inspect, and copy all of these records in the custody or control of a third party that reasonably pertain to the loss or damage. All information designated as confidential by the Insured Claimant provided to the Company pursuant to this Section shall not be disclosed to others unless, in the reasonable judgment of the Company, it is necessary in the administration of the claim. Failure of the Insured Claimant to submit for examination under oath, produce any reasonably requested information, or grant permission to secure reasonably necessary information from third parties as required in this subsection, unless prohibited by law or governmental regulation, shall terminate any liability of the Company under this policy as to that claim.

7. OPTIONS TO PAY OR OTHERWISE SETTLE CLAIMS; TERMINATION OF LIABILITY

In case of a claim under this policy, the Company shall have the following additional options:

(a) To Pay or Tender Payment of the Amount of Insurance or to Purchase the Indebtedness.

   (i)   To pay or tender payment of the Amount of Insurance under this policy together with any costs, attorneys' fees, and expenses incurred by the Insured Claimant that were authorized by the Company up to the time of payment or tender of payment and that the Company is obligated to pay; or

   (ii) To purchase the Indebtedness for the amount of the Indebtedness on the date of purchase, together with any costs, attorneys' fees, and expenses incurred by the Insured Claimant that were authorized by the Company up to the time of purchase and that the Company is obligated to pay. When the Company purchases the Indebtedness, the Insured shall transfer, assign, and convey to the Company the Indebtedness and the Insured Mortgage, together with any collateral security.

Upon the exercise by the Company of either of the options provided for in subsections (a)(i) or (ii), all liability and obligations of the Company to the Insured under this policy, other than to make the payment required in those subsections, shall terminate, including any liability or obligation to defend, prosecute, or continue any litigation.

(b) To Pay or Otherwise Settle With Parties Other Than the Insured or With the Insured Claimant.

   (i)   to pay or otherwise settle with other parties for or in the name of an Insured Claimant any claim insured against under this policy. In addition, the Company will pay any costs, attorneys' fees, and expenses incurred by the Insured Claimant that were authorized by the Company up to the time of payment and that the Company is obligated to pay; or

   (ii) to pay or otherwise settle with the Insured Claimant the loss or damage provided for under this policy, together with any costs, attorneys' fees, and expenses incurred by the Insured Claimant that were authorized by the Company up to the time of payment and that the Company is obligated to pay.

Upon the exercise by the Company of either of the options provided for in subsections (b)(i) or (ii), the Company's obligations to the Insured under this policy for the claimed loss or damage, other than the payments required to be made, shall terminate, including any liability or obligation to defend, prosecute, or continue any litigation.

8.   DETERMINATION AND EXTENT OF LIABILITY

This policy is a contract of indemnity against actual monetary loss or damage sustained or incurred by the Insured Claimant who has suffered loss or damage by reason of matters insured against by this policy.

(a) The extent of liability of the Company for loss or damage under this policy shall not exceed the least of

   (i)   the Amount of Insurance,
   (ii) the Indebtedness,
   (iii) the difference between the value of the Title as insured and the value of the Title subject to the risk insured against by this policy, or

(iv) if a government agency or instrumentality is the Insured Claimant, the amount it paid in the acquisition of the Title or the Insured Mortgage in satisfaction of its insurance contract or guaranty.

(b) If the Company pursues its rights under Section 5 of these Conditions and is unsuccessful in establishing the Title or the lien of the Insured Mortgage, as insured,

(i) the Amount of Insurance shall be increased by 10%, and
(ii) the Insured Claimant shall have the right to have the loss or damage determined either as of the date the claim was made by the Insured Claimant or as of the date it is settled and paid.

(c) In the event the Insured has acquired the Title in the manner described in Section 2 of these Conditions or has conveyed the Title, then the extent of liability of the Company shall continue as set forth in Section 8(a) of these Conditions.

(d) In addition to the extent of liability under (a), (b), and (c), the Company will also pay those costs, attorneys' fees, and expenses incurred in accordance with Sections 5 and 7 of these Conditions.

9. LIMITATION OF LIABILITY

(a) If the Company establishes the Title, or removes the alleged defect, lien, or encumbrance, or cures the lack of a right of access to or from the Land, or cures the claim of Unmarketable Title, or establishes the lien of the Insured Mortgage, all as insured, in a reasonably diligent manner by any method, including litigation and the completion of any appeals, it shall have fully performed its obligations with respect to that matter and shall not be liable for any loss or damage caused to the Insured.

(b) In the event of any litigation, including litigation by the Company or with the Company's consent, the Company shall have no liability for loss or damage until there has been a final determination by a court of competent jurisdiction, and disposition of all appeals, adverse to the Title or to the lien of the Insured Mortgage, as insured.

(c) The Company shall not be liable for loss or damage to the Insured for liability voluntarily assumed by the Insured in settling any claim or suit without the prior written consent of the Company.

10. REDUCTION OF INSURANCE; REDUCTION OR TERMINATION OF LIABILITY

(a) All payments under this policy, except payments made for costs, attorneys' fees, and expenses, shall reduce the Amount of Insurance by the amount of the payment. However, any payments made prior to the acquisition of Title as provided in Section 2 of these Conditions shall not reduce the Amount of Insurance afforded under this policy except to the extent that the payments reduce the Indebtedness.

(b) The voluntary satisfaction or release of the Insured Mortgage shall terminate all liability of the Company except as provided in Section 2 of these Conditions.

289

11. PAYMENT OF LOSS

When liability and the extent of loss or damage have been definitely fixed in accordance with these Conditions, the payment shall be made within 30 days.

12. RIGHTS OF RECOVERY UPON PAYMENT OR SETTLEMENT

(a) The Company's Right to Recover

Whenever the Company shall have settled and paid a claim under this policy, it shall be subrogated and entitled to the rights of the Insured Claimant in the Title or Insured Mortgage and all other rights and remedies in respect to the claim that the Insured Claimant has against any person or property, to the extent of the amount of any loss, costs, attorneys' fees, and expenses paid by the Company. If requested by the Company, the Insured Claimant shall execute documents to evidence the transfer to the Company of these rights and remedies. The Insured Claimant shall permit the Company to sue, compromise, or settle in the name of the Insured Claimant and to use the name of the Insured Claimant in any transaction or litigation involving these rights and remedies.

If a payment on account of a claim does not fully cover the loss of the Insured Claimant, the Company shall defer the exercise of its right to recover until after the Insured Claimant shall have recovered its loss.

(b) The Insured's Rights and Limitations

(i) The owner of the Indebtedness may release or substitute the personal liability of any debtor or guarantor, extend or otherwise modify the terms of payment, release a portion of the Title from the lien of the Insured Mortgage, or release any collateral security for the Indebtedness, if it does not affect the enforceability or priority of the lien of the Insured Mortgage.

(ii) If the Insured exercises a right provided in (b)(i), but has Knowledge of any claim adverse to the Title or the lien of the Insured Mortgage insured against by this policy, the Company shall be required to pay only that part of any losses insured against by this policy that shall exceed the amount, if any, lost to the Company by reason of the impairment by the Insured Claimant of the Company's right of subrogation.

(c) The Company's Rights Against Noninsured Obligors

The Company's right of subrogation includes the Insured's rights against non-insured obligors including the rights of the Insured to indemnities, guaranties, other policies of insurance, or bonds, notwithstanding any terms or conditions contained in those instruments that address subrogation rights.

The Company's right of subrogation shall not be avoided by acquisition of the Insured Mortgage by an obligor (except an obligor described in Section 1(e)(i)(F) of these Conditions) who acquires the Insured Mortgage as a result of an indemnity, guarantee, other policy of insurance, or bond, and the obligor will not be an Insured under this policy.

13. ARBITRATION

Either the Company or the Insured may demand that the claim or controversy shall be submitted to arbitration pursuant to the Title Insurance Arbitration Rules of the American Land Title Association ("Rules"). Except as provided in the Rules, there shall be no joinder or consolidation with claims or controversies of other persons. Arbitrable matters may include, but are not limited to, any controversy or claim between the Company and the Insured arising out of or relating to this policy, any service in connection with its issuance or the breach of a policy provision, or to any other controversy or claim arising out of the transaction giving rise to this policy. All arbitrable matters when the Amount of Insurance is $2,000,000 or less shall be arbitrated at the option of either the Company or the Insured. All arbitrable matters when the Amount of Insurance is in excess of $2,000,000 shall be arbitrated only when agreed to by both the Company and the Insured. Arbitration pursuant to this policy and under the Rules shall be binding upon the parties. Judgment upon the award rendered by the Arbitrator(s) may be entered in any court of competent jurisdiction.

14. LIABILITY LIMITED TO THIS POLICY; POLICY ENTIRE CONTRACT

(a) This policy together with all endorsements, if any, attached to it by the Company is the entire policy and contract between the Insured and the Company. In interpreting any provision of this policy, this policy shall be construed as a whole.

(b) Any claim of loss or damage that arises out of the status of the Title or lien of the Insured Mortgage or by any action asserting such claim shall be restricted to this policy.

(c) Any amendment of or endorsement to this policy must be in writing and authenticated by an authorized person, or expressly incorporated by Schedule A of this policy.

(d) Each endorsement to this policy issued at any time is made a part of this policy and is subject to all of its terms and provisions. Except as the endorsement expressly states, it does not (i) modify any of the terms and provisions of the policy, (ii) modify any prior endorsement, (iii) extend the Date of Policy, or (iv) increase the Amount of Insurance.

15. SEVERABILITY

In the event any provision of this policy, in whole or in part, is held invalid or unenforceable under applicable law, the policy shall be deemed not to include that provision or such part held to be invalid, but all other provisions shall remain in full force and effect.

16. CHOICE OF LAW; FORUM

(a) Choice of Law: The Insured acknowledges the Company has underwritten the risks covered by this policy and determined the premium charged therefor in reliance upon the law affecting interests in real property and applicable to the interpretation, rights, remedies, or enforcement of policies of title insurance of the jurisdiction where the Land is located.

Therefore, the court or an arbitrator shall apply the law of the jurisdiction where the Land is located to determine the validity of claims against the Title or the lien of the Insured Mortgage that are adverse to the Insured and to interpret and enforce the terms of this policy. In neither case shall the court or arbitrator apply its conflicts of law principles to determine the applicable law.

(b) Choice of Forum: Any litigation or other proceeding brought by the Insured against the Company must be filed only in a state or federal court within the United States of America or its territories having appropriate jurisdiction.

17. NOTICES, WHERE SENT

Any notice of claim and any other notice or statement in writing required to be given to the Company under this policy must be given to the Company at [fill in].

NOTE: Bracketed [ ] material optional

7. NOTES

a. FIXED RATE NOTE

NOTE

_____, _____   _____, _____

[Date]   [City]   [State]

_____

[Property Address]

1. BORROWER'S PROMISE TO PAY

In return for a loan that I have received, I promise to pay U.S. $_____ (this amount is called "Principal"), plus interest, to the order of the Lender. The Lender is _____
_____. I will make all payments under this Note in the form of cash, check or money order.

I understand that the Lender may transfer this Note. The Lender or anyone who takes this Note by transfer and who is entitled to receive payments under this Note is called the "Note Holder."

2. INTEREST

Interest will be charged on unpaid principal until the full amount of Principal has been paid. I will pay interest at a yearly rate of _____%.

The interest rate required by this Section 2 is the rate I will pay both before and after any default described in Section 6(B) of this Note.

3. PAYMENTS

(A) Time and Place of Payments

I will pay principal and interest by making a payment every month.

I will make my monthly payment on the _____ day of each month beginning on _____,
_____. I will make these payments every month until I have paid all of the principal and interest and any other charges described below that I may owe under this Note. Each monthly payment will be applied as of its scheduled due date and will be applied to interest before Principal. If, on _____, 20____, I still owe amounts under this Note, I will pay those amounts in full on that date, which is called the "Maturity Date."

I will make my monthly payments at _____
_____ or at a different place if required by the Note Holder.

(B) Amount of Monthly Payments

My monthly payment will be in the amount of U.S. $_____.

4. BORROWER'S RIGHT TO PREPAY

I have the right to make payments of Principal at any time before they are due. A payment of Principal only is known as a "Prepayment." When I make a Prepayment, I will tell the Note Holder in writing that I am doing so. I may not designate a payment as a Prepayment if I have not made all the monthly payments due under the Note.

I may make a full Prepayment or partial Prepayments without paying a Prepayment charge. The Note Holder will use my Prepayments to reduce the amount of Principal that I owe under this Note. However, the Note Holder may apply my Prepayment to the accrued and unpaid interest on the Prepayment amount, before applying my Prepayment to reduce the Principal amount of the Note. If I make a partial Prepayment, there will be no changes in the due date or in the amount of my monthly payment unless the Note Holder agrees in writing to those changes.

5. LOAN CHARGES

If a law, which applies to this loan and which sets maximum loan charges, is finally interpreted so that the interest or other loan charges collected or to be collected in connection with this loan exceed the permitted limits, then: (a) any such loan charge shall be reduced by the amount necessary to reduce the charge to the permitted limit; and (b) any sums already collected from me which exceeded permitted limits will be refunded to me. The Note Holder may choose to make this refund by reducing the Principal I owe under this Note or by making a direct payment to me. If a refund reduces Principal, the reduction will be treated as a partial Prepayment.

MULTISTATE FIXED RATE NOTE--Single Family--**Fannie Mae/Freddie Mac** UNIFORM INSTRUMENT　　　**Form 3200**　**1/01**　*(page 1 of 3 pages)*

6. **BORROWER'S FAILURE TO PAY AS REQUIRED**

    (A) **Late Charge for Overdue Payments**

    If the Note Holder has not received the full amount of any monthly payment by the end of _____ calendar days after the date it is due, I will pay a late charge to the Note Holder. The amount of the charge will be _____% of my overdue payment of principal and interest. I will pay this late charge promptly but only once on each late payment.

    (B) **Default**

    If I do not pay the full amount of each monthly payment on the date it is due, I will be in default.

    (C) **Notice of Default**

    If I am in default, the Note Holder may send me a written notice telling me that if I do not pay the overdue amount by a certain date, the Note Holder may require me to pay immediately the full amount of Principal which has not been paid and all the interest that I owe on that amount. That date must be at least 30 days after the date on which the notice is mailed to me or delivered by other means.

    (D) **No Waiver By Note Holder**

    Even if, at a time when I am in default, the Note Holder does not require me to pay immediately in full as described above, the Note Holder will still have the right to do so if I am in default at a later time.

    (E) **Payment of Note Holder's Costs and Expenses**

    If the Note Holder has required me to pay immediately in full as described above, the Note Holder will have the right to be paid back by me for all of its costs and expenses in enforcing this Note to the extent not prohibited by applicable law. Those expenses include, for example, reasonable attorneys' fees.

7. **GIVING OF NOTICES**

    Unless applicable law requires a different method, any notice that must be given to me under this Note will be given by delivering it or by mailing it by first class mail to me at the Property Address above or at a different address if I give the Note Holder a notice of my different address.

    Any notice that must be given to the Note Holder under this Note will be given by delivering it or by mailing it by first class mail to the Note Holder at the address stated in Section 3(A) above or at a different address if I am given a notice of that different address.

8. **OBLIGATIONS OF PERSONS UNDER THIS NOTE**

    If more than one person signs this Note, each person is fully and personally obligated to keep all of the promises made in this Note, including the promise to pay the full amount owed. Any person who is a guarantor, surety or endorser of this Note is also obligated to do these things. Any person who takes over these obligations, including the obligations of a guarantor, surety or endorser of this Note, is also obligated to keep all of the promises made in this Note. The Note Holder may enforce its rights under this Note against each person individually or against all of us together. This means that any one of us may be required to pay all of the amounts owed under this Note.

9. **WAIVERS**

    I and any other person who has obligations under this Note waive the rights of Presentment and Notice of Dishonor. "Presentment" means the right to require the Note Holder to demand payment of amounts due. "Notice of Dishonor" means the right to require the Note Holder to give notice to other persons that amounts due have not been paid.

10. **UNIFORM SECURED NOTE**

    This Note is a uniform instrument with limited variations in some jurisdictions. In addition to the protections given to the Note Holder under this Note, a Mortgage, Deed of Trust, or Security Deed (the "Security Instrument"), dated the same date as this Note, protects the Note Holder from possible losses which might result if I do not keep the promises which I make in this Note. That Security Instrument describes how and under what conditions I may be required to make immediate payment in full of all amounts I owe under this Note. Some of those conditions are described as follows:

    > If all or any part of the Property or any Interest in the Property is sold or transferred (or if Borrower is not a natural person and a beneficial interest in Borrower is sold or transferred) without Lender's prior written consent, Lender may require immediate payment in full of all sums secured by this Security Instrument. However, this option shall not be exercised by Lender if such exercise is prohibited by Applicable Law.

MULTISTATE FIXED RATE NOTE--Single Family--Fannie Mae/Freddie Mac UNIFORM INSTRUMENT   Form 3200   1/01   *(page 2 of 3 pages)*

If Lender exercises this option, Lender shall give Borrower notice of acceleration. The notice shall provide a period of not less than 30 days from the date the notice is given in accordance with Section 15 within which Borrower must pay all sums secured by this Security Instrument. If Borrower fails to pay these sums prior to the expiration of this period, Lender may invoke any remedies permitted by this Security Instrument without further notice or demand on Borrower.

WITNESS THE HAND(S) AND SEAL(S) OF THE UNDERSIGNED

_____(Seal)
- Borrower

_____(Seal)
- Borrower

_____(Seal)
- Borrower

[Sign Original Only]

MULTISTATE FIXED RATE NOTE--Single Family--Fannie Mae/Freddie Mac UNIFORM INSTRUMENT   **Form 3200   1/01**   *(page 3 of 3 pages)*

b. ADJUSTABLE RATE NOTE

ADJUSTABLE RATE NOTE
(1 Year Treasury Index - Rate Caps)

THIS NOTE CONTAINS PROVISIONS ALLOWING FOR CHANGES IN MY INTEREST RATE AND MY MONTHLY PAYMENT. THIS NOTE LIMITS THE AMOUNT MY INTEREST RATE CAN CHANGE AT ANY ONE TIME AND THE MAXIMUM RATE I MUST PAY.

_____, _____	_____,	_____
[Date]	[City]	[State]

_____
[Property Address]

1. BORROWER'S PROMISE TO PAY

In return for a loan that I have received, I promise to pay U.S. $_____ (this amount is called "Principal"), plus interest, to the order of the Lender. The Lender is _____ _____. I will make all payments under this Note in the form of cash, check or money order.

I understand that the Lender may transfer this Note. The Lender or anyone who takes this Note by transfer and who is entitled to receive payments under this Note is called the "Note Holder."

2. INTEREST

Interest will be charged on unpaid principal until the full amount of Principal has been paid. I will pay interest at a yearly rate of _____%. The interest rate I will pay will change in accordance with Section 4 of this Note.

The interest rate required by this Section 2 and Section 4 of this Note is the rate I will pay both before and after any default described in Section 7(B) of this Note.

3. PAYMENTS

(A) Time and Place of Payments

I will pay principal and interest by making a payment every month.

I will make my monthly payment on the first day of each month beginning on _____, _____. I will make these payments every month until I have paid all of the principal and interest and any other charges described below that I may owe under this Note. Each monthly payment will be applied as of its scheduled due date and will be applied to interest before Principal. If, on _____, 20_____, I still owe amounts under this Note, I will pay those amounts in full on that date, which is called the "Maturity Date."

I will make my monthly payments at _____ _____ or at a different place if required by the Note Holder.

(B) Amount of My Initial Monthly Payments

Each of my initial monthly payments will be in the amount of U.S. $_____. This amount may change.

(C) Monthly Payment Changes

Changes in my monthly payment will reflect changes in the unpaid principal of my loan and in the interest rate that I must pay. The Note Holder will determine my new interest rate and the changed amount of my monthly payment in accordance with Section 4 of this Note.

297

4. INTEREST RATE AND MONTHLY PAYMENT CHANGES

(A) Change Dates

The interest rate I will pay may change on the first day of _____, _____, and on that day every 12th month thereafter. Each date on which my interest rate could change is called a "Change Date."

MULTISTATE ADJUSTABLE RATE NOTE-ARM 5-2--Single Family--**Fannie Mae/Freddie Mac** UNIFORM INSTRUMENT   **Form 3502**   1/01   *(page 1 of 4 pages)*

(B)   The Index

Beginning with the first Change Date, my interest rate will be based on an Index. The "Index" is the weekly average yield on United States Treasury securities adjusted to a constant maturity of one year, as made available by the Federal Reserve Board. The most recent Index figure available as of the date 45 days before each Change Date is called the "Current Index."

If the Index is no longer available, the Note Holder will choose a new index which is based upon comparable information. The Note Holder will give me notice of this choice.

(C)   Calculation of Changes

Before each Change Date, the Note Holder will calculate my new interest rate by adding _____ percentage points (_____%) to the Current Index. The Note Holder will then round the result of this addition to the nearest one-eighth of one percentage point (0.125%). Subject to the limits stated in Section 4(D) below, this rounded amount will be my new interest rate until the next Change Date.

The Note Holder will then determine the amount of the monthly payment that would be sufficient to repay the unpaid principal that I am expected to owe at the Change Date in full on the Maturity Date at my new interest rate in substantially equal payments. The result of this calculation will be the new amount of my monthly payment.

(D)   Limits on Interest Rate Changes

The interest rate I am required to pay at the first Change Date will not be greater than _____% or less than _____%. Thereafter, my interest rate will never be increased or decreased on any single Change Date by more than two percentage points (2.0%) from the rate of interest I have been paying for the preceding 12 months. My interest rate will never be greater than _____%.

(E)   Effective Date of Changes

My new interest rate will become effective on each Change Date. I will pay the amount of my new monthly payment beginning on the first monthly payment date after the Change Date until the amount of my monthly payment changes again.

(F)   Notice of Changes

The Note Holder will deliver or mail to me a notice of any changes in my interest rate and the amount of my monthly payment before the effective date of any change. The notice will include information required by law to be given to me and also the title and telephone number of a person who will answer any question I may have regarding the notice.

5.   BORROWER'S RIGHT TO PREPAY

I have the right to make payments of Principal at any time before they are due. A payment of Principal only is known as a "Prepayment." When I make a Prepayment, I will tell the Note Holder in writing that I am doing so. I may not designate a payment as a Prepayment if I have not made all the monthly payments due under the Note.

I may make a full Prepayment or partial Prepayments without paying a Prepayment charge. The Note Holder will use my Prepayments to reduce the amount of Principal that I owe under this Note. However, the Note Holder may apply my Prepayment to the accrued and unpaid interest on the Prepayment amount, before applying my Prepayment to reduce the Principal amount of the Note. If I make a partial Prepayment, there will be no changes in the due dates of my monthly payment unless the Note Holder agrees in writing to those changes. My partial Prepayment may reduce the amount of my monthly payments after the first Change Date following my partial Prepayment. However, any reduction due to my partial Prepayment may be offset by an interest rate increase.

6.   LOAN CHARGES

If a law, which applies to this loan and which sets maximum loan charges, is finally interpreted so that the interest or other loan charges collected or to be collected in connection with this loan exceed the permitted limits, then: (a) any such loan charge shall be reduced by the amount necessary to reduce the charge to the permitted limit; and (b) any sums already collected from me which exceeded permitted limits will be refunded to me. The Note Holder may choose to make this refund by reducing the Principal I owe under this Note or by making a direct payment to me. If a refund reduces Principal, the reduction will be treated as a partial Prepayment.

MULTISTATE ADJUSTABLE RATE NOTE-ARM 5-2–Single Family--Fannie Mae/Freddie Mac UNIFORM INSTRUMENT   Form 3502   1/01   *(page 2 of 4 pages)*

7. BORROWER'S FAILURE TO PAY AS REQUIRED

(A) Late Charges for Overdue Payments

If the Note Holder has not received the full amount of any monthly payment by the end of _____ calendar days after the date it is due, I will pay a late charge to the Note Holder. The amount of the charge will be _____% of my overdue payment of principal and interest. I will pay this late charge promptly but only once on each late payment.

(B) Default

If I do not pay the full amount of each monthly payment on the date it is due, I will be in default.

(C) Notice of Default

If I am in default, the Note Holder may send me a written notice telling me that if I do not pay the overdue amount by a certain date, the Note Holder may require me to pay immediately the full amount of Principal which has not been paid and all the interest that I owe on that amount. That date must be at least 30 days after the date on which the notice is mailed to me or delivered by other means.

(D) No Waiver By Note Holder

Even if, at a time when I am in default, the Note Holder does not require me to pay immediately in full as described above, the Note Holder will still have the right to do so if I am in default at a later time.

(E) Payment of Note Holder's Costs and Expenses

If the Note Holder has required me to pay immediately in full as described above, the Note Holder will have the right to be paid back by me for all of its costs and expenses in enforcing this Note to the extent not prohibited by applicable law. Those expenses include, for example, reasonable attorneys' fees.

8. GIVING OF NOTICES

Unless applicable law requires a different method, any notice that must be given to me under this Note will be given by delivering it or by mailing it by first class mail to me at the Property Address above or at a different address if I give the Note Holder a notice of my different address.

Any notice that must be given to the Note Holder under this Note will be given by delivering it or by mailing it by first class mail to the Note Holder at the address stated in Section 3(A) above or at a different address if I am given a notice of that different address.

9. OBLIGATIONS OF PERSONS UNDER THIS NOTE

If more than one person signs this Note, each person is fully and personally obligated to keep all of the promises made in this Note, including the promise to pay the full amount owed. Any person who is a guarantor, surety or endorser of this Note is also obligated to do these things. Any person who takes over these obligations, including the obligations of a guarantor, surety or endorser of this Note, is also obligated to keep all of the promises made in this Note. The Note Holder may enforce its rights under this Note against each person individually or against all of us together. This means that any one of us may be required to pay all of the amounts owed under this Note.

10. WAIVERS

I and any other person who has obligations under this Note waive the rights of Presentment and Notice of Dishonor. "Presentment" means the right to require the Note Holder to demand payment of amounts due. "Notice of Dishonor" means the right to require the Note Holder to give notice to other persons that amounts due have not been paid.

11. UNIFORM SECURED NOTE

This Note is a uniform instrument with limited variations in some jurisdictions. In addition to the protections given to the Note Holder under this Note, a Mortgage, Deed of Trust, or Security Deed (the "Security Instrument"), dated the same date as this Note, protects the Note Holder from possible losses which might result if I do not keep the promises which I make in this Note. That Security Instrument describes how and under what conditions I may be required to make immediate payment in full of all amounts I owe under this Note. Some of those conditions are described as follows:

MULTISTATE ADJUSTABLE RATE NOTE-ARM 5-2--Single Family--Fannie Mae/Freddie Mac UNIFORM INSTRUMENT   Form 3502   1/01   *(page 3 of 4 pages)*

If all or any part of the Property or any Interest in the Property is sold or transferred (or if Borrower is not a natural person and a beneficial interest in Borrower is sold or transferred) without Lender's prior written consent, Lender may require immediate payment in full of all sums secured by this Security Instrument. However, this option shall not be exercised by Lender if such exercise is prohibited by Applicable Law. Lender also shall not exercise this option if: (a) Borrower causes to be submitted to Lender information required by Lender to evaluate the intended transferee as if a new loan were being made to the transferee; and (b) Lender reasonably determines that Lender's security will not be impaired by the loan assumption and that the risk of a breach of any covenant or agreement in this Security Instrument is acceptable to Lender.

To the extent permitted by Applicable Law, Lender may charge a reasonable fee as a condition to Lender's consent to the loan assumption. Lender may also require the transferee to sign an assumption agreement that is acceptable to Lender and that obligates the transferee to keep all the promises and agreements made in the Note and in this Security Instrument. Borrower will continue to be obligated under the Note and this Security Instrument unless Lender releases Borrower in writing

If Lender exercises the option to require immediate payment in full, Lender shall give Borrower notice of acceleration. The notice shall provide a period of not less than 30 days from the date the notice is given in accordance with Section 15 within which Borrower must pay all sums secured by this Security Instrument. If Borrower fails to pay these sums prior to the expiration of this period, Lender may invoke any remedies permitted by this Security Instrument without further notice or demand on Borrower.

WITNESS THE HAND(S) AND SEAL(S) OF THE UNDERSIGNED.

_____(Seal)
                                        - Borrower

_____(Seal)
                                        - Borrower

_____(Seal)
                                        - Borrower

[Sign Original Only]

MULTISTATE ADJUSTABLE RATE NOTE-ARM 5-2--Single Family--**Fannie Mae/Freddie Mac UNIFORM INSTRUMENT**   **Form 3502   1/01**   *(page 4 of 4 pages)*

8. MORTGAGE

After Recording Return To:

_____

_____

_____

_____

_____[Space Above This Line For Recording Data]_____

MORTGAGE

DEFINITIONS

Words used in multiple sections of this document are defined below and other words are defined in Sections 3, 11, 13, 18, 20 and 21. Certain rules regarding the usage of words used in this document are also provided in Section 16.

(A) **"Security Instrument"** means this document, which is dated _____, _____, together with all Riders to this document.
(B) **"Borrower"** is _____. Borrower is the mortgagor under this Security Instrument.
(C) **"Lender"** is _____. Lender is a _____ organized and existing under the laws of _____. Lender's address is _____ _____. Lender is the mortgagee under this Security Instrument.
(D) **"Note"** means the promissory note signed by Borrower and dated _____, _____. The Note states that Borrower owes Lender _____ _____ Dollars (U.S. $_____) plus interest. Borrower has promised to pay this debt in regular Periodic Payments and to pay the debt in full not later than _____.
(E) **"Property"** means the property that is described below under the heading "Transfer of Rights in the Property."
(F) **"Loan"** means the debt evidenced by the Note, plus interest, any prepayment charges and late charges due under the Note, and all sums due under this Security Instrument, plus interest.

(G) **"Riders"** means all Riders to this Security Instrument that are executed by Borrower. The following Riders are to be executed by Borrower [check box as applicable]:

☐ Adjustable Rate Rider ☐ Condominium Rider ☐ Second Home Rider
☐ Balloon Rider ☐ Planned Unit Development Rider ☐ Other(s) [specify] _____
☐ 1-4 Family Rider ☐ Biweekly Payment Rider

MASSACHUSETTS--Single Family--Fannie Mae/Freddie Mac UNIFORM INSTRUMENT   Form 3022   1/01   *(page 1 of 16 pages)*

(H) **"Applicable Law"** means all controlling applicable federal, state and local statutes, regulations, ordinances and administrative rules and orders (that have the effect of law) as well as all applicable final, non-appealable judicial opinions.

(I) **"Community Association Dues, Fees, and Assessments"** means all dues, fees, assessments and other charges that are imposed on Borrower or the Property by a condominium association, homeowners association or similar organization.

(J) **"Electronic Funds Transfer"** means any transfer of funds, other than a transaction originated by check, draft, or similar paper instrument, which is initiated through an electronic terminal, telephonic instrument, computer, or magnetic tape so as to order, instruct, or authorize a financial institution to debit or credit an account. Such term includes, but is not limited to, point-of-sale transfers, automated teller machine transactions, transfers initiated by telephone, wire transfers, and automated clearinghouse transfers.

(K) **"Escrow Items"** means those items that are described in Section 3.

(L) **"Miscellaneous Proceeds"** means any compensation, settlement, award of damages, or proceeds paid by any third party (other than insurance proceeds paid under the coverages described in Section 5) for: (i) damage to, or destruction of, the Property; (ii) condemnation or other taking of all or any part of the Property; (iii) conveyance in lieu of condemnation; or (iv) misrepresentations of, or omissions as to, the value and/or condition of the Property.

(M) **"Mortgage Insurance"** means insurance protecting Lender against the nonpayment of, or default on, the Loan.

(N) **"Periodic Payment"** means the regularly scheduled amount due for (i) principal and interest under the Note, plus (ii) any amounts under Section 3 of this Security Instrument.

(O) **"RESPA"** means the Real Estate Settlement Procedures Act (12 U.S.C. §2601 et seq.) and its implementing regulation, Regulation X (24 C.F.R. Part 3500), as they might be amended from time to time, or any additional or successor legislation or regulation that governs the same subject matter. As used in this Security Instrument, "RESPA" refers to all requirements and restrictions that are imposed in regard to a "federally related mortgage loan" even if the Loan does not qualify as a "federally related mortgage loan" under RESPA.

(P) **"Successor in Interest of Borrower"** means any party that has taken title to the Property, whether or not that party has assumed Borrower's obligations under the Note and/or this Security Instrument.

TRANSFER OF RIGHTS IN THE PROPERTY

This Security Instrument secures to Lender: (i) the repayment of the Loan, and all renewals, extensions and modifications of the Note; and (ii) the performance of Borrower's covenants and agreements under this Security Instrument and the Note. For this purpose, Borrower does hereby mortgage, grant and convey to Lender and Lender's successors and assigns, with power of sale, the following described property located in the _____

[Type of Recording Jurisdiction]

of _____ :

[Name of Recording Jurisdiction]

MASSACHUSETTS--Single Family--**Fannie Mae/Freddie Mac UNIFORM INSTRUMENT**   **Form 3022**   1/01   *(page 2 of 16 pages)* which currently has the address of _____

                                                                        [Street]
_____, Massachusetts _____ ("Property Address"):
              [City]   [Zip Code]

TOGETHER WITH all the improvements now or hereafter erected on the property, and all easements, appurtenances, and fixtures now or hereafter a part of the property. All replacements and additions shall also be covered by this Security Instrument. All of the foregoing is referred to in this Security Instrument as the "Property."

BORROWER COVENANTS that Borrower is lawfully seised of the estate hereby conveyed and has the right to mortgage, grant and convey the Property and that the Property is unencumbered, except for encumbrances of record. Borrower warrants and will defend generally the title to the Property against all claims and demands, subject to any encumbrances of record.

THIS SECURITY INSTRUMENT combines uniform covenants for national use and non-uniform covenants with limited variations by jurisdiction to constitute a uniform security instrument covering real property.

UNIFORM COVENANTS. Borrower and Lender covenant and agree as follows:

1.   Payment of Principal, Interest, Escrow Items, Prepayment Charges, and Late Charges. Borrower shall pay when due the principal of, and interest on, the debt evidenced by the Note and any prepayment charges and late charges due under the Note. Borrower shall also pay funds for Escrow Items pursuant to Section 3. Payments due under the Note and this Security Instrument shall be made in U.S. currency. However, if any check or other instrument received by Lender as payment under the Note or this Security Instrument is returned to Lender unpaid, Lender may require that any or all subsequent payments due under the Note and this Security Instrument be made in one or more of the following forms, as selected by Lender: (a) cash; (b) money order; (c) certified check, bank check, treasurer's check or cashier's check, provided any such check is drawn upon an institution whose deposits are insured by a federal agency, instrumentality, or entity; or (d) Electronic Funds Transfer.

Payments are deemed received by Lender when received at the location designated in the Note or at such other location as may be designated by Lender in accordance with the notice provisions in Section 15. Lender may return any payment or partial payment if the payment or partial payments are insufficient to bring the Loan current. Lender may accept any payment or partial payment insufficient to bring the Loan current, without waiver of any rights hereunder or prejudice to its rights to refuse such payment or partial payments in the future, but Lender is not obligated to apply such payments at the time such payments are accepted. If each Periodic Payment is applied as of its scheduled due date, then Lender need not pay interest on unapplied funds. Lender may hold such unapplied funds until Borrower makes payment to bring the Loan current. If Borrower does not do so within a reasonable period of time, Lender shall either apply such funds or return them to Borrower. If not applied earlier, such funds will be applied to the outstanding principal balance under the Note immediately prior to foreclosure. No offset or claim which Borrower might have now or in

MASSACHUSETTS--Single Family--Fannie Mae/Freddie Mac UNIFORM INSTRUMENT   Form 3022   1/01   *(page 3 of 16 pages)*

the future against Lender shall relieve Borrower from making payments due under the Note and this Security Instrument or performing the covenants and agreements secured by this Security Instrument.

    2.   **Application of Payments or Proceeds.** Except as otherwise described in this Section 2, all payments accepted and applied by Lender shall be applied in the following order of priority: (a) interest due under the Note; (b) principal due under the Note; (c) amounts due under Section 3. Such payments shall be applied to each Periodic Payment in the order in which it became due. Any remaining amounts shall be applied first to late charges, second to any other amounts due under this Security Instrument, and then to reduce the principal balance of the Note.

    If Lender receives a payment from Borrower for a delinquent Periodic Payment which includes a sufficient amount to pay any late charge due, the payment may be applied to the delinquent payment and the late charge. If more than one Periodic Payment is outstanding, Lender may apply any payment received from Borrower to the repayment of the Periodic Payments if, and to the extent that, each payment can be paid in full. To the extent that any excess exists after the payment is applied to the full payment of one or more Periodic Payments, such excess may be applied to any late charges due. Voluntary prepayments shall be applied first to any prepayment charges and then as described in the Note.

    Any application of payments, insurance proceeds, or Miscellaneous Proceeds to principal due under the Note shall not extend or postpone the due date, or change the amount, of the Periodic Payments.

3.   **Funds for Escrow Items.** Borrower shall pay to Lender on the day Periodic Payments are due under the Note, until the Note is paid in full, a sum (the "Funds") to provide for payment of amounts due for: (a) taxes and assessments and other items which can attain priority over this Security Instrument as a lien or encumbrance on the Property; (b) leasehold payments or ground rents on the Property, if any; (c) premiums for any and all insurance required by Lender under Section 5; and (d) Mortgage Insurance premiums, if any, or any sums payable by Borrower to Lender in lieu of the payment of Mortgage Insurance premiums in accordance with the provisions of Section 10. These items are called "Escrow Items." At origination or at any time during the term of the Loan, Lender may require that Community Association Dues, Fees, and Assessments, if any, be escrowed by Borrower, and such dues, fees and assessments shall be an Escrow Item. Borrower shall promptly furnish to Lender all notices of amounts to be paid under this Section. Borrower shall pay Lender the Funds for Escrow Items unless Lender waives Borrower's obligation to pay the Funds for any or all Escrow Items. Lender may waive Borrower's obligation to pay to Lender Funds for any or all Escrow Items at any time. Any such waiver may only be in writing. In the event of such waiver, Borrower shall pay directly, when and where payable, the amounts due for any Escrow Items for which payment of Funds has been waived by Lender and, if Lender requires, shall furnish to Lender receipts evidencing such payment within such time period as Lender may require. Borrower's obligation to make such payments and to provide receipts shall for all purposes be deemed to be a covenant and agreement contained in this Security Instrument, as the phrase "covenant and agreement" is used in Section 9. If Borrower is obligated to pay Escrow Items directly, pursuant to a waiver, and Borrower fails to pay the amount due for an Escrow Item, Lender may exercise its rights under Section 9 and pay such amount and Borrower shall then be obligated under Section 9 to repay to Lender any such amount. Lender may revoke the waiver as to any or all Escrow Items at any time by a notice

MASSACHUSETTS--Single Family--Fannie Mae/Freddie Mac UNIFORM INSTRUMENT   Form 3022   1/01   *(page 4 of 16 pages)*

given in accordance with Section 15 and, upon such revocation, Borrower shall pay to Lender all Funds, and in such amounts, that are then required under this Section 3.

Lender may, at any time, collect and hold Funds in an amount (a) sufficient to permit Lender to apply the Funds at the time specified under RESPA, and (b) not to exceed the maximum amount a lender can require under RESPA. Lender shall estimate the amount of Funds due on the basis of current data and reasonable estimates of expenditures of future Escrow Items or otherwise in accordance with Applicable Law.

The Funds shall be held in an institution whose deposits are insured by a federal agency, instrumentality, or entity (including Lender, if Lender is an institution whose deposits are so insured) or in any Federal Home Loan Bank. Lender shall apply the Funds to pay the Escrow Items no later than the time specified under RESPA. Lender shall not charge Borrower for holding and applying the Funds, annually analyzing the escrow account, or verifying the Escrow Items, unless Lender pays Borrower interest on the Funds and Applicable Law permits Lender to make such a charge. Unless an agreement is made in writing or Applicable Law requires interest to be paid on the Funds, Lender shall not be required to pay Borrower any interest or earnings on the Funds. Borrower and Lender can agree in writing, however, that interest shall be paid on the Funds. Lender shall give to Borrower, without charge, an annual accounting of the Funds as required by RESPA.

If there is a surplus of Funds held in escrow, as defined under RESPA, Lender shall account to Borrower for the excess funds in accordance with RESPA. If there is a shortage of Funds held in escrow, as defined under RESPA, Lender shall notify Borrower as required by RESPA, and Borrower shall pay to Lender the amount necessary to make up the shortage in accordance with RESPA, but in no more than 12 monthly payments. If there is a deficiency of Funds held in escrow, as defined under RESPA, Lender shall notify Borrower as required by RESPA, and Borrower shall pay to Lender the amount necessary to make up the deficiency in accordance with RESPA, but in no more than 12 monthly payments.

Upon payment in full of all sums secured by this Security Instrument, Lender shall promptly refund to Borrower any Funds held by Lender.

4. **Charges; Liens.** Borrower shall pay all taxes, assessments, charges, fines, and impositions attributable to the Property which can attain priority over this Security Instrument, leasehold payments or ground rents on the Property, if any, and Community Association Dues, Fees, and Assessments, if any. To the extent that these items are Escrow Items, Borrower shall pay them in the manner provided in Section 3.

Borrower shall promptly discharge any lien which has priority over this Security Instrument unless Borrower: (a) agrees in writing to the payment of the obligation secured by the lien in a manner acceptable to Lender, but only so long as Borrower is performing such agreement; (b) contests the lien in good faith by, or defends against enforcement of the lien in, legal proceedings which in Lender's opinion operate to prevent the enforcement of the lien while those proceedings are pending, but only until such proceedings are concluded; or (c) secures from the holder of the lien an agreement satisfactory to Lender subordinating the lien to this Security Instrument. If Lender determines that any part of the Property is subject to a lien which can attain priority over this Security Instrument, Lender may give Borrower a notice identifying the lien. Within 10 days of the date on which that notice is given, Borrower shall satisfy the lien or take one or more of the actions set forth above in this Section 4.

Lender may require Borrower to pay a one-time charge for a real estate tax verification and/or reporting service used by Lender in connection with this Loan.

5. **Property Insurance.** Borrower shall keep the improvements now existing or hereafter erected on the Property insured against loss by fire, hazards included within the term "extended coverage," and any other hazards including, but not limited to, earthquakes and floods, for which Lender requires insurance. This insurance shall be maintained in the amounts (including deductible levels) and for the periods that Lender requires. What Lender requires pursuant to the preceding sentences can change during the term of the Loan. The insurance carrier providing the insurance shall be chosen by Borrower subject to Lender's right to disapprove Borrower's choice, which right shall not be exercised unreasonably. Lender may require Borrower to pay, in connection with this Loan, either: (a) a one-time charge for flood zone determination, certification and tracking services; or (b) a one-time charge for flood zone determination and certification services and subsequent charges each time remappings or similar changes occur which reasonably might affect such determination or certification. Borrower shall also be responsible for the payment of any fees imposed by the Federal Emergency Management Agency in connection with the review of any flood zone determination resulting from an objection by Borrower.

If Borrower fails to maintain any of the coverages described above, Lender may obtain insurance coverage, at Lender's option and Borrower's expense. Lender is under no obligation to purchase any particular type or amount of coverage. Therefore, such coverage shall cover Lender, but might or might not protect Borrower, Borrower's equity in the Property, or the contents of the Property, against any risk, hazard or liability and might provide greater or lesser coverage than was previously in effect. Borrower acknowledges that the cost of the insurance coverage so obtained might significantly exceed the cost of insurance that Borrower could have obtained. Any amounts disbursed by Lender under this Section 5 shall become additional debt of Borrower secured by this Security Instrument. These amounts shall bear interest at the Note rate from the date of disbursement and shall be payable, with such interest, upon notice from Lender to Borrower requesting payment.

All insurance policies required by Lender and renewals of such policies shall be subject to Lender's right to disapprove such policies, shall include a standard mortgage clause, and shall name Lender as mortgagee and/or as an additional loss payee. Lender shall have the right to hold the policies and renewal certificates. If Lender requires, Borrower shall promptly give to Lender all receipts of paid premiums and renewal notices. If Borrower obtains any form of insurance coverage, not otherwise required by Lender, for damage to, or destruction of, the Property, such policy shall include a standard mortgage clause and shall name Lender as mortgagee and/or as an additional loss payee.

In the event of loss, Borrower shall give prompt notice to the insurance carrier and Lender. Lender may make proof of loss if not made promptly by Borrower. Unless Lender and Borrower otherwise agree in writing, any insurance proceeds, whether or not the underlying insurance was required by Lender, shall be applied to restoration or repair of the Property, if the restoration or repair is economically feasible and Lender's security is not lessened. During such repair and restoration period, Lender shall have the right to hold such insurance proceeds until Lender has had an opportunity to inspect such Property to ensure the work has been completed to Lender's satisfaction, provided that such inspection shall be undertaken promptly. Lender may disburse proceeds for the repairs and restoration in a single payment or in a series of progress payments as the work is completed. Unless an

MASSACHUSETTS--Single Family--Fannie Mae/Freddie Mac UNIFORM INSTRUMENT   **Form 3022**   **1/01**   *(page 6 of 16 pages)*

311

agreement is made in writing or Applicable Law requires interest to be paid on such insurance proceeds, Lender shall not be required to pay Borrower any interest or earnings on such proceeds. Fees for public adjusters, or other third parties, retained by Borrower shall not be paid out of the insurance proceeds and shall be the sole obligation of Borrower. If the restoration or repair is not economically feasible or Lender's security would be lessened, the insurance proceeds shall be applied to the sums secured by this Security Instrument, whether or not then due, with the excess, if any, paid to Borrower. Such insurance proceeds shall be applied in the order provided for in Section 2.

If Borrower abandons the Property, Lender may file, negotiate and settle any available insurance claim and related matters. If Borrower does not respond within 30 days to a notice from Lender that the insurance carrier has offered to settle a claim, then Lender may negotiate and settle the claim. The 30-day period will begin when the notice is given. In either event, or if Lender acquires the Property under Section 22 or otherwise, Borrower hereby assigns to Lender (a) Borrower's rights to any insurance proceeds in an amount not to exceed the amounts unpaid under the Note or this Security Instrument, and (b) any other of Borrower's rights (other than the right to any refund of unearned premiums paid by Borrower) under all insurance policies covering the Property, insofar as such rights are applicable to the coverage of the Property. Lender may use the insurance proceeds either to repair or restore the Property or to pay amounts unpaid under the Note or this Security Instrument, whether or not then due.

6.   **Occupancy.**   Borrower shall occupy, establish, and use the Property as Borrower's principal residence within 60 days after the execution of this Security Instrument and shall continue to occupy the Property as Borrower's principal residence for at least one year after the date of occupancy, unless Lender otherwise agrees in writing, which consent shall not be unreasonably withheld, or unless extenuating circumstances exist which are beyond Borrower's control.

7.   **Preservation, Maintenance and Protection of the Property; Inspections.** Borrower shall not destroy, damage or impair the Property, allow the Property to deteriorate or commit waste on the Property. Whether or not Borrower is residing in the Property, Borrower shall maintain the Property in order to prevent the Property from deteriorating or decreasing in value due to its condition. Unless it is determined pursuant to Section 5 that repair or restoration is not economically feasible, Borrower shall promptly repair the Property if damaged to avoid further deterioration or damage. If insurance or condemnation proceeds are paid in connection with damage to, or the taking of, the Property, Borrower shall be responsible for repairing or restoring the Property only if Lender has released proceeds for such purposes. Lender may disburse proceeds for the repairs and restoration in a single payment or in a series of progress payments as the work is completed. If the insurance or condemnation proceeds are not sufficient to repair or restore the Property, Borrower is not relieved of Borrower's obligation for the completion of such repair or restoration.

MASSACHUSETTS--Single Family--Fannie Mae/Freddie Mac UNIFORM INSTRUMENT   Form 3022   1/01   *(page 7 of 16 pages)*

Lender or its agent may make reasonable entries upon and inspections of the Property. If it has reasonable cause, Lender may inspect the interior of the improvements on the Property. Lender shall give Borrower notice at the time of or prior to such an interior inspection specifying such reasonable cause.

8.   Borrower's Loan Application.   Borrower shall be in default if, during the Loan application process, Borrower or any persons or entities acting at the direction of Borrower or with Borrower's knowledge or consent gave materially false, misleading, or inaccurate information or statements to Lender (or failed to provide Lender with material information) in connection with the Loan. Material representations include, but are not limited to, representations concerning Borrower's occupancy of the Property as Borrower's principal residence.

9.   Protection of Lender's Interest in the Property and Rights Under this Security Instrument.   If (a) Borrower fails to perform the covenants and agreements contained in this Security Instrument, (b) there is a legal proceeding that might significantly affect Lender's interest in the Property and/or rights under this Security Instrument (such as a proceeding in bankruptcy, probate, for condemnation or forfeiture, for enforcement of a lien which may attain priority over this Security Instrument or to enforce laws or regulations), or (c) Borrower has abandoned the Property, then Lender may do and pay for whatever is reasonable or appropriate to protect Lender's interest in the Property and rights under this Security Instrument, including protecting and/or assessing the value of the Property, and securing and/or repairing the Property. Lender's actions can include, but are not limited to: (a) paying any sums secured by a lien which has priority over this Security Instrument; (b) appearing in court; and (c) paying reasonable attorneys' fees to protect its interest in the Property and/or rights under this Security Instrument, including its secured position in a bankruptcy proceeding. Securing the Property includes, but is not limited to, entering the Property to make repairs, change locks, replace or board up doors and windows, drain water from pipes, eliminate building or other code violations or dangerous conditions, and have utilities turned on or off. Although Lender may take action under this Section 9, Lender does not have to do so and is not under any duty or obligation to do so. It is agreed that Lender incurs no liability for not taking any or all actions authorized under this Section 9.

Any amounts disbursed by Lender under this Section 9 shall become additional debt of Borrower secured by this Security Instrument. These amounts shall bear interest at the Note rate from the date of disbursement and shall be payable, with such interest, upon notice from Lender to Borrower requesting payment.

If this Security Instrument is on a leasehold, Borrower shall comply with all the provisions of the lease. If Borrower acquires fee title to the Property, the leasehold and the fee title shall not merge unless Lender agrees to the merger in writing.

10. Mortgage Insurance. If Lender required Mortgage Insurance as a condition of making the Loan, Borrower shall pay the premiums required to maintain the Mortgage Insurance in effect. If, for any reason, the Mortgage Insurance coverage required by Lender ceases to be available from the mortgage insurer that previously provided such insurance and Borrower was required to make separately designated payments toward the premiums for Mortgage Insurance, Borrower shall pay the premiums required to obtain coverage substantially equivalent to the Mortgage Insurance previously in effect, at a cost substantially equivalent to the cost to Borrower of the Mortgage Insurance previously in effect, from an alternate mortgage insurer selected by Lender. If substantially equivalent Mortgage Insurance

MASSACHUSETTS--Single Family--Fannie Mae/Freddie Mac UNIFORM INSTRUMENT   Form 3022   1/01   *(page 8 of 16 pages)*

coverage is not available, Borrower shall continue to pay to Lender the amount of the separately designated payments that were due when the insurance coverage ceased to be in effect. Lender will accept, use and retain these payments as a non-refundable loss reserve in lieu of Mortgage Insurance. Such loss reserve shall be non-refundable, notwithstanding the fact that the Loan is ultimately paid in full, and Lender shall not be required to pay Borrower any interest or earnings on such loss reserve. Lender can no longer require loss reserve payments if Mortgage Insurance coverage (in the amount and for the period that Lender requires) provided by an insurer selected by Lender again becomes available, is obtained, and Lender requires separately designated payments toward the premiums for Mortgage Insurance. If Lender required Mortgage Insurance as a condition of making the Loan and Borrower was required to make separately designated payments toward the premiums for Mortgage Insurance, Borrower shall pay the premiums required to maintain Mortgage Insurance in effect, or to provide a non-refundable loss reserve, until Lender's requirement for Mortgage Insurance ends in accordance with any written agreement between Borrower and Lender providing for such termination or until termination is required by Applicable Law. Nothing in this Section 10 affects Borrower's obligation to pay interest at the rate provided in the Note.

Mortgage Insurance reimburses Lender (or any entity that purchases the Note) for certain losses it may incur if Borrower does not repay the Loan as agreed. Borrower is not a party to the Mortgage Insurance.

Mortgage insurers evaluate their total risk on all such insurance in force from time to time, and may enter into agreements with other parties that share or modify their risk, or reduce losses. These agreements are on terms and conditions that are satisfactory to the mortgage insurer and the other party (or parties) to these agreements. These agreements may require the mortgage insurer to make payments using any source of funds that the mortgage insurer may have available (which may include funds obtained from Mortgage Insurance premiums).

314

As a result of these agreements, Lender, any purchaser of the Note, another insurer, any reinsurer, any other entity, or any affiliate of any of the foregoing, may receive (directly or indirectly) amounts that derive from (or might be characterized as) a portion of Borrower's payments for Mortgage Insurance, in exchange for sharing or modifying the mortgage insurer's risk, or reducing losses. If such agreement provides that an affiliate of Lender takes a share of the insurer's risk in exchange for a share of the premiums paid to the insurer, the arrangement is often termed "captive reinsurance." Further:

   (a)   **Any such agreements will not affect the amounts that Borrower has agreed to pay for Mortgage Insurance, or any other terms of the Loan. Such agreements will not increase the amount Borrower will owe for Mortgage Insurance, and they will not entitle Borrower to any refund.**

   (b)   **Any such agreements will not affect the rights Borrower has - if any - with respect to the Mortgage Insurance under the Homeowners Protection Act of 1998 or any other law. These rights may include the right to receive certain disclosures, to request and obtain cancellation of the Mortgage Insurance, to have the Mortgage Insurance terminated automatically, and/or to receive a refund of any Mortgage Insurance premiums that were unearned at the time of such cancellation or termination.**

MASSACHUSETTS--Single Family--Fannie Mae/Freddie Mac UNIFORM INSTRUMENT   **Form 3022**   **1/01**   *(page 9 of 16 pages)*

315

11.   Assignment of Miscellaneous Proceeds; Forfeiture.   All Miscellaneous Proceeds are hereby assigned to and shall be paid to Lender.

If the Property is damaged, such Miscellaneous Proceeds shall be applied to restoration or repair of the Property, if the restoration or repair is economically feasible and Lender's security is not lessened. During such repair and restoration period, Lender shall have the right to hold such Miscellaneous Proceeds until Lender has had an opportunity to inspect such Property to ensure the work has been completed to Lender's satisfaction, provided that such inspection shall be undertaken promptly. Lender may pay for the repairs and restoration in a single disbursement or in a series of progress payments as the work is completed. Unless an agreement is made in writing or Applicable Law requires interest to be paid on such Miscellaneous Proceeds, Lender shall not be required to pay Borrower any interest or earnings on such Miscellaneous Proceeds. If the restoration or repair is not economically feasible or Lender's security would be lessened, the Miscellaneous Proceeds shall be applied to the sums secured by this Security Instrument, whether or not then due, with the excess, if any, paid to Borrower. Such Miscellaneous Proceeds shall be applied in the order provided for in Section 2.

In the event of a total taking, destruction, or loss in value of the Property, the Miscellaneous Proceeds shall be applied to the sums secured by this Security Instrument, whether or not then due, with the excess, if any, paid to Borrower.

In the event of a partial taking, destruction, or loss in value of the Property in which the fair market value of the Property immediately before the partial taking, destruction, or loss in value is equal to or greater than the amount of the sums secured by this Security Instrument immediately before the partial taking, destruction, or loss in value, unless Borrower and Lender otherwise agree in writing, the sums secured by this Security Instrument shall be reduced by the amount of the Miscellaneous Proceeds multiplied by the following fraction: (a) the total amount of the sums secured immediately before the partial taking, destruction, or loss in value divided by (b) the fair market value of the Property immediately before the partial taking, destruction, or loss in value. Any balance shall be paid to Borrower.

In the event of a partial taking, destruction, or loss in value of the Property in which the fair market value of the Property immediately before the partial taking, destruction, or loss in value is less than the amount of the sums secured immediately before the partial taking, destruction, or loss in value, unless Borrower and Lender otherwise agree in writing, the Miscellaneous Proceeds shall be applied to the sums secured by this Security Instrument whether or not the sums are then due.

If the Property is abandoned by Borrower, or if, after notice by Lender to Borrower that the Opposing Party (as defined in the next sentence) offers to make an award to settle a claim for damages, Borrower fails to respond to Lender within 30 days after the date the notice is given, Lender is authorized to collect and apply the Miscellaneous Proceeds either to restoration or repair of the Property or to the sums secured by this Security Instrument, whether or not then due. "Opposing Party" means the third party that owes Borrower Miscellaneous Proceeds or the party against whom Borrower has a right of action in regard to Miscellaneous Proceeds.

Borrower shall be in default if any action or proceeding, whether civil or criminal, is begun that, in Lender's judgment, could result in forfeiture of the Property or other material impairment of Lender's interest in the Property or rights under this Security Instrument. Borrower can cure such a default and, if acceleration has occurred, reinstate as provided in Section 19, by causing the action or proceeding to be dismissed with a ruling that, in Lender's judgment, precludes forfeiture of the Property or other material impairment of Lender's interest in the Property or rights under this Security Instrument. The proceeds of any award or claim for damages that are attributable to the impairment of Lender's interest in the Property are hereby assigned and shall be paid to Lender.

All Miscellaneous Proceeds that are not applied to restoration or repair of the Property shall be applied in the order provided for in Section 2.

12.   Borrower Not Released; Forbearance By Lender Not a Waiver. Extension of the time for payment or modification of amortization of the sums secured by this Security Instrument granted by Lender to Borrower or any Successor in Interest of Borrower shall not operate to release the liability of Borrower or any Successors in Interest of Borrower. Lender shall not be required to commence proceedings against any Successor in Interest of Borrower or to refuse to extend time for payment or otherwise modify amortization of the sums secured by this Security Instrument by reason of any demand made by the original Borrower or any Successors in Interest of Borrower. Any forbearance by Lender in exercising any right or remedy including, without limitation, Lender's acceptance of payments from third persons, entities or Successors in Interest of Borrower or in amounts less than the amount then due, shall not be a waiver of or preclude the exercise of any right or remedy.

13.   Joint and Several Liability; Co-signers; Successors and Assigns Bound. Borrower covenants and agrees that Borrower's obligations and liability shall be joint and several. However, any Borrower who co-signs this Security Instrument but does not execute the Note (a "co-signer"): (a) is co-signing this Security Instrument only to mortgage, grant and convey the co-signer's interest in the Property under the terms of this Security Instrument; (b) is not personally obligated to pay the sums secured by this Security Instrument; and (c) agrees that Lender and any other Borrower can agree to extend, modify, forbear or make any accommodations with regard to the terms of this Security Instrument or the Note without the co-signer's consent.

Subject to the provisions of Section 18, any Successor in Interest of Borrower who assumes Borrower's obligations under this Security Instrument in writing, and is approved by Lender, shall obtain all of Borrower's rights and benefits under this Security Instrument. Borrower shall not be released from Borrower's obligations and liability under this Security Instrument unless Lender agrees to such release in writing. The covenants and agreements of this Security Instrument shall bind (except as provided in Section 20) and benefit the successors and assigns of Lender.

14. **Loan Charges.** Lender may charge Borrower fees for services performed in connection with Borrower's default, for the purpose of protecting Lender's interest in the Property and rights under this Security Instrument, including, but not limited to, attorneys' fees, property inspection and valuation fees. In regard to any other fees, the absence of express authority in this Security Instrument to charge a specific fee to Borrower shall not be construed as a prohibition on the charging of such fee. Lender may not charge fees that are expressly prohibited by this Security Instrument or by Applicable Law.

MASSACHUSETTS--Single Family--Fannie Mae/Freddie Mac UNIFORM INSTRUMENT   Form 3022   1/01   *(page 11 of 16 pages)*

If the Loan is subject to a law which sets maximum loan charges, and that law is finally interpreted so that the interest or other loan charges collected or to be collected in connection with the Loan exceed the permitted limits, then: (a) any such loan charge shall be reduced by the amount necessary to reduce the charge to the permitted limit; and (b) any sums already collected from Borrower which exceeded permitted limits will be refunded to Borrower. Lender may choose to make this refund by reducing the principal owed under the Note or by making a direct payment to Borrower. If a refund reduces principal, the reduction will be treated as a partial prepayment without any prepayment charge (whether or not a prepayment charge is provided for under the Note). Borrower's acceptance of any such refund made by direct payment to Borrower will constitute a waiver of any right of action Borrower might have arising out of such overcharge.

15. Notices. All notices given by Borrower or Lender in connection with this Security Instrument must be in writing. Any notice to Borrower in connection with this Security Instrument shall be deemed to have been given to Borrower when mailed by first class mail or when actually delivered to Borrower's notice address if sent by other means. Notice to any one Borrower shall constitute notice to all Borrowers unless Applicable Law expressly requires otherwise. The notice address shall be the Property Address unless Borrower has designated a substitute notice address by notice to Lender. Borrower shall promptly notify Lender of Borrower's change of address. If Lender specifies a procedure for reporting Borrower's change of address, then Borrower shall only report a change of address through that specified procedure. There may be only one designated notice address under this Security Instrument at any one time. Any notice to Lender shall be given by delivering it or by mailing it by first class mail to Lender's address stated herein unless Lender has designated another address by notice to Borrower. Any notice in connection with this Security Instrument shall not be deemed to have been given to Lender until actually received by Lender. If any notice required by this Security Instrument is also required under Applicable Law, the Applicable Law requirement will satisfy the corresponding requirement under this Security Instrument.

16. Governing Law; Severability; Rules of Construction. This Security Instrument shall be governed by federal law and the law of the jurisdiction in which the Property is located. All rights and obligations contained in this Security Instrument are subject to any requirements and limitations of Applicable Law. Applicable Law might explicitly or implicitly allow the parties to agree by contract or it might be silent, but such silence shall not be construed as a prohibition against agreement by contract. In the event that any provision or clause of this Security Instrument or the Note conflicts with Applicable Law, such conflict shall not affect other provisions of this Security Instrument or the Note which can be given effect without the conflicting provision.

320

As used in this Security Instrument: (a) words of the masculine gender shall mean and include corresponding neuter words or words of the feminine gender; (b) words in the singular shall mean and include the plural and vice versa; and (c) the word "may" gives sole discretion without any obligation to take any action.

    17.   **Borrower's Copy.**   Borrower shall be given one copy of the Note and of this Security Instrument.

18. Transfer of the Property or a Beneficial Interest in Borrower. As used in this Section 18, "Interest in the Property" means any legal or beneficial interest in the Property, including, but not limited to, those beneficial interests transferred in a bond for deed, contract for deed, installment sales contract or escrow agreement, the intent of which is the transfer of title by Borrower at a future date to a purchaser.

If all or any part of the Property or any Interest in the Property is sold or transferred (or if Borrower is not a natural person and a beneficial interest in Borrower is sold or transferred) without Lender's prior written consent, Lender may require immediate payment in full of all sums secured by this Security Instrument. However, this option shall not be exercised by Lender if such exercise is prohibited by Applicable Law.

If Lender exercises this option, Lender shall give Borrower notice of acceleration. The notice shall provide a period of not less than 30 days from the date the notice is given in accordance with Section 15 within which Borrower must pay all sums secured by this Security Instrument. If Borrower fails to pay these sums prior to the expiration of this period, Lender may invoke any remedies permitted by this Security Instrument without further notice or demand on Borrower.

19. Borrower's Right to Reinstate After Acceleration. If Borrower meets certain conditions, Borrower shall have the right to have enforcement of this Security Instrument discontinued at any time prior to the earliest of: (a) five days before sale of the Property pursuant to any power of sale contained in this Security Instrument; (b) such other period as Applicable Law might specify for the termination of Borrower's right to reinstate; or (c) entry of a judgment enforcing this Security Instrument. Those conditions are that Borrower: (a) pays Lender all sums which then would be due under this Security Instrument and the Note as if no acceleration had occurred; (b) cures any default of any other covenants or agreements; (c) pays all expenses incurred in enforcing this Security Instrument, including, but not limited to, reasonable attorneys' fees, property inspection and valuation fees, and other fees incurred for the purpose of protecting Lender's interest in the Property and rights under this Security Instrument; and (d) takes such action as Lender may reasonably require to assure that Lender's interest in the Property and rights under this Security Instrument, and Borrower's obligation to pay the sums secured by this Security Instrument, shall continue unchanged. Lender may require that Borrower pay such reinstatement sums and expenses in one or more of the following forms, as selected by Lender: (a) cash; (b) money order; (c) certified check, bank check, treasurer's check or cashier's check, provided any such check is drawn upon an institution whose deposits are insured by a federal agency, instrumentality or entity; or (d) Electronic Funds Transfer. Upon reinstatement by Borrower, this Security Instrument and obligations secured hereby shall remain fully effective as if no acceleration had occurred. However, this right to reinstate shall not apply in the case of acceleration under Section 18.

20. Sale of Note; Change of Loan Servicer; Notice of Grievance. The Note or a partial interest in the Note (together with this Security Instrument) can be sold one or more times without prior notice to Borrower. A sale might result in a change in the entity (known as the "Loan Servicer") that collects Periodic Payments due under the Note and this Security Instrument and performs other mortgage loan servicing obligations under the Note, this Security Instrument, and Applicable Law. There also might be one or more changes of the Loan Servicer unrelated to a sale of the Note. If there is a change of the Loan Servicer, Borrower will be given written notice of the change which will state the name and address of

MASSACHUSETTS--Single Family--**Fannie Mae/Freddie Mac UNIFORM INSTRUMENT**   Form 3022   1/01   *(page 13 of 16 pages)*

the new Loan Servicer, the address to which payments should be made and any other information RESPA requires in connection with a notice of transfer of servicing. If the Note is sold and thereafter the Loan is serviced by a Loan Servicer other than the purchaser of the Note, the mortgage loan servicing obligations to Borrower will remain with the Loan Servicer or be transferred to a successor Loan Servicer and are not assumed by the Note purchaser unless otherwise provided by the Note purchaser.

Neither Borrower nor Lender may commence, join, or be joined to any judicial action (as either an individual litigant or the member of a class) that arises from the other party's actions pursuant to this Security Instrument or that alleges that the other party has breached any provision of, or any duty owed by reason of, this Security Instrument, until such Borrower or Lender has notified the other party (with such notice given in compliance with the requirements of Section 15) of such alleged breach and afforded the other party hereto a reasonable period after the giving of such notice to take corrective action. If Applicable Law provides a time period which must elapse before certain action can be taken, that time period will be deemed to be reasonable for purposes of this paragraph. The notice of acceleration and opportunity to cure given to Borrower pursuant to Section 22 and the notice of acceleration given to Borrower pursuant to Section 18 shall be deemed to satisfy the notice and opportunity to take corrective action provisions of this Section 20.

21. Hazardous Substances. As used in this Section 21: (a) "Hazardous Substances" are those substances defined as toxic or hazardous substances, pollutants, or wastes by Environmental Law and the following substances: gasoline, kerosene, other flammable or toxic petroleum products, toxic pesticides and herbicides, volatile solvents, materials containing asbestos or formaldehyde, and radioactive materials; (b) "Environmental Law" means federal laws and laws of the jurisdiction where the Property is located that relate to health, safety or environmental protection; (c) "Environmental Cleanup" includes any response action, remedial action, or removal action, as defined in Environmental Law; and (d) an "Environmental Condition" means a condition that can cause, contribute to, or otherwise trigger an Environmental Cleanup.

Borrower shall not cause or permit the presence, use, disposal, storage, or release of any Hazardous Substances, or threaten to release any Hazardous Substances, on or in the Property. Borrower shall not do, nor allow anyone else to do, anything affecting the Property (a) that is in violation of any Environmental Law, (b) which creates an Environmental Condition, or (c) which, due to the presence, use, or release of a Hazardous Substance, creates a condition that adversely affects the value of the Property. The preceding two sentences shall not apply to the presence, use, or storage on the Property of small quantities of Hazardous Substances that are generally recognized to be appropriate to normal residential uses and to maintenance of the Property (including, but not limited to, hazardous substances in consumer products).

Borrower shall promptly give Lender written notice of (a) any investigation, claim, demand, lawsuit or other action by any governmental or regulatory agency or private party involving the Property and any Hazardous Substance or Environmental Law of which Borrower has actual knowledge, (b) any Environmental Condition, including but not limited to, any spilling, leaking, discharge, release or threat of release of any Hazardous Substance, and (c) any condition caused by the presence, use or release of a Hazardous Substance which adversely affects the value of the Property. If Borrower learns, or is notified by any governmental or regulatory authority, or any private party, that any removal or other

MASSACHUSETTS--Single Family--**Fannie Mae/Freddie Mac UNIFORM INSTRUMENT**   **Form 3022**   1/01   *(page 14 of 16 pages)*

remediation of any Hazardous Substance affecting the Property is necessary, Borrower shall promptly take all necessary remedial actions in accordance with Environmental Law. Nothing herein shall create any obligation on Lender for an Environmental Cleanup.

NON-UNIFORM COVENANTS. Borrower and Lender further covenant and agree as follows:

22. Acceleration; Remedies. Lender shall give notice to Borrower prior to acceleration following Borrower's breach of any covenant or agreement in this Security Instrument (but not prior to acceleration under Section 18 unless Applicable Law provides otherwise). The notice shall specify: (a) the default; (b) the action required to cure the default; (c) a date, not less than 30 days from the date the notice is given to Borrower, by which the default must be cured; and (d) that failure to cure the default on or before the date specified in the notice may result in acceleration of the sums secured by this Security Instrument and sale of the Property. The notice shall further inform Borrower of the right to reinstate after acceleration and the right to bring a court action to assert the non-existence of a default or any other defense of Borrower to acceleration and sale. If the default is not cured on or before the date specified in the notice, Lender at its option may require immediate payment in full of all sums secured by this Security Instrument without further demand and may invoke the STATUTORY POWER OF SALE and any other remedies permitted by Applicable Law. Lender shall be entitled to collect all expenses incurred in pursuing the remedies provided in this Section 22, including, but not limited to, reasonable attorneys' fees and costs of title evidence.

If Lender invokes the STATUTORY POWER OF SALE, Lender shall mail a copy of a notice of sale to Borrower, and to other persons prescribed by Applicable Law, in the manner provided by Applicable Law. Lender shall publish the notice of sale, and the Property shall be sold in the manner prescribed by Applicable Law. Lender or its designee may purchase the Property at any sale. The proceeds of the sale shall be applied in the following order: (a) to all expenses of the sale, including, but not limited to, reasonable attorneys' fees; (b) to all sums secured by this Security Instrument; and (c) any excess to the person or persons legally entitled to it.

23. Release. Upon payment of all sums secured by this Security Instrument, Lender shall discharge this Security Instrument. Borrower shall pay any recordation costs. Lender may charge Borrower a fee for releasing this Security Instrument, but only if the fee is paid to a third party for services rendered and the charging of the fee is permitted under Applicable Law.

24. Waivers. Borrower waives all rights of homestead exemption in the Property and relinquishes all rights of curtesy and dower in the Property.

MASSACHUSETTS--Single Family--Fannie Mae/Freddie Mac UNIFORM INSTRUMENT   Form 3022   1/01   *(page 15 of 16 pages)*

BY SIGNING BELOW, Borrower accepts and agrees to the terms and covenants contained in this Security Instrument and in any Rider executed by Borrower and recorded with it.

Witnesses:

_____   _____(Seal)
                                                        - Borrower

_____   _____(Seal)
                                                        - Borrower

_____**[Space Below This Line For Acknowledgment]**_____

9. DEED OF TRUST

After Recording Return To:

_____

_____

_____

_____

_____[Space Above This Line For Recording Data]_____

DEED OF TRUST

DEFINITIONS

Words used in multiple sections of this document are defined below and other words are defined in Sections 3, 11, 13, 18, 20 and 21. Certain rules regarding the usage of words used in this document are also provided in Section 16.

(A) **"Security Instrument"** means this document, which is dated _____, _____, together with all Riders to this document.

(B) "Borrower" is _____. Borrower is the trustor under this Security Instrument.

(C) **"Lender"** is _____. Lender is a _____ organized and existing under the laws of _____. Lender's address is _____ _____. Lender is the beneficiary under this Security Instrument.

(D) **"Trustee"** is _____.

(E) **"Note"** means the promissory note signed by Borrower and dated _____, _____. The Note states that Borrower owes Lender _____ _____ Dollars (U.S. $_____) plus interest. Borrower has promised to pay this debt in regular Periodic Payments and to pay the debt in full not later than _____.

(F) **"Property"** means the property that is described below under the heading "Transfer of Rights in the Property."

(G) **"Loan"** means the debt evidenced by the Note, plus interest, any prepayment charges and late charges due under the Note, and all sums due under this Security Instrument, plus interest.

(H) **"Riders"** means all Riders to this Security Instrument that are executed by Borrower. The following Riders are to be executed by Borrower [check box as applicable]:

☐ Adjustable Rate Rider   ☐ Condominium Rider   ☐ Second Home Rider
☐ Balloon Rider   ☐ Planned Unit Development Rider   ☐ Other(s) [specify] _____
☐ 1-4 Family Rider   ☐ Biweekly Payment Rider

CALIFORNIA--Single Family--**Fannie Mae/Freddie Mac UNIFORM INSTRUMENT**   **Form 3005**   **1/01**   *(page 1 of 16 pages)*

(I) **"Applicable Law"** means all controlling applicable federal, state and local statutes, regulations, ordinances and administrative rules and orders (that have the effect of law) as well as all applicable final, non-appealable judicial opinions.

(J) **"Community Association Dues, Fees, and Assessments"** means all dues, fees, assessments and other charges that are imposed on Borrower or the Property by a condominium association, homeowners association or similar organization.

(K) **"Electronic Funds Transfer"** means any transfer of funds, other than a transaction originated by check, draft, or similar paper instrument, which is initiated through an electronic terminal, telephonic instrument, computer, or magnetic tape so as to order, instruct, or authorize a financial institution to debit or credit an account. Such term includes, but is not limited to, point-of-sale transfers, automated teller machine transactions, transfers initiated by telephone, wire transfers, and automated clearinghouse transfers.

(L) **"Escrow Items"** means those items that are described in Section 3.

(M) **"Miscellaneous Proceeds"** means any compensation, settlement, award of damages, or proceeds paid by any third party (other than insurance proceeds paid under the coverages described in Section 5) for: (i) damage to, or destruction of, the Property; (ii) condemnation or other taking of all or any part of the Property; (iii) conveyance in lieu of condemnation; or (iv) misrepresentations of, or omissions as to, the value and/or condition of the Property.

(N) **"Mortgage Insurance"** means insurance protecting Lender against the nonpayment of, or default on, the Loan.

(O) **"Periodic Payment"** means the regularly scheduled amount due for (i) principal and interest under the Note, plus (ii) any amounts under Section 3 of this Security Instrument.

(P) **"RESPA"** means the Real Estate Settlement Procedures Act (12 U.S.C. §2601 et seq.) and its implementing regulation, Regulation X (24 C.F.R. Part 3500), as they might be amended from time to time, or any additional or successor legislation or regulation that governs the same subject matter. As used in this Security Instrument, "RESPA" refers to all requirements and restrictions that are imposed in regard to a "federally related mortgage loan" even if the Loan does not qualify as a "federally related mortgage loan" under RESPA.

(Q) **"Successor in Interest of Borrower"** means any party that has taken title to the Property, whether or not that party has assumed Borrower's obligations under the Note and/or this Security Instrument.

TRANSFER OF RIGHTS IN THE PROPERTY

This Security Instrument secures to Lender: (i) the repayment of the Loan, and all renewals, extensions and modifications of the Note; and (ii) the performance of Borrower's covenants and agreements under this Security Instrument and the Note. For this purpose, Borrower irrevocably grants and conveys to Trustee, in trust, with power of sale, the following described property located in the _____ of _____:

       [Type of Recording Jurisdiction]   [Name of Recording Jurisdiction]

CALIFORNIA--Single Family--Fannie Mae/Freddie Mac UNIFORM INSTRUMENT   Form 3005   1/01   *(page 2 of 16 pages)*

which currently has the address of _____

[Street]

_____, California _____ ("Property Address"):

[City]   [Zip Code]

TOGETHER WITH all the improvements now or hereafter erected on the property, and all easements, appurtenances, and fixtures now or hereafter a part of the property. All replacements and additions shall also be covered by this Security Instrument. All of the foregoing is referred to in this Security Instrument as the "Property."

BORROWER COVENANTS that Borrower is lawfully seised of the estate hereby conveyed and has the right to grant and convey the Property and that the Property is unencumbered, except for encumbrances of record. Borrower warrants and will defend generally the title to the Property against all claims and demands, subject to any encumbrances of record.

THIS SECURITY INSTRUMENT combines uniform covenants for national use and non-uniform covenants with limited variations by jurisdiction to constitute a uniform security instrument covering real property.

UNIFORM COVENANTS. Borrower and Lender covenant and agree as follows:

1.   **Payment of Principal, Interest, Escrow Items, Prepayment Charges, and Late Charges.** Borrower shall pay when due the principal of, and interest on, the debt evidenced by the Note and any prepayment charges and late charges due under the Note. Borrower shall also pay funds for Escrow Items pursuant to Section 3. Payments due under the Note and this Security Instrument shall be made in U.S. currency. However, if any check or other instrument received by Lender as payment under the Note or this Security Instrument is returned to Lender unpaid, Lender may require that any or all subsequent payments due under the Note and this Security Instrument be made in one or more of the following forms, as selected by Lender: (a) cash; (b) money order; (c) certified check, bank check, treasurer's check or cashier's check, provided any such check is drawn upon an institution whose deposits are insured by a federal agency, instrumentality, or entity; or (d) Electronic Funds Transfer.

Payments are deemed received by Lender when received at the location designated in the Note or at such other location as may be designated by Lender in accordance with the notice provisions in Section 15. Lender may return any payment or partial payment if the payment or partial payments are insufficient to bring the Loan current. Lender may accept any payment or partial payment insufficient to bring the Loan current, without waiver of any rights hereunder or prejudice to its rights to refuse such payment or partial payments in the future, but Lender is not obligated to apply such payments at the time such payments are accepted. If each Periodic Payment is applied as of its scheduled due date, then Lender need not pay interest on unapplied funds. Lender may hold such unapplied funds until Borrower makes payment to bring the Loan current. If Borrower does not do so within a reasonable period of time, Lender shall either apply such funds or return them to Borrower. If not applied earlier, such funds will be applied to the outstanding principal balance under the Note immediately prior to foreclosure. No offset or claim which Borrower might have now or in the future against Lender shall relieve Borrower

CALIFORNIA--Single Family--Fannie Mae/Freddie Mac UNIFORM INSTRUMENT   Form 3005   1/01   *(page 3 of 16 pages)*

from making payments due under the Note and this Security Instrument or performing the covenants and agreements secured by this Security Instrument.

    2.   Application of Payments or Proceeds. Except as otherwise described in this Section 2, all payments accepted and applied by Lender shall be applied in the following order of priority: (a) interest due under the Note; (b) principal due under the Note; (c) amounts due under Section 3. Such payments shall be applied to each Periodic Payment in the order in which it became due. Any remaining amounts shall be applied first to late charges, second to any other amounts due under this Security Instrument, and then to reduce the principal balance of the Note.

    If Lender receives a payment from Borrower for a delinquent Periodic Payment which includes a sufficient amount to pay any late charge due, the payment may be applied to the delinquent payment and the late charge. If more than one Periodic Payment is outstanding, Lender may apply any payment received from Borrower to the repayment of the Periodic Payments if, and to the extent that, each payment can be paid in full. To the extent that any excess exists after the payment is applied to the full payment of one or more Periodic Payments, such excess may be applied to any late charges due. Voluntary prepayments shall be applied first to any prepayment charges and then as described in the Note.

    Any application of payments, insurance proceeds, or Miscellaneous Proceeds to principal due under the Note shall not extend or postpone the due date, or change the amount, of the Periodic Payments.

3. **Funds for Escrow Items.** Borrower shall pay to Lender on the day Periodic Payments are due under the Note, until the Note is paid in full, a sum (the "Funds") to provide for payment of amounts due for: (a) taxes and assessments and other items which can attain priority over this Security Instrument as a lien or encumbrance on the Property; (b) leasehold payments or ground rents on the Property, if any; (c) premiums for any and all insurance required by Lender under Section 5; and (d) Mortgage Insurance premiums, if any, or any sums payable by Borrower to Lender in lieu of the payment of Mortgage Insurance premiums in accordance with the provisions of Section 10. These items are called "Escrow Items." At origination or at any time during the term of the Loan, Lender may require that Community Association Dues, Fees, and Assessments, if any, be escrowed by Borrower, and such dues, fees and assessments shall be an Escrow Item. Borrower shall promptly furnish to Lender all notices of amounts to be paid under this Section. Borrower shall pay Lender the Funds for Escrow Items unless Lender waives Borrower's obligation to pay the Funds for any or all Escrow Items. Lender may waive Borrower's obligation to pay to Lender Funds for any or all Escrow Items at any time. Any such waiver may only be in writing. In the event of such waiver, Borrower shall pay directly, when and where payable, the amounts due for any Escrow Items for which payment of Funds has been waived by Lender and, if Lender requires, shall furnish to Lender receipts evidencing such payment within such time period as Lender may require. Borrower's obligation to make such payments and to provide receipts shall for all purposes be deemed to be a covenant and agreement contained in this Security Instrument, as the phrase "covenant and agreement" is used in Section 9. If Borrower is obligated to pay Escrow Items directly, pursuant to a waiver, and Borrower fails to pay the amount due for an Escrow Item, Lender may exercise its rights under Section 9 and pay such amount and Borrower shall then be obligated under Section 9 to repay to Lender any such amount. Lender may revoke the waiver as to any or all Escrow Items at any time by a notice given in accordance with Section 15 and, upon such revocation, Borrower shall pay to Lender all Funds, and in such amounts, that are then required under this Section 3.

CALIFORNIA--Single Family--Fannie Mae/Freddie Mac UNIFORM INSTRUMENT   Form 3005   1/01   *(page 4 of 16 pages)*

Lender may, at any time, collect and hold Funds in an amount (a) sufficient to permit Lender to apply the Funds at the time specified under RESPA, and (b) not to exceed the maximum amount a lender can require under RESPA. Lender shall estimate the amount of Funds due on the basis of current data and reasonable estimates of expenditures of future Escrow Items or otherwise in accordance with Applicable Law.

The Funds shall be held in an institution whose deposits are insured by a federal agency, instrumentality, or entity (including Lender, if Lender is an institution whose deposits are so insured) or in any Federal Home Loan Bank. Lender shall apply the Funds to pay the Escrow Items no later than the time specified under RESPA. Lender shall not charge Borrower for holding and applying the Funds, annually analyzing the escrow account, or verifying the Escrow Items, unless Lender pays Borrower interest on the Funds and Applicable Law permits Lender to make such a charge. Unless an agreement is made in writing or Applicable Law requires interest to be paid on the Funds, Lender shall not be required to pay Borrower any interest or earnings on the Funds. Borrower and Lender can agree in writing, however, that interest shall be paid on the Funds. Lender shall give to Borrower, without charge, an annual accounting of the Funds as required by RESPA.

If there is a surplus of Funds held in escrow, as defined under RESPA, Lender shall account to Borrower for the excess funds in accordance with RESPA. If there is a shortage of Funds held in escrow, as defined under RESPA, Lender shall notify Borrower as required by RESPA, and Borrower shall pay to Lender the amount necessary to make up the shortage in accordance with RESPA, but in no more than 12 monthly payments. If there is a deficiency of Funds held in escrow, as defined under RESPA, Lender shall notify Borrower as required by RESPA, and Borrower shall pay to Lender the amount necessary to make up the deficiency in accordance with RESPA, but in no more than 12 monthly payments.

Upon payment in full of all sums secured by this Security Instrument, Lender shall promptly refund to Borrower any Funds held by Lender.

4.   **Charges; Liens.** Borrower shall pay all taxes, assessments, charges, fines, and impositions attributable to the Property which can attain priority over this Security Instrument, leasehold payments or ground rents on the Property, if any, and Community Association Dues, Fees, and Assessments, if any. To the extent that these items are Escrow Items, Borrower shall pay them in the manner provided in Section 3.

Borrower shall promptly discharge any lien which has priority over this Security Instrument unless Borrower: (a) agrees in writing to the payment of the obligation secured by the lien in a manner acceptable to Lender, but only so long as Borrower is performing such agreement; (b) contests the lien in good faith by, or defends against enforcement of the lien in, legal proceedings which in Lender's opinion operate to prevent the enforcement of the lien while those proceedings are pending, but only until such proceedings are concluded; or (c) secures from the holder of the lien an agreement satisfactory to Lender subordinating the lien to this Security Instrument. If Lender determines that any part of the Property is subject to a lien which can attain priority over this Security Instrument, Lender may give Borrower a notice identifying the lien. Within 10 days of the date on which that notice is given, Borrower shall satisfy the lien or take one or more of the actions set forth above in this Section 4.

Lender may require Borrower to pay a one-time charge for a real estate tax verification and/or reporting service used by Lender in connection with this Loan.

CALIFORNIA--Single Family--Fannie Mae/Freddie Mac UNIFORM INSTRUMENT   **Form 3005**   **1/01**   *(page 5 of 16 pages)*

5. **Property Insurance.** Borrower shall keep the improvements now existing or hereafter erected on the Property insured against loss by fire, hazards included within the term "extended coverage," and any other hazards including, but not limited to, earthquakes and floods, for which Lender requires insurance. This insurance shall be maintained in the amounts (including deductible levels) and for the periods that Lender requires. What Lender requires pursuant to the preceding sentences can change during the term of the Loan. The insurance carrier providing the insurance shall be chosen by Borrower subject to Lender's right to disapprove Borrower's choice, which right shall not be exercised unreasonably. Lender may require Borrower to pay, in connection with this Loan, either: (a) a one-time charge for flood zone determination, certification and tracking services; or (b) a one-time charge for flood zone determination and certification services and subsequent charges each time remappings or similar changes occur which reasonably might affect such determination or certification. Borrower shall also be responsible for the payment of any fees imposed by the Federal Emergency Management Agency in connection with the review of any flood zone determination resulting from an objection by Borrower.

If Borrower fails to maintain any of the coverages described above, Lender may obtain insurance coverage, at Lender's option and Borrower's expense. Lender is under no obligation to purchase any particular type or amount of coverage. Therefore, such coverage shall cover Lender, but might or might not protect Borrower, Borrower's equity in the Property, or the contents of the Property, against any risk, hazard or liability and might provide greater or lesser coverage than was previously in effect. Borrower acknowledges that the cost of the insurance coverage so obtained might significantly exceed the cost of insurance that Borrower could have obtained. Any amounts disbursed by Lender under this Section 5 shall become additional debt of Borrower secured by this Security Instrument. These amounts shall bear interest at the Note rate from the date of disbursement and shall be payable, with such interest, upon notice from Lender to Borrower requesting payment.

All insurance policies required by Lender and renewals of such policies shall be subject to Lender's right to disapprove such policies, shall include a standard mortgage clause, and shall name Lender as mortgagee and/or as an additional loss payee and Borrower further agrees to generally assign rights to insurance proceeds to the holder of the Note up to the amount of the outstanding loan balance. Lender shall have the right to hold the policies and renewal certificates. If Lender requires, Borrower shall promptly give to Lender all receipts of paid premiums and renewal notices. If Borrower obtains any form of insurance coverage, not otherwise required by Lender, for damage to, or destruction of, the Property, such policy shall include a standard mortgage clause and shall name Lender as mortgagee and/or as an additional loss payee and Borrower further agrees to generally assign rights to insurance proceeds to the holder of the Note up to the amount of the outstanding loan balance.

In the event of loss, Borrower shall give prompt notice to the insurance carrier and Lender. Lender may make proof of loss if not made promptly by Borrower. Unless Lender and Borrower otherwise agree in writing, any insurance proceeds, whether or not the underlying insurance was required by Lender, shall be applied to restoration or repair of the Property, if the restoration or repair is economically feasible and Lender's security is not lessened. During such repair and restoration period, Lender shall have the right to hold such insurance proceeds until Lender has had an opportunity to inspect such Property to ensure the work has been completed to Lender's satisfaction, provided that such inspection shall be undertaken promptly. Lender may disburse proceeds for the repairs and restoration in a single payment or in a series of progress

CALIFORNIA--Single Family--Fannie Mae/Freddie Mac UNIFORM INSTRUMENT   Form 3005   1/01   *(page 6 of 16 pages)*

payments as the work is completed. Unless an agreement is made in writing or Applicable Law requires interest to be paid on such insurance proceeds, Lender shall not be required to pay Borrower any interest or earnings on such proceeds. Fees for public adjusters, or other third parties, retained by Borrower shall not be paid out of the insurance proceeds and shall be the sole obligation of Borrower. If the restoration or repair is not economically feasible or Lender's security would be lessened, the insurance proceeds shall be applied to the sums secured by this Security Instrument, whether or not then due, with the excess, if any, paid to Borrower. Such insurance proceeds shall be applied in the order provided for in Section 2.

If Borrower abandons the Property, Lender may file, negotiate and settle any available insurance claim and related matters. If Borrower does not respond within 30 days to a notice from Lender that the insurance carrier has offered to settle a claim, then Lender may negotiate and settle the claim. The 30-day period will begin when the notice is given. In either event, or if Lender acquires the Property under Section 22 or otherwise, Borrower hereby assigns to Lender (a) Borrower's rights to any insurance proceeds in an amount not to exceed the amounts unpaid under the Note or this Security Instrument, and (b) any other of Borrower's rights (other than the right to any refund of unearned premiums paid by Borrower) under all insurance policies covering the Property, insofar as such rights are applicable to the coverage of the Property. Lender may use the insurance proceeds either to repair or restore the Property or to pay amounts unpaid under the Note or this Security Instrument, whether or not then due.

6.   **Occupancy.**   Borrower shall occupy, establish, and use the Property as Borrower's principal residence within 60 days after the execution of this Security Instrument and shall continue to occupy the Property as Borrower's principal residence for at least one year after the date of occupancy, unless Lender otherwise agrees in writing, which consent shall not be unreasonably withheld, or unless extenuating circumstances exist which are beyond Borrower's control.

7.   **Preservation, Maintenance and Protection of the Property; Inspections.** Borrower shall not destroy, damage or impair the Property, allow the Property to deteriorate or commit waste on the Property. Whether or not Borrower is residing in the Property, Borrower shall maintain the Property in order to prevent the Property from deteriorating or decreasing in value due to its condition. Unless it is determined pursuant to Section 5 that repair or restoration is not economically feasible, Borrower shall promptly repair the Property if damaged to avoid further deterioration or damage. If insurance or condemnation proceeds are paid in connection with damage to, or the taking of, the Property, Borrower shall be responsible for repairing or restoring the Property only if Lender has released proceeds for such purposes. Lender may disburse proceeds for the repairs and restoration in a single payment or in a series of progress payments as the work is completed. If the insurance or condemnation proceeds are not sufficient to repair or restore the Property, Borrower is not relieved of Borrower's obligation for the completion of such repair or restoration.

Lender or its agent may make reasonable entries upon and inspections of the Property. If it has reasonable cause, Lender may inspect the interior of the improvements on the Property. Lender shall give Borrower notice at the time of or prior to such an interior inspection specifying such reasonable cause.

8.   Borrower's Loan Application. Borrower shall be in default if, during the Loan application process, Borrower or any persons or entities acting at the direction of Borrower or with Borrower's knowledge or consent gave materially false, misleading, or inaccurate information or statements to Lender (or failed to provide Lender with material information) in

CALIFORNIA--Single Family--Fannie Mae/Freddie Mac UNIFORM INSTRUMENT   Form 3005   1/01   *(page 7 of 16 pages)*

connection with the Loan.   Material representations include, but are not limited to, representations concerning Borrower's occupancy of the Property as Borrower's principal residence.

9.   Protection of Lender's Interest in the Property and Rights Under this Security Instrument. If (a) Borrower fails to perform the covenants and agreements contained in this Security Instrument, (b) there is a legal proceeding that might significantly affect Lender's interest in the Property and/or rights under this Security Instrument (such as a proceeding in bankruptcy, probate, for condemnation or forfeiture, for enforcement of a lien which may attain priority over this Security Instrument or to enforce laws or regulations), or (c) Borrower has abandoned the Property, then Lender may do and pay for whatever is reasonable or appropriate to protect Lender's interest in the Property and rights under this Security Instrument, including protecting and/or assessing the value of the Property, and securing and/or repairing the Property. Lender's actions can include, but are not limited to: (a) paying any sums secured by a lien which has priority over this Security Instrument; (b) appearing in court; and (c) paying reasonable attorneys' fees to protect its interest in the Property and/or rights under this Security Instrument, including its secured position in a bankruptcy proceeding.   Securing the Property includes, but is not limited to, entering the Property to make repairs, change locks, replace or board up doors and windows, drain water from pipes, eliminate building or other code violations or dangerous conditions, and have utilities turned on or off.   Although Lender may take action under this Section 9, Lender does not have to do so and is not under any duty or obligation to do so. It is agreed that Lender incurs no liability for not taking any or all actions authorized under this Section 9.

Any amounts disbursed by Lender under this Section 9 shall become additional debt of Borrower secured by this Security Instrument.   These amounts shall bear interest at the Note rate from the date of disbursement and shall be payable, with such interest, upon notice from Lender to Borrower requesting payment.

If this Security Instrument is on a leasehold, Borrower shall comply with all the provisions of the lease. If Borrower acquires fee title to the Property, the leasehold and the fee title shall not merge unless Lender agrees to the merger in writing.

10. **Mortgage Insurance.** If Lender required Mortgage Insurance as a condition of making the Loan, Borrower shall pay the premiums required to maintain the Mortgage Insurance in effect. If, for any reason, the Mortgage Insurance coverage required by Lender ceases to be available from the mortgage insurer that previously provided such insurance and Borrower was required to make separately designated payments toward the premiums for Mortgage Insurance, Borrower shall pay the premiums required to obtain coverage substantially equivalent to the Mortgage Insurance previously in effect, at a cost substantially equivalent to the cost to Borrower of the Mortgage Insurance previously in effect, from an alternate mortgage insurer selected by Lender. If substantially equivalent Mortgage Insurance coverage is not available, Borrower shall continue to pay to Lender the amount of the separately designated payments that were due when the insurance coverage ceased to be in effect. Lender will accept, use and retain these payments as a non-refundable loss reserve in lieu of Mortgage Insurance. Such loss reserve shall be non-refundable, notwithstanding the fact that the Loan is ultimately paid in full, and Lender shall not be required to pay Borrower any interest or earnings on such loss reserve. Lender can no longer require loss reserve payments if Mortgage Insurance coverage (in the amount and for the period that Lender requires) provided by an insurer selected by Lender again becomes available, is obtained, and Lender requires separately designated payments toward the premiums for Mortgage Insurance. If Lender required Mortgage Insurance as a condition of making the Loan and Borrower was required to make separately designated payments toward the premiums for Mortgage Insurance, Borrower shall pay the premiums required to maintain Mortgage Insurance in effect, or to provide a non-refundable loss reserve, until Lender's requirement for Mortgage Insurance ends in accordance with any written agreement between Borrower and Lender providing for such termination or until termination is required by Applicable Law. Nothing in this Section 10 affects Borrower's obligation to pay interest at the rate provided in the Note.

Mortgage Insurance reimburses Lender (or any entity that purchases the Note) for certain losses it may incur if Borrower does not repay the Loan as agreed. Borrower is not a party to the Mortgage Insurance.

Mortgage insurers evaluate their total risk on all such insurance in force from time to time, and may enter into agreements with other parties that share or modify their risk, or reduce losses. These agreements are on terms and conditions that are satisfactory to the mortgage insurer and the other party (or parties) to these agreements. These agreements may require the mortgage insurer to make payments using any source of funds that the mortgage insurer may have available (which may include funds obtained from Mortgage Insurance premiums).

As a result of these agreements, Lender, any purchaser of the Note, another insurer, any reinsurer, any other entity, or any affiliate of any of the foregoing, may receive (directly or indirectly) amounts that derive from (or might be characterized as) a portion of Borrower's payments for Mortgage Insurance, in exchange for sharing or modifying the mortgage insurer's risk, or reducing losses. If such agreement provides that an affiliate of Lender takes a share of the insurer's risk in exchange for a share of the premiums paid to the insurer, the arrangement is often termed "captive reinsurance." Further:

(a) **Any such agreements will not affect the amounts that Borrower has agreed to pay for Mortgage Insurance, or any other terms of the Loan. Such agreements will not increase the amount Borrower will owe for Mortgage Insurance, and they will not entitle Borrower to any refund.**

(b) **Any such agreements will not affect the rights Borrower has - if any - with respect to the Mortgage Insurance under the Homeowners Protection Act of 1998 or any other law. These rights may include the right to receive certain disclosures, to request and obtain cancellation of the Mortgage Insurance, to have the Mortgage Insurance terminated automatically, and/or to receive a refund of any Mortgage Insurance premiums that were unearned at the time of such cancellation or termination.**

11.   **Assignment of Miscellaneous Proceeds; Forfeiture.**   All Miscellaneous Proceeds are hereby assigned to and shall be paid to Lender.

If the Property is damaged, such Miscellaneous Proceeds shall be applied to restoration or repair of the Property, if the restoration or repair is economically feasible and Lender's security is not lessened. During such repair and restoration period, Lender shall have the right to hold such Miscellaneous Proceeds until Lender has had an opportunity to inspect such Property to ensure the work has been completed to Lender's satisfaction, provided that such inspection shall be undertaken promptly.   Lender may pay for the repairs and restoration in a single disbursement or in a series of progress payments as the work is completed.   Unless an agreement is made in writing or Applicable Law requires interest to be paid on such Miscellaneous Proceeds, Lender shall not be required to pay Borrower any interest or earnings on such Miscellaneous Proceeds.   If the restoration or repair is not economically feasible or Lender's

CALIFORNIA--Single Family--Fannie Mae/Freddie Mac UNIFORM INSTRUMENT   Form 3005   1/01   *(page 9 of 16 pages)*

security would be lessened, the Miscellaneous Proceeds shall be applied to the sums secured by this Security Instrument, whether or not then due, with the excess, if any, paid to Borrower. Such Miscellaneous Proceeds shall be applied in the order provided for in Section 2.

In the event of a total taking, destruction, or loss in value of the Property, the Miscellaneous Proceeds shall be applied to the sums secured by this Security Instrument, whether or not then due, with the excess, if any, paid to Borrower.

In the event of a partial taking, destruction, or loss in value of the Property in which the fair market value of the Property immediately before the partial taking, destruction, or loss in value is equal to or greater than the amount of the sums secured by this Security Instrument immediately before the partial taking, destruction, or loss in value, unless Borrower and Lender otherwise agree in writing, the sums secured by this Security Instrument shall be reduced by the amount of the Miscellaneous Proceeds multiplied by the following fraction: (a) the total amount of the sums secured immediately before the partial taking, destruction, or loss in value divided by (b) the fair market value of the Property immediately before the partial taking, destruction, or loss in value. Any balance shall be paid to Borrower.

In the event of a partial taking, destruction, or loss in value of the Property in which the fair market value of the Property immediately before the partial taking, destruction, or loss in value is less than the amount of the sums secured immediately before the partial taking, destruction, or loss in value, unless Borrower and Lender otherwise agree in writing, the Miscellaneous Proceeds shall be applied to the sums secured by this Security Instrument whether or not the sums are then due.

If the Property is abandoned by Borrower, or if, after notice by Lender to Borrower that the Opposing Party (as defined in the next sentence) offers to make an award to settle a claim for damages, Borrower fails to respond to Lender within 30 days after the date the notice is given, Lender is authorized to collect and apply the Miscellaneous Proceeds either to restoration or repair of the Property or to the sums secured by this Security Instrument, whether or not then due. "Opposing Party" means the third party that owes Borrower Miscellaneous Proceeds or the party against whom Borrower has a right of action in regard to Miscellaneous Proceeds.

Borrower shall be in default if any action or proceeding, whether civil or criminal, is begun that, in Lender's judgment, could result in forfeiture of the Property or other material impairment of Lender's interest in the Property or rights under this Security Instrument. Borrower can cure such a default and, if acceleration has occurred, reinstate as provided in Section 19, by causing the action or proceeding to be dismissed with a ruling that, in Lender's judgment, precludes forfeiture of the Property or other material impairment of Lender's interest in the Property or rights under this Security Instrument. The proceeds of any award or claim for damages that are attributable to the impairment of Lender's interest in the Property are hereby assigned and shall be paid to Lender.

All Miscellaneous Proceeds that are not applied to restoration or repair of the Property shall be applied in the order provided for in Section 2.

12. **Borrower Not Released; Forbearance By Lender Not a Waiver.** Extension of the time for payment or modification of amortization of the sums secured by this Security Instrument granted by Lender to Borrower or any Successor in Interest of Borrower shall not operate to release the liability of Borrower or any Successors in Interest of Borrower. Lender shall not be required to commence proceedings against any Successor in Interest of Borrower or to refuse to extend time for payment or otherwise modify amortization of the sums secured by this Security Instrument by reason of any demand made by the original Borrower or any

Successors in Interest of Borrower. Any forbearance by Lender in exercising any right or remedy including, without limitation, Lender's acceptance of payments from third persons, entities or Successors in Interest of Borrower or in amounts less than the amount then due, shall not be a waiver of or preclude the exercise of any right or remedy.

13. **Joint and Several Liability; Co-signers; Successors and Assigns Bound.** Borrower covenants and agrees that Borrower's obligations and liability shall be joint and several. However, any Borrower who co-signs this Security Instrument but does not execute the Note (a "co-signer"): (a) is co-signing this Security Instrument only to mortgage, grant and convey the co-signer's interest in the Property under the terms of this Security Instrument; (b) is not personally obligated to pay the sums secured by this Security Instrument; and (c) agrees that Lender and any other Borrower can agree to extend, modify, forbear or make any accommodations with regard to the terms of this Security Instrument or the Note without the co-signer's consent.

Subject to the provisions of Section 18, any Successor in Interest of Borrower who assumes Borrower's obligations under this Security Instrument in writing, and is approved by Lender, shall obtain all of Borrower's rights and benefits under this Security Instrument. Borrower shall not be released from Borrower's obligations and liability under this Security Instrument unless Lender agrees to such release in writing. The covenants and agreements of this Security Instrument shall bind (except as provided in Section 20) and benefit the successors and assigns of Lender.

14. **Loan Charges.** Lender may charge Borrower fees for services performed in connection with Borrower's default, for the purpose of protecting Lender's interest in the Property and rights under this Security Instrument, including, but not limited to, attorneys' fees, property inspection and valuation fees. In regard to any other fees, the absence of express authority in this Security Instrument to charge a specific fee to Borrower shall not be construed as a prohibition on the charging of such fee. Lender may not charge fees that are expressly prohibited by this Security Instrument or by Applicable Law.

If the Loan is subject to a law which sets maximum loan charges, and that law is finally interpreted so that the interest or other loan charges collected or to be collected in connection with the Loan exceed the permitted limits, then: (a) any such loan charge shall be reduced by the amount necessary to reduce the charge to the permitted limit; and (b) any sums already collected from Borrower which exceeded permitted limits will be refunded to Borrower. Lender may choose to make this refund by reducing the principal owed under the Note or by making a direct payment to Borrower. If a refund reduces principal, the reduction will be treated as a partial prepayment without any prepayment charge (whether or not a prepayment charge is provided for under the Note). Borrower's acceptance of any such refund made by direct payment to Borrower will constitute a waiver of any right of action Borrower might have arising out of such overcharge.

15. **Notices.** All notices given by Borrower or Lender in connection with this Security Instrument must be in writing. Any notice to Borrower in connection with this Security Instrument shall be deemed to have been given to Borrower when mailed by first class mail or when actually delivered to Borrower's notice address if sent by other means. Notice to any one Borrower shall constitute notice to all Borrowers unless Applicable Law expressly requires otherwise. The notice address shall be the Property Address unless Borrower has designated a substitute notice address by notice to Lender. Borrower shall promptly notify Lender of Borrower's change of address. If Lender specifies a procedure for reporting Borrower's change

CALIFORNIA--Single Family--**Fannie Mae/Freddie Mac UNIFORM INSTRUMENT** **Form 3005** 1/01 *(page 11 of 16 pages)*

of address, then Borrower shall only report a change of address through that specified procedure. There may be only one designated notice address under this Security Instrument at any one time. Any notice to Lender shall be given by delivering it or by mailing it by first class mail to Lender's address stated herein unless Lender has designated another address by notice to Borrower. Any notice in connection with this Security Instrument shall not be deemed to have been given to Lender until actually received by Lender. If any notice required by this Security Instrument is also required under Applicable Law, the Applicable Law requirement will satisfy the corresponding requirement under this Security Instrument.

16.   Governing Law; Severability; Rules of Construction.   This Security Instrument shall be governed by federal law and the law of the jurisdiction in which the Property is located. All rights and obligations contained in this Security Instrument are subject to any requirements and limitations of Applicable Law. Applicable Law might explicitly or implicitly allow the parties to agree by contract or it might be silent, but such silence shall not be construed as a prohibition against agreement by contract. In the event that any provision or clause of this Security Instrument or the Note conflicts with Applicable Law, such conflict shall not affect other provisions of this Security Instrument or the Note which can be given effect without the conflicting provision.

As used in this Security Instrument: (a) words of the masculine gender shall mean and include corresponding neuter words or words of the feminine gender; (b) words in the singular shall mean and include the plural and vice versa; and (c) the word "may" gives sole discretion without any obligation to take any action.

17.   Borrower's Copy.   Borrower shall be given one copy of the Note and of this Security Instrument.

18.   Transfer of the Property or a Beneficial Interest in Borrower.   As used in this Section 18, "Interest in the Property" means any legal or beneficial interest in the Property, including, but not limited to, those beneficial interests transferred in a bond for deed, contract for deed, installment sales contract or escrow agreement, the intent of which is the transfer of title by Borrower at a future date to a purchaser.

If all or any part of the Property or any Interest in the Property is sold or transferred (or if Borrower is not a natural person and a beneficial interest in Borrower is sold or transferred) without Lender's prior written consent, Lender may require immediate payment in full of all sums secured by this Security Instrument. However, this option shall not be exercised by Lender if such exercise is prohibited by Applicable Law.

If Lender exercises this option, Lender shall give Borrower notice of acceleration. The notice shall provide a period of not less than 30 days from the date the notice is given in accordance with Section 15 within which Borrower must pay all sums secured by this Security Instrument. If Borrower fails to pay these sums prior to the expiration of this period, Lender may invoke any remedies permitted by this Security Instrument without further notice or demand on Borrower.

19.   Borrower's Right to Reinstate After Acceleration. If Borrower meets certain conditions, Borrower shall have the right to have enforcement of this Security Instrument discontinued at any time prior to the earliest of: (a) five days before sale of the Property pursuant to any power of sale contained in this Security Instrument; (b) such other period as Applicable Law might specify for the termination of Borrower's right to reinstate; or (c) entry of a judgment enforcing this Security Instrument. Those conditions are that Borrower: (a) pays Lender all sums which then would be due under this Security Instrument and the Note as if no acceleration

CALIFORNIA--Single Family--Fannie Mae/Freddie Mac UNIFORM INSTRUMENT   Form 3005   1/01   *(page 12 of 16 pages)*

had occurred; (b) cures any default of any other covenants or agreements; (c) pays all expenses incurred in enforcing this Security Instrument, including, but not limited to, reasonable attorneys' fees, property inspection and valuation fees, and other fees incurred for the purpose of protecting Lender's interest in the Property and rights under this Security Instrument; and (d) takes such action as Lender may reasonably require to assure that Lender's interest in the Property and rights under this Security Instrument, and Borrower's obligation to pay the sums secured by this Security Instrument, shall continue unchanged. Lender may require that Borrower pay such reinstatement sums and expenses in one or more of the following forms, as selected by Lender: (a) cash; (b) money order; (c) certified check, bank check, treasurer's check or cashier's check, provided any such check is drawn upon an institution whose deposits are insured by a federal agency, instrumentality or entity; or (d) Electronic Funds Transfer. Upon reinstatement by Borrower, this Security Instrument and obligations secured hereby shall remain fully effective as if no acceleration had occurred. However, this right to reinstate shall not apply in the case of acceleration under Section 18.

     20.   Sale of Note; Change of Loan Servicer; Notice of Grievance. The Note or a partial interest in the Note (together with this Security Instrument) can be sold one or more times without prior notice to Borrower. A sale might result in a change in the entity (known as the "Loan Servicer") that collects Periodic Payments due under the Note and this Security Instrument and performs other mortgage loan servicing obligations under the Note, this Security Instrument, and Applicable Law. There also might be one or more changes of the Loan Servicer unrelated to a sale of the Note. If there is a change of the Loan Servicer, Borrower will be given written notice of the change which will state the name and address of the new Loan Servicer, the address to which payments should be made and any other information RESPA requires in connection with a notice of transfer of servicing. If the Note is sold and thereafter the Loan is serviced by a Loan Servicer other than the purchaser of the Note, the mortgage loan servicing obligations to Borrower will remain with the Loan Servicer or be transferred to a successor Loan Servicer and are not assumed by the Note purchaser unless otherwise provided by the Note purchaser.

     Neither Borrower nor Lender may commence, join, or be joined to any judicial action (as either an individual litigant or the member of a class) that arises from the other party's actions pursuant to this Security Instrument or that alleges that the other party has breached any provision of, or any duty owed by reason of, this Security Instrument, until such Borrower or Lender has notified the other party (with such notice given in compliance with the requirements of Section 15) of such alleged breach and afforded the other party hereto a reasonable period after the giving of such notice to take corrective action. If Applicable Law provides a time period which must elapse before certain action can be taken, that time period will be deemed to be reasonable for purposes of this paragraph. The notice of acceleration and opportunity to cure given to Borrower pursuant to Section 22 and the notice of acceleration given to Borrower pursuant to Section 18 shall be deemed to satisfy the notice and opportunity to take corrective action provisions of this Section 20.

21. **Hazardous Substances.** As used in this Section 21: (a) "Hazardous Substances" are those substances defined as toxic or hazardous substances, pollutants, or wastes by Environmental Law and the following substances: gasoline, kerosene, other flammable or toxic petroleum products, toxic pesticides and herbicides, volatile solvents, materials containing asbestos or formaldehyde, and radioactive materials; (b) "Environmental Law" means federal laws and laws of the jurisdiction where the Property is located that relate to health, safety or

CALIFORNIA--Single Family--Fannie Mae/Freddie Mac UNIFORM INSTRUMENT   Form 3005   1/01   *(page 13 of 16 pages)*

environmental protection; (c) "Environmental Cleanup" includes any response action, remedial action, or removal action, as defined in Environmental Law; and (d) an "Environmental Condition" means a condition that can cause, contribute to, or otherwise trigger an Environmental Cleanup.

Borrower shall not cause or permit the presence, use, disposal, storage, or release of any Hazardous Substances, or threaten to release any Hazardous Substances, on or in the Property. Borrower shall not do, nor allow anyone else to do, anything affecting the Property (a) that is in violation of any Environmental Law, (b) which creates an Environmental Condition, or (c) which, due to the presence, use, or release of a Hazardous Substance, creates a condition that adversely affects the value of the Property. The preceding two sentences shall not apply to the presence, use, or storage on the Property of small quantities of Hazardous Substances that are generally recognized to be appropriate to normal residential uses and to maintenance of the Property (including, but not limited to, hazardous substances in consumer products).

Borrower shall promptly give Lender written notice of (a) any investigation, claim, demand, lawsuit or other action by any governmental or regulatory agency or private party involving the Property and any Hazardous Substance or Environmental Law of which Borrower has actual knowledge, (b) any Environmental Condition, including but not limited to, any spilling, leaking, discharge, release or threat of release of any Hazardous Substance, and (c) any condition caused by the presence, use or release of a Hazardous Substance which adversely affects the value of the Property. If Borrower learns, or is notified by any governmental or regulatory authority, or any private party, that any removal or other remediation of any Hazardous Substance affecting the Property is necessary, Borrower shall promptly take all necessary remedial actions in accordance with Environmental Law. Nothing herein shall create any obligation on Lender for an Environmental Cleanup.

NON-UNIFORM COVENANTS. Borrower and Lender further covenant and agree as follows:

22. **Acceleration; Remedies. Lender shall give notice to Borrower prior to acceleration following Borrower's breach of any covenant or agreement in this Security Instrument (but not prior to acceleration under Section 18 unless Applicable Law provides otherwise). The notice shall specify: (a) the default; (b) the action required to cure the default; (c) a date, not less than 30 days from the date the notice is given to Borrower, by which the default must be cured; and (d) that failure to cure the default on or before the date specified in the notice may result in acceleration of the sums secured by this Security Instrument and sale of the Property. The notice shall further inform Borrower of the right to reinstate after acceleration and the right to bring a court action to assert the non-existence of a default or any other defense of Borrower to acceleration and sale. If the default is not cured on or before the date specified in the notice, Lender at its option may require immediate payment in full of all sums secured by this Security Instrument without further demand and may invoke the power of sale and any other remedies permitted by Applicable Law. Lender shall be entitled to collect all expenses incurred in pursuing the remedies provided in this Section 22, including, but not limited to, reasonable attorneys' fees and costs of title evidence.**

If Lender invokes the power of sale, Lender shall execute or cause Trustee to execute a written notice of the occurrence of an event of default and of Lender's election to cause the Property to be sold. Trustee shall cause this notice to be recorded in each county

CALIFORNIA--Single Family--Fannie Mae/Freddie Mac UNIFORM INSTRUMENT   Form 3005   1/01   *(page 14 of 16 pages)*

in which any part of the Property is located. Lender or Trustee shall mail copies of the notice as prescribed by Applicable Law to Borrower and to the other persons prescribed by Applicable Law. Trustee shall give public notice of sale to the persons and in the manner prescribed by Applicable Law. After the time required by Applicable Law, Trustee, without demand on Borrower, shall sell the Property at public auction to the highest bidder at the time and place and under the terms designated in the notice of sale in one or more parcels and in any order Trustee determines. Trustee may postpone sale of all or any parcel of the Property by public announcement at the time and place of any previously scheduled sale. Lender or its designee may purchase the Property at any sale.

Trustee shall deliver to the purchaser Trustee's deed conveying the Property without any covenant or warranty, expressed or implied. The recitals in the Trustee's deed shall be prima facie evidence of the truth of the statements made therein. Trustee shall apply the proceeds of the sale in the following order: (a) to all expenses of the sale, including, but not limited to, reasonable Trustee's and attorneys' fees; (b) to all sums secured by this Security Instrument; and (c) any excess to the person or persons legally entitled to it.

23.   **Reconveyance.** Upon payment of all sums secured by this Security Instrument, Lender shall request Trustee to reconvey the Property and shall surrender this Security Instrument and all notes evidencing debt secured by this Security Instrument to Trustee. Trustee shall reconvey the Property without warranty to the person or persons legally entitled to it. Lender may charge such person or persons a reasonable fee for reconveying the Property, but only if the fee is paid to a third party (such as the Trustee) for services rendered and the charging of the fee is permitted under Applicable Law. If the fee charged does not exceed the fee set by Applicable Law, the fee is conclusively presumed to be reasonable.

24.   **Substitute Trustee.** Lender, at its option, may from time to time appoint a successor trustee to any Trustee appointed hereunder by an instrument executed and acknowledged by Lender and recorded in the office of the Recorder of the county in which the Property is located. The instrument shall contain the name of the original Lender, Trustee and Borrower, the book and page where this Security Instrument is recorded and the name and address of the successor trustee. Without conveyance of the Property, the successor trustee shall succeed to all the title, powers and duties conferred upon the Trustee herein and by Applicable Law. This procedure for substitution of trustee shall govern to the exclusion of all other provisions for substitution.

25.   **Statement of Obligation Fee.** Lender may collect a fee not to exceed the maximum amount permitted by Applicable Law for furnishing the statement of obligation as provided by Section 2943 of the Civil Code of California.

CALIFORNIA--Single Family--Fannie Mae/Freddie Mac UNIFORM INSTRUMENT   Form 3005   1/01   *(page 15 of 16 pages)*

BY SIGNING BELOW, Borrower accepts and agrees to the terms and covenants contained in this Security Instrument and in any Rider executed by Borrower and recorded with it.

Witnesses:

_____   _____(Seal)
                                                                        - Borrower

_____   _____(Seal)
                                                                        - Borrower

_____**[Space Below This Line for Acknowledgment]**_____

CALIFORNIA--Single Family--**Fannie Mae/Freddie Mac UNIFORM INSTRUMENT**   **Form 3005**   **1/01**   *(page 16 of 16 pages)*

10. SUBORDINATION AGREEMENT

———— SPACE ABOVE THIS LINE FOR RECORDER'S USE ————

SUBORDINATION AGREEMENT

NOTICE: THIS SUBORDINATION AGREEMENT RESULTS IN YOUR SECURITY INTEREST IN THE PROPERTY BECOMING SUBJECT TO AND OF LOWER PRIORITY THAN THE LIEN OF SOME OTHER OR LATER SECURITY INSTRUMENT.

THIS AGREEMENT, made this _____ day of _____, 19___, by _____

_____ owner of the land hereinafter described and hereinafter referred to as "Owner," and _____

_____ present owner and holder of the deed of trust and note first hereinafter described and hereinafter referred to as "Beneficiary";

WITNESSETH

THAT WHEREAS, _____ did on _____, execute a deed of trust to _____, as trustee, covering:

_____

to secure a note in the sum of $_____, dated _____

_____, in favor of _____, which deed of trust was recorded _____, in book _____ page _____, Official Records of said county and is subject and subordinate to the deed of trust next hereinafter described; and

WHEREAS, _____, did on _____ execute a deed of trust to _____ as trustee, covering said land and securing an indebtedness in the amount of $_____ in favor of _____, hereinafter referred to as "Lender," which deed of trust was recorded _____ in book _____ page _____, Official Records of said county and provides among other things that it shall also secure additional loans and advances thereafter made upon the terms and conditions therein set forth; and

WHEREAS, Owner has executed, or is about to execute, a note in the amount of $_____, dated _____, in favor of Lender, payable with interest and upon the terms and conditions described therein, which note evidences an additional loan to be made by Lender to Owner under the terms and provisions of, and secured by, said deed of trust in favor of Lender; and

WHEREAS, it is a condition precedent to obtaining said additional loan that said deed of trust in favor of Lender, securing all obligations recited therein as being secured thereby, including but not limited to said additional loan, shall unconditionally be and remain at all times a lien or charge upon the land hereinbefore described, prior and superior to the lien or charge of the deed of trust first above mentioned; and

WHEREAS, Lender is willing to make said additional loan provided the deed of trust securing the same is a lien or charge upon said land prior and superior to the lien or charge of the deed of trust first above mentioned and provided that Beneficiary will specifically and unconditionally subordinate the lien or charge of the deed of trust first above mentioned to the lien or charge of said deed of trust in favor of Lender; and

WHEREAS, it is to the mutual benefit of the parties hereto that Lender make said additional loan to Owner; and Beneficiary is willing that the deed of trust securing the same shall constitute a lien or charge upon said land which is unconditionally prior and superior to the lien or charge of the deed of trust first above mentioned.

SUBORDINATION, DEED OF TRUST TO ADDITIONAL LOAN UNDER PRIOR DEED OF TRUST.

NOW, THEREFORE, in consideration of the mutual benefits accruing to the parties hereto and other valuable consideration, the receipt and sufficiency of which consideration is hereby acknowledged, and in order to induce Lender to make the additional loan above referred to, it is hereby declared, understood, and agreed as follows:

(1) That said deed of trust in favor of Lender, as to said additional loan as well as all other obligations recited as being secured thereby, and any renewals or extensions thereof, shall unconditionally be and remain at all times a lien or charge on the property therein described, prior and superior to the lien or charge of the deed of trust first above mentioned.

(2) That Lender would not make its additional loan above described without this subordination agreement.

(3) That this agreement shall be the whole and only agreement between the parties hereto with regard to the subordination of the lien or charge of the deed of trust first above mentioned to the lien or charge of the deed of trust in favor of Lender as to the additional loan above referred to and shall supersede and cancel any prior agreements as to such subordination.

Beneficiary declares, agrees, and acknowledges that

(a) He consents to and approves (i) all provisions of the note evidencing said additional loan and the deed of trust securing same, and (ii) all agreements, including but not limited to any loan or escrow agreements, between Owner and Lender for the disbursement of the proceeds of Lender's additional loan;

(b) Lender in making disbursements pursuant to any such agreement is under no obligation or duty to, nor has Lender represented that it will, see to the application of such proceeds by the person or persons to whom Lender disburses such proceeds and any application or use of such proceeds for purposes other than those provided for in such agreement or agreements shall not defeat the subordination herein made in whole or in part;

(c) He intentionally and unconditionally waives, relinquishes, and subordinates the lien or charge of the deed of trust first above mentioned in favor of the lien or charge upon said land of the deed of trust in favor of Lender, as to said additional loan as well as all other obligations recited therein as being secured thereby, and understands that in reliance upon and in consideration of this waiver, relinquishment and subordination specific loans and advances are being and will be made and, as part and parcel thereof, specific monetary and other obligations are being and will be entered into which would not be made or entered into but for said reliance upon this waiver, relinquishment and subordination; and

(d) An endorsement has been placed upon the note secured by the deed of trust first above mentioned that said deed of trust has by this instrument been subordinated to the lien or charge of the deed of trust in favor of Lender above referred to.

NOTICE: THIS SUBORDINATION AGREEMENT CONTAINS A PROVISION WHICH ALLOWS THE PERSON OBLIGATED ON YOUR REAL PROPERTY SECURITY TO OBTAIN A LOAN, A PORTION OF WHICH MAY BE EXPENDED FOR OTHER PURPOSES THAN IMPROVEMENT OF THE LAND.

_____   _____

_____   _____
               Beneficiary   Owner

(ALL SIGNATURES MUST BE ACKNOWLEDGED)

IT IS RECOMMENDED THAT, PRIOR TO THE EXECUTION OF THIS SUBORDINATION AGREEMENT, THE PARTIES CONSULT WITH THEIR ATTORNEYS WITH RESPECT THERETO.

C. PROBLEMS

PROBLEM 1

On September 1, Alice Barnes, as buyer, and Harold Simkin, as seller, entered into a contract for the sale to Barnes of Simkin's house and lot. The purchase price was $50,000 and the closing date, January 1. After executing the contract, Barnes gave Simkin a certified check for $5,000 as a deposit. On November 20, Barnes informed Simkin, in writing, of her intention not to perform the contract. What recourse would you counsel Simkin to take under each of the following circumstances:

A. The value of the parcel on November 20 was $40,000 and, because of local planning developments, threatened to decline even more in the next few months. By January 1, Simkin has

   1. found another buyer, Geoff Gorman, who is willing to enter into a contract immediately for a purchase price of $38,000;

   2. been unable to find a new buyer at a price above $30,000. (Would your answers to 1 and 2 differ if you knew that Barnes was

      a. a prospering business executive?

      b. insolvent?)

B. On November 30, Simkin was approached by Nina Felton who

   1. offered him $45,000 for the property;

   2. offered him $50,000 for the property.

C. Between November 30 and December 10, Simkin was approached with offers from five different people, ranging from $38,000 to $40,000. On December 11, Joan Maxon offered him $60,000 for the property which she says is ideally situated for her law offices. You discover that Barnes' breach was prompted by

   1. her inability to obtain financing;

   2. her financial distress.

PROBLEM 2

A.

It is November 5. Your clients, John and Sara Buchanan, husband and wife, want to sell their home at 272 Moody Street in the City of Watertown. Mrs. Buchanan recently accepted a new job that will require the family to move across the country early in December. The Buchanans have listed their home with a real estate broker, Harmony Homes, under an "exclusive right to sell" listing and Harmony Homes submitted the listing to the Watertown Multiple Listing Service of which it is a member. Ethan Davidson, a salesperson for Kellog Realty, which is also a member of the Watertown MLS, subsequently showed the house to Sam and Tina Ford, husband and wife. This was one of many houses which Davidson had shown to the Fords. The Fords, who own and live in a house at 1743 Main Street, Watertown, have accepted an offer to sell their own home and are interested in purchasing the considerably larger, more luxurious Buchanan residence. The Fords are particularly attracted by the Buchanan's swimming pool, and they intend, if they buy the house, to build a small cabana next to it.

Aided by one salesperson each from Harmony Homes and Kellog Realty, the Buchanans ("sellers") and the Fords ("buyers") have had a preliminary discussion regarding the terms of the proposed sale of the Buchanan home and have informed their respective attorneys as follows:

1. They have orally agreed on a price of $127,500.

2. The sellers have not specified the amount that they will require as a deposit, and have asked you to advise on this.

3. The Fords do not want to be committed to go through with the deal unless and until the sale of their Main Street residence has been closed. The anticipated closing date on that transaction is November 15.

4. The prospective purchasers of the Ford's Main Street residence insist on taking possession on November 15. Accordingly, the Fords want to move into the Buchanan home on that date. It is expected that the closing on the sale of the Buchanan home cannot take place until about three weeks later, roughly, December 6. The idea of prior possession by the Fords is agreeable to the sellers but they seek your advice as to how this should be worked out.

5. The buyers do not want to be committed to the purchase of the Buchanan home unless they can obtain a commitment for a conventional loan, secured by a mortgage or deed of trust, from an institutional lender in the amount of $102,000, repayable over a period of 30 years at a rate of interest no higher than 9½%. They are informed that there is plenty of

356

home mortgage money available, and that these terms are generally acceptable to local lenders.

The sellers have asked you to help negotiate the contract of sale with the buyers and their lawyer. Using either the form of Contract of Sale or the form of Deposit Receipt reprinted in this Supplement, draft a proposed form of sale agreement for submission to the buyers that incorporates or resolves the five points set forth above and any other points that you think will be important to address. Also, draft a cover letter to your clients explaining, where you think it necessary, the reasons for your use of any particular clauses. You should in this letter also indicate any objections that the buyer is likely to make to your proposed language, and your suggested reactions to these objections.

B.

It is now November 25. The contract of sale has been signed. The Fords moved into the Buchanan house on November 15. The sale of the Ford's Main Street home has been completed. The Fords have just obtained a mortgage commitment from the Bank of Watertown in the amount they requested and the mortgage is set to close December 6, at the time set for the closing of the sale.

As attorney for sellers you have obtained, and supplied the buyers' attorney with, a preliminary title report on the Buchanan property issued by the Great Northern Title Insurance Company. The report contains proposed exceptions from coverage relating to the following matters:

1. A mechanic's lien for $1,000 against the Buchanan property has been filed by the Hydra Corporation to protect its claim as a contractor in connection with its relining and resurfacing of the Buchanan swimming pool. Mr. Buchanan tells you that he withheld the $1,000 payment because he will not be sure until next spring whether the work will withstand the rigors of winter. The Hydra Corporation undertook to do the job in early September, but did not perform the work until the middle of October, after cold weather had set in.

2. Two years before the Buchanans acquired the 272 Moody Street parcel, John Hammond, a single man, their predecessor in interest, had granted the benefit of a right of way easement over the parcel to a neighbor, Clyde Stokes. Stokes did not record the instrument creating the easement until after the Buchanans had acquired the parcel and recorded their deed. While the Buchanans did not know of the easement, Great Northern Title did come across it in the course of their search on behalf of the Fords and, for this reason, noted it as an exception on the preliminary report.

You have also given the buyers' attorney an updated survey of the Buchanan property. The survey shows no encroachments on the Buchanan property or by the Buchanans on neighboring property. The buyers' attorney is satisfied that the buyers would be getting the property that they bargained for, with one exception. As a result of an error in an earlier site survey that was used in connection with building the Buchanan house, the rear of the house is set back 50´ from the adjoining neighbor's property line, not 65´ as the Buchanans had thought, and as they had represented to the Ethan Davidson, the Kellog Realty salesperson; Davidson had repeated this assertion to the Fords when showing them the property. Addition of a cabana, as intended by the Fords, would reduce the setback by 10´,

357

to 40´. While a 50´ setback is permissible under the Watertown zoning ordinance, a 40´ setback would not be permitted.

During the first week the Fords occupied the Buchanan home, a severe wind storm toppled a tree, part of which fell into the swimming pool, causing approximately $850.00 damage.

Prepare a letter to your client, sellers, outlining the possible objections that the buyers may make prior to or at the closing; the relative merits of these objections; the rights and remedies available to the buyers and to the sellers; the negotiating strategies that you would suggest the sellers employ in dealing with the buyers; and the most promising areas for compromise. Your letter should also advise the sellers of their possible liability to the brokers involved in this transaction as well as the possible liability of the brokers to the buyers and sellers. Please also identify any facts, not given, that would aid you in preparing your letter.

PROBLEM 3

Three years ago your client, Mary Haseltine, purchased a house situated at 831 Girard Avenue. Ms. Haseltine is an architect, employed by a local architecture firm. She also "moonlights," doing work for some private clients. Ms. Haseltine uses one room in the house, comprising approximately twenty percent of the total square footage, exclusively for this moonlighting work.

The purchase price was $100,000, of which Ms. Haseltine paid $20,000 from her own funds and financed $80,000 through a loan, evidenced by a note and secured by a mortgage on the premises, from Fidelity Savings & Loan Association. The note has a 30–year term and calls for level monthly payments of $559.40. The note contains the following clause:

14. Obligor agrees to repay the principal sum of $80,000 and to pay interest at the rate of 7.5% per annum on the unpaid balance until the balance is completely paid. Obligor may at any time prepay the principal balance outstanding hereunder but, in the event of such prepayment at any time before the expiration of five years from the date of this instrument, obligor shall pay an additional sum equivalent to 12% of the amount of principal then outstanding. Said additional sum shall be due and payable whether said prepayment is voluntary, involuntary, or is required by the lender's exercise of any acceleration clause provided for in this note or in the mortgage securing this note.

The mortgage contains the following clause:

17. In the event the mortgagor sells, conveys, transfers, disposes of or further encumbers said property, or any part thereof, or any interest therein, without the written consent of mortgagee being first obtained, then mortgagee shall have the right, at its option, to declare all sums secured hereby immediately due and payable.

Ms. Haseltine recently decided to sell the house and to buy a unit in a condominium development. One month ago she entered into a contract to purchase a condominium unit for $135,000. The condominium purchase contract is by its terms to close one month from today. Two weeks ago, Ms. Haseltine entered into a contract to sell the 831 Girard house to a young couple, Ted and Sally Hertz. That contract, by its terms, is to close one month from today.

The Haseltine–Hertz contract, prepared for the parties by the real estate broker who listed the property for Ms. Haseltine, specifies a purchase price of $150,000, payable as follows:

1. Buyers to take subject to outstanding note and mortgage to Fidelity Savings & Loan: $76,720

359

2. Buyers to execute note to seller, secured by a second mortgage, with a term of 10 years and an interest rate of 14%: $46,280

3. Buyers to pay cash to seller: $27,000

$150,000

The contract requires the Hertzs, at closing, to deliver a guaranty executed by Ted Hertz's father to the benefit of Ms. Haseltine, guaranteeing the couple's performance on the note to Haseltine and also on the note to Fidelity.

Yesterday Ms. Haseltine spoke with a vice president at Fidelity Savings & Loan who informed her that the Hertzs are unacceptable to Fidelity because of their low net worth and the fact that they will require second lien financing to purchase the house. He added, "Anyway, it would be crazy for us to be stuck with a 7.5% mortgage in the present 9.5% mortgage market." He further informed Ms. Haseltine that, in the event she closed the sale with the Hertzs, Fidelity would declare the loan due and payable under Paragraph 17 of the mortgage, and would require her to pay 12% of the unpaid balance under Paragraph 14 of the note.

Ms. Haseltine has come to you today for advice. She tells you that she will need the cash generated by the sale of the Girard Avenue house to close the condominium purchase. Because the real estate market is slow, she thinks she will not be able to get new buyers for, and close the contract on, the Girard Avenue house before the date on which she must close her purchase of the condominium unit. Indeed, she fears that unless she closes with the Hertzs she may have to sell her house at a sharply reduced price. Also, she tells you, she has become fond of the Hertzs and would like to go through with the deal with them whether or not required to do so by the terms of her contract with them. The jurisdiction's usury statute bars interest rates over 10% for residential mortgage loans.

1. Advise Ms. Haseltine as to the strength of Fidelity's position with respect to its contemplated action under Paragraph 14 of the note and Paragraph 17 of the mortgage. Advise her as to how she might try to convince Fidelity to change its position respecting the sale to the Hertzs.

2. On the assumption that the Hertzs will be allowed to buy the property subject to the Fidelity mortgage, and that the sale will close, advise Ms. Haseltine as to her rights against the Hertzs on the second mortgage, and against Ted Hertz's father on his guaranty, in the event of default on the second mortgage.

3. Advise Ms. Haseltine of the federal income tax consequences of her sale of the 831 Girard property and her purchase of the condominium unit.

PROBLEM 4

Your client, Charles Caldwell, owns a shopping center encumbered by a first mortgage securing a loan with an outstanding principal balance of $1,500,000. His adjusted basis in the center, for federal income tax purposes, is $1,750,000.

Barbara Baker would like to purchase the shopping center for $2,750,000, contingent upon her ability to refinance the center with a mortgage loan for 75% of the purchase price. At closing, she would prepay the existing first mortgage, and would pay Caldwell with her own cash and with the proceeds of the refinancing.

While Caldwell is willing to part with the center at Baker's price, he is reluctant to sell it because of the tax consequences of a sale. He is, however, willing to enter into a tax-deferred exchange at the exchange value represented by Baker's offer. He understands that it may not be possible to avoid all of the gain, but would like to minimize the recognition of capital gains to the extent possible. He also does not want to pay the prepayment penalty of $27,000 that will accrue when the existing first mortgage is paid off.

To facilitate the exchange, Caldwell has asked Baker to acquire an apartment complex, from Alfred Angell, to trade for the shopping center. The apartment complex is on the market at a price of $4,000,000, with an existing first mortgage loan having an outstanding principal balance of $3,000,000. Angell is willing to sell the apartment complex to Baker in connection with such an exchange for cash subject to the existing loan.

Caldwell comes to you today with the information that Baker has obtained a commitment for the 75% financing for the shopping center, that all other conditions precedent have been met, and that all parties are now ready to close.

At Caldwell's request:

    1. Prepare a memorandum describing the federal income tax consequences of the transaction.

    2. Draft a set of joint escrow instructions that will constitute the instructions of all the parties to the transaction. The instructions should direct the escrow officer in every respect concerning the documents and funds he will receive and the manner in which they should be handled.

361

PROBLEM 5

You are counsel for Aragon Development which has just received the commitment letter set out below. Aragon has an option to purchase a site in Gotham for construction of a hotel, and a conditional commitment from Host International Hotels to manage a hotel built on the site under a long term management contract. The architectural firm of Tassie, Elrod & Lewis has completed a set of preliminary plans and specifications, and Aragon has a letter of intent from a reputable contractor to build the hotel for $19 million. The land will cost $3 million, soft costs will amount to $2.5 million to $3 million, and the management contract proposal by Host will require another $1.5 million in working capital and other funds. Aragon will provide $5 million in equity for the project. All of the additional money required to complete the project is expected to come from the proceeds of financing.

Your client has informed you that it will be able to borrow interim loan funds equal to the amount of the permanent loan commitment and the amount of committed equity provided that the loan and equity commitments are legally binding, and are either unconditional or conditioned solely on "construction risks." Aragon Development has asked you to tie up the package so that it may be presented to an interim lender as leaving the interim lender with nothing but construction risks.

Define each of the risks to which you must address your attention. Describe how each of these risks can be eliminated or reduced so that the interim lender will be confident that the building will be completed at a cost within the terms of the permanent financing and other available money, and that when it is completed at that cost, the permanent loan will fund and the interim lender will be repaid.

Fidelity Life Assurance Society

Dear Aragon Development:

We are pleased to inform you of our commitment to loan to Aragon Development the sum of Twenty Million Dollars ($20,000,000.00) in the form of first mortgage financing in connection with the proposed construction of the Aragon Resort Hotel. The commitment is made upon the following terms, covenants and conditions:

1. Unpaid principal on our note shall bear interest at the rate of ten and one quarter percent (10.25%) per annum with principal and interest payable in level monthly payments of principal and interest at a rate which would amortize the loan over a term of twenty-five (25) years, with all unpaid principal on the twentieth (20th) anniversary date thereupon becoming due and payable. No prepayment of principal shall be permitted during the first ten (10) years of the term. Thereafter, prepayment only of the entire principal (and not of portions thereof) may be permitted with a premium of three percent (3%) of the unpaid

362

principal after the tenth (10th) anniversary and before the eleventh (11th) anniversary date of the note; two and three quarters percent (2.75%) after the eleventh (11th) anniversary but before the twelfth (12th) anniversary date of the note with the premium to decrease one quarter point (.25) per year thereafter until the maturity date.

2. All of the improvements shall have been completed in accordance with final plans and specifications prepared by Messrs. Tassie, Elrod & Lewis pursuant to its Job Order No. 15728. No change in plans and specifications shall occur without our prior written consent, which we reserve the right to refuse in our absolute and sole discretion. Completion in accordance with the plans and specifications shall be deemed to have occurred when all of the following have occurred and it has been certified to us in form satisfactory to us that:

(a) The premises have been accepted as complete by Host International Hotels;

(b) Host International Hotels has taken possession of the premises pursuant to a management contract;

(c) A Certificate of Completion shall have been issued by the building inspector and all other officials of the City and County of Gotham whose certification is required to establish completion of the building in accordance with the plans and specifications; and

(d) Completion shall have been certified by our architectural supervisor and representative, Ms. Lucia Del Roggia of Messrs. Handy, Gordon, Stockwell & Lindeman of Gotham.

3. The hotel shall have been completely fixturized with furniture, fixtures, equipment and hotel consumables sufficient for operation. Aragon shall have entered into a management contract with Host International Hotels for a term of not less than twenty (20) years, and upon other terms, covenants and conditions satisfactory to us which we shall approve in our sole discretion. Among other things, the management contract shall provide for payment to Aragon of sufficient monies to service our debt, pay real estate property taxes and pay insurance premiums on insurance required to be maintained pursuant to our loan documents and, as additional security for our loan, we shall have an assignment of Aragon Development's rights pursuant to the management contract.

4. At your cost and expense, you shall provide title insurance with respect to our mortgage document establishing that it stands of record as a valid first lien encumbrance, insured under extended coverage lender's form policies of title insurance, with co-insurance satisfactory to us and with title insurers of sufficient financial standing and reputation to meet our requirements. The title insurance shall be based upon a survey acceptable to us and prepared by a surveyor of whom we approve.

5. All documentation for the loan shall be in form satisfactory to our counsel, Thatcher & Voit. You agree to pay the fees of said counsel and all of its cost in connection with document preparation. At the request of the interim lender that you select to provide you with construction funds for construction of the hotel, we will agree to enter into a note purchase or "buy-sell" agreement in form satisfactory to us and our counsel. Due execution and delivery of all documents and instruments shall be supported by such corporate resolutions and opinions of counsel as our counsel shall require in its sole discretion, provided by counsel of whom we approve.

6. This commitment will be void unless it is funded in accordance with the terms hereof on or before the expiration of two years from the date hereof.

This commitment is good for a period of fifteen (15) days. To accept the commitment, you must return to us a duly executed copy of it together with a commitment fee of One Hundred Thousand Dollars ($100,000.00). The commitment fee shall be non-refundable except that you shall be entitled to a credit of up to Seventy–Five Thousand Dollars ($75,000.00) on closing costs in the event the loan is consummated.

Very truly yours,

Fidelity Life Assurance Society

By _____
        Vice President
        Investment Department

Accepted:

Aragon Development Corp.

By _____
    Vice President

Dated: _____

PROBLEM 6

Manchester Bank was the construction lender and now holds the permanent mortgage on an office building developed and currently owned by Chauncey Development. The face amount of the mortgage is $3 million, $2.9 million of which has been advanced by Manchester to Chauncey.

Due to a weak market for office space, the building is only 60% rented and has been operating at a loss. Chauncey has already borrowed additional funds from Second Bank in exchange for a second mortgage on the property. Despite current problems, Chauncey hopes to be operating at a break even point in a year from now when some additional tenants, who have already signed leases, move in and start paying rent.

In the meantime, Chauncey has been unable to pay county real estate taxes in the amount of $25,000. Tax liens have been filed and the county has threatened foreclosure. As a result, Chauncey has recently requested that Manchester advance it funds for the payment of taxes under Paragraph 25 of the mortgage:

"25. Lender shall advance any funds to Borrower that Lender deems necessary for the construction and maintenance of the improvements to be erected hereunder, and such funds shall be secured under this Mortgage."

The mortgage also provides that failure to pay taxes when due is a default under the mortgage.

A. Assume you are a new member of the office of the general counsel of Manchester. Write a memo to the general counsel addressing the following issues:

1. Must Manchester make the requested advance? What risks will Manchester face if it makes or refuses to make the advance?

2. Describe the remedies available to Manchester against Chauncey and their advantages and disadvantages, and recommend how the company should proceed.

B. You have just learned that during the construction phase, bulldozers unearthed some leaking barrels which contained hazardous substances. The barrels were removed but contaminated earth was spread around the property.

1. Do any of the parties face liability for the contamination?

2. Give your recommendation on how Manchester can best protect itself from liability in this regard.

PROBLEM 7

Your client, Gerard Developers, Inc. (GDI), would like to develop a shopping center in the town of Emoryville, a growing suburb. A preliminary market survey and an investigation of available land indicate that the land shown on the plot plan below represents the most desirable available site for GDI's purposes.

Parcel A, shown on the plan, is farmland owned by Lester Raiche, a truck farmer. Sally Bender, a local real estate broker, presently holds an option to purchase Parcel A from Mr. Raiche for $225,000. Bender acquired this option shortly after she had been approached by a GDI representative with inquiries as to the availability of various sites in Emoryville. Mr. Raiche had previously listed the property for sale through Ms. Bender for $200,000, but that listing had expired a few months before Ms. Bender acquired the option. Mr. Raiche lives in a house on Parcel B and does not wish to sell this parcel. Parcel C is owned by Alice Cuomo, a local developer and land speculator.

Parcels D, E, F and G were at one time owned by Alan Paris who subsequently sold Parcels D, F, and G, but continues to reside on Parcel E. Paris sold Parcel G to Big Burgers, Inc., a fast food chain which has operated a hamburger stand on the premises for 15 years. Five years ago, Paris conveyed Parcel D to Signal Oil Company by a deed containing a covenant by Paris, "for himself, his heirs, successors and assigns," that none of the grantor's lands within 500 feet of Parcel D would be used for the sale of gasoline, oil or other products commonly sold at automobile service stations. Last year Paris sold Parcel F to Ronald Steck, a land speculator. Parcel F remains vacant.

GDI's marketing survey convinces it that the proposed shopping center must have direct access to Interurban Highway, the principal north-south route in the Town of Emoryville, and that the highway will have to be widened to accommodate an extra turn-off lane so that drivers travelling south can make a left-hand turn directly into the shopping center.

Ms. Bender has informed GDI that Parcel A can be obtained for $250,000 and, further, has offered her services in assembling the parcel for GDI for a $20,000 fee. Signal Oil Company will not sell Parcel D and Mr. Paris has not been receptive to inquiries as to the sale of his home on Parcel E. However, Ms. Bender believes that Parcel E could be purchased for $50,000 to $75,000. Mr. Steck refuses to sell Parcel F but has offered a long term ground lease at a $15,000 annual rental. Big Burgers is willing to sell Parcel G for $100,000, but insists on a $75,000 twenty-year purchase money mortgage as partial payment.

Ms. Cuomo estimates that the present fair market value of Parcel C is $350,000. She refuses to sell the parcel outright, but would be interested in leasing it to GDI under a

366

twenty-five year net ground lease, at a monthly rental of $3,947 with an option in GDI to purchase the parcel at the end of the term for $25,000. (In evaluating this proposal, and comparing the lease terms to mortgage terms, GDI estimates that a twenty-five year, fully amortized note for $350,000 requiring monthly payments of $3,947, would have an interest rate of 13%.) Cuomo has shown some interest in reducing the proposed, fixed monthly payments in return for receiving a part of any of the percentage rentals received by GDI from tenants situated on Parcel C.

GDI has approached Disco–City, an operator of a nationwide chain of discount stores, about leasing a 100,000 square foot store in the proposed shopping center at a base rent of $2.25 per square foot. Disco–City is interested but insists that its lease include a satellite facility for automotive repair and for the sale of tires, batteries and other automobile accessories, to be located near a busy highway. Disco–City would also require that no other stores in the shopping center be leased for a general discount sales type operation. Hansen's, a locally-based discount store chain, has also expressed interest in the center. Specifically they would be interested in a 90,000 square foot store at a $2.00 per square foot base rent, but with a higher percentage rental than Disco–City.

GDI has also interested Super–Save, a large supermarket chain, in leasing a 30,000 square foot store at $2.35 per square foot base rent. GDI also believes that it will be able to obtain other nationwide chain tenants for another 30,000 square feet, at an average rental of $4.50 per square foot, before it starts construction, and that another 40,000 square feet could later be rented at a comparable rent.

The proposed site is within a CD–2, Commercial Development, district under the Emoryville Zoning Ordinance. Within a CD–2 district, the ordinance allows 5,000 square feet of retail store floor area for each 1 acre of land.

GDI estimates that construction costs, including architectural and engineering services and site work, would run about $22 per square foot of building area, and that construction would be completed within twelve to fifteen months after it begins.

The Bank of Emoryville, a local commercial bank, has told GDI that it would be willing to provide up to $5,000,000 in construction financing at 2% over its prime interest rate, plus a 1% fee, and would require a firm takeout commitment for permanent financing from a reputable institutional lender. Union Life, a large insurance company, has expressed interest in purchasing a 200,000 square foot development fully rented for $5,000,000 and leasing it back to GDI for 30 years at an annual rent of $450,000. Fidelity Savings, a mutual savings bank, indicates that it would consider a $4,000,000, thirty-year mortgage at 9½% interest if a minimum net annual rental of $425,000 is achieved, and a $5,000,000 loan on similar terms, if a minimum net annual rental of $550,000 is achieved by the time the loan is funded. The Bank of Emoryville and Fidelity Savings both contemplate first freehold mortgage liens. Union Life contemplates an unencumbered fee interest.

Please select one scheme for acquiring, developing, financing and leasing the shopping center project, and indicate:

    1.   Why you think it is the most attractive alternative;

    2.   What legal instruments will be necessary to effectuate the alternative chosen and what clauses it will be particularly important for those instruments to contain; and

367

3. What major legal pitfalls, if any, surround the scheme, and what additional instruments, changes or steps you would propose for avoiding them.

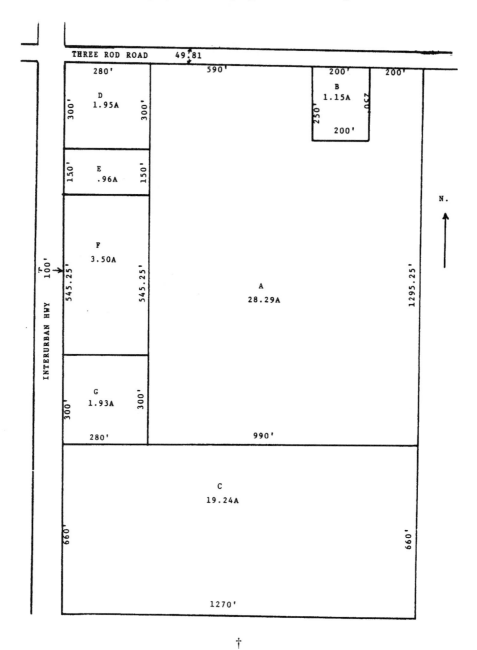